The Lean IT Expert
Leading the Transformation
to High Performance IT

The Lean IT Expert
Leading the Transformation
to High Performance IT

By

Niels Loader

Routledge
Taylor & Francis Group

A PRODUCTIVITY PRESS BOOK

First edition published in 2019
by Routledge/Productivity Press
711 Third Avenue New York, NY 10017, USA
2 Park Square, Milton Park, Abingdon, Oxon OX14 4RN, UK

© 2019 by Niels Loader
Routledge/Productivity Press is an imprint of Taylor & Francis Group, an Informa business

---

Library of Congress Cataloging-in-Publication Data

Names: Loader, Niels, author.
Title: The lean IT expert : leading the transformation to high performance IT
/ Niels Loa.
Description: 1 Edition. | New York : Taylor & Francis, [2019] | Includes
bibliographical references and index.
Identifiers: LCCN 2018030495 (print) | LCCN 2018034202 (ebook) | ISBN
9780429506369 (e-Book) | ISBN 9781138549524 (hardback : alk. paper)
Subjects: LCSH: Total quality management. | Information
technology--Management. | Six sigma (Quality control standard)
Classification: LCC HD62.15 (ebook) | LCC HD62.15 .L64 2019 (print) | DDC
004.068/4--dc23
LC record available at https://lccn.loc.gov/2018030495

Visit the Taylor & Francis Web site at
http://www.taylorandfrancis.com

Contents

PART II   Starting Out

PART III   Leadership Transformation

PART IV   Team Transformation

PART V   Continuous Improvement

Foreword

When I first coauthored the book *Lean IT: Enabling and Sustaining Your Lean Transformation*, I could never have imagined the impact the application of Lean thinking might have on IT professionals around the world. Today Lean IT is well known and embraced alongside Service Management, Agile and DevOps. At the core of these disciplines are the ideas and methods of Lean Manufacturing, which can be traced back hundreds of years.

An early mentor of mine once said to me, "All of Lean can be summarized as follows: *to create and manage the flow of customer value.*" As a practitioner of Lean in the IT space for over 25 years, I have come to understand the great wisdom in these simple words. But understanding concepts such as customer value and flow do not always position us to effectively manage or drive enterprise-wide transformation. Often the challenge is on our focus: when we lead with tools (e.g., value stream maps, A3s, leader standard work, visual boards, etc.) we lose focus on *what* we are trying to create and *why* we are creating it. But continuous improvement methods and tools are not enough to create an authentic, lasting change in an organization's culture. So what is needed? At its heart, Lean IT is about People, Process and Technology in that specific order.

Countless Lean IT, Service Management, Agile and DevOps initiatives have overpromised and underdelivered because too much emphasis was placed on tools and bottom-line results around cost reduction. True transformation emphasizes the journey as much as the finish-line results. In fact, there is no end point. I like to say, "Transformation is a verb, not a noun!" A key takeaway of this book is the emphasis on behavior and the critical importance of reinforcing the change you are trying to achieve. This seems like an obvious point, but it is often missed as we grasp the shiny new ideas and tools of Lean.

A Lean IT transformation is really a misnomer because an IT transformation is a business transformation. IT impacts every element of the value stream including stakeholders, the business, partners, vendors, suppliers, internal users, external customers and customers' customers. Radical changes to the way we approach the work of IT mean radical changes to the way everyone works.

What leaders do and prioritize creates an indelible mark on employees. Over time it becomes the setting employees know they live and work in. Each contact between leader and employee adds to the body of understood assumptions about what's done and not done, said and not said, asked and not asked. This makes up the culture of the team, group, department and organization. Over time it becomes clear to employees whether it's prudent, safe and really expected that they engage and take initiative in continuous improvement and structured problem solving.

As you read on, you will discover the ideas and methods of Lean IT and, more importantly, how to create the conditions for a lasting, deep transformation in the way leaders lead, people and teams interact and ultimately how great IT work gets done. This book contains a collection of learnings on Lean IT that will assist the reader in developing a Lean Thinking mindset as they approach the IT value stream.

Michael Orzen
Portland, Oregon

Preface

It is difficult to mark a moment when the turmoil in the world of Information Technology (IT) started. The introduction of the iPhone, the coming of age of the Internet, the financial crisis can all lay claim. One thing is certain: The term *digital transformation* is on the lips of most business leaders. And herein lies the difference between all previous moments of excitement with IT. Digital transformation is a business concern; it is no longer just IT that needs to get things done.

Add to this the disruptive force of start-ups focusing on IT-based services that can be consumed through mobile devices. These start-ups eat away at the high-margin services provided by incumbents, leaving lower-margin products and services that are rapidly being commoditized. This is happening in all industry sectors and it is the ones who are best able to adjust, innovate, and improve their service offerings that will survive.

So far, so good. This is probably a story you have read or heard a thousand times before.

The question is: What do you need to do to ensure that your organization is one of the survivors?

Over the past 20 years, I have had the privilege to work with tens of IT organizations. The focus of this work was primarily to improve the performance of the IT organizations toward their customers, who were their colleagues in the business departments. In the last ten years, a complication was added to IT organizations: The business's customer became a direct user of IT services that previously were only used by colleagues. The demand for better, even excellent, IT services became louder, mainly because complaints from business customers go to the Board of Directors and not to the IT Manager or CIO, as they previously did when it was mainly colleagues using IT services.

Over the same period, one of the enduring themes within IT has been getting "a seat at the table," meaning being heard by top business management, and being part of strategic decision-making at an early stage. Well, that moment has come: Business customers have ensured that IT has a seat at the table. Now, IT needs to deliver, and deliver excellently. But delivering is not something that IT can do on its own; delivering the value needed by the business means that the business and IT need to work together.

And this is where the problem resides: It has not always been very easy to work with IT. The main complaints include (but are not limited to) a high level of bureaucracy in processes and procedures that stifle business improvements, being reactive instead of proactive, not understanding business needs and therefore the right level of the solution, delivering too late, no time to truly support innovation within the business, and, lastly, IT people who do not listen and think they know what needs to happen. These are largely the customer's interpretation of the behavior of people within IT.

There is obviously a different side to this coin. The processes and procedures are increasingly a response to legal or regulatory requirements, for example, the Sarbanes-Oxley Act, healthcare industry regulations, financial sector regulations, and the general cry for IT to be compliant with COBIT controls. The reactive nature of IT is a result of how loud customers shout when there is a disruption of the IT service and is an effect of whimsically changing business priorities. Lack of time is a result of excessive and often senseless demand from the business. And so we can go on explaining why IT is the way it is. But this does not solve the problem.

The core of the solution to the problem is to radically improve the way the IT organization works together with the business. To be clear, the digital transformation of your business depends on that relatively small group of people in the basement, or other out-of-the-way location, who make sure that your IT services work. So, building a cooperative model is vital for the success of the business. Which model has proven its worth in many industries? It is the application of Lean principles that gives organizations an advantage in delivering their products and services to their customers.

In the years that I have been applying Lean principles to IT organizations, I have witnessed improvements in the performance of IT organizations, ranging from substantial to impressive, as a result of adopting the Lean philosophy and applying it to their work environment. The journey tends to start with getting the internal workings of the IT organization sorted out, and quite quickly leads to a different interaction between IT and business. This gives way to a cooperative environment in which the desired or required improvements to business processes and services are implemented in rapid succession. The last two sentences could give the impression that applying Lean principles to IT is a "walk in the park." This is not the case, and throughout this book I will try to guide you through the difficulties you may encounter. However, the effects and results make the difficult moments of the journey worthwhile.

Every digital transformation of a business has its foundations in the Lean transformation of the IT organization into a High Performance IT Organization, and this transformation is first and foremost a behavioral change.

This book aims to ensure that you build that foundation for your digital transformation, and I will focus on the behaviors that are necessary in this context. I have chosen to describe the transformation as it tends to happen in practice in IT organizations. The first part will cover the basics of Lean and describe the aim of the Lean IT transformation. This is the phase in which the realization sets in that the current way of working has reached its limits and, in order to better serve customers, a new paradigm is needed. Part II looks at what happens when you start with Lean within an IT organization. This section may feel somewhat messy, and that is because this phase of moving towards a Lean IT organization is exactly that, messy. I will however attempt to bring method to the madness that is the transformation of an IT organization. Part II ends with the step to defining an integral approach to the transformation. Parts III and IV describe the real work of transforming your IT organization. The transformation is described from two different perspectives: Leadership (Part III) and Team (Part IV). The final part looks at what happens when you have gone through the transformation and are looking to maintain and improve on your achievements so far.

Acknowledgments

As a first-time author, I am indebted to the people at Taylor & Francis for their patience in this process, particularly Meredith Norwich, Michael Sinocchi, and Katherine Kadian. Thanks also to Joseph Gautham and Michelle van Kampen at Deanta for their support during the production process.

This book would not have been possible without the experiences afforded me through the work I have done for Quint Wellington Redwood. This work has given me the opportunity to interact with many IT organizations where the ideas in this book have been tried out and improved. In addition, the support and challenge of my past and current colleagues have been instrumental in developing the area of Lean IT. The examples and figures in this book are presented courtesy of Quint Wellington Redwood.

Regarding the IT organizations, I wish to thank the IT leaders who knowingly, and sometimes unknowingly, party to the development and improvement of the ideas, techniques and tools described in this book. I am deeply grateful for the opportunity you have afforded me. Specifically, I would like to thank Eugen Boon, Kees Bink, Walther Rasche, Marcel Verbunt, Wytze-Jan de Jong, Enno Soeren, Esther Ruis-Odenkirchen, Jeroen Janssen, Catharina Adriaans, and Annemiek van Duurling-Horck for their drive to improve their organizations. These leaders in Lean IT, Agile, and DevOps organizations have been instrumental (whether you knew it or not) in improving the understanding of how Lean principles are applied to IT organizations. Other IT leaders, who are too many to name, have helped by providing the environments in which newly developed capabilities could be confirmed in their effectiveness. For this, I thank you all.

Quint has also put me in the circumstance that I have been able to train hundreds of people in Lean IT. The participants in those training sessions have all helped to develop Lean IT through their questions, personal anecdotes, stories of success and failure, and in the way they enthusiastically carry out the exercises during the training sessions. The insights have been a source of inspiration for me.

To ensure that this book can also be used to achieve the Lean IT certifications, some of the passages in this book are extracts from the three publications I wrote for the Lean IT Association. These publications were achieved with the help of many people. The privilege of being involved in the conception and development of both the Lean IT Association (LITA) has also been a cause to "raise the bar". My deep thanks go out to the LITA Content Board members Mike Orzen, Reni Friis and John Terry for your contributions and challenges that have helped develop the Lean IT body of knowledge. Special thanks in this context go out to the final member of the LITA Content Board, Troy DuMoulin, whose ideas, wisdom and drive I value deeply. Thank you all for your support from the start.

In getting LITA up and running, I am grateful for the existence of a formidable force, Deborah Burton. Deborah, thank you for your continued support, help and advice in all of the ventures we have been involved in together. You have been an inspiration and source of amazing energy for the Lean IT Association and the DevOps Agile Skills Association, and the content they promote.

Another group of people I wish to recognize are my current and former colleagues at Quint Wellington Redwood. For the twenty-five years of its existence, Quint has operated at the leading edge of the improvement of IT organizations. As part of this, I have been free to develop the application of Lean in IT organizations. At the same time, my colleagues have elicited challenges that have been instrumental in moving our thinking and capabilities forward. In no specific order, because you have all played a significant role at one time or another, I would like to thank Hans Smorenburg, Natasja Soselisa, Willem Wouter Gerritse, Diederick Dekker, Rob Kobussen, Jan Hendriks, Alex van Kampen, Karlijn Bruns, Bart Stofberg, Meindert Duker, Charlotte van der Kooij, Natasja Soselisa, Corne Pol(†), Eline Zweers, Eric Rozemeijer, Frederik Schukken, Harriette Blaauboer, Karlijn Bruns, Wijnand Kamerling(†), Tim Wiegel, Alex Mazurek, Dave van Herpen, and Tijs Clous. Thank you all for helping to develop and improve the application of Lean to IT organizations. To Jeroen Janssen and Hans Kompier, without you, there would not have been a Lean IT Foundation; you believed when very few others did. Thanks to Maurice Boon, CEO of Quint Wellington Redwood, whose support in both Quint and LITA made this journey possible. Last but not least, special thanks to Dragana Mijatovic for being the best sparring partner someone could possibly hope for over the last fifteen years. You are a rock star.

My acknowledgments end with the people who suffer most when a book is written: the people who are nearest and dearest. To my wonderful children, Daniel and Diana, and my fabulous wife, Jolanda, thank you for your support and patience.

Introduction: Transformation

Never [...] has so much been owed by so many to so few.

Winston Churchill
Speech to the House of Commons, 20 August 1940

As Steven Covey (1989) recommended, it is important to "start with a clear understanding of your destination." Your destination, in a generic sense, is a high performance IT organization that is capable of ensuring that your business thrives (or at least survives), and the premise is that applying Lean principles will ensure that your IT organization will become a high performance IT organization.

For the purposes of this book, we will define the "End" as an IT organization that has developed itself into an environment that works according to Lean principles and has a Lean Management System in place. The goal is, therefore, a transformed IT organization, that can be recognized by different behavioral patterns, along with improved measurable performance. An example of this can be found in the continuous improvement of streaming services delivered by a national broadcaster, based on the application of Lean principles. This meant not just improving the discipline of the operational processes but building a management system that embedded and promoted a customer-centric approach to understanding what aspects of the services needed to be addressed. This was followed by focused action based on a systemic view of the service, meaning not simply focusing on getting the technology right but also instilling the behavior necessary to provide the service in an ever-improving manner, in the team members and managers.

As we will see throughout this book, you will need to define more specific goals for your IT organization. These goals may be the achievement of a particular level of performance (as a milestone on the way to even better performance), a particular capability (as a milestone on the way to a greater capability) or a level of satisfaction (as a milestone on the way to higher levels of satisfaction). The overall status of your transformation may, of course, also be one of your goals, as a milestone on the way to a greater level of integration of Lean thinking and acting in your way of working.

Transformation is something that happens to all industries. It appears to be a relatively natural phenomenon that occurs as the capabilities within an industry develop, the use of the product or service becomes more widespread, and the complexity of the product increases. Transformation is by nature disruptive and creates opportunities for new entrants based on new visions of how the product or service can be delivered to customers.

If we look at how industries develop, the current situation of the IT industry no longer appears so random. In fact, we see a logical progression of phases. Unfortunately, each phase in the progression has survivors and victims. The key question is: What does it take to be a survivor? How can you ensure that your organization makes the step to the new phase? Taking a broad look at the development of industries and using the car industry as an example, we can identify three major phases of the development of an industry. Industries tend to develop along a relatively predictable path from Artisan, through Mass Production to Lean Production.

As a new industry emerges, it starts in its Artisan phase. In this phase, a new product or service has been identified and there are pioneers who see that there is a market to be created and conquered. The key characteristics of this phase are that there are low barriers to entry and entrepreneurs who operated in related industries take up the challenge of developing the new product or service. This is a phase in which learning is done on the job and most of the work is manual. The learning curve is steep and, in the case of a new product, there will be one or more technicians who understand the entire product. They will do much of the work in designing the product, creating the (new) parts and assembling these parts into the final product. In the Artisan phase, products are often one-off or limited-series production, with new and improved versions coming in relatively rapid succession. In fact, the succeeding product is different to its predecessor. The market appears to be small but lucrative with high-wealth individuals and businesses purchasing the new product.

Looking at the car industry, we see the first car companies emerge during the 1890's. The diversity of products is large as each company develops its products. In the Artisan phase, there was a great amount of experimentation with a variety of fuels and propulsion methods, not to mention size, numbers of wheels, gears, seats and other attributes. Towards the end of the 1890's, the larger car companies were producing a couple of thousand cars per year. There is a better understanding of how cars need to be produced, and the industry is ripe for its first transformation: The move to the Mass Production phase.

The Mass Production phase is the phase in which industry standards are created; we see strong standardization of an iconic product (e.g. Model T Ford, Sony Walkman, IBM PC), which forms the basis for further development. The principal organizational characteristics of this phase are specialization and coordination. Specialization means that the creation of the product is broken down into small steps with individuals taking account for carrying out these small steps. A "specialist" will focus on a single task, which has been standardized. Since there are many small tasks that need to be carried out to create the final product, there are many people involved in assembling the final product. All these activities and, therefore, people need to be coordinated. In the beginning, this coordinating role is carried out by a chief engineer who oversees the technical execution of activities. As standards become embedded, the engineer's role is transformed into a managerial role in which production targets and people management take a more prominent position than the technical aspects of the job. Managers collect and collate information to create reports on which they make decisions regarding production. The chief engineer focuses more on design and the creation of the production mechanism.

Through the combination of standards, specialization and coordination, the industry is able to reduce the learning curve dramatically. The introduction of standards means that much work can be mechanized, with people ensuring that the machines do the work correctly and intervening when the machine goes wrong. People are also used for those activities that cannot be easily mechanized. This is the phase in which the product has proven itself to be useful for more than just the high-wealth individuals and businesses and, at the right price, is attractive for a much larger group of consumers. The mechanization of the industry means that the price per unit plummets and the demand can increase. The number of models is limited and the variations on these models are more cosmetic than substantial. The focus of the industry is very much on production and less on what the market actually wants.

The longevity of the Model T Ford is a testament to this way of working: The engines remained the same for a long time (33 years with evolutionary improvements), the colors remained limited (Ford (1922) famously said: "You can have any color as long as it's black") and the bodywork was adjusted to cope with different customer needs (coupes, sedans, pick-ups, vans). In the car industry, we see the Mass Production phase starting around 1910. The guiding force is primarily Henry Ford, with his Ford

Motor Company, who used the ideas and methods for which Frederick W. Taylor is well known to develop into a Mass Production business. Based on the successes achieved (growth of both business and market, higher wages for employees, more production at lower costs), Mass Production becomes the modus operandi for the car industry.

With the increase in production and sales, the customer base of the product grows and with it the number of people who have an opinion about the product. There is demand for customization. Initially, producers cannot deliver this customization effectively and much of it is done post-production at specialized customizing shops. This includes relatively simple, but lucrative, modifications. The exploding customer base with its increasing diversity of demand is the trigger for the second transformation.

The move from Mass Production to, what we shall call, Lean Production is the next phase in the development of an industry. Spurred by the demands of customers, the industry turns from an internal focus, producing as much as possible as cheaply as possible, to an external, customer-oriented focus. In this new paradigm, production is about delivering exactly what the customer wants and doing it as quickly as possible. This means removing waste from the system and ensuring that people are able to oversee and execute more than one activity in the process. One of the key facilitators of this second transformation is automation. Where Mass Production thrives on mechanization, Lean Production is powered by the automation of machinery and processes. This automation allows the people working in the industry to rapidly gain insight into their performance and, subsequently, adjust their way of working to improve performance.

The result is an organization in which teams become responsible for larger steps in the production of the product, thus reducing the need for coordination. The specialists from the Mass Production phase become generalized specialists who work together to create the entire product. The need for managerial oversight reduces as teams are provided with real-time information feedback on their work.

The car industry went through this transformation during the 1970's and 1980's. Any car company not producing in a Lean manner by the 1990's was effectively obsolete and destined for failure. The Lean Production transformation of the car industry was started by the Toyota Motor Corporation at the end of the 1940's. The Toyota Production System (TPS) is the classic example of Lean Production, because of its enduring success. Interestingly, Taiichi Ohno, considered to be the "father" of the Toyota Production System, was a great fan of Henry Ford – "I, for one, am in awe of Ford's greatness." He devoured the writings on Ford and concludes in his own book (Ohno, 1988) that Ford would have developed Lean production at Ford, had he not died.

Ford died in 1947, around the time that Ohno and others within Toyota were looking to emulate the American car manufacturers. Around this time, Toyota leadership had given the company a three-year goal of "catching up with the Americans." They realized that by doing exactly the same as the American manufacturers they would not be able to compete since they lacked the resources. They would need to do something different. Ford, General Motors and the other American manufacturers seem to have taken the "never change a winning formula" approach, choosing to optimize their Mass Production-based system rather than transform the industry to Lean Production. And this stood the American manufacturers in good stead for a long time.

However, the space opened for Toyota to use the standards developed in the industry to that point and create a new modus operandi in which the delivery of the value that customers require is embedded in the system, from development through production to the servicing of the car in use.

If we briefly look at the history of the car industry, we see a large amount of turmoil in the 1970's and 1980's. The result of this turmoil was that companies that did not make the transition to Lean Production of their own accord simply disappeared: The car industries in Britain, Spain, Czechoslovakia, Russia, and other countries effectively ceased to exist, were replaced by or were taken over by companies that did make the transition. Where the customer base permitted, Mass Production lingered longer than it probably should have. Nowadays, every car manufacturer uses its own form of Lean Production.

In summary, we see that the car industry moved from an Artisan phase, through a Mass Production phase, to a Lean Production phase. The question, of course, is: What is the transformation after the move to Lean Production? I believe the fourth step is the one in which robotization and automation facilitate the customer in producing their own product. The role of people other than the consumer in the production of these products and services is minimized. One example is the processing of a financial transaction. This service has changed from being one in which a customer would go to a bank and instruct a teller to transfer funds from one account to another. Nowadays, the process has been fully robotized/automated so that I, as a customer, can transfer money from my account to any other account in the world without the intervention of another human being.

This is possible for services and there is no reason why I should not be able to configure my car and have it produced, in a fully automated/robotized factory, without the intervention of another human being at some time in the future. Admittedly, this is a more complicated proposition than a financial transaction, but it is the future of the car industry which now employs a fraction of the people that it once employed, during its Mass Production phase.

But we are getting ahead of ourselves.

What does this development of industries mean for the IT industry and IT organizations in particular?

The short answer is that we see exactly the same evolution marked by a couple of disruptive transformations. In fact, we are currently in our transformation from Mass Production to Lean Production, and the purpose of this book is to help you guide your IT organization into the Lean Production phase.

The IT industry burgeoned in the 1950's. Before this time, automation had been the realm of speculation and academic research. The development of automation as a response to cryptography during the World War II is when automation started becoming a serious force. From the 1950's, we see the IT industry in its Artisan phase, with the creation of many different hardware platforms that initially were programmed mechanically, but were rapidly replaced by code that could be stored as zeroes and ones. Through experimentation and focused development, information technology products were created. At this time, the expectation was that there was a limited market for large-scale computing.

By the early 1980's however, the IT industry had developed attractively priced products that were useful for a large group of customers, whether those customers realized it or not at the time. The introduction of the personal computer (PC) in 1982 marks the moment that the IT industry moved into its Mass Production phase. With the advent of server-based computing, the use of computers exploded, both within businesses and at home. As we saw, the key characteristics of the Mass Production phase are standardization, specialization and coordination. From a technology perspective, we see standardization in terms of hardware (microprocessors) and platforms (Windows, Unix), making a proliferation of software possible. But even with software, we see standards emerge, such as Microsoft Office. But the development of industries is more about the way we work. One of the key standards was TCP/IP for communication purposes and the development of the Internet. This brought the possibility of computers to every home. The classic artifact of the Mass Production phase of the IT industry is the IT Infrastructure Library (ITIL). Conceived during the 1980's, the first version of ITIL was published in 1989, after development started in 1986.

ITIL describes *what* the IT industry does. In short, it delivers information technology products and services. In doing so, the organization that delivers these products and services needs to support and maintain the existing services, it needs to improve them, it needs to create and deliver new products and services and it must advise its customers on the use of IT products and services. The IT organization also needs to plan for the future use of these products and services. In describing these activities (in substantial detail), ITIL chose the Mass Production paradigm to describe *how* the industry works. The activities were described as processes carried out by technical staff and were described as standards to be implemented in IT organizations. These processes needed to be coordinated by a process manager (supported by process coordinators). The technical staff were positioned as specialists (service desk, application, infrastructure). Unfortunately, ITIL failed to explicitly describe one of the key processes within IT: The software development process. Although this process is generically included in Change Management, software professionals did not sufficiently recognize their work in the ITIL process descriptions. This led to a lack of adoption of ITIL within the application development parts of the IT organization. The use of the word "Infrastructure" in ITIL will undoubtedly have contributed to the conviction that ITIL is not applicable to application development.

The world of application development followed a slightly different path. Initially, the method of choice was Waterfall in which a development team would sequentially design, build, test and then deploy a piece of software. This method is fine when small pieces of software need to be created. When it comes to large designs, the lead times for deployment become disastrously long, with the design phase alone sometimes taking years to complete. The resulting dissatisfaction of customers led to the development of iterative models that aimed to deliver software more quickly, thus providing customers with the value they require. In essence, later models (e.g. Rapid Application Development, Agile Software Development, Lean Software Development, Extreme Programming, Rational Unified Process, Scrum Development) all aim to get working software to customers more quickly, a characteristic of Lean Production. Unfortunately, applying the characteristics of Lean Production to one part of an industry, in this case application development, does not mean the entire industry is in its new phase. It is the same as a car manufacturer basing its engine manufacturing department on Lean Production with the rest working with the Mass Production paradigm.

Moving forward to 2010, we see a number of developments that signal the advent of the Lean Production phase of the IT industry: 2009 sees the start of the DevOps "movement" which recognizes the need for applying Lean Production methods throughout the value chain of IT and 2010 saw the publication of the book entitled *Lean IT* (Bell and Orzen, 2010). It is important to note that *what* IT does has not changed, it still provides IT products and services for which it carries out changes, solves incidents, does operational work and gives advice. It is the *how* that is changing, from specialization and coordination (Mass Production) to value delivery and flow (Lean Production). If we look at the years since 2010, we see an explosion of automation capabilities within IT. Where previously, the IT industry focused on automating its customers, it now applies a significant effort to automating its own key processes. The emergence of Continuous Delivery (Humble and Farley, 2010) with the associated automation is a testament to this development (Figure 0.1).

Why is this happening? In the Artisan phase, it was principally academia, government agencies and large businesses that used computers. In the Mass Production phase, there was an increase in use within the initial users of IT, and some innovators and early adopters among private individuals. The number of people using IT products and services has increased exponentially, especially with the explosion of the use of smartphones and other mobile devices. The needs of this group have proliferated and these customers want more diversified capabilities in their IT products

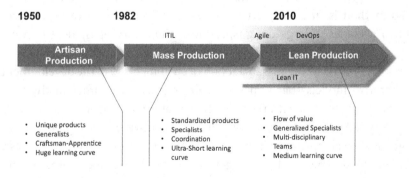

FIGURE 0.1
Development of IT industry.

and services. In fact, the ease with which customers can switch from one IT service to another means that the market for a particular provider can dry up overnight if a better proposition is created. This means that IT organizations have been forced into an environment where customer value is key and the speed with which services must be improved needs to increase dramatically. The capabilities of end-consumer-oriented IT organizations create a huge expectation from business IT organizations. With substantial legacy systems and processes, these IT organizations have a hill to climb when it comes to achieving the same performance as their end-consumer-oriented IT counterparts.

Another development of the past decade has been one of dependence. Businesses are dependent on their IT systems. No IT means no transactions, which essentially means no business. There are very few businesses that can thrive without IT, e.g. websites, electronic fulfillment, financial processes. In the past, businesses could still perform well in spite of a poorly performing IT organization. The balance has tipped. A poorly performing IT organization will now cause your business to perform poorly and, ultimately, fail.

The message is clear: As a business using IT products and services, you must ensure that you have a highly capable group of people ("the IT organization") providing excellent IT products and services to your organization. This IT organization may be internal or external, but you have no choice regarding their ability to perform. As with the car industry, a failure to move to the Lean Production paradigm will mean the demise of the IT organization and, in all likelihood, the business it works for. Remember, in most businesses, the people working in IT constitute no more than 5% of the total workforce. This small group of people bears a large part of the responsibility for the IT systems that allow businesses to thrive and develop. It is absolutely vital that businesses invest not just in the technical capabilities but also in the abilities of IT people (management and team members) to ensure that products and services are developed rapidly and maintained in a way that meets the requirements of the current environment.

Up to this point, I have used the word "business" and it may appear that the move to Lean Production is only valid for for-profit organizations. Nothing could be less true. Governments, NGOs and not-for-profit organizations are all in a race for survival. The intervention of foreign countries in elections in other countries is an example of the fight for survival. The fact that countries become more attractive as places to "settle" based on their technological capabilities, making it easy for organizations to do business. The ability of charities to attract funding and dispense it in a transparent and cost-efficient way, so that donors know that their donations are ending up where they are intended. These are all examples of how organizations other than businesses are also caught up in the development of the IT industry.

It is critical to realize: This race for survival depends on the ability of a relatively small group of technical professionals.

The vast majority of businesses currently operate their IT organizations in the Mass Production paradigm. Many of these businesses will, as a result, fail as other businesses with high performance IT organizations are able to develop new business capabilities more quickly, and deploy and support them more successfully. One of the "canary in a coal mine" indicators that you need to start your own Lean IT transformation is a difficulty in recruiting and retaining top talent in your IT organization. There is a generation of IT professionals who simply do not want to work in IT organizations that do not promote collaboration, autonomy, improvement and innovation. They are looking for inspiring environments in which they can take responsibility for a product or service together with a team.

One message I hope you have taken from the above description of the development of industries is that the move to Lean Production is not a "fad," "management toy" or "something that will blow over." If you believe that the transition to Lean Production is a whim, you are likely to end up not being one of the survivors. Lean Management and Lean Production in IT is here and it is here to stay, until the transformation to the next fundamentally different paradigm.

In the previous section, I introduced the term High Performance IT organization. The question is: What is this entity? Is it a mythical beast or does it actually exist? A high performance IT organization is one that is able to provide the products and services that its customer requires with an ever-decreasing delay. To achieve this, the high performance IT organization must apply Lean principles which, essentially, means increasing the rate of learning and the application of the lessons learned to the delivery of IT products and services. You may have spotted the error in the previous sentence: Organizations cannot apply principles and, despite assertions elsewhere, organizations do not learn. It is people who apply principles and people who learn and pass on learning to others. Turning your IT organization into a high performance IT organization is all about creating an environment in which people are helped, supported, encouraged and led in such a way that "potential" is turned into "actual." This is often communicated as a need to change the "culture" of the organization.

Changing culture has been the subject of a huge amount of publications. It seems that directly trying to work on creating a new culture is a task of monstrous proportions. In the move from Mass Production IT organization to Lean Production IT organization (High Performance IT), the way to achieve the transformation is based on Craig Larman's Law of Organizational Behavior that "Culture follows structure" (Larman, n.d.). The term "structure" must be taken in its broadest sense. The organizational structure is one aspect, and the aim is to organize in a customer-oriented way. This organizational structure needs to be supplemented by other structures. In Lean IT, we find a number of these structures in the form of visual management, the Cascade, structured problem-solving, performance indicators and value streams. These structures help to remind people of what needs to be done. Every structure can be bureaucratized in such a way that causes it to work in a slow and cumbersome fashion. The aim of a high performance IT organization is to constantly be aware of the principles that drive the structures. This is the difficult bit, and this is where leaders truly earn their compensation: They are accountable for the fact that the organization adheres to the agreed principles, and makes them work as intended.

But somebody has to do the helping, supporting, encouraging and leading. The premise of this book is that Lean IT Experts will do much of this work. The "trick" for the sustainability of your transformation to Lean Production within IT is that everyone must be a Lean IT Expert. That sounds like a lot of work. And transforming your IT organization requires dedication. However, for most people in your IT organization, much of the learning will happen on the job under the guidance of Lean IT Experts. Most of your Lean IT Experts will emerge as a result of others having the discipline to apply Lean principles, methods and tools within the IT organization. In the end, everyone in the IT organization will need to know the foundations of Lean IT, be able to solve problems and improve on a daily basis, be able to lead whether it is in a technical area, a team or a set of teams and be able to coach colleagues to better performance.

So, what is a Lean IT Expert? A simple description is: someone who is capable of acting as a Lean IT coach, a Lean IT leader and a Lean IT kaizen lead, based on a thorough understanding of the basics of Lean IT.

But let us not leave it to my subjective judgment. There is an International Standard for Lean Experts which can obviously be used for Lean IT Experts as well. The standard is ISO18404. Annex B.3 provides the requirements for a Lean Expert:

> The role of the Lean expert is to support the Lean leaders in the application of Lean principles and the selection and use of techniques required.
> In particular, the Lean expert will
>
> - lead improvement initiatives as required,
> - determine if any training activities are appropriate and effective,
> - provide training in Lean approaches to Lean leaders as required,
> - assist in the identification of suitable areas for Lean implementation,
> - assist in periodic reviews of the implementation,
> - provide "internal" consultancy in Lean,
> - provide support so that improvements identified are realized and maintained,
> - coach and mentor the Lean leaders in the implementation of Lean principles and the selection and
> - use of the techniques required,
> - work regularly with senior management to build Lean awareness, Lean skills, and support for
> - implementation,
> - perform Lean audits at site level and use the results to identify future Lean events,
> - benchmarking, and
> - instigate/coordinate reward and recognition as appropriate.

This standard describes a host of competencies required by the Lean (IT) Expert. All of these competencies are covered in this book.

You are probably one of the people leading the transformation of your IT organization to Lean Production. This does not necessarily mean that you are hierarchically responsible for the IT organization, but you are interested in delivering more value to your customers. As you may have surmised, this book is about what you need to do to help your business survive.

This book is about you.

Part I

The Goal

The greatest thing in this world is not so much where we stand as in what direction we are moving.

Johann Wolfgang von Goethe

1

Lean IT

One of the success factors of a Lean IT transformation is building a common basis among everyone within the IT organization. This common basis is made up of definitions, knowledge and stories. In this section, we will lay down that common basis. We will define Lean IT and investigate the specifics of the IT context in which Lean is being applied. We will take a high-level look at what it means to transform an IT organization, what are the phases you will go through and how to identify the success of the transformation.

In order to ensure that the rest of the book makes sense, we must describe some basic concepts. Lean principles, dealing with waste and different types of activities are fundamental to creating a solid basis for your Lean IT transformation. We will also take a look at the relationship between Lean IT and a number of other trends in the world of IT, particularly Agile, DevOps and IT Service Management.

This book is definitely not exhaustive when it comes to Lean. A brief look at the Lean Community and the materials available to help you make your Lean IT transformation successful concludes this part of the book.

Before we dive into the process of transforming your IT organization, we need to define Lean IT. The Lean IT Association (2014) defines Lean IT as:

> Lean IT is the extension of Lean manufacturing and Lean services principles to the development and management of information technology products and services. Its goal is to continuously improve the value delivered by IT organizations to their customers, and the professionalism of people working in IT.

What this means is that Lean IT is principally about improving the capabilities of the people working within IT, their way of working and the information technology products and services, in order to deliver more value to customers. Many of the principles, methods and tools have been borrowed from other industries where Lean has been applied. There are a few tools that are specific to Lean IT.

One interesting aspect of Lean is that despite the similarities between the application of Lean principles in manufacturing, healthcare or other services, there are differences. Initially, the term Lean was synonymous with what is now called Lean Manufacturing. As Lean principles were applied to industries other than manufacturing, variations such as Lean Services, Lean Healthcare, Lean Government and of course, Lean IT developed. This proliferation comes from the fact that the context within which Lean principles, tools and methods are applied is important in determining how they are applied. Even though the tools used in Lean Manufacturing and Lean IT may be exactly the same, for example, Value Stream Mapping, kaizen problem-solving and visual management, it is necessary for a Lean practitioner from a different context to understand the IT context to be effective within IT.

Why has Lean been so successful in manufacturing industries? Manufacturing mainly deals with machines that create products. Increasingly, the human factor is removed from the production equation; robots, automated processes and machinery are all aimed at removing, or helping to remove, the variability of humans and ensuring consistent quality. Machines are designed for efficiency, i.e. they create large amounts of products at a speed that humans cannot match. Unfortunately, in the process, they tend to produce more waste than people, who adapt quickly to re-use or reduce waste. The machines are subsequently tuned to ensure that they work better, producing more products per hour or less waste per product. This is, in general, a rational, scientific process, which deals with tangible products that are produced in a predictable, structured manner. It is also relatively easy to measure how the products are made. After many improvement iterations, the goal is to obtain a defined percentage increase in improvement each time. These characteristics explain why the Six Sigma methodology developed within the manufacturing industry.

Compare this with an IT organization and we find different challenges. Firstly, an IT service is an intangible entity. Even at the core of the service, software is not something you can pick up and look at. It is only by installing it and using it that the value can be understood. To a large extent, IT is unpredictable; we do not know when it will fail; we do not know how it needs to be improved. Within IT, we are also not used to measuring the service as a whole. We measure the performance of machines but that is only part of the service. The "people" part remains largely unmeasured. This is precisely where IT differs from manufacturing: The most critical component is still the people delivering the service. The software industry continues to make inroads into reducing the people effect, but people still make up a substantial part of where the IT service can fail.

Applying Lean to IT is thus a paradoxically different proposition. The paradox is that despite our focus on the technology, Lean IT is about applying the Lean approach to people, and to a much lesser extent to machines. Aiming for perfection means raising the level of professionalism of the people involved. This means improving their ability to solve problems, to deliver and provision services in a predictable time frame and quality, to work autonomously and in a team, and to improve their mastery of the subject matter. Aside from skills training, this means embedding a new mindset focused on Lean principles.

Since the context is so important, we will start by taking a look at the IT context and what it means to transform an IT organization, followed by a dive into the basics of Lean.

2

The IT Context

What makes applying Lean to IT different to applying Lean to other sectors or industries?

As we saw earlier, the success of a business is closely linked to the ability of its IT organization to deliver business needs quickly. There is an increasingly flawed assumption that IT is a supporting and sometimes non-core or non-essential "department." The flaw in this assumption exists in two respects.

Firstly, IT is treated as separate from the business. IT products and services have become so intertwined with business processes, that the IT organization can no longer be seen as a separate entity from the business. The need for cooperation is so intense as a result of the intimate link between business process and the associated automation which together enable business outcomes. Most business decisions or functions have been built into information systems for efficiency, consistency and quality control purposes. The people building and maintaining these systems are no longer just there to execute requests from "the business" but are increasingly knowledgeable about the business process and can contribute to the improvement and further automation of the business process. In summary, information systems and services are a critical part of every business process.

Secondly, IT is seen as a simple, supporting function. IT has the characteristics of a business-within-a-business. In contrast to other "supporting" departments (such as HR, Legal or Finance), IT contains the full range of business functions. It designs and develops products and services. The IT organization ensures that IT services run in production and it provides support and maintenance for these products and services. IT usually manages its own finances, as a result of complicated cost allocation and budgeting, based on economies of scale. Human Resources

Management for IT is increasingly seen as a separate, specialist discipline, as can be seen from the development of the e-Competence Framework. IT departments have their own specialized purchasing and legal support to deal with the requirements for contracting external parties.

One useful model that illustrates the complexity of the IT environment quite well is described in the Lean IT book *Run, Grow, Transform* (Bell, 2012). The Flows of Value model defines five different levels of flow within an IT organization. The five levels are described in Figure 2.1.

The key premise of this model is that the focus of IT strategy, governance, organizational structures and measures change as IT organizations increase their scope from technological through enterprise to external customer focus. The model does not imply that each IT organization must achieve Level 5, although this is sometimes forced on the organization by external use of IT products and services. It simply describes the characteristic of each level of flow.

At the first level (Technology Focused), the value of IT flow is seen from the departmental level, and the focus is on technology domains. At the core of IT, the basic components of IT, the hardware and software, must work correctly. At this level, we find the various technologies required to make IT services work. From a value stream perspective, process improvement will focus on IT Operations and basic support processes and functions such as the Service Desk.

Level	Type of Flow	Focus of Flow	The Value of IT Flow
5	External Market Flow	External Customer Focused	• Business revenue is directly generated by IT services • IT is key part of business process • Image, and value of business influenced by IT capability
4	Business Process Flow	Business Partner Focused	• IT part of strategic business planning process • CIO responsible for more than traditional IT function • IT and business KPIs overlap
3	Enterprise IT Flow	Business Customer Focused	• IT services support the business process • IT organization is enterprise function common processes & tools, with enforced standards • IT is taking and fulfilling orders from its business customers
2	Application vs. Infrastructure Flow	System/Service Focused	• Common services, tools and processes • Service-based Service Level Agreements • IT services defined as infrastructure and users based services
1	Departmental Flow	Technology Focused	• IT Technology domains (Infrastructure / Applications) • IT Operations and Service Desk

FIGURE 2.1
Five flows of IT value as defined by Bell (2012).

The next level (System/Service Focused) focuses on the coherent cooperation of the IT components into IT systems and IT services, meaning that infrastructure and applications work together in the eyes of the customer. IT services are typically initially defined as infrastructure and user-based services, such as workplace services or a service concerning an application of which the name is recognizable for the end-user. At this level, the IT organization perceives two forms of flow: Plan and Build processes on the one hand and Run processes on the other. The various IT groups largely split themselves into two camps, Application Development or Infrastructure, and there is limited connection between the camps.

Level 3 is focused on the Business Customer. The customers of IT are the employees of the IT Department's colleagues in different parts of the business, who gain real value when the two camps of the IT organization come together to deliver services that support business processes. Unfortunately, at this level, there is a false belief that IT is a service provider that is somehow a disconnected supplier to the actual business. This delivery of value typically involves IT taking and fulfilling orders from its business customer. The business customer is gaining a better understanding of the fact that IT is a function made up of both internal and external suppliers using common processes and tools. IT is seen as a single entity (Enterprise IT Flow) but still separate from the other business units.

At level 4, IT is seen as an integral part of the business. As IT becomes focused on its business partners, IT becomes an integral part of the strategic business planning processes. IT measures its success in terms that are relevant for the business, for example, end-to-end availability of IT services rather than just the uptime of IT components. Value is based on ensuring that IT services match business processes and the two (business process and IT service) are considered as one. There is a focus on flow across the entire business ecosystem, with IT-enabled value streams.

The highest level of value delivered by IT (level 5: External customer focused) is when IT services can be sold in the market. The IT organization may be part of a larger enterprise or a commercial IT service provider, and is explicitly focused on the external customer. Business revenue is directly generated by the sale of IT services to customers outside the enterprise. IT-based services and their digital transactions are perceived to be integral and synonymous with the business processes they support. This means that websites and apps that are made available to external customers are part of this level of value, even though the organization may not charge separately for their use. At this level of value, it is possible for market share and stock price to be influenced by the market's perception of the quality and stability of IT capability. Value streams directly involve external customers as well as internal partners and stakeholders.

The complexity of IT is found in the fact that all five levels can be found in different parts of an IT organization at the same time. This causes challenges in prioritization and collaboration, as different parts of the IT organization have a different view at different times of their role in supporting overall business value stream and the improvement of flow. The first three levels (Technology, Systems/Service and Business Customer) are absolutely essential for any value to be delivered.

As a Lean IT Expert within IT, you will work with individuals who will be working at different levels of this model and may be confronted with the challenge of getting the various stakeholders to a common level of understanding. A team leader of a team responsible for a part of the IT infrastructure may be focused solely on technological issues. A Service Manager will likely look at the IT context from a system/service focus. Although, depending on the way the IT organization has deployed its Service Managers, they may even have a business customer focus. The cooperation between the team leader and the Service Manager (and between their teams) is challenging. This challenge can be made more difficult by leaders looking at the IT organization from the business partner or external customer perspective. A Product Owner may look at the world from a business process flow or an enterprise IT flow perspective.

The dynamics of IT also mean that there is a wide range in the characteristics of IT people. Some are focused on fire-fighting while others take a more long-term view of IT. In my experience, people in IT inherently have a strong curiosity; they adore puzzles especially when they have the time to investigate and solve them. They tend to be methodical in their approach to problems, although everyone has their own method. This relationship with problems and puzzles does have a shadow side: IT people seem to like being the one who can identify the new or associated problems with any solution to a given problem, however unlikely the situation is to arise. Depth of knowledge is a status-enhancing quality for IT people, both in their own estimation and the estimation of others. This aspect, specifically, is also a minefield for managers within IT, which I refer to as the "knowledge trap." If the manager has too much technical knowledge, team members tend to feel undervalued and unrecognized; if he has too little, team members will not respect his decisions. Managers must have "technical understanding," a capability that manifests itself in the ability to ask the right questions and make the right judgment calls when required. Here, we see that leadership behaviors like asking the right questions, listening carefully to the answers and making decisions based on broad input can serve as a balance to the knowledge "trap."

Like many experts, IT experts have a tendency to overestimate the understanding that another person has regarding their area of expertise. This means that they end up not getting their message across or, rather, the other party is confirmed in their belief that if you ask an IT engineer a question you will no longer understand your own question once you have heard the answer. Having said that, this style of communication is grounded in the engineer's desire to be complete, i.e. to explain the solution and all the pitfalls surrounding it. In most cases, I have found that this behavior is based on a sincere need to be helpful; although in some cases, it is just showing off expertise.

Another complexity within IT is the fact that IT people tend to be confronted with many different units of work. These units of work include smaller, less time-consuming ones such as operational activities, incidents, service requests and standard changes, but also larger ones like non-standard changes, projects or advisory work. Not only are IT people confronted with this diverse range of units of work, they may have to work on all of these units of work within a single working day. This can lead to a confusing work dynamic, since each unit of work has different requirements, from high-stress – incidents that need to be solved instantly – to high thought-intensity planning related to the delivery of a complicated business automation solution, requiring careful consideration.

One of the key characteristics that differentiates Lean IT from Lean in other areas of business is the units of work. These units of work are the inputs for processes. The standard units of work are derived to a certain extent from ITIL (Table 2.1).

Each unit of work is processed through one or more IT processes. These processes have different dynamics. Plotted on a scale of customer involvement against repeatability, we see that IT operations has a high repeatability but low customer involvement whereas application development has high customer involvement and low repeatability (Figure 2.2).

As a result of the explosion of technological capabilities within IT, language has been developed to ensure that IT professionals can distinguish between the various technologies and possibilities. IT people speak their own jargon and have their own rituals and behaviors, to such an extent that

TABLE 2.1

Units of Work

Unit of Work	Definition
Incident	A technical malfunction of the IT service affecting the customer
Service Request	A request from the customer, not being a technical malfunction
Problem	The root cause of incident(s)
Standard Change	Change that is carried out according to a checklist or standard operating procedure
Non-Standard Change	Any change that is not a standard change
Operational Activity	Any activity necessary to keep the current IT service running, not being an incident or service request. This category includes events, monitoring and other daily/weekly activities that ensure the health of an IT service.
Advice	A document detailing options for a solution, based on a customer request
Plan	A document covering a course of action in the future (availability, capacity, continuity, security)

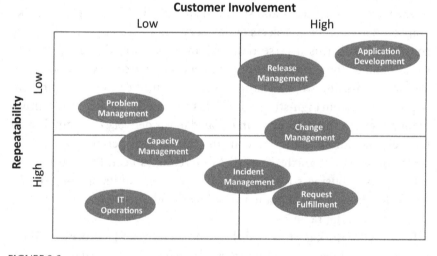

FIGURE 2.2

Dynamics of IT processes.

in a large IT organization, infrastructure and application departments may have difficulties understanding one another. The problem is compounded when we include the service desk, agile development teams or DevOps teams. The proliferation of jargon, of course, leads to communication difficulties with non-IT colleagues.

Lastly, and possibly most important, IT is "invisible." The intangible nature of IT makes it hard to observe the work within IT. This often leads to a lack of understanding of what IT people do all day. The visible parts of IT development and operations are basically people and hardware. But what these visible parts actually do is not always easy to grasp. The consequence is that the IT *gemba*, the place where the work is done, needs to be studied and understood before you can apply Lean principles.

The question is: What does the IT gemba look like?

If we take a bird's eye view of an IT organization, we can identify four distinct parts of the IT gemba: The software development gemba, the service desk gemba, the IT operations gemba and the supporting staff gemba. Each part has its own characteristics.

This Software Development part of the IT gemba is made up of people principally working on changes to IT services or creating new IT services. They are strongly deliverable-oriented. Creating these deliverables will entail both individual work and project-based teamwork. These people tend not to work on production systems, and generally see their involvement in the resolution of an incident on a production system as a disruption to their workflow. The focus of this gemba is to create high-quality deliverables that meet the needs of the customer. What will you see at this gemba? Individuals working on various phases of the software development process (designing, coding, testing). An effective development gemba has small teams of people working together. Software developers tend to use different tools than the rest of the IT organization. However, with the development of a continuous delivery pipeline, we see the software development gemba becoming integrated with the IT operations gemba.

The IT operations gemba is the production gemba, the place where IT services that are used by customers are operated and supported. This may be split into various technology-oriented teams that together encompass the IT production gemba. This is what makes the IT gemba a difficult place to interpret. Different parts of the delivery of IT services take place in different departments. The most obvious part of the IT operations gemba is the data center. Here we find the machines running the various environments, with relatively few people. Most of the people working at the IT operations gemba can be found in their respective (technology-oriented) team rooms. Ultimately, this means that the people running a particular IT service may be dotted throughout the IT organization, increasing the difficulty of actually understanding what is going on.

To complicate matters, there may also be an overlap between these teams and the software development gemba, in that people from IT operations may be involved in software development projects, or developers may be required for solving incidents and problems in the operation. The IT operations gemba tends to be a highly process-oriented environment in which standards are important, and the focus is on ensuring the right capabilities (both in a technological and people sense).

The third part of the IT gemba is the service desk, which tends to be the most dynamic part. You will see people on the phone talking to customers about their issues when using the IT services, or processing questions received by email or through a self-service portal. These people have the most intense contact with customers and, consequently, are often those most focused on meeting the customers' expectations. They are interested in the status of the IT services in production. Depending on the responsibilities of the service desk, part of the team may be carrying out standard changes. The service desk gemba can be hectic when a major incident hits the IT services. The primary tool used by the service desk is the IT service management tool and their focus is on ensuring that incidents, service requests, and standard changes are executed as quickly as possible. The units of work they process will be recorded in the IT service management tool so that they can be routed to other teams if the service desk is unable to process the unit of work. In most IT organizations, the IT operations teams use the IT service management tool as well. The communication is relatively straightforward. Software development teams tend to use different software (other than the IT service management tool) to process their work. This often leads to delays and miscommunication between the service desk, IT operations and software development.

Throughout the IT organization, there are people who do not directly work on producing or operating IT services, but are nonetheless vital for the flow of IT processes. I refer to this group of people collectively as supporting staff, and these are people focused on ensuring that policy is created, implemented and followed. There is a high level of expertise in these roles. The supporting staff gemba is essentially made up of expert and coordination roles, both technological and managerial. The supporting staff coordinate processes, projects, architecture and teams. An example is the role of the IT architect, an expert responsible for creating architectures that are needed to identify the risks involved with a large change or project. In this respect, they have a direct impact on the ability of the IT organization as a whole to deliver value on time. In traditional

IT organizations organized in technology silos, there will be roles in place focused on ensuring the coordination of the technologies into a coherent and functioning service to the customer. When looking at this gemba, it is vital to understand what is being coordinated and how this is being done.

With the integration of Lean principles into IT organizations, there will be a natural tendency of these archetypes to overlap and even merge. In the case of DevOps teams, we see that the different focuses are brought together with the aim of producing high-quality IT services that meet the expectations of the internal and external customers of IT. This is the result of the increased explicit focus on achieving flow by every means available, including organizing teams differently, integrating all necessary aspects into a completely new gemba. The new gemba will look and feel completely different to the traditional gembas we know, as described above. The new gemba will include all of the activities, however, as a result of the diversity of activities, the structures, activities and behaviors will overlap and evolve into something more holistic.

A final word on the impact of context on Lean: In his book *Developing Lean Leaders at All Levels*, Jeffrey Liker himself refers to an IT example of the application of Lean principles as an example of "non-traditional Lean" (2014).

3

Lean IT Transformation

The starting point I choose for your Lean IT transformation is a Mass Production IT organization. You may already have taken steps within your IT organization, for example, using Scrum in your application development or doing daily stand-ups in your Operations department. Although there is a more pressing reason for transforming your IT organization, namely survival, we need to have some kind of business rationale for starting what is an arduous journey.

There are essentially three components to the business case for Lean IT: Customer satisfaction, strategic advantages and cost advantages. All three play a role in creating the sense of urgency and ambition to start the transformation.

Internal IT organizations and external IT service providers have all had, at some time, problems with customer satisfaction. These issues tend to be related to excessive disruptions in existing IT services, long lead times in the delivery of new capabilities and the insufficient delivery of promised capabilities. The benefits that Lean IT brings to increasing customer satisfaction start with the increased focus on customer value. This shift in focus can be particularly seen in a shift of behavior and attitude of everyone within the IT organization away from individual targets and goals towards a goal-sharing mentality, in which customer value is central. In a more practical sense, the behavior and attitude of all employees, when combined with the Lean IT tools, leads to the structural elimination of defects and other dissatisfiers. This, in turn, leads to the increase in reliable and predictable delivery of services and the development of superior IT products and services. For external IT service providers, Lean IT can bring a better market position due to increased loyalty from satisfied customers and a new or sustained reputation for high-quality services.

Lean also brings what can be described as strategic advantages; advantages that allow the IT organization to operate in a way that leaves it less liable to substitution (outsourcing) or other effects of competition. Strategic advantages are principally achieved through the development of competencies that are difficult for other organizations to copy. Although the adoption of Lean IT may be similar for all IT organizations, the effects will undoubtedly be different. Lean IT provides strategic value because it encourages competence building with the continual improvement of products and services. Lean IT also delivers higher productivity due to increased efficiency as a result of removing waste from the system. The removal of waste delivers time advantages, allowing the IT organization to provide new IT functionality and capabilities more rapidly. Lastly, and maybe most importantly, Lean IT has been proven to improve employee and managerial involvement and motivation. This brings a strategic advantage since it is an aspect that cannot be copied.

No business case is complete without a financial aspect. There is an almost automatic reaction that when increasing quality, costs will rise. Lean paradoxically works on the opposite premise: Applying Lean principles reduces waste and increases flow leading to better quality of processes and resulting products and services. This, in turn, leads to lower costs or at the very least the ability of the IT organization to produce more with the same people. If it does not, you are not doing it right or you are not finished transforming yet. Lean IT aims to optimize value-add work, so that there is time for other activities. Focus on reducing work-in-progress and inventory leads to improvements in the financial position of the organization. One word of warning: Cost reduction is never a reason to embark on transforming to a Lean IT organization, it is a consequence of driving waste out of the organizational system.

All in all, there is a strong business case for Lean IT. However, it is vital for the IT management team to identify the business case for its own organization. Each IT organization must define its own reasons for starting the Lean journey. It is this preliminary discussion of the reasons for Lean IT that provide the longer-term vision and goals to which the managers within IT can and must commit, both individually and collectively.

It is obvious that moving towards a Lean IT organization will be a departure from the current way of working; a change that requires effort and dedication to achieve the intended goals. One of the widely used and insightful publications on the general rules of change is John Kotter's 2007 article "Leading Change: Why Transformation Efforts Fail." He clearly describes eight reasons for failure and proposes a corresponding eight-step model to mitigate the key mistakes. Let us look at the eight mitigations that can have a huge effect on the results of the change.

- Create a sense of urgency and ensure that people understand the need for the change. This is more difficult than it may seem. A sense of urgency must not create an environment in which fear takes over; this leads to inaction, rather than the action we are looking for. The sense of urgency should contain a strong element of challenge and ambition.
- Establish a guiding coalition that is powerful enough. This guiding coalition must consist of both management and team members and, in the case of a Lean IT transformation, it is useful if these people are all actively in the process of becoming Lean IT Experts. Throughout the organization, there must be people supporting the need for change.
- There must be a clear vision for the future. This is the responsibility of the leaders of the organization. This vision means having a narrative describing how a Lean IT organization should work and which results are being aimed for. This vision must be consistent with the sense of urgency created to encourage action.
- Communicate, communicate, communicate the vision. Leaders have a tendency to think that it is enough to tell people a few times where the organization is going and what needs to be. Experience from a number of Lean IT transformations confirms that reminding people of the vision on a daily basis is no luxury, rather a necessity.
- Remove obstacles to the new vision. This is a difficult aspect of a transformation because this is where leadership must make it easy for the organization to work in the new way. This means truly committing to the chosen vision and getting rid of previously successful ways of working that do not promote the Lean way of working.
- Plan for and create short-term wins. Regular successes help people to maintain their enthusiasm for Lean IT. The problem is that we need to tell ourselves that we have been successful. Leaders must be aware of the successes, especially the small ones, that are being achieved and celebrate them.
- Do not declare victory too soon. In fact, do not declare victory at all. A Lean IT transformation will not be completed in the short term

and stating that you are now a Lean IT organization is a sure sign that you are not there yet.

- Anchor changes in the organization's way of working. The Lean way of working must be part of the habits and routines of the organization. It must be part of the way people think and act.

Lean IT actually includes methods and tools to support all of these remedies to the problems associated with transforming organizations. We will discuss this in more detail throughout this book.

4

The Basics of Lean

As a Lean IT Expert, one of the first things you must be able to do is to explain where Lean came from, what its premises are and its relation to the current frame of reference that people are familiar with. Much of what follows has been told many TIMES before in other publications. I will therefore try to stick to the essentials.

Towards the end of the 19th century, Frederick Winslow Taylor investigated workplace efficiencies. His ideas included dividing work and specifying tasks to be performed, training workers so they could perform these tasks, and installing supervisors to ensure that tasks were performed as specified. Henry Ford used these ideas, introducing interchangeable parts with standardized work and moving conveyance to create what he called flow production. This type of production, Mass Production, thrived on the division of labor and specification of tasks.

As the people at Toyota looked at this situation in the 1930's, and more intensely after World War II, it occurred to them that a series of innovations might make it more possible to provide both continuity in process flow and a wide variety in product offerings. The goal for Toyota was to catch up with the rest of the world, particularly America. Due to scarcity in a general sense, Toyota focused on minimizing the amount of raw materials required to produce cars and on minimizing the time between purchasing raw materials and sending an invoice to the customer. The system Toyota developed became known as the Toyota Production System (TPS). This system shifted the focus from individual machines and their utilization, to the flow of the product through the total process, ensuring that customer demand became a key driver of this system. The Toyota Production System was based on two basic principles: Just-in-time production and jidoka. As Toyota improved, TPS became part of the *The Toyota Way*, that was published in 2001. Today, the jidoka and just-in-time principles remain; however, the Toyota Way philosophy within which they now reside has included two higher principles: Respect for People and Continuous Improvement.

W. Edwards Deming is regarded as having provided the basis for Lean through the introduction of the Plan–Do–Check–Act (PDCA) cycle (Imai, 1997). The PDCA cycle is an iterative four-step management method used in business for the control and continuous improvement of processes and products. The Deming cycle is an integral part of the Lean philosophy and embodies the goal for continuous improvement.

In the Plan step, business process components are designed or revised to improve results. Do involves implementing the plan and measuring the resulting performance. Check means assessing the measurements and reviewing them. Act is all about deciding which changes are needed to improve the process.

The PDCA cycle creates a feedback loop for both management and teams to ensure that improvements are identified and implemented. Deming showed that organizations could increase quality and reduce costs by reducing waste, rework and staff attrition while increasing customer loyalty. The key was to improve continuously and think of manufacturing as a system, not as a series of parts to be optimized.

Lean is a way of thinking and behaving. It revolves around the following key concepts: Improving customer value, continuous improvement in small steps, decreasing peaks and troughs in production, reducing waste, involving everybody, developing people and focusing on long-term goals.

As discussed earlier, there are a variety of reasons for organizations to be Lean. The business case components, customer satisfaction and strategic value are a great place to start. Poor quality can also be a driver for the adoption of Lean. Poor quality has its effects both within and outside the organization. Aspects such as reputational damage and loss of customer trust may cause the organization to incur large costs or penalties. Also, waste of talent or an unexpected number of defects cause stress within the organization. Consequently, costs increase due to inspections, rework or demotivation.

An outcome of applying Lean principles is a paradigm shift in the way we think. Lean challenges our assumptions of how work is supposed to be done and how responsibilities are supposed to be executed. A traditional paradigm is that knowledge is power. An organization may find itself depending on a few critical resources that have the knowledge of how processes operate. Lean organizations understand that it is more powerful to work on the continuous involvement of all employees and to maximize the transparency of information by use of, for example, visual management techniques. In a traditional context, management decides what needs to be done and how to operate, while workers just need to follow orders. This division of labor and specification of tasks originate from the interpretation of the studies of Taylor. In Lean organizations, managers facilitate the teams at the operational level. They lead as a coach and teacher, and allow their teams to take on the responsibility to figure out how processes are best optimized to deliver results for the customer.

In order to effectively facilitate a team, managers need to be present at the gemba. This kind of managerial behavior is in sharp contrast with the more traditional style of management, where managers are found in their offices or in meetings mainly with other managers. This latter behavior causes them to lose touch with what is actually happening in the organization.

Traditional organizations aim to maximize the utilization of resources. In the case of IT, this means ensuring that "expensive" people like programmers must be given as much work as possible so that no time is "wasted." This kind of thinking derives from the scarcity and cost of resources, so we should make the best use of them. However, it often leads to inefficiencies because people produce more than is actually needed, and filling people up with work reduces their flexibility. Lean organizations focus first on maximizing the efficiency of flow, i.e. ensuring that work is moved through the process so as to deliver value to the customer as quickly as possible.

Another aspect of the paradigm shift is how people regard defects or mistakes and how to deal with problems. In traditional organizations, the focus is on avoiding problems, even though they occur. Problems are seen as "not good." At the same time, there is acceptance of a certain, undefined, rate of defects. Lean organizations welcome problems and learn from mistakes. They make it a collaborative exercise and share what they have learned across the organization. It is up to management to ensure that the mistakes are embraced and used to continually improve the capabilities of the people and the organization as a whole. This openness to seeing, accepting, and solving problems is strongly related to an ongoing pursuit of perfection.

Lean contains elements that appear counterintuitive, such as the increase in quality accompanied by a reduction in cost. Another element is that Lean thrives in environments with scarcity of resources such as time, money, talent, or materials. Toyota's pioneering ideas come from a time where they could not afford to produce inventory simply because there was not enough material. A scarcity of resources is a reason for the development of Lean and a reason to apply Lean principles and use Lean tools. The key perceived scarce resource within IT is time. Interestingly, lack of resources (particularly time and/or money) is one of the most touted reasons for *not* beginning to apply Lean to IT. In fact, the slowest and least successful adoptions of Lean within IT are in organizations with the most resources. While we are on the subject of reasons not to start your Lean journey, one of the most enigmatic I have come across is lack of maturity (whatever that means). This is like saying: "This IT organization is so bad that we cannot even attempt improving it." Obviously, this is a complete fallacy from a Lean perspective. Starting the journey to Lean IT can start anywhere, any time and at any (perceived) level of capability. There are no prerequisites, bar the enduring desire to improve.

LEAN PRINCIPLES – PART 1

The essence of Lean is delivering value to customers and continuously improving the ability to do this, by removing waste from the entire system that produces the value. In the landmark publication on the philosophy of Lean, *Lean Thinking: Banish Waste and Create Wealth in Your Corporation* by Womack and Jones (1996), the authors describe the key principles of Lean.

Value is defined by the customer and represents the requirements that a customer has regarding a specific product or service delivered. The value of a product or service is its ability to help the user of the product or service to deliver value to his or her customers. We, therefore, need to continuously focus on the value for the customer and the value they perceive from a product or service. If that value is insufficient, customers will seek out another organization to provide it.

Value is delivered through a value stream. This is an end-to-end process triggered by the customer that ensures the delivery of the required value. A value stream contains all tasks and activities used to bring a product or service from concept to customer, and includes all information, work and material flows.

In order for a value stream to deliver value, it must have flow. This means that the activities must follow each other with minimal interruptions and minimal intermediate stockpiles. The value stream must be designed so that each unit of work that enters the value stream is carried to its conclusion without interruption. The ultimate form of flow is working with a so-called "single piece flow," i.e. each unit of work goes through the process on its own. This is the opposite of working in batches where multiple units of work are processed through a particular step together, or work is started, set aside and then resumed at a later moment, as is often the case in IT.

Flow is interrupted mostly by the following types of waste: Handoffs, inspections and waiting times. Work In Progress (WIP) is both a result of a lack of flow and an obstacle to achieving flow. It is often generated by differences in work tempo. A surplus of inventory can result from a work tempo that is faster than customer demand in production environments (produce to inventory), or a work tempo that is slower than customer demand in service (and IT) environments (inability to process demand). Flow is about getting the right materials and the right information to the right people, with the right skills, in the right place, at the right time, every time; in short: Just in Time. One word of caution: Even if a process has flow, it is vital to monitor demand to ensure that the work can be carried out, as a change in customer demand can alter the flow in the process.

It is also vital to understand that the customer can trigger the value stream when the value is required. This is the essence of pull. A pull production system is one that explicitly limits the amount of work in the value stream to that which can be processed by the system. Nothing is to be produced until the next step really requires it. For service industries like IT, this is less problematic than for production industries, since a service is consumed as it is produced and is generally started when requested by the customer. In IT, pull is particularly used to manage the capacity in the process.

Last but not least, Lean aims for perfection. This does not mean that multiple quality controls need to be in place to generate quality. This would only cause delays. It means that each person in the value stream must know their task and the associated quality requirements. The essence of perfection is doing things right the first time and, in the case that this does not happen, stopping the process to resolve the problem. This aspect also ensures that there is a focus on continuously improving the ability to deliver value. Transparency supports the goal for perfection because transparency ensures useful feedback is obtained to understand where delivery does not meet expectations. We need to create an environment where learning from mistakes is a powerful element of continuous improvement. There is no end to the process of reducing effort, time, space, cost and mistakes to offer a product that is aligned with what the customer wants and values.

WASTE

As part of delivering as much value as possible to customers and working towards perfection, Lean IT is focused on ensuring that the waste that often accompanies and hinders the creation of customer value is removed. Therefore, the value to customers is increased in two ways, by reducing the proportion of wasteful activities to value-adding activities and by increasing the absolute amount of value-related activities.

Waste within IT includes the traditional categories: Transportation, Inventory, Motion, Waiting Time, Overprocessing, Overproduction and Defects & Rework (TIMWOOD). There is an important additional type of waste in IT: Talent (or Skills). This is when the skills and abilities of the resources in the IT organization are lacking or not used to their full extent (Table 4.1).

In addition to traditional definitions of waste (or muda), there are two other categories of loss: Variability (mura) and Overburden (muri).

Mura (variability) occurs when incoming work is not matched to the right number of people with the appropriate skills, thus leading to a wide range of possible outcomes in quality. Variability is about fluctuation, in cost, quality, or throughput times. Variability in IT is directly related to the fact that customer demand can vary significantly and unpredictably. For example, an IT organization may be able to estimate how many units

TABLE 4.1

Eight Types of Waste

Waste	Description
Transportation	Movement of work product, information, or materials
Inventory	Work in progress, having more than strategic levels of products
Motion	Unnecessary physical movement
Waiting	Stopping or slowing down for work to arrive
Overproduction	Producing more or sooner than is needed
Overprocessing	Excessive or unnecessary work
Defects	Reworking to correct mistakes, inspect and scrap
Talent (or Skills)	Unused human creativity and potential

of work (e.g. incidents, changes, service requests) will be received in a particular time frame. However, predicting when these units of work will arrive is a more difficult prospect. This causes variability.

Muri (overburden) is caused by fixed service timeframes, release windows and other such time constraints. The ability to scale a team up or down to match workload also plays a role in being flexible. Large inventories and a batch processing system cause overburden and inflexibility, reducing the ability of processes to have flow. Muri is largely policy-based waste. It is caused by constraints that the organization chooses to use, for example, team composition or size, organizational structure and the aforementioned release windows.

To remove waste from an IT organization, it is vital for management to initiate a review of muri before tackling mura, followed by muda. Attempting to remove, for example, an excess of changes (inventory waste) may be frustrated by a policy-based choice to allow people to submit any number of changes.

THE VALUE OF ACTIVITIES

Customers put a demand for value on your organization. In carrying out the work to deliver this value, we can identify three types of activities: Activities that add value from a customer perspective (Value-Add Activities, VA), activities that do not add value from a customer perspective (Non-Value-Add Activities, NVA) and activities that do not add value but need to be done nevertheless, often according to an organization's policy (Necessary Non-Value-Add Activities, NNVA). Necessary Non-Value-Add activities include steps or changes made to the product for future or subsequent steps to ensure compliance with policies, but which are not noticed by the final customer.

Examples of Value-Add activities:

Activity	Example
Application Development	Delivering new functionality for the customer
Operational Activities	Ensuring the service keeps working by checking log files, cleaning up temporary files
Delivery of a laptop	Meaning a new employee can start working
Advice	Providing understanding and insight into the use of IT so that decisions can be made

Examples of Necessary Non-Value-Add activities:

Activity	Example
Recruiting Staff	Recruiting and selecting new people ultimately helps the organization to deliver value
Finance and Accounting	These activities mean we can finance the delivery of value to customers
Application Testing	Ensuring that the product works before it is delivered to the customer
Conducting Problem and Root Cause Analysis	Resolving the root cause incidents to avoid re-occurrence

Examples of Non-Value-Add activities:

Activity	Example
Inventory	Managing large backlogs of incidents
Doing more than Required	Providing functionality that is not necessary
Rework	Bugs in software and subsequent solving of IT incidents
Waiting	Delay between programming and testing.
General Non-Value-Add	Sick leave, smoking breaks

Our goal is to optimize value-adding activities, minimize necessary non-value-add activities and remove non-value-adding activities. The expenditure of resources for any goal other than the creation of value is considered to be wasteful. Value-adding activity is any action or process that a customer would be willing to pay for, and that is performed right the first time.

Understanding the nature of a particular activity helps people within IT to focus on activities that add value to the customer. Lean aims to remove Non-Value-Adding activities, which Taiichi Ohno stated was not work at all (Ohno, 2012). Necessary Non-Value-Add work must be optimized and reduced, where possible. The difficult part is that we may not be able to identify an entire activity as being Non-Value-Add or necessary Non-Value-Add. We will often need to look deeper at activities that appear to be value-adding but end up having all manner of sub-activities that do not add value.

LEAN PRINCIPLES –PART 2

There are a few concepts that will be referred to repeatedly in this book. These are fundamental to thinking and acting within a Lean environment. Next to the seven words that you should be able to recite at will, Customer Value – Value Stream – Flow – Pull – Perfection, these concepts are at the heart of Lean. The great thing about principles is that they always help you. Take a random situation and apply a principle to it. For example, I do not know which change to work on first. Throw "customer value" at it first, which of the changes has the highest customer value? Throw "pull" at it: How can we ensure this piece of work is ready to be pulled into the next process step? Throw "perfection" at it: How can you ensure that this change can be delivered first time right? The following principles complement the five basic principles.

Jidoka

The focus of a Lean organization is on the team members creating value for the customers. Team members are empowered to operate effectively. Team members are made responsible for the quality and value of their work. Ideas and ongoing development and improvement of team members are also important.

A clear way in which this empowerment is stimulated is jidoka. Jidoka is about creating an environment in which problems cannot remain unseen and supports the use of visual management. An associated concept is autonomation or "automating with a human touch," which helps to make problems visible. This is where automation is used to help people understand when something has gone wrong in the process or is about to go wrong. This ensures that errors do not get passed to next steps in the process. This is the core of creating quality at the source. Jidoka is one of the two pillars of the Toyota Production System, along with just-in-time production. Jidoka highlights the causes of problems because work is stopped immediately when a problem is uncovered. This leads to improvements in the processes that build in quality by eliminating the root causes of defects. With jidoka, team members are asked to take responsibility for stopping the line to ensure there is quality at the source. Everyone is expected to take responsibility for embedding quality at the source.

A central concept within jidoka is the andon cord. This is a physical cord that employees can pull to stop the production line. In fact, pulling the andon cord initially only affects a single station in the production line. The team at that station has a limited amount of time to solve the problem before the stations upstream and downstream are affected. The andon cord is pulled some 3,500 times per day in a typical Toyota manufacturing plant. The principal effect of the andon cord is that it gives the people closest to the work the authority to ensure quality at the source. There is no excuse for passing defective work forward.

The question is: What are the andon cords within the Lean IT organization? Certainly, with regard to changes, the Change Advisory board meeting must act as an andon cord, stopping changes that will introduce new errors into the IT infrastructure from progressing in the process. The advent of Continuous Delivery (CD) pipelines is one of the ways that IT creates jidoka. The CD pipeline is a structure that needs to be continuously improved so as to ensure that all software conforms to the standards that are necessary for bug-free operation. The CD pipeline must ensure that defective code is not passed forward into production. It helps the developers to identify where code contains errors, so that they can pull the andon cord.

Just-In-Time

As we have seen, inventory is one of the wastes in an organization. Just-in-time is a principle that aims to ensure that inventory approaches zero. In a production environment, this means ensuring that the right parts are available in exactly the right amount at the right moment, thereby reducing inventory to the bare minimum. Within IT, where we do not talk about parts, just-in-time is a more difficult concept. It means dealing with units of work as and when they need to be dealt with.

For operational activities, incidents, service requests and standard changes, this means dealing with them without delay, i.e. process what you receive each and every day ensuring that no inventory grows. For advice, plans and non-standard changes, it means processing the unit of work so that the value is delivered exactly when the customer needs it. Combine this with the principle of flow and the need for an excellent understanding of time usage becomes clear.

For decades, IT has worked in batches. Based on the argument that introducing changes into the production environment inevitably causes disruptions to users, IT has limited the moments for introducing changes. Consequently, IT has needed to bundle multiple changes into a release (a batch) to be introduced together. Paradoxically, the effect is that there are more disruptions and the time needed to resolve them is longer since it is not always clear which change in the release caused the disruption. Lean encourages single piece flow or small batch processing. Again, the CD pipeline is a structure that helps to achieve the goal of just-in-time working.

Just-in-time within IT means having the capability to adjust each and every system at any moment of the day with a single small change that has minimum disruption for the customer. Many of the legacy systems do not readily facilitate such a capability. However, this does not mean that the responsible teams should not take steps to achieve this capability. In fact, in a Lean IT organization, it is their duty to take steps on a daily basis to make working to the principle of just-in-time possible.

Kaizen

In Lean IT, our mindset is that we accept that our world is filled with problems and we act to solve the problems on a continuous basis. This is kaizen and is the heart of continuous improvement. Continuous improvement means never being satisfied with the current situation, always on the lookout for ways to deliver more value, improve the quality, or simply make the work easier.

Kaizen forms the basis of incremental continuous improvement in organizations and contains an approach for solving problems. Kai means "change," zen means "for the better." Kaizen is about continuously improving: Everyday, everyone, everywhere. Many small improvements implemented results in faster innovation and more competitive advantage for both IT and the business with far lower risks.

IT people spend most of their days solving problems. However, there tends to be little structure in how this is done, which inevitably leads to "jumping to conclusions." In the case of more complicated incidents, for example, we see technical people throwing solutions at one another rather than doing a thorough analysis of the situation. More about this in Part V.

The starting point of kaizen is developing a kaizen mindset. What do we mean by this? We mean that there must be a belief throughout the IT organization, both among managers and employees, that improving IT services and the way they are delivered can and must be done on a daily basis.

What are the core behaviors that turn a kaizen mindset into effective action?

- Seeing and prioritizing problems: Are both managers and team members truly prepared to uncover problems, accept them as a part of daily life and initiate action to identify the problems that most need solving?

- Solving problems: Are both managers and team members prepared to invest time and other resources to understand the root causes of problems and resolve problems completely?
- Sharing lessons learned: Are both managers and team members driven to share the lessons learned as a result of solving problems with others in the IT organization, so that they may benefit from the lessons learned?

It is important to note at this point that problem solving is not about reactively waiting for problems to appear and then resolving them as they occur. A problem-solving mindset is to first establish a desired state of the IT service or process, understand the current baseline and gap and, then, to incrementally close the gaps towards the desired state through kaizen improvement steps. The essence is that identifying problems and solving their root cause drives individual and organizational learning.

Respect for People

This is one area where IT organizations have not always excelled. Respect for people is about valuing the contributions made by people within the IT organization and recognizing their needs and satisfaction. Respect for people obviously extends outside the IT organization to customers, colleagues, suppliers and other stakeholders. The key to respect is ensuring that there is trust in the relationships built between people. This is done by, among other ways, being open to the differences between people, encouraging individual initiative and being prepared to listen to other people's opinions. It also means being accountable for the required performance. Here, we see that IT management who have grown up through the ranks of the IT organization have a tendency to "know the solutions." Rather than letting the engineers and experts determine the answers and solutions, management gets involved in all manner of technical details, often making decisions that do not make sense.

Respect for people is also about development of skills and knowledge. In many IT organizations, people are assigned to support legacy systems that are being phased out. Unfortunately, this phasing out can take a long time. During this period, those assigned to the system are often not included in the new developments. By the time the new system is implemented, the "legacy people" are completely out of touch with the new world and IT management generally writes these people off, by either removing them from the system or finding a way to bundle them into an outsourcing deal. Rarely is a concerted effort made to re-skill these people. This aspect of respect is best described as the development of teams and the ensurance of teamwork, and positioning the development of the individual as part of a larger group. We will discuss teamwork and the development of teams in more detail in part IV.

5

Lean IT and Its Relations

Since the advent of the Mass Production IT organization, there have been many efforts to standardize and ensure that high-quality services are delivered. Frameworks and standards, particularly in the area of IT Service Management, aim to ensure quality. Most frameworks have some element of continuous improvement. However, their focus is on what to do rather than on methods and approaches to improve and to ensure long-term relevance and evolution. These frameworks present the principles and the need for continuous improvement but fall short in delivering the practical methods and tools to achieve it.

Quality systems all begin and end with the same goal of establishing a rhythm and cycle of continuous improvement. There are many different quality systems available such as the PDCA cycle, Total Quality Management, ISO9000, or Lean. Note that Toyota reviewed early versions of ISO 9000 and found that they "did not add value to the Toyota Production System" (Seddon, 2003).

It is important to note that the various quality systems and process frameworks are co-dependent and complementary. Without the application of a quality system, a process framework is at risk of not being applied with the controls necessary to sustain and keep it relevant. Likewise, without the use of an IT management framework, the quality system is less effective due to the lack of external best practice reference models which support the goal of establishing best and common practices.

IT best practice frameworks deliver content on how topics like architecture, service management or security should be approached. They present an ideal end-state picture of the way the world of IT should look and operate. Unfortunately, most IT organizations struggle to achieve this end-state, leaving them with a feeling that they are not making progress.

Lean IT is an improvement approach uniquely focused on pursuing the delivery of value to customers with the least amount of effort. In other words, Lean IT while similar in nature to other quality systems balances both the concept of effectiveness with efficiency with a goal to establish a "Fit for Purpose" approach to continuous improvement. This gives the people involved the feeling they are making steps towards delivering more value in the most efficient way possible. In this quest for improvement, the best practice frameworks and standards can provide input for the long-term vision.

The second benefit of combining Lean IT with an IT best practice framework is that Lean IT brings a strong focus on behavior and attitude within IT environments. Lean IT is applied to all aspects of the IT domain, which makes it inclusive rather than restrictive, as most IT best practices have been designed to be, i.e. dealing with a single aspect of IT. Applying Lean IT involves the entire management and all the team members. Attitude and behavior elements are often not explicitly covered in these frameworks, and if they are the tools to improve are not provided. This, consequently, makes the combination of Lean IT and IT best practices very powerful.

Lean tools are used to optimize processes and reduce waste. The IT best practices guide us, for example, on how the process should be structured. Frameworks, models, standards and quality systems offer guidelines for demonstrating compliance, good practices, a common language and measurements for improvement. But, as Taiichi Ohno said: "If you think of the standard as the best you can do, it's all over. The standard is only a baseline for doing further kaizen [continuous improvement]" (Ohno, 2013).

IT Service Management is constructed around the need for standardized IT processes. However, from a Lean perspective not all of the processes are actually value streams. By using Lean IT, we can focus on the right processes to deliver the maximum value to customers. Even though Lean IT practices evolved independently, IT Service Management is highly supportive of them as there are many shared objectives. IT Service Management best practices may serve as a "future state" for process improvement while Lean IT keeps the IT processes fresh and continually relevant.

In the last ten years, there has been an explosion of interest in methods such as Agile and DevOps. These methods are strongly related to the Lean principles. Agile has its roots in the application of Lean principles to the area of software development. We see that a focus on customer value ("working software") is at the heart of Agile. As with Lean, Agile aims to ensure that the processes ("value streams") work in such a way that software is delivered quickly ("flow") and that teams deliver the software that is required at that moment ("pull"). There is also a clear continuous improvement mindset within Agile, based on the delivery and improvement of a "minimum viable product" that delivers the value that customers are seeking. However, applying Lean principles to software development is a suboptimal solution since the entire value stream from a customer's perspective includes the daily use of the software, not just its development. Here is where Agile met its limitations, and since this came to light, the Agile community has done its best to extend the reaches of Agile beyond the confines of software development, initially across IT and increasingly across entire enterprises.

As with Agile, DevOps is also about the application of Lean principles to the delivery of IT products and services. In fact, one could go so far as to say that DevOps is actually all about achieving the flow of value to customers of IT. Every possible method for achieving flow is used within DevOps. We reorganize, combining previously separate departments, to improve flow. We optimize and automate the processes to improve flow. We focus behavior and mindset on achieving flow. In fact, every choice made in a DevOps environment is about delivering value as quickly as possible to a customer, and here lies an intimate connection to the principles of Lean we saw earlier.

The fundamental reason the concept of DevOps has developed is to focus on the delivery of Customer Value across the entire IT value stream. Over the decades, many things have been tried within IT to satisfy customers. One of the aspects of DevOps is that we bring people working on delivering the same service together in a single team. The reason is to optimize coordination and collaboration throughout the value stream, without adding the need for coordinating roles. If people work closely together, they are positioned to shorten the time to deliver value because there are no barriers in the form of organizational silos, and fewer and shorter moments when we transfer work from one step to the next in the value stream. This all stems from our desire to truly understand and work in an all-encompassing value stream that ensures the shortest distance between value demand and value delivery. This brings us to the pivotal principle: Flow. DevOps is the ultimate search for flow in the delivery of IT services. Everything we do in DevOps is aimed at ensuring the flow of value to customers. We cut out as much waste as possible, minimize variation, stop overburdening people, and automate everything possible in an attempt to reduce the lead time of value delivery. Bringing people together in autonomous cross-functional teams is all about facilitating flow. Giving these teams end-to-end responsibility is about removing blockages due to outside decision-making, which stop work and reduce flow.

Pull is another aspect of Lean that we find embedded in DevOps. Pull means carrying out the actions within the value stream as and when the customer requires it. It is all about doing and delivering work at the pace the customer is asking for. We principally see this within DevOps teams as they manage work through their process. Pull within the team is all about ensuring there are no work-in-progress inventories; it is about working towards single piece flow based on customer demand. The ubiquitous use of Kanban and Agile Scrum are evidence of our intent to fulfill the pull principle. The role of the Product Owner is aimed at identifying the value to be delivered and at creating leveled production (another Lean aim) from the user community to the DevOps team.

Last but certainly not least, the Lean principle of perfection is very clearly a vital part of DevOps. DevOps teams spend a lot of time not just delivering value to the customer but improving their ability to do so; continuously seeking ways to make work easier or better. In this way, DevOps teams reduce waste (in the form of rework or incidents) as much as possible. Continuous improvement, the way to work towards perfection and a mainstay of both Lean and DevOps, means ensuring impediments to value delivery are removed, thus improving flow. We see DevOps teams working intensively with performance measures to assess their ability to deliver and flow IT value that meets or exceeds the expectations of their customers. The "Fail Fast" adage is all about perfection, it means understanding where things go wrong as early as possible and taking action to understand cause and effect before "fixing things." This is a key element of Lean Thinking.

Based on the Lean principles, we see that Lean IT and DevOps (and Agile for that matter) share a common basis in the principles that drive the concepts. The differences are principally found at the level of the tools and techniques that have developed. Clearly, the developments of the past decade have been focused, intentionally or not, on integrating Lean principles into the fabric of the IT industry. An example of a difference that can lead to major discussions is the use of roles. Both Agile and DevOps work with the concept of a Product Owner, the person who decides which value is to be delivered next by the team. Lean IT only specifies the role of leader, coach, kaizen lead and team member. These generic roles are aimed at helping the organization to structure learning and do not exclude the possibility of using the Product Owner in a Lean IT organization. The question we need to answer is: Do we have a problem that is best solved using the role of a Product Owner? Or is there a different mechanism by which we can guarantee that a team is giving priority to the work that has the highest business value?

Another relative of Lean is Six Sigma. Originating at Motorola in the 1980's, Six Sigma today is widely adopted in many industries and sectors. Six Sigma is a disciplined, data-driven approach for eliminating variability, defects and waste from processes delivering value. Six Sigma improvement projects help to increase performance and decrease process variation, leading to defect reduction and considerable improvements in profits, employee morale and the quality of a product. Six Sigma is often mentioned in combination with Lean. The two concepts have a large overlap; however, there are differences in the approach on various aspects. Where Six Sigma pays significant attention to the statistical analysis of processes in order to eliminate variation, Lean IT primarily focuses on establishing flow of value, particularly in conjunction with the behavior and attitude of the people involved.

One of the methodologies developed in Six Sigma, and inspired by the PDCA cycle, is a problem-solving method called DMAIC (Define, Measure, Analyze, Improve and Control). There are a number of possibilities when it comes to problem-solving. The A3 method is very much based on the four steps of the PDCA cycle (Sobek and Smalley, 2008), sometimes referred to as the Toyota's seven-step problem-solving methodology. There is also a five-step Toyota problem-solving method as described in *Toyota Kata* (Rother, 2009). Other practitioners describe a method used by Toyota using eight steps (Goldsmith, 2014). Lean IT makes use of some elements of Six Sigma, for example the aforementioned problem-solving method. The intuitive nature of the five steps makes DMAIC an easy-to-adopt method for problem-solving.

An abundance of associations, consultancy firms and educational organizations are well established in the world of Lean. Many of them provide websites filled with insights, tools, discussion platforms, training propositions and certifications. There is an increasing number of communities coming together on a regular basis to discuss Lean topics and new insights into the application of principles and tools.

In the world of Lean, the Shingo Institute (www.shingo.org) with its Shingo Model is one of the foremost Lean standards. The world of Lean is also constantly evolving and still growing in popularity. Since all work is a process, and all value is delivered as a result of a process, the application of Lean is relevant to all industries and businesses. The Shingo Model contains two components: The Shingo "House," a set of guiding and supporting principles, and the Shingo "Diamond," a guideline for the transformational process.

The Shingo House contains principles that we will return to in this book (Figure 5.1).

The concept of the Lean "house" is one that has been around for many years. Pioneered by Toyota as a visualization of the key principles, you can now find hundreds of variations on the theme of Lean houses.

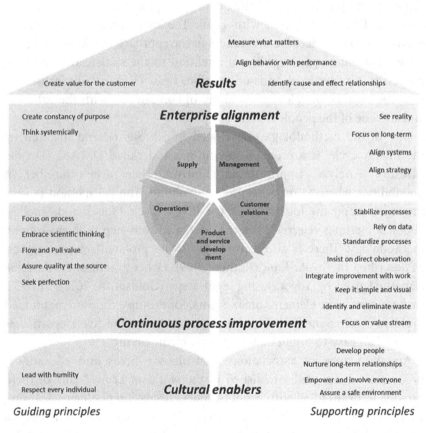

FIGURE 5.1
Shingo house with principles.

Some have two pillars, others have more. Principles are sometimes seen as the foundations, sometimes as a pillar or part of the capstone. Fortunately, one part is always the same: The top of the capstone is always about the results for the customer. It is not so much about the visualization; the most important aspect is that the key principles are in place.

Lean IT was brought to prominence by the 2010 book *Lean IT* by Steven Bell and Michael Orzen. This came after a number of years of growing interest in using Lean within IT, and many practitioners applying Lean principles within IT organizations. Since then, tens of books and thousands of articles and blogs have been published on the application of Lean principles within IT.

Established in 2014, the Lean IT Association (www.leanitassociation. com) aims to develop and promote the application of Lean principles in the IT industry, by providing a body of knowledge with standardized curricula for key roles in the transformation from Mass Production IT to Lean IT. The Lean IT Association has defined four qualifications that together amount to a Lean IT Expert designation: Lean IT Foundation, Lean IT kaizen, Lean IT leadership and Lean IT coach. With the achievement of the certifications, you take steps towards becoming a Lean IT Expert. The most important step cannot be achieved through certification and that is the practical application of what you learn in your own organization. In the Appendix, you will find the syllabi containing the knowledge you need to acquire to pass the exams.

The importance of the Lean community is that there are many people, like yourself, who are making a similar choice to move their IT (or other) organization to a Lean way of working. Reach out to the community to find solutions for problems you are facing.

6

Becoming Lean

As we have discussed numerous times so far, Lean is a way of thinking and acting. Lean behavior starts with acquiring Lean knowledge, applying the knowledge to thinking about the way your organization works (Lean thinking) followed by Lean acting. The Lean mindset has the following characteristics. It seeks perfection by acknowledging that good is not an end state but a step towards further improvement. Perfection is about delivering quality at the source. The eradication of waste through continuous improvement leads to the Lean principles of flow and perfection. In the same way, problems are seen as opportunities to improve customer value, rather than a reason to apportion blame. Lean challenges people to think differently in the process of delivering value. In Lean organizations, people do not talk about the procedure but the "best known way" of doing something. This implies that there is a better way, only we do not know it yet. Thinking counter-intuitively can lead to new "best known ways" of doing work. In the process of delivering value for people who are prepared to buy your product and, by continuously removing waste from the system producing the value, profit takes care of itself. Invest in people to create long-term relationships and benefits for all stakeholders. In IT, we also need to look at how we develop long-term relationships with external service providers. They can play a crucial role in the value delivered to customers. Being Lean in the long-term depends very much on what you do in the next five minutes. If you behave in such a way as to deliver value in the short term in accordance with the values of the organization, the ability to meet long-term goals will be much easier. In this way, we can sustainably deliver value.

Within (IT) organizations, we have a tendency to look at our department or immediate surroundings. It is vital to look at the whole picture to avoid sub-optimization. For IT, this means at least taking an integral view of a service towards a customer. The cornerstone behavior underlying these characteristics is learning. People working within Lean IT organizations distinguish themselves from other organizations by the fact that they are prepared to learn and that their environment encourages them to learn.

Let's go one step deeper and take a look at the attitude that contributes to a Lean environment. We have seen the characteristics of a Lean mindset. But the mindset is nothing without the right attitude. Attitude is largely built up from the way we see the world and the beliefs that we have. The beliefs of Lean are relatively universal and can be summarized by the words of Kiichiro Toyoda, founder of the Toyota Motor Corporation (2001): "Do whatever you please. Just take responsibility."

The following are beliefs that are consistent with a Lean attitude.

If we believe that improvement is possible, it is a small step to take the responsibility to make the improvement happen. The vast majority of IT people come to work to do the right thing, especially if it means having a happy customer. Adding value is therefore a fundamental attitude to most people. One of the more difficult aspects of a Lean attitude is to be critical *and* to be solution-oriented, i.e. focused on actually solving the point on which you have criticism. The last two beliefs are related to a positive view of people: Their ability to rise above themselves and to work together to produce better results than what an individual can do alone.

The essential difference between attitude and behavior is that attitude determines the way people approach the situations they meet and behavior is how they act and react. Behavior is influenced by these beliefs. However, the behavior will become part of the organizational culture if, and only if, leaders and colleagues reinforce the fact that people go looking for waste, treat others with respect and share knowledge. The Figure 6.1 lists a non-exhaustive list of Lean and non-Lean behaviors.

What makes a Lean transformation a long-term success? When an organization starts with Lean, the first improvement proposals are often evolutionary. These are often quite quickly identified and these quick wins are swiftly implemented. At the start, the success of Lean is particularly visible. As time goes by and many improvements are identified and implemented, it becomes more difficult to identify new improvement opportunities. The low hanging fruit (or "quick wins") are taken. This leads to comments such as "we're finished with Lean; there's nothing left to improve." Generally, people forget that each percentage improvement is an improvement. Organizations like Toyota do so well because they

Non-Lean behaviors	Lean behaviors
• Respond with negative comments	• Exercise patience in interactions
• Exact revenge	• Reflect on events
• Distrust the opinions of others	• Trust others
• Criticize actions	• Engage in constructive dialogue
• Evaluate people based on interpretations and hearsay	• Show compassion for difficulties of others
• Gossip about people	• Ensure arguments are fact based
• Deliver sarcastic remarks	• Show respect
• Decide based on prejudice	• Listen actively to others
• Act to achieve individual glory	• Share knowledge with others
• React cynically to suggestions	• Reflect on own behavior
	• Be visible and transparent in action

FIGURE 6.1
Lists of Lean and non-Lean behaviors.

improve each and every year. Remember that Toyota is more than sixty years down the road with Lean. That is a lot of improvement!

How do organizations succeed in integrating the Lean way of thinking into a long-term source of success and truly adopt a continuous improvement attitude? One of the key challenges is for Lean principles to become an integral part of the paradigm used by managers for steering the organization. This means that the consistent set of models and theories used as the thought framework (paradigm) to steer reality must be enriched with Lean principles and methods. Lean, as part of the management paradigm for IT organizations, means managing based on the results produced for the customer. We will discuss the Lean Management System in Part III. The Lean transformation means a significant change in the way managers do their work. This has proven to be one of the more difficult aspects of moving to an IT organization based on Lean principles.

Part II

Starting Out

The secret to getting ahead is getting started.

Anonymous

7

The First Steps

Starting with Lean IT is largely a hesitant affair. There are very few IT organizations that decide to go for a full-blown transformation once the decision has been made to start the journey. In all but one of the Lean journeys I have experienced, the start was toe-dipping; testing the water to see how cold it is. This Starting Out section is about the first three to six months, sometimes longer, of your relationship with Lean IT. In this first period, there is much uncertainty, but also excitement. When the IT management announces that "we're going to do something with Lean," there is a surprisingly large group of people that responds positively as a result of the frustration with the current way of working. They may have resigned themselves to the stove-piped organization and may seem to have accepted the inefficiencies and lack of customer satisfaction, but given the chance to change their environment they jump at the opportunity. The level of enthusiasm will also depend on "re-organization fatigue." Many leadership teams see re-organization as the solution to any number of problems. Sometimes, they encumber the organization with this phenomenon every year. If your IT organization has recently been through a re-organization, there is a large chance that the enthusiasm for Lean will be mild. Remember: A re-organization is simply a solution to a problem. The question therefore is: What problem are you trying to solve and are there solutions other than re-organizing that may deliver a better result?

Do not worry, there is also a group that has no intention of joining you on this journey that they perceive as arduous and senseless. It is far too much like hard work and disruption to the current comfortable way of working that is known. And, generally speaking they will say "we are not doing such a bad job. OK, some customers are not particularly happy but we are no worse than other IT organizations. And we do our best." In fact, the group that has no intention of joining you slowly crystallizes into a group that is prepared to see the benefits and a small group that still has no intention of helping you on the journey.

In this phase, there are people who see their opportunity to take the lead and, preferably, sideline the managers to a certain degree. In this period of hesitancy and trepidation, people will play the top-down/bottom-up "card." The key to this "card" is that some people state that Lean is a bottom-up improvement method, implying that any management involvement is an assault of the core idea of Lean which is to let the teams do their thing. This is a somewhat one-sided presentation of the facts, as we will see later. Surprisingly, this card gets played by both team members and managers for different reasons. Team members do it to create space for themselves to take more control over their own lives and environments. Managers do it as a response to a lack of clarity regarding responsibility and lack of understanding of what the transformation to Lean actually means.

At this stage of the transformation, moving to Lean is shrouded in myths and perceptions that slowly get unshrouded and debunked as both managers and team members gain experience with the Lean tools. Let us look at a few of the more common perceptions.

"Lean is about processes, it does not concern managers." This is, in fact, a golden oldie. This argument was used during the IT Service Management process improvement projects. Based on cursory information about Lean principles (value stream), the first part of the perception is not incorrect. The second part, however, is blatantly wrong. In fact, this is one of the problems in many IT organizations, the management team has paid insufficient attention to processes over the past years. This is not entirely unexpected since the Mass Production paradigm promotes specialization and coordination, and this means there is generally a specialized process manager for coordinating the individual processes. Understanding and improving processes became a delegated responsibility. Consequently, many IT management teams are no longer used to looking at the efficacy of their own processes. Moving to Lean Production changes this situation. Managers become more intimately involved in the processes. In fact, taking a value stream view of the world is the manager's responsibility; it is an example of systemic thinking.

"Lean is for Operations/Infrastructure, Agile is for Application Development." Emphasizing the differences within an IT organization seems to be the automatic primary response to any proposed change. In this case, each part of the myth may appear to be correct but it does not help you in your aim to move your IT organization to the Lean Production paradigm, since Lean means looking holistically at the IT organization and the delivery of IT services. Does this mean that Application Development should be forced to ignore Agile? Of course not, the key is to emphasize the similarities and the flow of value for the customer across the entire IT organization. Tools and methods traditionally associated with Agile support the Lean IT transformation, and they can be used in all parts of IT organizations. Good examples are learning to think in backlogs, iterative creation of value for the customer and the attention to the work process through the role of the Scrum Master.

"When solving problems, the teams are in the lead." Again, this perception is strictly speaking not wrong. However, by giving teams the impression that they are in the lead, we plant the seeds for doubt, uncertainty and misunderstanding. As teams learn how to solve problems and take decisions based on their investigations, managers get involved at a late stage often questioning whether the work that has been done was rigorous enough or whether all possibilities have been researched, or outright proclaiming of a preferred suggested solution: "We are not going to do that!" This leads to all manner of demotivation and turns previously enthusiastic team members into skeptics who say: "I told you, this Lean thing is all for show. Management doesn't really want this change themselves so why should we make the effort."

"Management takes a back seat because it's all about autonomous teams." The rise of DevOps has brought the term autonomous teams to prominence. It is very important to realize that autonomous teams are something that may be achieved as a result of the Lean IT transformation. It is not a pre-defined configuration that needs to be put in place first before starting with the transformation. In fact, in a number of cases, a declaration of the autonomy of teams led to chaos because no attention was paid to building common ground on which to base the autonomy and the cooperation. In one case, team autonomy was proclaimed in a situation where the teams retained their original technical orientation. This meant that the teams did not support a defined service or set of services, nor did they contain the necessary skills and knowledge to support the customer completely. These are two of the main preconditions for autonomy. It is, therefore, recommended to steer clear of the term "autonomous teams" at this very early phase of the transformation.

A central underlying theme of the above myths is the decision as to whether the Lean IT transformation is a top-down affair or whether the initiatives should be bottom-up. Initially, when being introduced to Lean, much emphasis is laid on the devolution of responsibility and authority to the operational teams. In addition, we look more to team members to provide solutions to problems and ask them for initiative. A detailed plan guiding both the overall organizational transformation and the transformation of individual teams seems to contradict the bottom-up power of Lean.

It is important to communicate that Lean, and Lean IT, has always been a combination of both styles. In a broad sense, the guidance for the overall transformation comes from the top and improvement initiatives tend to be driven from the teams, i.e. bottom-up. Both lead to a combined and coordinated drive to improve the quality and performance of the IT organization. One cannot do without the other (Figure 7.1).

As Figure 7.1 shows, the top-down and bottom-up aspects principally ensure that improvements are identified from both directions, thus ensuring a steady stream of improvement projects to be carried out. This need for a combination of styles means that starting a Lean IT transformation without buy-in from both management and team members is inadvisable. Does this mean that everyone needs to be on board? Not necessarily, since we have seen that there will always be people who are not enthusiastic about the change. It is all about creating a guiding coalition with sufficient power to drive the first steps of the change and engage the

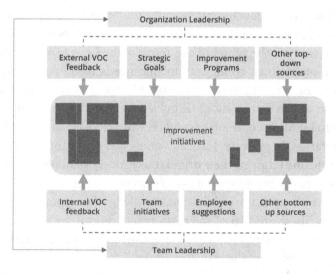

FIGURE 7.1
Top-down or bottom-up.

people who are not yet convinced. One thing is certain: Management must take a proactive, guiding role at this phase.

There is only one way to get rid of myths and misconceptions: Learn and gain experience. The word of warning is to ensure that none of these (or other) misconceptions or myths becomes entrenched in the organization. It becomes difficult to get rid of these convictions once they have become embedded in the way people see the world.

So, given that you as a budding Lean IT Expert are faced with a situation in which there are probably more people who are not actually waiting for your message to transform the organization, how do you go about starting? Based on my experience, there are basically two ways that IT organizations start with Lean.

The first way is to introduce visual management and the associated rituals in teams. This is the preferred method for IT organizations that have little control over the work that needs to be done. This lack of control manifests itself in a variety of ways. The most notable are team members who work on units of work of their own choosing irrespective of the priorities, customers who come into the IT department and give people work personally thereby pressuring people to change priorities, stressed out teams who complain about too much work and managers who have little insight into what work is being done and, therefore, what work is not being picked up.

The second method is to introduce problem-solving as a precursor to actions that lead to kaizen. This is the method of choice for managers who are in a bit of hurry and who want results quickly. Solving problems is indeed the shortest route to improvements. However, this is still just an introduction to Lean IT, not the definitive step to continuous improvement. It is similar to building a prototype application as a try-out then bringing it to production and being surprised that it does not work properly. This method tends particularly to be focused on tackling process problems, which provides the opportunity to introduce Value Stream Mapping as a tool.

Both of these methods are, in fact, excellent ways to get people to experience what the Lean way of working can bring. It is important to understand that just because you have been doing either of these methods, you are half-way through your transformation. This is most definitely not the case.

I have experienced two other starting points but these are less frequently chosen. One transformation was started by training everyone in Lean IT.

Now, do not get me wrong, training is extremely important and is an integral part of every transformation, but its return on investment is relatively low if it is done before anyone has experienced what Lean can mean. Another transformation was started with a pilot in two teams using a selection of tools including visual management, Skills and Knowledge Analysis and Earning Capacity Analysis.

Interestingly, it is very rare for the IT Management Team to start with itself. This is one of the reasons why the starting points as described above are in themselves insufficient to truly trigger a lasting change. I am not saying that managers are not involved in these starts, after all, they have initiated the introduction of Lean. It is just that the involvement is non-committal. The most heard argument is that there are so many other things to do and, as someone who has been an IT manager, I fully commiserate with this position. However, from a leadership perspective, this transformation to Lean Production in IT is *the* most important task of the leaders. The question, therefore, is: Why are you giving a bad example by not focusing the lion's share of your time on your most important task?

Towards the end of this Part, we will look in more detail at the steps that managers need to take in this, Starting Out, phase.

8

Ways to Start

VISUAL MANAGEMENT IN TEAMS

Picture a team of database administrators (DBAs). There are ten people in the team: four seniors, three experienced and three juniors. They have a team leader who has been on the job for the best part of a year. They have a common office space where they spend part of their time. Much of the time of each individual DBA is spent with the application team(s) that they support. Each DBA has been allocated to one or more application teams based on the database technology used. There are three brands of database in use and one is present in multiple versions. Their manager, the head of IT Shared Services, has agreed with the team leader that the team of DBAs will be the place where visual management will be tried out first.

As Lean IT experts, we were asked to support their first steps on the Lean journey.

We set up a kick-off meeting of three hours in which the five core Lean principles were explained. We also spent part of the meeting discussing the issues they faced; what were the most pressing problems for the DBAs? As with so many teams, there was a feeling that there was too much work, and no time to spend on professional development or the improvement of the products, services and way of working. During the kick-off, we explained the fundamentals of visual management and its intended effects.

In order to improve performance, early feedback and the knowledge of what is happening are key elements of operational management. The biggest change when transforming to Lean IT is the introduction of visual management. Visual management fulfills a crucial role in Lean. It ensures we can achieve jidoka, the aim of which is to create a visible and clear view to ensure that any disturbances to flow can be identified. In effect, Visual management is about effective team communication. Transparency and visibility within IT are created by a smooth flow of information. This ensures that everyone can follow the progress of work which makes for an efficient coordination of the work. Visual management is about steering work, planning and reviewing progress and managing improvements.

The first significant effect of visual management for the team is that it enables the team members to see which tasks are progressing and which are blocked. In traditional IT organizations, we find team meetings that happen once a week, sometimes fortnightly. These meetings lead to a list of action points. The rule tends to be that most action points do not get carried out by the next meeting. The owner of the action point is then put under pressure to carry out the action. This may happen multiple times but the result may be that an intended action never gets carried out, due to shifting priorities and new action points. Visual management ensures that action points are reviewed on a daily basis and that time is reserved for the goals that are set.

Related to the aforementioned benefit, visual management helps to share information on the progress, priorities and problems of the team. However, this brings an obligation to the team members to ensure that the information is as current as possible, preferably with real-time status updates. This means that team members update the tickets on the board as and when their status changes.

This frequent updating of information establishes effective and short feedback loops within the team, based on common knowledge of what is going on in the team. The knowledge is common because it is continually visible and up-to-date. It plays a major role in connecting management to the day-to-day operation of the team, ensuring that managers are also aware of the state of value delivery to customers. The effect of well-maintained visual management is that not only that the team members feel on top of their work, but managers feel more "in control" without having to ask for reports or other administrative burden. In fact, it strongly reduces the need for reports because the information is there on the wall.

This brings us to the fifth benefit: Visual management helps to create consistent and effective communication not only between team members, but particularly between the team and management. It removes the need for a host of one-to-one communication that inherently contain the risk of an inconsistent message.

Finally, visual management also facilitates dialogues that are more fact-based. Through the clear definition of work, the team is better able to identify what has been done, what is being done and what still needs to be done. As a result, they can see more clearly when they need help and what with.

Not unimportantly, these aims of visual management have the effect of making the allocation and execution of work transparent and inclusive, which is vital in building trust.

At the outset, a team generally uses three boards to create a visually managed workplace: The week board, the day or kanban board and the improvement or kaizen board. Based on these boards, even someone who is relatively unfamiliar with the work of a team can, upon seeing the boards, scan and quickly ascertain which aspects of the processes are under control and which are not. The initial boards tend to be best practice templates. The goal is, however, to develop visual management that specifically suits the work done by the team. Once team members are engaged in the creation, maintenance and improvement of their own boards, they commit to their success.

When starting with visual management in a team, the best board to start with is the week board. The power of the week board is that it provides information on the team's objectives for the week to come at a glance. It includes a limited set of performance indicators that offer insight into the development of, for example, the team's quality, timeliness or cost. The team chooses its own performance indicators. These indicators must be under the control of the team and must, given an improving score, be a source of pride regarding the ability of the team to deliver the required value. The week board must also include information on both customer satisfaction and employee satisfaction.

The week board visually supports a meeting called the week start. The week start tends to replace traditional team meetings and tends to last one hour to one and a half hours, depending on the needs of the team. The first goal of the week start is to evaluate whether the goals of the previous week were achieved. Where this is not the case, the team briefly discusses what needs to be done in the coming week to ensure that goals are achieved.

The next step is to determine the goals for the current week. In most of the teams I have experienced, when discussing the new goals of the week, team members talk about "What I am going to do this week." The process of dealing with the goals of the week is individualistic and seemingly disjointed. Team members have the tendency to talk in activities rather than the objectives to be achieved. A recurring example is the fact that people have goals of the week like "Have meeting with [customer] to discuss [change/project]." The coaching question is: What *deliverable* will be ready at the end of the week? This has proven to be quite a difficult question to answer for many people, but it is an important change in behavior, thinking in "finished products" rather than "activities to be carried out." As the team becomes more experienced, the discussion of objectives moves from what "I" need to do to what "we" need to do as a team.

Aside from their objectives, the team discusses its performance based on the team's performance indicators, specifically including the way the team works and what the customer thinks of the team's performance. Employee and customer satisfaction are the aspects that need to be understood. During the discussion of these aspects, problems and possible improvements will be mentioned. These need to be identified as work that needs to be added either to the goals of the week or to the improvement board, depending on how clear the solution is and the need for direct action (Figure 8.1).

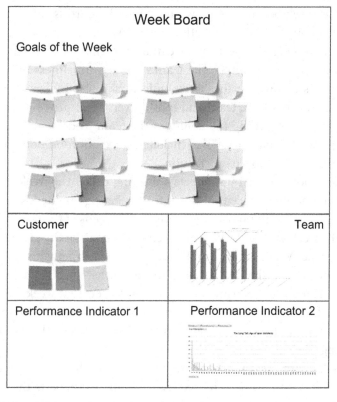

FIGURE 8.1
Week board.

In Part IV, we will discuss the full mechanics of the week start in more detail.

The second element in the standard set of visual management is the day board. The day board (or kanban board) is the tool that visualizes the short-term work. It is used to support a brief meeting that starts the day's activities. A 15-minute time-boxed daily meeting, known as day start or daily standup, offers the team a moment to discuss operational performance and allows for synchronization of workload among team members. Impediments that block the flow of work can be identified and either mitigated or escalated if the team members cannot solve the blockage themselves. The meeting is always done standing up. The effect is that people have an active stance that reflects their attitude to the subject matter and it keeps the meeting short.

There are two ways of designing the board used on a daily basis.

The first is based on the days of the week. This supports a team that needs to do work on a specific day or wishes to plan work for specific days in the week. We call this a day board. Each team member records all the deliverables they are going to create that day. On the day board, work is represented with tickets; small cards which make it possible to see which work is progressing and which is not. Regular work is posted, for example, on yellow tickets, ad-hoc or unplanned work on pink tickets (Figure 8.2).

The second type of visualization of daily work represents the process. The team's aim is to ensure that tickets "flow" across the board as the work progresses. This board helps to identify where there is spare capacity for work to be pulled into the next step in the process, and is known as a kanban board. The design of the board is dependent on the team and type of work they perform. In software development, we may find alternative versions of the kanban board. These will generally be designed along the lines of the software development process. They may include Backlog, Ready to Code, Coding and Complete or a simpler variation on this theme: To Do, Doing, Done (Figure 8.3).

The day start is the daily, (generally) morning ritual during which each team member shares with the group their daily tasks and goals, as posted on the day board. It is also an opportunity to determine if the previous day was successful and to ask for or offer help if needed. The facilitation of the day start is the responsibility of the team leader. However, as time goes by and the team is accustomed to the board and the ritual, team members may deputize for the team leader. Typical questions to be asked at the day start are: Were the goals of the previous work day achieved? What went

Name	Monday	Tuesday	Wednesday	Thursday	Friday	Done	Blocked

Problems		Tip of the day		Manager's Agenda		☺ ☺ ☹

FIGURE 8.2
Day board.

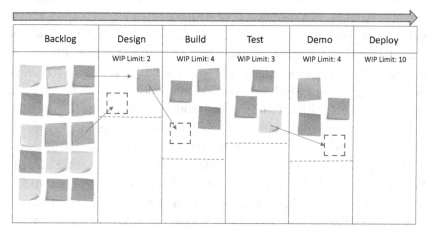

FIGURE 8.3
Kanban board.

well and what can be improved? What did we learn? What is the objective for this day and when are we successful? Who needs help on what and who will offer help?

At a day start, a problem may be identified. This should be posted in the problems section and, at the end of the day start, a decision should be made regarding all problems posted: Does the problem need to be acted on directly or does it represent an improvement that needs to be discussed in more detail? Generally, the team leader's calendar is posted on the day board so that the team members know when the leader is available.

During the day start, the team also takes time to check the morale within the team. In this way, the team leader can identify and act on any problems as they arise. Discussing morale is initially quite difficult. The initial response is that everything is fine, not great but fine. However, as team members get used to the question and, once one of the team members breaks the ice, they will increasingly be prepared to discuss morale issues. This is a sign that the team has a higher level of trust. The first time a team member indicates that their morale is low tends to be a key moment in the development of the team. Particularly the response of the team leader and other team members is telling for the state of the team. A lack of compassion and understanding in the response is rare, but does indicate the work that needs to be done in promoting the Respect for People principle.

As we have seen, during both day and week starts, problems or improvements may be identified. Some of these can be directly tackled by putting them on the day or week board as actionable items for that day or week. Others may require more consideration because the problem is not clear or the solution is not obvious. This category of problems and improvements find their way to the improvement board

The kaizen or improvement board is the last in the trilogy of standard visual management boards. Each improvement is evaluated by assessing the business impact of its possible solution and then looking at the impact for the IT organization and the feasibility for the team to implement the solution. During a regular meeting, usually weekly or fortnightly, the team evaluates the problems and improvements that have been added to the board. This is one of the methods to drive continuous improvement. Typically, the team will look at the new tickets that have been added to the board as described. They will also check the status of ongoing improvements and results of implemented improvements (Figure 8.4).

Figure 8.5 shows the role of each board and the relationship between the boards.

At all three of the meetings, both team and individual performance are openly discussed. The emphasis must be on team performance. Where individual performance is an issue, this is an opportunity for further coaching to ensure that the personal capabilities are improved. Initially, the openness is certainly not welcomed by all of the team members, especially since the team leader is present at these discussions. Some team members feel exposed as their contribution (or lack of it) is made clear on the board. Again, this is an opportunity to coach and raise the level of

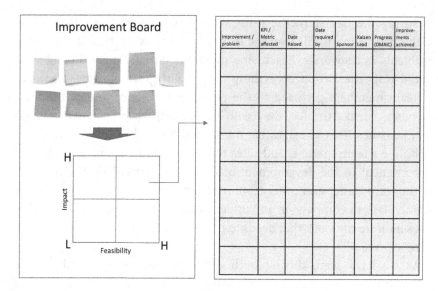

FIGURE 8.4
Kaizen or improvement board.

performance. It is all the more important that the team leader shows some vulnerability to encourage the openness.

Getting back to the DBAs at the start of this section. How did they fare? They started with the week board, and almost immediately a problem started to manifest itself. There were two types of tickets. Tickets that had to do with daily work, primarily related to the application teams, and tickets that were related to internal DBA work. After a couple of weeks in which many of the week goals were not achieved, the team agreed that having a meeting more frequently than once a week would be beneficial. This was the sign to introduce the day board and the day starts. It took a number of weeks before the team members were thinking in terms of finished products and, all the while, the behavior during the meeting became clearer. When individual DBAs talked about their goals for the week, the attention of the other team members would diminish quite rapidly. The DBA would have the feeling that he or she was talking only to the team leader, turning what should have been a team meeting into a series of one-on-ones. At the end of each week start, we would evaluate how it went. In the beginning, the responses were "social," meaning that everyone thought it went OK.

After about five weeks, one of the seniors said "This is pointless. I don't really care about what the other DBAs are doing in their application teams."

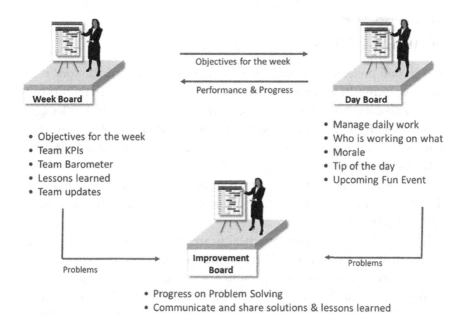

FIGURE 8.5
Tryptic of visual management in teams.

The rest of the team admitted that they had the same experience. This led to a re-think of the team and, particularly, its purpose. If the team members were not interested in each other's daily work, what then was the reason for them to be put together in a team of DBAs? The team determined that their common purpose was to ensure that databases were designed, implemented and maintained based on a set of defined practices that would be enforced by the team itself. The result of the soul-searching was that the visual management was completely redesigned. The week board was stripped of the work done in the application teams (Later, visual management was introduced into those teams and the DBAs were able to put their work/tickets on the boards of the application teams, where they were more relevant), and was filled with the work related to the purpose of the team. This change also led to the creation of an improvement board on which improvements and problems related to multiple databases were posted. Problems that concerned a single application or database found their way to the application team's improvement board.

The fundamental question, which we will deal with in Parts III and IV, is what constitutes a team? The answer to this question is absolutely essential when trying to engage people in the transformation.

PROBLEM-SOLVING

The second preferred way of kick-starting Lean in IT organizations is to solve problems. In the end, embedding problem-solving as a habit in your IT organization is the central part of continuous improvement or kaizen. Next to the relatively quick results, this is an enticing proposition: "If I start with continuous improvement, then I can take a short cut through this Lean IT transformation malarkey." Unfortunately, solving problems as a kick-starter does not mean you have become a Lean IT organization. It means you have kick-started your Lean IT transformation with problem-solving.

Take the IT organization of a healthcare organization. They chose to approach the introduction of Lean principles through problem-solving. The aim was to improve the capabilities of two key IT processes, incident management and change management. The goals were to improve customer satisfaction through the reduction of the impact of incidents i.e. reducing the number of incidents and shortening their lead times, and increasing the ability to deliver changes on time. The improvements were to be determined using three consecutive improvements cycles per process. Each improvement cycle consisted of a total of eight meetings over a period of four weeks. The first four meetings of two hours each were concerned with defining the problem, measuring the key aspects of the problem, analyzing the measurements to understand the key drivers of the problem and identifying the most suitable improvements. These meetings took place over a period of two weeks. The last four meetings were shorter meetings that were aimed at ensuring the progress of the implementation of the improvements.

Continuous improvement focused on improving the flow of value requires both the ability to measure and analyze a specific situation (scientific thinking) and the capacity to identify and eliminate waste. The most essential precondition for improvement is the pursuit of clear and agreed goals: Make things better, faster, cheaper, create more meaning in our work and leave a healthier environmental footprint.

Problem-solving starts with a problem statement, and ends with embedded improvements implemented in the relevant parts of the organization, using the DMAIC method.

In the Define step, we define the problem statement, describe the goal statements, analyze the cost of poor quality, define the scope of the problem, establish the kaizen project team, create the kaizen charter and planning, get stakeholders' support and start.

In the Measure step, we build understanding of current performance, write a data collection plan, we try to understand process behavior and variation, and relate current performance to customer requirements.

In the Analyze step, we collect data and verify the measurement system, analyze the process, identify the types of waste, develop hypotheses about the root cause, analyze and identify the data distribution and study correlation

In the Improve step, we generate potential solutions by brain-storming, design assessment criteria for impact and feasibility, decide the improvement to implement, implement or pilot the improvement and measure the impact on the customer.

In the Control step, we implement ongoing measurement, we anchor the change in the organization, we quantify the improvement, capture the learning and replicate it where necessary.

The findings are summarized in the form of an A3 Problem-solving report and we close the actions for our project. For more details on kaizen, DMAIC problem-solving and A3, see Part V.

So what happened in the healthcare organization? The improvement cycles were executed as planned with each cycle of both incident and change management providing a small set of improvements that were implemented directly. Regarding the incident process, the results were substantial: A reduction of open incidents by 60% and a reduction of average lead time by almost 50%. The results for change management were less spectacular simply because the overall lead time of changes is longer which means the effects are less easily seen in the short term. On top of this, it transpired in the first improvement cycle that actually recording an agreed implementation date and reporting on the ability to meet the agreed deadline was not possible. Other improvements did have a qualitative effect on the delivery of changes to customers.

When kicking off Lean with problem-solving, there are a number of challenges. First and foremost, it is getting people into the frame of mind to actually tackle and solve problems. In this, and many other, IT organizations, a sort of immunity to problems has developed over the years. This immunity manifests itself in that people no longer actually see the problems. If they do see a problem, there is one of two automatic reactions. The first is to just accept that that is the way the world is ("We can't change ..."), the second is to determine a way around the problem

("We have a workaround, so there is no need to actually solve the problem"). Either way the effect is to leave the problem and its cause in place. This means that when the choice is made to actually tackle problems head-on and solve them, people react with some skepticism (a fairly non-Lean behavior). And this behavior is, maybe surprisingly, not limited to team members, but affects all levels of the organization. This institutionalization of this kind of undesirable behavior is one of the effects that Lean IT aims to address and correct.

Generally, there is quite a relief that problems are being dealt with and the DMAIC method provides a logical set of steps that everyone understands. As the improvement team reached the Improve phase in which solutions are defined, the skepticism grew again. There is disbelief that the rest of the organization will accept the solutions. As stated earlier, this is the moment that managers tend to get cold feet. When it comes to causing waves in the organization as a result of implementing the improvement team's recommendations, all manner of doubt comes to the surface. This is the moment that IT management can destroy its own attempts to kick-start Lean. By questioning the results of the improvement team, management sends a signal that the improvement teams are just a smokescreen and everything stays the same in terms of decision-making and responsibility. Questioning the results of intense research, as is done during the D–M–A phases of DMAIC, is a blatant expression of distrust (not-Lean behavior).

In the case of the healthcare organization, with the benefit of some coaching, management unequivocally supported the improvement teams in their choice of improvements. The effect was that the enthusiasm for continuing to determine and implement improvements remained in place. Of course, there were dips in motivation when implementation proved more difficult than anticipated. The improvements chosen by the teams have been proven to have an effect on both the results and the cooperation across the various departments of the IT organization.

TRAINING

Strange as it may seem, most Lean IT transformations do not actually start with training. You may expect that this is the start of choice because, as we have seen, Lean is all about learning. Talking with IT managers a number of months after the start of their Lean journey, it was found that when training occurs too early, i.e. before anybody has experienced Lean in a practical way, the effect of the learning is present but low. This is where we really see that Lean is a way of thinking and acting. Embedding the thinking (based on understanding created through training) only happens when people have the space to act in a Lean way.

To be clear, training needs to be organized within the first six months of kicking off your Lean journey. The question is: What type of training does an IT organization need? Focus on ensuring your key roles (kaizen lead, coach and leader) are clear on what they need to do, and that everyone has basic knowledge of Lean.

In terms of delivery, experience has shown that classroom training is substantially more effective for the effect of your Lean IT transformation than e-learning. Why is this the case? The move from Mass Production to Lean Production within IT is a paradigm shift and paradigm shifts take time and attention to assimilate. One of the best ways to assimilate the new way of thinking and acting is by sharing thoughts, discussing concepts and, then, trying them out in practice. The investment in classroom training in terms of time spent is worth substantially more than it costs. Not only does it give you the time to digest the subject matter but it also gives you the opportunity to discuss with colleagues or other organizations and to ask clarification questions.

Let me get one irritation off my chest at this point: Executive sessions. Executive sessions are management jargon for "tell me what I need to know but in a shorter time than my employees." Although I recognize that most executives are highly intelligent and capable people, I see them struggling with their roles in the new paradigm. Often, it ends up being the executives and managers who form the biggest brake on the transformation simply because they are late in truly understanding the effect of the change, developing the vision for the rest of the organization to buy into and practicing the behaviors that support the transformation. I say "late" because they are certainly not slow once the urgency hits home. The average executive session does enough to provide executives with the jargon but not the capability; it allows executives to "talk the talk" but not "walk the talk" and Lean IT is about the latter. Use executive sessions in the same way that you organize awareness sessions to introduce people to the goals that need to be achieved or the problems that need to be solved. In short, executive sessions do not replace the training as it was intended.

9

Leadership Awakens

This is the moment that leaders are confronted with what they have set in motion. Whether you try out Lean IT with visual management, problem-solving, training or a combination of all three, having triggered interest and activity in this area, most IT management teams find that they have opened Pandora's box. Although management takes a healthy interest in what happens in the "try-out," it mostly does not take a particularly active role. Leadership is woken up by two key themes: performance and direction.

Teams working with visual management that include (rudimentary) performance indicators and teams that solve problems both tend to approach management with the same question: When is the performance good enough? As we will see in Part V, this is not a particularly Lean question (since it may be construed as meaning there is no need to improve beyond "good enough") but we are just starting so it is alright to ask it.

The second question they both ask is: What's next; where are we going?

Realizing they have not yet formulated answers to these questions, managers are faced with their own development needs, which at this phase tend to be vague. Before the Lean IT transformation can start, management must get itself in shape. Fundamentally, there are three concrete things that happen. Key Performance Indicators (KPIs) are created, a transformation plan is drawn up and there is a request for commitment.

PERFORMANCE

A financial institution had kicked off their transformation. The belief was that the full-blown transformation had been started. Although the leadership had been involved with the decision to hire coaches to help execute the transformation, the fact was that teams were largely practicing with visual management and also using some Agile tools and techniques. They also dabbled in problem-solving. The organization's leadership was still quite busy with other priorities. It was only after about four months that the aforementioned questions (What performance is good enough? Where are we going?) arose.

This was when workshops were organized for the management teams of the four departments. During these workshops, the principal topics were Lean and performance, with the aim of creating direction. Surprisingly, the knowledge of Lean was very low and the management teams benefited greatly from the opportunity to discuss the five basic Lean principles. Simply the effort of translating these generic principles to their own work brought insights to the management teams. The next step in the workshop was to define performance indicators. Each of the management teams had spent time eight months earlier defining the purpose of their departments and the goals they aimed to achieve. Defining purpose is a vital step in determining direction and performance. Purpose becomes valuable to the organization when it is clearly linked to the customer value.

Performance is a critical component of Lean. It is about ensuring that decisions are based on facts and figures rather than opinion and conjecture. Performance, like all other dimensions of Lean IT, starts with the customer. We need to choose the right indicators. Performance indicators must be related to agreed objectives and/or critical success factors. They must be consistent throughout the IT organization and must reflect the IT organization's strategy and its customers' needs.

So what do we mean by performance? It is the completion of a chosen objective or obligation. The performance includes both the result and the way the result is achieved, whereby the result is the outcome of a process.

Measuring performance enables us to achieve objectives. In relation to the Plan–Do–Check–Act cycle, you will find that, in the Check step, you must form an opinion of how the organization did in comparison to the plan. The only way to do this objectively is to include the way to check whether the plan was achieved at the conception of the plan. This means that while we are doing the work, measurements are being carried out that form the basis for an evaluation.

Within the Lean IT organization, we aim to make performance information available to everyone involved. Primarily, the team producing the performance must get frequent feedback so that the team members are able to understand whether the performance meets the requirements.

Leaders must also be aware of the numbers so that they can help to identify whether there is a reason to investigate possible shortcomings with the team. Lastly, the team must be prepared to share performance information with customers. Based on these insights, the customer can help to define what level of performance represents the value they are looking for.

Let's take a brief look at a common example. Customers of IT generally indicate that they would like to have an incident resolved the moment they report it to the service desk. The IT organization cannot deliver on this requirement each time. The customer indicates that the current level of performance is good, even though the IT organization does not live up to the ultimate expectation. By measuring the performance, the IT organization can put a concrete number to the general feeling of the customer. We may find, for example, based on the measurement of the average time to resolve incidents, that 90% of calls are resolved within one day. This measure can be equated to a "good" level of performance. Sharing this information with the customer can help the customer put their own thoughts and experience into perspective.

Later, the customer may indicate that the expectation has changed and now expects a better level of performance. Not that calls must be solved more quickly but that a higher percentage must be solved within one day. Obviously, there are more aspects to the service than the speed of resolution of the incident. Friendliness of the service desk agent and how quickly the telephone is answered are also part of the total performance.

Central to the measurement of performance is a concept that is often underestimated: the Performance Indicator. Clearly-defined performance measures (or indicators) are vital in order to understand whether the organization is achieving its goals. Performance indicators can and must be used at all levels of the organization. Measuring performance is, in fact, relatively straightforward. We need to understand whether we are measuring the right things and whether the measurement helps the organization to continuously improve. If we do not take action based on the results of the measurement, then there is no point to measuring. It is particularly the definition and use of performance indicators that are underestimated.

First, we need to distinguish between general performance indicators and Key Performance Indicators (KPIs). A KPI is a performance measure that supports the execution of the strategy. A KPI cascades from the strategic level to the operational level and is consistent across the organization. It must be measured with a clearly defined measurement procedure so that everyone knows how the KPI is created and, most importantly, how it can be influenced. Ideally, a KPI should be long lasting. This is to ensure that we can follow the trend of the KPI over a longer period of time, especially since the achievement of a strategy is a longer-term objective. In this way, performance can be consistently tracked over a longer period of time allowing the organization to see whether improvement measures have a sustained impact. The use of performance indicators should be Specific, Measurable, Achievable, Realistic and Time-bound (SMART).

KPIs are derived from the strategic intent or purpose of the IT organization and measure the performance of a key organizational objective. At the same time, a performance indicator should be controllable by the team that is being measured according to the indicator. This may be a technical team but also a management team.

We saw in relation to the week board that teams within the IT organization have freedom to choose the performance indicators that they can directly influence. The requirement is that the team can explain how their chosen performance indicators are related to the KPIs of the IT organization. An example is a team that is responsible for delivering development, test and acceptance environments (a kind of department that will disappear with the advent of software-defined data centers). Their principal performance indicator may be the ability to deliver a new environment within one day. This contributes to the ability of the IT organization to meet the time-to-market goals of its customers, a Key Performance Indicator for many IT organizations.

Once we have performance indicators, we need to make them work for us. This means ensuring that measurements become part of the organizational or team Plan–Do–Check–Act cycle. We also need to ensure that measurements become embedded in the visual management, as a daily reminder of what is important. KPIs are vital for monitoring performance in relation to the delivery of customer value. Having said this, contributing to customer value is more important than achieving the specific goal or target of a KPI. This also means that managing the long-term development of the trend of a particular KPI measurement is more important than meeting a particular target.

Managing with KPIs is a balancing act. Within IT, a common occurrence is that the number of incidents has a tendency to increase as a result of an increased number of changes. The IT organization will only truly be successful if the number of incidents does *not* increase in line with the number of changes. On the contrary, we should be aiming to reduce the number of incidents with an increased number of changes since at least some of these changes will be related to problems that have been solved, and our aim is to implement changes that do not introduce new errors into the IT infrastructure. Another example of the balancing act may be the ability to deliver more changes at the same level of cost. The balancing act ensures that there is tension between the KPIs. If all of the KPIs display their intended trend, we know that no area is improving at the expense of another.

The next step is to actually define the KPIs of the IT organization. Defining a KPI has proven to be not as straightforward as it may seem. Management teams tend to spend insufficient time and attention getting the right performance indicators in place. A clear symptom of a Management Team that is still in the Starting Out mode is one that delegates the creation of KPIs to a working group. In one such situation, I was given such a working group in which there were no managers. The group worked diligently to define an excellent set of KPIs. The group was very pleased with the result, having not only defined the KPIs but also created a baseline measurement. The group presented their KPIs and associated dashboard to the Management Team and were met with a resounding silence followed by the memorable words of the head of Application Development: "But I want to know how many incidents we receive every day." The lesson learned was that managers need to define their own KPIs so that they can tell the story about *why* particular KPIs have been chosen and what the intended effect is of measuring these KPIs. To be complete, defining a solid set of KPIs including the story around the KPIs takes between three and five three-hour workshops with a Management Team. If you feel this is too much time, then do not start until you are prepared to put in the effort. The result will only be disappointing.

Getting back to actually defining KPIs. First, the goal of the KPI must be described. The goal of a performance indicator is always to influence behavior towards the achievement of an organizational objective. For example, the time-to-market of changes will help us to understand whether we are meeting our part of the customer's goal to innovate quickly and will help people to focus their behavior on getting changes done within the time required by customers. This in turn will drive the behavior to ensure that we know when the change needs to be delivered. This is obviously a different, although compatible, measure to ensuring that changes do not cause more incidents.

The definition of the KPI tells what the KPI is about. The time-to-market KPI is defined as the ability to meet an agreed implementation date.

Alternatively, we may choose to define it as the ability to continually shorten the time between the request for and the delivery of new functionality. The definition obviously has an impact on the formula, the way the KPI is calculated. The two definitions described above will lead to different formulae for determining the performance. Related to the formula, it is vital to define which data is used to calculate the KPI. This is to ensure that each time the KPI is measured, it is measured consistently. The data collection process includes both the data and the way it is processed as it is turned into the performance indicator. Are there, for example, any exclusions? If we are measuring the performance of changes, do we include or exclude standard changes?

A KPI must have a unit of measurement. Do we want an absolute number, an index or a percentage? This choice can influence the way a KPI is read. Is it, for example, the amount of open incidents (an absolute number) that gives us useful information, or does the percentage of incidents still open from this month tell us more?

We must know with what frequency a KPI is reported. Within Lean, we need KPIs that are refreshed on a frequent basis. Only KPIs that provide a new reading at least once a week can be used to actually steer performance. Preferably KPIs must be measurable on a continuous basis, providing an updated reading every time we check.

The KPI must have an owner. This is the person who is responsible for the quality of the KPI and preferably also someone who takes overall responsibility for the performance regarding the KPI across the organization. This almost inevitably means that a member of the senior management team will be the owner.

In order to ensure that KPIs are balanced, it is advisable to consider multiple perspectives. Preferably, the categories should be taken directly from the strategy, to increase their recognition and the consistency of steering.

We must also define the measurement accuracy. Will we round percentages up or down to the nearest integer or will we present a percentage to hundredths of a percent? This will depend on what kind of improvement is possible. Moving the performance from 60% to 80% is unlikely to depend on 10ths of a percent. Going from 98.7% to 99.5% may even make it interesting to measure 100ths of a percent, to understand progress of improvements.

Lastly, under the euphemism of "issues," we need to understand how the KPI can be manipulated. Knowing how to fudge the numbers will enable us to be alert to any manipulation. Discussing the way a KPI can be manipulated also creates an open atmosphere in which the intent of the KPI and the way in which it should be used can be shared with teams. Teams, then, have the opportunity to give their views on whether the performance indicator is likely to achieve its intended goal (Figure 9.1).

You may feel that a key aspect is missing: the norm. Within Lean IT, norms are used as improvement goals rather than absolute levels of performance. It is therefore not necessary to record this in the definition of the performance indicator since it will continuously change as performance is continuously improved.

In one IT organization, I met a team manager and asked how he was doing regarding his ability to solve incidents within the agreed time limits. He showed me a graph that resembled a healthy heart monitor display: a repeating pattern of a flat line with a dip down followed by a peak with the line returning to the "flat" level. My interest piqued, I asked him to explain what was happening. He gladly explained that the flat level was 80% that he was evaluated on. The dip to around 70% was after every fortnightly release and the subsequent peak to about 90% was an "overshoot in performance" to compensate for the dip. Together with his team, he neatly managed the performance back down to 80%. In fact, this manager was impressive in his ability to speed up and slow down his team, but this has nothing to do with delivering customer value. In the end, customer value is represented not by solving 80% of incidents on time, but 100%. And once this has been achieved to reduce the lead time associated with being "on time."

KPI : Lead Time	
Goal: To influence behaviour towards ensuring that customers get the value they have requested as quickly as possible	**Formula:** • Date/time the request is submitted by the customer subtracted from the date/time the request is fulfilled. This gives the Lead time. • For each type of unit of work, the average lead time is calculated per week.
Definition: Measure the lead time of all units of work in order to understand where improvements in processes can be made to decrease lead time	
Category: process, customer	**Data collection process:** [including source of information, timing and responsible] - Extract data (request submission date and request completion date) from [system in which unit of work is recorded] - Calculate Lead time according to formula - Present data as a trend graph showing at least the last 13 weeks
Level at which the performance indicator is used: Management Team, Teams	
Unit of measurement (%, number, index): Number	**Measurement Accuracy:** 1 decimal
Frequency of reporting: Daily (data is available real-time)	**Issues:** • Request submission and request completion dates are not accurately recorded giving a wrong lead time • Requests are not registered, meaning no data is available
KPI owner: Management Team	

FIGURE 9.1
KPI lead time.

It is therefore vital to manage the trend of a KPI, not just look at a single data point or a norm. When managing the trend, we must not only ask ourselves what to do when the trend goes the wrong way, but also ask ourselves what we are doing *right* when the trend goes in the right way. In the latter case, we need to understand what we did right and how we can continue to do the right thing.

The financial institution at the start of this chapter created performance indicators for each of the departments. These were consolidated at the highest level to a set of seven KPIs that represented the strategy of the entire organization. This two-phased exercise led to the realization that the transformation they had envisaged had had a suitable start, but that the real transformation needed to be designed and planned.

There are two key aspects at this point: commitment and a plan. The order is not particularly important, but both need to be present to have a credible story for the rest of the organization.

COMMIT

Commitment has proven to be easy to give but tough to live up to, especially when it means changing behavior, and that is exactly what a transformation entails. The big question for the members of a leadership team is: What am I committing to? In essence, leaders need to commit to the goal of transforming the IT organization from a Mass Production style IT organization to a Lean Production-based IT organization with a Lean Management System. There is, however, an underlying commitment that is much more important. Each individual manager needs to commit to the goals of the IT organization, but also commit to developing as a Lean IT Leader and, consequently, as a Lean IT Expert.

Committing to self-development is the pre-requisite for the success of Lean within any organization, and it is no different for IT organizations. By self-development, we mean the act of reflecting honestly on one's own actions, thoughts, behavior and attitude with the aim of making these more effective. Self-development is an activity that requires both individual reflection and feedback from outside. This is why committing to self-development is more difficult than it may seem. Committing to self-development does not mean, for example, that you commit to reading a book about how to be a better leader and then doing your best to implement some of the ideas or suggestions; it means taking steps to change behavior. It is an activity that needs to be planned and carried out on a regular basis.

Toyota believes that the key trait that distinguishes potential leaders from everyone else is self-development (Liker and Convis, 2011). Leaders actively seek to improve themselves and their skills. Potential leaders need to be given the opportunity to self-develop and they need to be supported along the way of their development. The paradoxical aspect of self-development is that you do not self-develop on your own. You need to find the right challenges for self-development, allow space for self-development, and receive coaching at the right times in the process.

Self-development is not necessarily something that comes naturally; it is not self-evident. In fact, everyone aims to live their life using routines and habits that make living easier and less tiring.

Self-development has two aspects: developing yourself to become a Lean IT Leader and helping team members to become Lean IT Leaders themselves. Self-development takes time, and dedication to understanding one's behavior and changing it where necessary. You cannot teach someone who does not want to learn (including oneself); a person must be passionate about becoming a Lean IT Leader. Becoming a Lean IT Leader does not happen overnight; learning is a process that goes in small steps. Learning cannot be rushed. Start with learning basic routine patterns of behavior followed by more detailed and extensive learning.

This is one of the most difficult moments when dealing with IT managers who want to make the step to Lean IT Leader. Managers need to make time available for learning. My estimation is that somewhere between 8 and 16 hours a week is necessary at the start of the transformation. This is time necessary for individual and team-based reflection on what needs to happen. Unsurprisingly, most managers react with complete incredulity, with the comment "That's impossible." Earlier, we briefly discussed solving problems and how important this is in Lean. And that is my response to the comment: "If you are committed, solve the problem."

Ask yourself the same question: Could you make 8 to 16 hours available to learn how to transform your organization and lead your IT organization to a Lean IT organization? Are you prepared to reconsider your current work in such a way that this time becomes available?

Are you committed?

Learning requires reflection and reflection means getting feedback from others. The learning process is facilitated by engaging others in the process. In the Lean tradition, each leader has a sensei, a teacher or coach, who helps to guide the leader's learning process. The sensei collaborates intensely with the leader to turn problems into learning moments by embodying the values, principles and techniques of Lean. You need a coach to develop yourself and you need to be or to become a coach to develop other Lean leaders. A coach helps to uncover blind spots and helps to maintain the commitment to self-development, simply by being there.

In Lean, every manager is expected to figure out what they have to learn to become a Lean leader. What is their personal challenge to better align their people's work with customer value, to ensure flow of that value and, in so doing, aligning sustainable, profitable growth with employee satisfaction? Each manager needs to learn through observation of their teams. This learning style is deeply embedded in personally observing daily operations; the manager's learning evolves from providing support for team-level learning activities. As the teams solve their problems or show initiative, the manager is expected to interpret their conclusions in the wider context of the business, as well as support further learning activities in the workplace. In other terms, if they learn, you learn. Lean's learning approach is very clearly learning-by-doing

As a leader, you must create a learning environment for your team members. Learning on the job is never easy, particularly not with the pressures of today's business environments. Consequently, one of the key roles of a Lean IT leader is to create a visual environment together with team members in which the abnormal is easily distinguishable from the normal and where opportunities for small-step continuous improvement are clearly visible to all. A learning environment also means an environment in which mistakes are *not punished* but seen as sources of learning, and where employees feel they can thrive without fearing arbitrary, sudden changes.

Finally, you need to practice. In the Western style of management, leaders are expected to be infallible; they do not make mistakes and they know everything they need to know. This means that admitting you do not know what it means to create and lead a Lean IT organization may be difficult. The only way to learn and improve is by practicing. Practicing Lean leadership implies that the leader does not know everything and is likely to make mistakes. It also means trying out new behaviors that may cause team members to be surprised or caught off guard. An example is doing a gemba walk. This is a new behavior in most IT organizations and both team members and leaders need to get used to it. The only way to turn the gemba walk into unremarkable behavior is by doing it every day.

And, yes, as a leader, you will make mistakes, but you will have a chance to do it better the next day, when you have your next gemba walk planned.

In order to truly be able to start the Leadership transformation, the leaders must commit to self-development. It is only once this happens that leadership can move forward. Until that time, leaders are just starting out. In many Lean IT transformations, an interesting phenomenon occurs: Teams tend to move into their transformation earlier than the leaders do. Even though leaders may also dabble in visual management with a rudimentary obeya (see Part III) as teams do when they start out, without the commitment to self-development which manifests itself as a desire to gain knowledge, leaders are not yet transforming themselves.

In developing leaders, the PDCA (Plan–Do–Check–Act) cycle can be used to support learning. The PDCA starts at a different point and the A takes on a different meaning; it starts with the A and goes on as follows:

Advance: A job is selected that fits the leader's next development step, to advance learning and growth.

Prepare: The leader must then understand gaps between the current situation and the vision by gaining deep understanding of what is actually happening in the teams. This involves building relationships with the team members.

Do: The leader then leads and develops others to achieve challenging goals. This is where the practical experience of leading is tested.

Check: The leader then discusses their leadership experiences with the coach. This is often done during the "doing" so that the leader can reflect, learn and apply the lessons learned.

Let's look at an example of how this works in practice:

Jane is a highly competent team leader for her team of developers. She has proven her ability to manage the team to a good level of performance. It is time for her to take the next step. Alice was a developer herself, and is seen by her team members as the logical choice for team leader with the previous team leader leaving. The senior management recognizes her ability but needs to feel sure that she can use and develop her skills in a different environment. To further develop leadership skills, Jane is asked to manage a different department: a newly created team supporting the IT services for the Finance department (Advance). The IT organization has chosen to create a DevOps team to deliver end-to-end support for all of the Financial systems and business processes. The Finance department uses two main systems. In the past, there were ongoing conflicts about whether a change should be carried out in one or the other system, detracting from the fact that IT needs to deliver value to Finance. The first thing Jane must do is gain insights from the work floor in what the team actually does, and what the issues are that they face (Plan). An additional challenge is that this is a completely new team, made up of IT engineers who previously have barely spoken to one another, despite working on closely related topics. Together with the team, Jane develops a vision of where the team needs to be and ensures that this vision is aligned with the overall goals of the IT organization. Subsequently, she leads and coaches the team members to shift their focus from their respective systems to a collective responsibility for delivering value to the Finance department (Do).

Jane spends many hours sitting together with her team, often simply observing what happens. She coaches her team members in improving their interactions and cooperation. She does this based on the collective vision of providing high value IT services to support the Finance processes. Jane regularly asks her team for feedback. She also involves her manager (her coach) in helping to improve her capabilities as a team leader (Check). This process of development creates what is known as T-type leaders. These are leaders with deep technical knowledge In a particular area of the work (vertical bar), supplemented by broad leadership skills (horizontal bar). When senior leadership focuses on create leaders with a T-type profile, they are in fact developing a pipeline of leadership potential. The most challenging aspect is building leadership capabilities onto excellent technical skills. As with Jane, putting leaders into positions outside their areas of expertise, forces them to listen and coach, as they are no longer the technical experts. This helps to develop their skills at motivating people and building teams.

In Part III, we will investigate in more detail what it means to develop into a Lean IT Leader. At this point in the steps towards getting your IT organization to a state in which it can transform to a Lean IT organization, it is important to realize that you will have to commit to something (becoming a Lean IT Leader) without knowing exactly what it means, partly because much of understanding exactly what Lean IT Leadership is, is the journey itself.

So, in order to not to feel part of Alice in Wonderland, you will need to decide where you are going, and then decide which path you are going to take. Deciding where you are going is about having a purpose supported by the values of the organization and deciding which path to take means creating a plan.

10

Transformation Plan

Transforming the IT organization into a Lean IT organization is not easy. It requires changing multiple aspects: the way the IT organization interacts with the customer, the way processes work, the way performance is measured and steered, the way the IT organization is organized and, most importantly, the change in behavior and attitude of everyone involved. A transformation is a stressful time and it is easy for leaders to lose focus. Especially during a transformation, a plan is helpful in managing the change effort to become Lean. Lean IT transformations are designed in multiple phases. Each phase should address the points identified by Kotter (2007).

Typical questions for which answers will need to be provided are:

- What phasing do we use for our transformation?
- In what order will parts of the organization participate in the transformation?
- What is the optimal timeline and planning for the transformation?
- Should the transformation be top-down or do we rely on bottom-up initiative?
- What kind of activities and interventions are part of our roll-out?
- Who will do what during the transformation?

The transformation must be designed at an organizational level. In this way, we can provide everyone in the IT organization with the vision and a plan, and with a timeframe in which they can expect to get involved (Figure 10.1).

At an organizational level, there are essentially three phases for the transformation: the Leadership transformation, Team transformation and

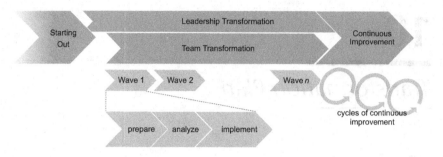

FIGURE 10.1
Lean IT transformation model.

Continuous Improvement. At this point, it is useful to have a high-level insight into each of the phases. We will deal with the details in Parts III, IV and V.

LEADERSHIP TRANSFORMATION

We start with preparing the change. This can only be done by the leaders of the IT organization. They are fully accountable for initiating and sustaining the chosen direction. In practice, this means that the leadership goes through a full cycle of the Lean Leadership Development Model, discussing and trying out new structures and behaviors as part of choosing to commit to the change. This Development Model takes leaders through a cycle of four core activities: Commit to Self-Development, Coach and Develop Others, Support Daily Kaizen and Create Vision and Align Goals (for more detail, see Part III). It is only as a result of this first step that the IT leadership team can truly state that they intend to move forward with Lean IT and have shown the required commitment.

The key result of the Lean Leadership transformation is a common change story in which the urgency and need for change are communicated, together with a vision for the future. Each leader has their own change story. The Lean Leadership transformation is not just a phase; the development of Lean IT Leaders is a *continuous process*. The first steps in the Lean Leadership phase ensure that true commitment is voiced and that the first iteration of Leader Standard Work is defined. The change story, commitment and Leader Standard Work are the three anchors that ensure leaders can help each other to stick to the changes agreed upon.

Consequently, the plan for the Leadership team takes the form of a track during which a number of topics are dealt with. Experience has shown that a combination of learning, seeing and doing helps to support leaders in their own behavioral change. Learning is about spending time discussing specific aspects of Lean IT and deciding how to use these aspects within the IT organization. Seeing gets leaders going to the teams and observing what is actually going on with the aim of gaining a true understanding of capabilities and problems. Doing is where learning and seeing come together in the form of practicing new behaviors.

During this time, it is important that the initiatives that were tested during the try-out are continued and that bottom-up initiatives are encouraged. This fosters the start of a collaborative learning environment, in which teams and leaders learn from different perspectives. The next phase is the transformation of the teams. This is the phase in which teams are helped to adopt the Lean way of working.

TEAM TRANSFORMATION

It is important for the development of the teams that the leaders decide on whether teams go through their initial transformation based on volunteering or whether the leaders determine a roadmap in which the sequence of team transformation is dictated. In larger organizations, it is often simply not feasible for all teams to start the transformation at the same time. The resources to support the teams are simply not available. Transitioning large organizations usually involve so-called "waves." If the transformation is carried out in waves, they should be logically sequenced. The teams in a single wave will need to be selected in a non-random way. Key considerations for teams to be in the same wave are whether teams are dependent on one another, whether they serve the same customer or form part of the same value stream.

In many cases, the transformation takes place in a traditionally organized IT organization in which there is huge interconnectedness between the technical departments. IT leadership may then choose to transform functional areas one at a time, for instance first the development teams, then the IT operations teams (or the other way round). Leadership must ensure that teams are supported throughout the *entire* transformation period. There is a risk that once the team of Lean IT Experts helping the leaders to drive the transformation have finished in one area and move on to the next, the transformed teams will be left to their own devices; leaders declare victory too soon.

At the team level, it is important to provide a clear outline of what activities will take place to help the team to adopt Lean IT principles and ways of working.

It is important to be clear on what is going to happen. Some people only need a vague roadmap, but the majority of people gain confidence from a detailed plan on which the transformation is based. As with any plan, the value of the plan is created more in the planning process than in the plan itself. My experience is that teams should be presented with a detailed plan that is input for a further fine-tuning session together with the team. This detailed planning process works for both the leadership team and for the technical and support teams.

The aim of the fine-tuning planning session is to enlist the cooperation of the team in planning their own transformation. The planning session gives the team a measure of control, which encourages more buy-in for the transformation. Always communicate that the detailed plan for the transformation is just the beginning of Lean working.

Per technical team, we follow a three-step process of preparing, analyzing and implementing. This is done together with the team and ensures that the team goes through its initial transformation. The ambition is to get the team to be confident at the Know What level of understanding. The preparation will include training and understanding the particularities of the team. It also means discussing the activities of the Analyze and Implement steps. Much attention is paid to ensuring the team leader is fully aware of what is expected. The Prepare step usually takes between two and four weeks, depending on how quickly basic Lean IT training and other meetings can be planned. Difficulties in planning must be promptly addressed by senior management; this is a situation in which the leaders' commitment to the transformation must be clear.

The next step is to analyze the team using Lean tools and techniques, so that the team comes to terms with the reality of their situation. Seeing reality, or genchi genbutsu, is a fundamental Lean principle. This means analyzing, at least, the units of work processed by the team, the processes that run through the team, including identification of muda, mura and muri, the requirements of the customer, regulators and other teams regarding the team's performance, the overall performance and time usage of the team, and the skills and knowledge in the team. This analysis establishes a baseline from which improvements must be made. In this step, visual management boards are prepared and other necessary artifacts are put in place.

The Analyze step takes four weeks and is always slightly longer than strictly necessary to ensure that the team is ready to make improvement steps in the Implement step. The Implement step is about embedding the behaviors both amongst the team members and the team leader.

The Lean IT Transformation plan for a team should be based on the five Lean dimensions. These dimensions provide a clear basis for *why* activities are carried out. It is important to show the team that the analysis and implementation cover all aspects of Lean IT. It also helps the team to realize that, although it may seem like there is a lot of work to be done, the work is spread out in an achievable way within the timeframe set for the analysis and implementation.

The dimensions of Lean IT are Customer, Process, Performance, Organization and Behavior & Attitude. There is no business without a customer. The purpose of any business is to find and keep customers. For any business improvement to be effective we therefore need to start by looking at it from a customer's point of view. The Customer dimension deals with all aspects of understanding the customer and the value they are seeking and includes tools such as Voice of the Customer and Critical to Quality (CTQ).

Once we know the customer, the IT organization will need to perform a sequence of activities that result in products and services for which the customer is willing to pay for. Process looks at how value is delivered through value streams, integrating the principles of flow, pull and perfection. Tools used are Supplier, Input, Process, Output and Customer (SIPOC) and Value Stream Mapping (VSM) to ensure that a process is correctly scoped (SIPOC) and detailed with the addition of quantitative data (VSM). The VSM is subsequently used to identify where there is waste in the process.

To make a process flow, it requires resources of any kind, like time, money, people and their talents, and materials. Aligning these resources around the process output requires organization. The Organization dimension investigates the aspects needed to ensure that we can steer the resources. This includes visual management techniques supplemented with the performance dialog. Also, we need to decide how to organize people for maximum value delivery to customers. This means understanding the effect of siloed organizations versus organizing for customer-orientation.

Performance, as we have seen is a key aspect of Lean. From our understanding of the customer value and process, we can determine the performance measures needed to understand, manage and steer the performance of the organization. Key aspects are defining (Key) Performance Indicators to understand, at the very least, the output of processes, understanding and measuring the use of time within an IT organization and, lastly, identifying the availability and requirements for the skills and knowledge of the workforce.

Behavior and Attitude has been found to be one of the most important success factors for Lean (and Lean IT) transformations. There are many tools available to help steer behavior. The first step is for everybody within the organization to understand the key characteristics of Lean behavior, in particular for those in leadership positions. Leaders must also understand how behavior and attitude may change during a transformation.

These five dimensions have ongoing importance in our improvement activities. We will see that, particularly in the teams, the dimensions play an important role in structuring the activities during the analysis and implementation. After the Leadership and Team Transformation phases, it is up to the team to identify what help they need to further improve their performance and capabilities.

CONTINUOUS IMPROVEMENT

A wave ends with putting all mechanisms in place to ensure that gains are consolidated and further improved. This is when the Continuous Improvement phase starts. The Continuous Improvement phase focuses on keeping the cycles that were started in the Leadership Transformation and Team Transformation going. The Continuous Improvement phase builds on all the behaviors, tools, methods and rituals that have been used in the Leadership and Team transformations, and uses them together with problem-solving to ensure that improvements are continuously embedded in the fabric of the IT organization. It is likely that further Lean tools will be added as and when necessary, or tools will be repeated to renew and update insights.

Continuous improvement begins by clearly defining value in the eyes of customers, both internal and external. Expectations must be clearly and unambiguously communicated so that processes can be designed to meet customer need. Continuous improvement focuses on how the flow of value requires both scientific thinking and the capacity to identify and eliminate waste. The most essential precondition for improvement is the pursuit of clear and agreed goals: Make things better, faster, cheaper, create more meaning in our work and leave a healthier environmental footprint. Incremental continuous improvement, or kaizen, in organizations is about developing a series of behaviors among which is problem-solving. Kai means change, Zen means for the better. Kaizen is about continuously improving: everyday, everyone, everywhere. Many small improvements implemented with kaizen result in faster innovation and more competitive advantage for the business with fewer risks.

The main objective is to improve the delivery of value to the customer. For this, we apply Lean principles, tools and techniques to the work of IT. We use five dimensions to support the effectiveness of our improvement activities. The DMAIC steps are used in a disciplined way to solve problems and learn from them. This is how we implement and adapt Lean IT, and how we continuously improve business performance.

The real challenge of Continuous Improvement is maintaining the pressure on the status quo, with both teams and leadership working together to ensure that standards are continuously brought to a higher level of performance. In IT, there is one sure way in which we see continuous improvement: the automation of manual tasks. The dedication of leaders and teams to reserve time to automate manual tasks is an important signal that the IT organization is moving towards being a Lean IT organization. This dedication means helping customers (the user community and their leaders) to realize that long-term success of the organization as a whole depends on the IT organization continually spending time on automating tasks so as to free up more time for increasing the speed and volume of delivery of customer requirements.

ROLES

So, you are committed to transforming to Lean IT. But who is meant to do what in this transformation? This question needs to be answered at the organizational level. The premise of this book is that everyone in a Lean IT organization should eventually become a Lean IT Expert, i.e. that everyone has a kaizen mindset with the ability to solve problems in a structured way, everyone should be able to show some degree of (Lean) leadership and everyone should be able to coach a colleague to a certain extent. Obviously, these activities are based on a foundation of Lean knowledge. In the period before the Lean IT transformation starts, it is unrealistic to expect that everyone is capable of doing everything; that everyone is a Lean IT Expert from day one. This is why the people involved in the transformation take on a specific role. The problem with roles in the Lean IT transformation is that they tend to evolve into permanent jobs. This is explicitly not the aim of the roles described.

The team member role is the fundamental role that everyone has at the beginning of the transformation. Everyone is a member of a team; technical experts and engineers are members of technical or product teams, and managers are members of both management teams and technical or product teams. As we saw earlier with the case of the DBAs, there may be a question as to whether you are a member of the right team.

The role of the team member is to fully understand Lean principles, tools and methods, and support their use within the IT organization. This means active contribution to problem-solving and continuous improvement, an understanding of, for example, Value Stream Mapping and general support for finding waste and removing it. This role is absolutely vital because everyone should be able to help others to maintain the focus on becoming a Lean IT organization and this means that everyone, leaders and team members alike, must have the same basic Lean IT training.

The second key role is the kaizen lead. Initially, using a structured problem-solving method does not come naturally to IT organizations. Especially when starting out with problem-solving, it is useful to have people who know the DMAIC method and can guide small teams through the process. This role needs to initially be filled by one or more experienced kaizen leads who help others to understand how the process works. It takes three or four kaizens for someone to build up sufficient experience to be able to run a kaizen on their own. Be aware that this does not mean that the individual is a fully-fledged kaizen lead; more experience is needed. On average, each team will have someone who knows the structured problem-solving method.

In a traditional IT organization, there are both "line" managers and "process" managers. When planning an IT transformation, I generally include the process managers in the category of people being trained up for the role of kaizen lead. The main effect is to change their way of working from ITSM process "policeman" to process problem-solver. This approach entails a substantially different way of looking at the world of processes. Whereas the focus of the ITSM process manager tends to be on defining the "ideal" process and then hammering away at the organization to ensure that everyone uses the process as described, the kaizen lead approach means that process managers seek out the problems in processing units of work (for example, incidents, service request, changes) and, together with the people who are experiencing these problems, try to solve the problems.

At first, the role of Lean IT leader, the third key role, is one fulfilled by the current managers in the IT organization. It is important to include everyone in a managerial position from executives to team leaders in this category. The reason is that there needs to be consistency in the way leadership is experienced throughout the organization. As we will see, the role of Lean IT leader brings new challenges. It is easier to deal with these new challenges if a larger group of people are dealing with them together at the same time. They are better able to discuss the new requirements and help each other to stay on track. We will discuss the challenge of Lean IT leadership more extensively in Part III.

During a Lean IT transformation, there is much to be learned. For both leaders and team members, there are many activities to be practiced in order to create a new way of working. Experience has shown that it is very useful to assign a number of people to the role of Lean IT coach.

A Lean IT coach is definitely a member of the guiding coalition. However, the Lean IT coach does not have the hierarchical position of the managers. The Lean IT coach is usually trained during the Leadership transformation, together with the managers. It is a good idea to select people who have leadership potential for the role of Lean IT coach. In this way, if there happens to be a leader who does not wish to adopt the Lean philosophy, there is someone else suitable for the position. Growing the leadership potential ensures that the Lean IT Transformation is not jeopardized by the absence of a leader in an important position at a critical moment.

Lean IT coaches play the role of the conscience of the IT organization during the transformation. They help the leaders to stay on track and to stick to the commitments they have made. Lean IT coaches tend to be team members who have informal networks among the teams and can help individuals and teams to understand the transformation to a Lean IT organization. Especially at the start of a transformation, as traditional managers make their first steps to becoming Lean IT leaders, the coach can play a critical role. The coach can ensure that the manager is given a chance to learn and grow as a Lean IT leader. Ideally, Lean IT leaders play both roles: Lean IT leader and Lean IT coach. In part III, we will look at how leadership contains a substantial coaching component.

The role of Lean IT coach is not the easiest of roles since it requires people who are prepared to give feedback to management on how they are doing with their own Lean development. Since the environment, often, has yet to evolve to one in which people can freely speak their minds, the role of Lean IT coach can feel risky for the person fulfilling the role. The answer is to take small steps in expanding the mandate of coaches. The steps include agreeing which behaviors will be subject to feedback and which will not. As we will see in the leadership transformation, gradually more behaviors become part of the coaching assignment. The expansion of the mandate of coaches is a sign of increasing trust in the organization. It is not uncommon for leaders to deem their coaches capable of coaching teams, but not capable of coaching leaders. In most cases, this is a trust and vulnerability issue inherent in the leaders.

In some cases, the leaders choose to supplement their internal Lean IT coaches with one or more experienced external Lean IT coaches. This lowers the risk of failure as experienced coaches help to avoid common pitfalls.

11

Transforming to Lean IT

Having got a plan, worked out who is going to do what and, especially importantly, having committed to the transformation, managers tend to become impatient. Having spent long enough talking and thinking out what needs to happen, it is time for action. Unfortunately, the transformation is dependent on the cooperation of individuals and teams. People are notably fickle: One day they may be positive, the next they may be less cooperative, as a result of other influences in their lives. This makes a Lean IT transformation a complex problem to be solved.

Fortunately, research has shown that people react in fundamentally similar ways when confronted with change.

In their article *Beyond the Peter Principle—Managing Successful Transitions*, Lewis and Parker (1981) describe a transition curve experienced by someone who has been promoted to a new managerial position. This curve can help us to understand the experiences people go through when the organization changes. The problem with change is that it is never all positive or all negative. During a transformation, it is also the case that some parts of the change are planned and others happen by accident. In Figure 11.1, each of the phases is described.

This figure is very important for Lean IT leaders. First and foremost, they will be experiencing these phases themselves. Leaders also go through shock that the "business as usual" world is changing, even though they often cause the change as a result of the desire to provide more value more quickly to customers. In many cases, the denial of the change may take the form of the manager *believing* that they are experienced, and that they already carry out many Lean IT activities. As a result, they feel that they have already been through their change. This is almost always *not* the case.

As more and more new information about Lean IT enters the organization, the leader can feel incompetent. This results in anger and frustration.

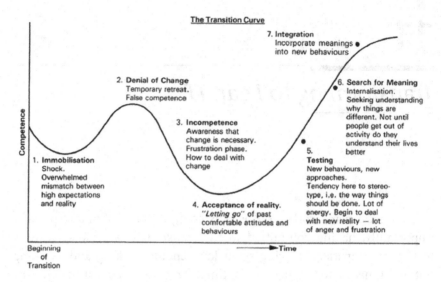

FIGURE 11.1
Transition curve (Parker and Lewis, 1981).

Without support, the manager may become a destructive rather than constructive force. It may help to realize that as you, as a leader, become more competent in Lean IT leadership, you will be able to recognize non-Lean behavior. As the leadership team helps one another to take the Lean IT Leadership steps, the new reality becomes accepted. Through trying out new behaviors, you can define a new meaning for yourself, followed by the integration of Lean behaviors into day-to-day work.

This experience will help the Lean IT leader to relate to what people in the teams are going through. The idea is to show understanding and show the way forward, rather than joining in with the complaining. Lean behavior is about identifying problems and looking for solutions on a daily basis; going back to the practices of yesterday is not a long-term solution. Choosing for Lean means letting go of many of the pre-Lean behaviors, even though it means hard work in adopting the new Lean practices.

According to Parker and Lewis, people go through three broad phases: Farewell, Letting Go and Moving Forward. They must leave the current way of working (Farewell). This can be done by looking carefully at the current situation and by putting the present and the past into perspective. The best way to do this is to show respect for the efforts people have made and results they have achieved, and to explain why the new step is necessary. Deming (1982) already recognized this phenomenon: "The management needs to learn that the main responsibility is theirs from now on to improve the system." It is critical to spend time informing and communicating the vision for the *future*. The Lean IT leader must show understanding and sympathy for the loss people are likely to feel.

The next step is to help the team let go of the past (Letting Go). This is done by providing help, support and motivation. One of the best ways to take this step is to engage the team in carrying out long desired improvements that are in line with the Lean principles. The Lean IT leader must continue to inform but should also reassure the team that the right steps are being taken. The moment where the energy levels and motivation to continue are lowest is sometimes referred to as the Valley of Despair.

Finally, the Lean IT leader must help the team to take steps to create a new reality (Moving Forward). This means encouraging kaizen and helping individuals to develop further. In this step, the Lean IT leader must be clear about celebrating successes and ensuring that the team is supported in its further development.

Generally, the Analysis step of team transformation will cause the first three steps of the Lewis and Parker curve to happen in the team. The team members will be faced with the reality of their situation, leading to denial and potentially a feeling of incompetence. Therefore, it is vital to involve the team in the analysis. Insight into the team's actual performance, combined with actual solutions will allow the beginning of an internalized sense of why the transition is happening. Often, the analysis will show a poorer performance than team members envisaged. There may be some finger-pointing to other teams that are deemed to be the cause of the poor performance of the team being analyzed. The team leader must help to manage the negative feelings or shock toward carrying out improvements and taking control of the team's situation.

Finally, what counts in the adoption of new technologies and ideas, counts for the adoption of Lean IT as well. People will adopt Lean IT at different speeds. It is well known that people fall into one of the following five categories of adopters when it comes to adopting new ideas and technologies, based on Roger's classification in *Diffusion of Innovations* (2003):

- Innovators: These are the people who take the risk to first adopt new ideas. These people may be critical but will be enthusiastic for the change.
- Early Adopters: Will try out new ideas but in a more considered or careful way than the innovators. They tend to see the positive aspects in the change.

- Early Majority: These are the people who carefully look at the development. They are generally susceptible to a high level of "what's in it for me?" They accept that the change is likely to bring more good than bad.
- Late Majority: These are people who are skeptical of the change and will follow once a clear majority has decided to take the leap.
- Laggards: These are the people who will resist the change both actively and passively. They will always be able to say why the old ways were better and that the new way is nothing new.

The guiding coalition will generally be made up of people in the first two categories. However, it is also likely that among the leadership team, there are people from the other categories. When designing a transformation, it is important to take the different rates of adoption of change into account. It is important that there are also people from the Early (or even Late) Majority in the guiding team because they represent the speed of adoption of a large group in the organization. This is one of the reasons why a transformation should include revisiting teams that have been through their first iteration; to ensure that the late majority and laggards are given the chance to join in. The Know What, Know How, Know Why phases are testament to this difference in adoption rates.

The topic of speed of adoption of Lean is one that comes up in all Lean IT transformations. This is because of two key aspects: disruption and cost. Most management teams are eager to be able to say they have finished their Lean IT transformation as quickly as possible so as to remove the expense of external support or lower production. This is a poor reason to "declare victory"; the main reason should be "we have learned enough to sustain the level of use of Lean principles, tools and techniques ourselves." This means focusing on learning rather than a specific period of time of a specific budget. Disruption is an interesting aspect which centers on the availability and use of time. We have already seen that time is an important factor within IT, and we will return to it later in this book. Certainly, creating the time to work on learning about and practicing Lean causes time pressures in the delivery of IT services, but the learning and practicing also frees up time.

The stance an individual takes towards the change depends on their experiences with organizational change in the past. IT has seen many different technological and organizational hypes, which together make the longer-serving IT employees skeptical or even immune to the change. The position on the adoption curve will also be affected by whether a person volunteers for the change or is "planned for change." One thing is certain; stopping, pausing or otherwise hesitating after the initial try-out causes people to lump the Lean IT transformation in with all the other attempts at change. Teams positioned in one of the later waves may feel they are not important enough and may think that everything will have been decided by the time the transformation reaches them. In addition, even if people are early adopters of new technology, this does not always mean that they are early adopters in Lean.

STAGES OF TRANSFORMATION

We can identify three broad stages of development. These stages take anywhere from six months to three years depending on the size of the IT organization and the amount of time dedicated to learning and translating the lessons learned into practice.

The first stage is the "Know What" stage. In this stage, there is a group of people who believe that Lean IT is the way to go. This group will include leaders and employees who may previously have informally discussed using Lean principles. At a certain point in time, the choice is made to start using Lean tools and techniques in some specific areas of the IT organization. This may include adopting Lean for software development, complete with techniques such as Scrum to facilitate the more reliable delivery of new software, or the use of visual management in an IT operations department to better monitor the flow of units of work through processes. Some people will be immediately engaged, because they see benefits for themselves. However, the principal reason for involvement for most people is that they are asked to join in. This may happen under guidance from Lean IT consultants. People do Lean IT, at least initially, because others are doing it.

There is often a substantial amount of skepticism, even among leaders, as to the ability of this new "fad" to deliver results and benefits. Many IT people have seen a variety of models, trends and hypes, and have also seen many blow over. It is extremely important for IT management to realize that starting on the journey to Lean IT is a long-term commitment and not the new management trend that may or may not blow over when the next new thing comes along. In this stage, the key is to maintain the discipline of using the Lean methods and principles, so that these can be turned into habits. The presence of the leader as coach, supporter and teacher is vital. In this stage, trust and respect must be built. Keep in mind that this foundation stage requires time, effort and close attention of the leadership team.

The second, "Know How," stage is when Lean tools are integrated across the various parts of the IT organization and value streams. People have "automated" a number of the Lean tools and principles into their daily work. Teams will carry out rituals such as day starts, daily kaizen and other such activities independently of the presence of the leader because they have fully understood the working and benefits of the Lean way of working. The Lean way of working provides a new predictability for the IT organization; people know what to expect. In this second stage, Lean IT is recognized as the IT organization's mode of operation. There is widespread belief that Lean IT is the right thing to do. However, there will still be pockets in the organization where Lean IT is not fully adopted and there will be moments and situations in which people (engineers and leaders) will revert to old, non-Lean behavior. People increasingly recognize these situations and coach each other to adopt and adhere to the agreed new behaviors.

The third and final stage ("Know Why") is when Lean principles have been fully embraced by the whole IT organization and a deeper understanding of Lean IT is present throughout the entire organization. Practicing Lean IT has become the way of life, the new "normal," the new "business as usual." Lean is not negotiable; it is who you are as an organization; it is how you do what you do. The collective and individual ways of thinking and acting are recognizably determined by Lean principles. Everyone in the IT organization contributes to, supports and teaches Lean IT and its further evolution within the organization.

These three stages all require a similar amount of effort. The effort is focused on different aspects moving from acquiring knowledge and skills ("Know What") through embedding the discipline ("Know How") to continually improving ("Know Why"). In my experience, around 10% of the IT organization's time should be reserved for these activities. This is the first major difference between the traditional IT organization and the Lean IT organization: Time is explicitly set aside to improve the way of working on a continuous basis rather than periodically. This means that the first improvements made must have the effect of freeing up time to reflect, learn and develop.

The goal is to achieve the third level in which Lean becomes the standard way of working in the IT organization. But when is the transformation to Lean IT finished? The short answer is: never. A Lean IT transformation is complete when no more improvements can be made. This is a rather facetious answer since a Lean IT organization will always find something to improve.

12

Change Story

We have seen how the journey to Lean IT can start, often tentatively. This start tends to cause leaders to understand that they have started something that needs to be continued. Creating a high-level plan defines intent especially when people are encouraged to take on roles that are necessary for the Lean IT transformation to succeed. Obviously, leaders need to take into account that the transformation will not be embraced by everyone from day one, and helping people to understand the journey ahead is vital for success.

One of the preconditions to starting a Lean IT transformation is the existence of a so-called change story. The change story is a leader's way of describing what changes need to be made and why. It gives direction to the organization. A change story must describe the motivation behind the desire to change, giving people a sense of urgency. The important message is that "business as usual" is over, and a new business as usual needs to be created. A change story is written by leaders with their team members in mind. It is not a polished product from a Communications department. It is often raw and to-the-point, infused with the passion and inspiration of the leader. One of the important reasons for creating a change story is that it is a source of continuity during periods of uncertainty during the transformation. In periods of stress, leaders have been known to go back to their change story to help themselves get back on track. It is also a powerful tool for aligning the organization, since leaders include similar elements in their stories.

How does this work in practice? Change stories evolve over time, but they tend to start in a change story workshop in which the managers discuss their specific reasons for starting the Lean IT transformation. Many of the arguments used in Part I will be part of the discussion. The basic change story is one that a management team should develop together. In defining the reason for the transformation, management is able to create a common statement that they can all use in their individual change stories. The development of the change story is an iterative process that delivers many insights into how the managers individually see the transformation. Once a common basis has been created, managers use the materials created in the change story workshop to develop their own change stories.

A change story must be compelling to the audience. As I said, the process is iterative and generally the first attempts tend to be very functional ("I want us to be the best IT organization, providing the best IT services") and not particularly inspirational. It is only once managers find their specific "angle" that the change story really starts to work. Of course, a change story should be a call to action.

The following change story is from the manager of a Software Development department.

> The past months have not been easy for the management team, nor for me personally. The pressure on the teams to deliver major projects faster has had a huge impact. The re-organizations in Sales and Production have also been disruptive. I have seen team members almost buckle under the pressure of the sponsor in his efforts to deliver a new release of the system. Delivering performance is fine, but incessant discussions on the policy choices, scope and the continuous battles about the budget are energy killers. Because of the pressure, we work chaotically in the short term. The last straw for me personally was the incident last week, where our main customer was offline for seven hours. The pressure and the lack of focus on quality, shorten our testing and make me unhappy. I'm fed up, it's time to change course. What do I want to change? I want to focus on customers, the quality of the product and the process, and say "No" to things that we can't deliver. Plan work, less unnecessary meetings and coordination, more time on development work. The passion for our expertise must come first! If people are disappointed or have to wait a moment, then so be it! This change will cause resistance with our colleagues, but I want to fight this battle together with you. Because I am convinced that we have to do this. I invite you to join me. Let's start a new direction together!

Without actually mentioning Lean, this manager does identify a number of Lean principles (particularly customer value and perfection) and talks about removing waste.

When it comes to change story, one piece of advice: Please, no "burning platforms." Lean is about building a learning environment. You only need to watch the last fifteen minutes of the film Deepwater Horizon to realize that burning platforms are a place where you live in mortal fear and, above all, hope you come out alive. This is not the environment in which learning happens; it is not a Lean environment.

Part III

Leadership Transformation

I cannot say whether things will get better if we change; what I can say is they must change if they are to get better.

Georg C. Lichtenburg

13

The Challenge for Leaders

Transforming the leadership of an IT organization has proven to be the most difficult aspect of the Lean IT transformation. The reasons I have encountered are fairly self-evident and many current leaders will recognize, even – sometimes grudgingly – acknowledge, that one or more of these reasons is valid in their situation.

When we discuss the transformation of teams, we will see that the initial response to change is to externalize the need for change. Teams tend to point to others who need to change first, before they can actually change effectively. Leaders are not immune to this thinking, especially in larger organizations. At a management level, the most heard argument is that IT may become "Lean" but if customers and suppliers do not follow suit, the transformation will be pointless because the entire value stream is not Lean. To a certain extent, this is true. However, from the starting point of being a Mass Production style IT organization, there is so much that needs be done within the IT organization before we need to start influencing customers and suppliers, that this argument is largely based on uncertainty about the magnitude of the task ahead. By creating dependencies with the outside world, an argument is created that causes and reinforces inertia.

In the same vein, another argument I have been confronted with is that the 'environment' will not allow a change in behavior. The environment is principally made up of business colleagues who have their own structures. Changing the way of working within IT does almost inevitably mean that there will be times when there is a mismatch in the relationship between customer and IT. This may temporarily cause a degradation in service. It may cause miscommunication. There may be problems. But these things are happening now as well. One of the best arguments is that if we improve the way of working within IT, we will need to change the SLA (Service Level Agreement) and that "will open a whole can of worms."

On top of this, continues the argument, it will entail changing the contracts with suppliers and, if there is one thing that is disastrously difficult, it is changing these contracts. And so, we have developed another reason to not embark on the transformation of leadership. The paradoxical aspect of this argument is that these leaders do expect their teams to improve. I have found that the "environment" is largely ecstatically happy if IT leadership improves and encourages the teams to improve.

Like most people, leaders are not immune to their own successes. They have achieved their positions as a result of past successes and behavior that has been seen to be successful. These past successes reinforce past behavior. It is quite difficult for anyone, leaders included, to truly look themselves in the mirror and recognize that successful behavior actually needs to be changed, simply because it is hard to envisage what the new behavior looks like. I have had occasion to explain Lean leadership behaviors to many leaders and in more than half of the cases the response has been "Yeah ... I already do that." This is an unfortunate response that blocks learning in the leader. This leads to the next issue with leaders.

Leaders tend to have got to their position because they are capable, knowledgeable, often steadfast and have a belief in their own ability. In short, the egos of leaders are strong which means they are quite certain of their own opinion. As a result, they have a relatively clear idea of where they are going based on an internal frame of reference. When introducing new elements to this frame of reference, mostly the new elements are compared to existing ones and found to be similar. As with the behaviors, the new elements being added to the frame of reference are linked to existing ideas and labelled with the statement "Yeah ... I already know that." Again, the value of the new element is destroyed.

Leaders tend to be clever people which means they understand topics conceptually very well. They are extremely capable of talking the right talk. The problem here is you can learn and use a bunch of adopted Japanese words as is certainly the case in Lean IT, and then pretend to be knowledgeable. However, Lean IT is about putting new behaviors into practice, and this is where many leaders, initially, do not take the required steps. They do not build the discipline to try out new behaviors. As with most adults, leaders do not practice behaviors for fear of failure, desire to avoid making mistakes or looking foolish, thereby potentially losing face in front of the rest of the IT organization or, worse, in front of customers.

This brings us to the most heard argument of all: "I'm a busy person. I certainly do not have time to sit in a class for three days. And spending a morning or afternoon with my entire management team once a week to learn about Lean, and then having to spend time practicing, is out of the question." I agree. Leaders are "busy" people. The key question is: are they busy with the right things? The answer is that in order to have the illusion of control, leaders are "on top" of everything. For mid-level leaders, this is especially difficult because top-level leaders tend to ask for intimate details of all projects, critical incidents and so on. Meaning that these leaders feel they need to be at all meetings in order to grasp what is happening in the organization. Honest reflection often reveals that many leaders feel they are in meetings where they do not need to be, or where they feel that they do not add any value. This feeling of time-wasting is a fundamental cause of the "busy" feeling. The most difficult aspect is coming down from the adrenaline rush of being busy. As leaders find more time for reflection and other Lean behaviors, a feeling of inadequacy and doubt has been known to set in, until time has been reallocated in a productive way. In this context, reflection is a productive way for a leader to spend their time. It is vital to ensure that the leaders understand the principles of Lean in such a way that they fill their time with work that is productive from a Lean point of view.

The consequence of these arguments is that leaders learn more slowly than teams. They start later with their learning and learn poorly. Frankly, it is more often than not the leaders who "sabotage" the transformation that they claim to want. Until they make the commitment to themselves to actually take the transformation to Lean IT and their own role in making it a success seriously, the whole endeavor remains a slow and difficult process. It is important for leaders to realize that not taking a step is more damaging than taking a small step and finding that it may not have been the right step. This is one of the fundamental – lead by example – behaviors that ensures the Lean IT transformation actually happens.

In this part, we will look at how Lean IT actually contains the elements necessary to feel and be "in control", to feel less "busy" and be more productive.

People, in general, consistently believe they perform better than they actually do (the self-serving bias), and leaders are not immune. Timely, relevant, and actionable feedback provides for the enlightening and revealing truth about our behavior and drives the changing of what we think. It is up to Lean IT leaders to ensure that they lead by example and show that changing behavior is one of the keys to achieving the benefits possible from applying Lean principles to IT organizations. As a leader, your impact on organizational performance and culture is known to be considerable. People take their cues from those they consider significant and model their behavior on what they see. The various levels of leadership within an IT organization, and particularly the first line IT leader (the team leader), represent a crucial, "significant", role model and influencer of sustainable success. In combination with the effect of first line leaders, what senior IT leaders do and how they act has a powerful symbolic value. They help create stories about the Lean thinking and acting that will spread throughout the IT organization.

As I described in Part II, the transformation of leaders works best in the form of a flow of knowledge sessions alternated with sessions in which experience is shared. In between, there will undoubtedly be some form of individual coaching. I aim to give a flavor of what this process looks and feels like in practice. In this section, I will use the word "leader" to denote anyone in a hierarchical position of responsibility. Senior leaders or Management Team members are the top level of leadership, moving through mid-level leaders to team leaders. These together form the leadership hierarchy.

The leadership transformation I will describe is focused on the senior leaders. This leadership program needs to be cascaded through the organization to all levels of leadership. The first interesting aspect is that, eventually, senior leaders tend to pay sufficient attention to their own development, and then cascade an "executive" version of the program to lower levels of leadership. This defeats the point of the leadership transformation. If senior leaders do not spend the time and effort to transform their mid-level and team leaders, the transformation will peter out. Senior leaders must coach other levels of management extensively.

The best way to start the Leadership transformation is with Lean IT Leadership training. It is partly about building a common knowledge platform on which further discussion and development of thinking and acting can be based. The greatest value is the fact that the management team is together for three days, not discussing projects or technological developments, but focusing on how to actually run the IT organization, how to ensure that it will be able to deliver the customer demand, how people will work together across both hierarchy and teams. Most of the aspects dealt with in the training need to return in the workshops. For the sake of this storyline, we will skip the training and investigate the transformation. If you do the training with your leadership team, the discussion in the next section happens at the end of the training, and will tend to be more focused and lead to consensus in the planning more quickly.

14

Before Starting the Leadership Transformation

The IT organization has been practicing with either visual management in the teams or problem-solving with improvement teams that are either within a team or, preferably, cross-functional in terms of participants. Since the leaders have not paid a lot of attention to what is going on in the organization, the start of their own transformation is a bit of a surprise. What follows is a mad scramble to, grudgingly, free up time for their own program as designed at the end of the starting out phase. I have found that this is a period in which the CIO/IT Director needs to voice his or her intent clearly and take the opportunity to lead by example. Clear a space in the calendar and ensure that other senior leaders do the same. This sounds simple, but it more often than not leads to heated discussions. In effect, this is a negotiation in which the senior leaders test the resolve of the top leader in their will to go ahead with what will lead to a considerable upheaval in the organization.

What are common arguments? For each given moment planned for knowledge and experience sessions, at least one member of the management team will say: "Oooh, that's not going to work in my schedule, I have [insert name of very important meeting] and there's no way I can move that one because there are so many other people at the meeting." As a coach, these comments provide insights because they show how individually focused the senior leaders are at that point. The next is: "Can we delay for [insert a number of your choosing] months because we have this really important 'go live' and I'm sure I won't have time to attend all the meetings?" Again, the resolve of the top leader is being tested. The argument that a leader cannot do something because a project is going live is a curious one. The question is: Why is the leader so ensconced in the content of a project? A more generic argument is simply: "My calendar is full. I can't scrap anything. Just set some dates and I will see whether I can make it." Again, as a coach, these are the signs that doing the leadership transformation is a dire necessity and will end up, after some struggle, having a significant effect on the daily lives of some of the leaders. Once again, the resolve of the top leader is being tested. This negotiation has been known to take the best part of a regular management team meeting to get sorted out, and the discussions provide the coach with very revealing insights into how committed the leaders are to the Lean IT transformation, especially now that it is getting closer to them personally.

The series of meetings is set. If there is a substantial time (more than two weeks) until the first session, it is worthwhile for the coach to plan individual meetings with each of the senior leaders to understand their individual goals and motivations. In these meetings, very few leaders voice skepticism regarding the transformation and, in some cases, it is being saved up for later. Again, these interviews can be very educational for the coach as leaders state their concerns about the commitment of colleagues, the "real" reasons for the transformation – mostly, a suggestion that it is only a cost-cutting exercise, or an indication that the urgency of this transformation is being blown out of all proportion. Having said this, these preparatory interviews also trigger a passion in most of the leaders I have met. When they are asked what they want to achieve, there are personal stories of changing the way they interact with the teams, goals they wish to help their teams reach, personal development goals or simply regaining the pleasure of being a leader. Interestingly, these stories have not yet found their way into the change story, which at this point tends to still be a fairly dry, factual abstract of the IT organization's strategy document.

Let us assume that the management team has chosen to do their knowledge and experience sessions on a Wednesday afternoon, from 14:00 to 17:00. The agreement is that everyone will be there, and no one will set a meeting after the session so that, if necessary, continuing beyond 17:00 is possible. These are basic ground rules that need to be made explicitly, in order to ensure that the leaders can give each other feedback.

The next discussion concerns the order in which topics will be dealt with. Each management team has different priorities. Some will wish to focus on flow first, others on problem-solving, still others on team-forming. There is one common thread, the list is created in a fairly rational way with very few of the leaders voicing a concern that a particular problem needs to be tackled quickly. And this is a fairly universal observation: Most IT leaders are concerned about the ability to deliver projects and critical incidents, if there are too many. Other than that, IT leaders tend to be acceptant of the ability of the IT organization to perform, rather than taking an active stance in creating a structural approach to changing the way people and teams work and interact, in order to improve the ability to deliver. It is particularly the – angry – voice of the customer that spurs action. But delivering the value is a team responsibility and the responsibility of leadership is to ensure that they can do this. It is vital to understand that delivering the value and ensuring that someone is able to deliver value are two separate, but interrelated, topics.

Taking a typical leadership transformation, the first session always covers the basics of Lean Leadership, the core principles and goals that the leadership team wishes to achieve. The second session will generally focus on creating the environment to fulfill the commitment made. Fundamentally, this means making time to learn and practice. The third session is about the gemba walk. Once this foundation has been laid, it is time for leaders to start interacting with the teams. The fourth session looks at leadership use of visual management and the cascade. The fifth session goes into the details of flow and capacity management, a perennial issue in every IT organization. Later sessions will be defined based on the needs of the management team, and topics will include creating high performance teams, kaizen and problem-solving, performance dialog, KPIs and managing performance, and behavior and habits. To be clear, the sequence of the topics from the second session on depends on the focus of the management team. However, the first sessions must all focus on the behaviors required of leaders, building from understanding principles and their effect on behavior to actually practicing Lean behaviors.

Below is an example of a plan for Lean IT Leadership transformation (Figure 14.1).

	Weeks 1-2	Weeks 3-4	Weeks 5-6	Weeks 7-8	Weeks 9-10	Weeks 11-12	Week 13-14
	Leadership Transformation						
Learning	Deep Dive Lean Principles & Goals	Deep Dive Leader Standard Work	Deep Dive Gemba Walk & Performance Dialog	Deep Dive Visual Mgmt & Cascade	Deep Dive Flow and Capacity	Deep Dive Kaizen	Deep Dive High Performance Team
Seeing			Gemba Walk: Customer	Gemba Walk: Visual Management	Gemba Walk: Variability	Gemba Walk: Inflexibility	Gemba Walk: Lean Team
			Gemba Walk: Waste		Gemba Walk: Waste		Gemba Walk: Waste
Doing	Change Story Set direction KPIs	Change Story Leader Standard Work	Change Story Visual Mgmt Week Start	Visual Mgmt Obeya	Visual Mgmt Improvement	Engage in kaizen	Engage in kaizen
				Performance Dialogue	Performance Dialogue	Performance Dialogue	Performance Dialogue

FIGURE 14.1
Leadership transformation plan.

15

Change Story: Revisited

It is Wednesday afternoon. The clock ticks 14:02 … 14:04. The leaders trickle into the meeting room. By 14:09, all the leaders are seated. There is a diversity of body language around the table, from active in anticipation to reclined in reluctant expectation of what is to come.

> It's a date three to six months in the future. What will make you say that the transformation has been a success? What has it brought you? And your teams? In what way have you improved? What will you still need to do?

Before we can get into the details of what we need to do, it is important to have a high-level vision of what you as a leader aim to achieve. Having said that, these questions are actually quite difficult to answer at this moment. At this point in the proceedings, the answers are quite generic: "I want to be less busy," "I want to spend more time with my teams," "I want us to act more as a team," "I want to help my teams be more productive." This is a good start which will be revisited in the coming sessions.

First, we take a look at what Lean (IT) leadership is and how it differs from traditional perceptions of leadership. Any publication on the application of Lean principles within any organization in any industry will mention the critical importance of leadership in the success of the initiative, or the lack of success if leadership is absent. Experience supports this observation entirely. There are thousands of publications on leadership, many on leadership in IT, less on Lean leadership and very few on Lean leadership within the IT context. Among the pre-eminent work done on Lean leadership, two books stand out: *The Toyota Way to Lean Leadership* (2011) and *Developing Lean Leaders at all Levels* (2014). These books, both written by Jeffrey Liker, present a model of developing leadership. The first book describes the way leadership is developed at Toyota; the second is a more generic description of the key aspects of Lean leadership. The model presented by Liker has been used for developing leaders within IT organizations and has proven to be very suitable.

The question then is: What defines Lean leadership specifically? The key to Lean leadership is that it is principle-based. A principle is a rule or core belief governing one's personal behavior, described in a clear statement. This means that leaders are expected to base their decisions and actions on clear statements that describe the core beliefs of the IT organization. The clear statements do however leave room for interpretation and the leader's discretion. The idea is that leaders think and act according to the spirit of the principle.

The discussion of principles provides an interesting perspective on leadership for the leaders. Leadership tends to focus on either what you need to be (character traits) or how you need to act (e.g. direct, coach, support, delegate). By starting with the principles, we can identify how we need to think about the world and then we can link the actions and behaviors to the principles. If leaders understand and act in accordance with the principles, it does not actually matter what I do as long as I acted in the spirit of the principles.

Looking at the Shingo Model, we find four guiding principles that we can clearly and directly link to the challenge of leadership: Respect Every Individual, Lead with Humility, Create Constancy of Purpose and Think Systemically.

Respect is a principle that provides the space for people to develop and creates an environment for people to feel confident about being accountable for their actions. Respect must become something that is deeply felt by every person in the organization. One of the most basic forms of respect is being grateful and showing it, for the contributions that people make. Other forms of respect include trusting another person's judgment, reacting positively to not just the results, but also the effort people put into their work, and giving honest and objective feedback when results and effort do not match the agreed goals. Respect for people is about demonstrating an honest interest in people combined with performance objectives. Structurally showing true interest in how team members execute their tasks, but not telling them how to do their work distinguishes Lean leaders from traditional leaders. Respect does not mean being nice if it means that people are left with the impression that they have performed well when it is not the case. Respect does however mean using non-offensive language and behavior in giving feedback.

Respect must be felt at the individual level, because it is individuals who drive continuous improvement throughout an organization. Respect for every individual naturally includes respect for individuals representing customers, suppliers, the community and society in general. Individuals are energized when they are respected.

Leading with humility is a guiding principle that precedes learning and improvement. Humility is best described as a leader's behavior that demonstrates a willingness to seek input, to listen carefully and to continuously learn. There is also a need for humility on the part of all members of an organization. In many cases, IT leaders have come up through the ranks, often based on extensive knowledge of the technological landscape. Such a leader lacking humility will be first to present solutions, options and ideas, and will ensure these points are followed by the teams, often to the exclusion of ideas from the team members. It is important to realize that ideas can come from anywhere. Something new can be learned from anyone. Leading with humility occurs when people are willing to abandon judgment, bias and prejudice in their pursuit of a better way.

W. Edwards Deming (2000) recognized the need to create constancy of purpose (the first of his "14 points"). It is the responsibility of leaders to find agreement on the organizational values and strategic direction to provide a unifying vision. Once this unifying vision is created, performance measures that are tied to the attainment of that vision should also be established. Changes in the vision and associated performance measures should be treated like changing a national constitution, with extreme care. Frequently redirecting values and strategies causes a tremendous amount of waste associated with instability. Lean practitioners frequently use the term "True North" to represent the important and constant focus that organizations should have. As organizations maintain a True North focus, they will attain competitive and financial advantages that separate them from the competition. Common categories in which customer-focused True North metrics are developed include: morale, safety, quality, delivery and cost. Lean leaders stimulate and inspire employees through dialog and by setting challenging expectations at the individual level. Through the focus on purpose, they inspire people to change from "just doing my work" to "my work makes a difference; it is necessary to achieve our long-term goals." They build systems and processes that cascade responsibility and embed the constancy. Lean leaders influence by being knowledgeable, by getting into messy details, by coaching and teaching.

Think systemically is the principle that unifies all the other principles of operational excellence and enables companies to sustain Lean and develop constancy of purpose centered on continuous improvement. This principle is based on the fact that the impact of synergy—of all parts working together—is far greater than the sum of the parts. This appreciation requires managers to move from thinking analytically about systems to thinking systemically. Systemic thinking occurs between parts of a system that occur over time, rather than snap-shot events, and consists of three parts. The first is holistic thinking which concerns understanding the interconnectedness of the aspects of larger systems. Holistic thinking means looking at "the big picture" and being aware of the relationships between the components. The second is dynamic thinking which focuses on creating a vision and aims to increase understanding of what has happened, what is happening and identifying what may happen in the future. It means understanding the dynamics of a situation and how these may be shifting. The final part is closed-loop thinking that requires understanding how changes within the system ripple across the value stream, affecting the work and behavior of other employees in the same department, in other departments, external customers, suppliers and other stakeholders.

As leaders practice systemic thinking, the full value of operational excellence is realized as it moves across the organization, the enterprise it operates within, and ultimately the entire value chain. As employees at all levels of the organization adopt systemic thinking practices, they are better able to understand the impact of improvements. Ultimately, this understanding is what allows the improvement effort to move from being solely top-down to include more effort from the teams.

These principles are the basis for Lean leadership and come on top of the Lean principles we saw earlier. This all adds up to a lot of principles. It is important to realize that you will need to integrate these principles into your way of working in a step-by-step manner. I have found that the basic five Lean principles (customer value – value stream – flow – pull – perfection) become relatively easy to remember and live by as the whole of the IT organization adopts them. This also goes for the more advanced principles, leaving leaders the space to focus on the leadership principles.

One Lean IT leader commented that his most difficult challenge was sticking to the principles when things go wrong. There does not even need to be a crisis; time pressures and mistakes have the effect of pushing the principles to the background. If you recognize and experience this, then you know that you are making progress. Knowing that you are deviating from principles is the first step towards embedding those principles in your way of working. At the same time, it emphasizes that you still have work to do in increasing your own level of Lean leadership (know what – know how – know why). The principles need to become your modus operandi and not something you forget in difficult times. In fact, these are the times that you most need to make use of the principles.

It is vital when you start practicing Lean leadership that you ensure you have sufficient time set aside to reflect on experiences, occurrences and problems. During these moments of reflection, it is useful to review a situation, preferably together with a coach, and identify which principles you applied or, at the beginning in many cases, should have applied. This helps to embed the principle so that, the next time you encounter the same or similar situation, you can more readily apply the principle. At this point, some of the leaders in the workshop invariably reiterate that they have no time. In this phase, it is not so much about time, it is about attention and alertness to what is going on around the leader that is important.

If we look at the effect of Lean leadership when truly practiced according to the principles, there are substantial differences in both the feel and performance of IT organizations that do use Lean principles and those that do not. Lean IT organizations achieve both a more positive "feel" in terms of better collaboration, higher customer satisfaction, employee satisfaction and higher acceptance of decisions, and better results in terms of lead times, inventory and quality of products and services, i.e. both "noticeable" and "measurable" improvements.

To understand the concept of Lean leadership, we should take a look at the differences between traditional Western leadership and Lean leadership. Traditional Western leaders are expected to be strong and act like a superhero in order to achieve results repeatedly. They must achieve financial objectives in order to climb the organizational ladder. Traditional Western leaders tend to work to a financial plan or budget and focus on achieving the numbers. They are also expected to have detailed knowledge of the work, without having to rely on the teams, leading to a "knowledge is power" culture. It is also seen as a badge of honor and pride to have risen rapidly through the hierarchy of a large organization, based on quick results that have been achieved through any means and at all costs, usually at the expense of others. There is a good chance that the results are not sustainable, as a result of the organization's dependence on a charismatic leader.

In comparison, a Lean leader is humble and patient in achieving results and focuses on ensuring that the right process is in place that delivers the results consistently, even without the presence of the leader. The Lean leader learns deeply and earns their way up the ladder through the demonstration of Lean leadership behavior. Along the way to reaching for the organization's vision, the Lean leader focuses on developing other people through (process) improvement work. This does not mean that the leader does not know what is going on in the organization; the leader relies more on the structures and the expertise of team members, power is in sharing knowledge.

In Toyota's experience, it takes about ten years before a leader can act like a mature leader (Liker and Convis, 2011). The leader must have all of the routines etched into his or her brain to be successful. The leadership approach at Toyota expects leadership from, and grants authority to, individuals at much lower levels of the hierarchy than is typical in Western organizations. This approach to leadership is exactly what is needed in the current development of the IT industry. IT organizations working with Agile and DevOps (and Lean IT, obviously) aim to grant authority and accountability at a much lower level in the organization. In fact, we see that the role of Product Owner at the team level is a highly influential role with substantial responsibilities and associated decision-making power. In order to make Agile and DevOps work in IT, it is absolutely vital that leaders take a Lean IT leadership view of and approach to their work as leaders.

The Lean leadership approach produces three key outcomes. Firstly, the dispersal of power and the expectation that leadership will come from the base of the hierarchy ensures that there is a constantly growing set of potential future senior leaders who gain experience on a daily basis. Secondly, it ensures that change is driven by people closest to the problem which results in better problem solving, more sustainable solutions and the possibility of continuous improvement. Lastly, it ensures that the vision is cascaded through the organization and that the principles and values that are being pursued are the organization's goals, not the goals of an individual leader.

In many of the transformations that I have seen, there are people from the operational level who have taken on the role of kaizen lead or Lean/ Agile coach, who end up in a hierarchical leadership position. This is based on their proven ability to solve problems and make change stick, and how they are able to communicate the Lean vision in a way that resonates with colleagues and helps to move the IT organization towards its goals. These coaches also have a high level of knowledge and insight into the "new" way of working and are capable of communicating its importance.

This is the marked difference between Lean leadership and "traditional" Leadership. Much research into leadership focuses on identifying specific character and personality traits that should be considered key success factors of effective leaders. Lean leadership focuses on behavior. It does not matter what the situation is, the behaviors are still relevant, whereas character or personality traits may be counterproductive or insufficient for the situation. Behavior can be practiced, observed and feedback can be given on the quality and effect of the behavior. This leads to learning which leads to adjusting less successful (parts of) behavior. Changing character and personality traits is notoriously difficult, if not impossible.

We have looked at what defines Lean leadership. However, is Lean leadership so different from other types of leadership? If we look at the intent of other leadership models then there are no great differences.

Taking Jim Collins' Level 5 Leadership as one example of a leadership model not directly based on Lean principles, but derived from practices in the great companies of the world, we see many similarities to Lean leadership. The term "Level 5 Leadership" refers to the top of a five-level hierarchy. Level 1 relates to individual capability, Level 2 to team skills, Level 3 to managerial competence and Level 4 to leadership as traditionally conceived. Level 5 leaders possess the skills of levels 1 to 4 but also have an "extra dimension." Under the title *The Triumph of Humility and Fierce Resolve*, Collins' 2001 article in the *Harvard Business Review* describes Level 5 Leadership in the following terms: "The level 5 executive 'builds enduring greatness through the paradoxical blend of personal humility and professional will'."

In this excerpt, we can recognize the Lean principles lead with humility and create constancy of purpose. In the details, Collins describes personal humility in terms of a leader who

> demonstrates a compelling modesty, shunning public adulation. The leader acts with quiet, calm determination; relies principally on inspired standards to motivate; channels ambition into the company, not the self; and looks in the mirror to apportion responsibility for poor results, never blaming others.

"Professional will" includes creating superb results by being a clear catalyst in the transition. A leader who demonstrates an unwavering resolve to do whatever must be done to produce the best long-term results. Collins continues: "The Level 5 Leader sets the standard of building an enduring great company. The leader looks out the window, not in the mirror, to apportion credit for success of the company – to other people." In other words, the Level 5 Executive sees and respects the contributions that others make. In this, we can recognize the principle "respect every individual."

Lastly, the Level 5 Executive creates an environment of disciplined thought, disciplined people and disciplined action. They also use technology both conservatively and in a pioneering way. The Level 5 Leader thus considers multiple aspects and selects the right choice based on what provides the most value; an example of "thinking systemically" (Figure 15.1).

The interesting perspective is that Collins suggests through his model that team leaders cannot be Level 5 Executives. Lean leadership aims for a different level of ambition. The aim is for all levels of leadership within a Lean organization to have the same or similar behaviors, thereby creating a consistent leadership environment in which leaders at all levels can share experiences and lessons learned concerning the key behaviors. Behaviors at which a team leader can excel just as easily as an executive.

Many IT managers have developed under the Western leadership culture and are strongly influenced by the Mass Production leadership and organization paradigm. This fact alone means that integrating Lean principles into the way of working will not only be hampered by unfamiliarity, but will be subject to the mental models currently in use.

Characteristics of a Level 5 Leader

1. Humble and modest
2. Determined
3. 'Work horse' rather than 'Show horse'
4. Enough confidence to make sure his/her successor will flourish in the future
5. Dedicates success to others and takes personal responsibility for inferior results

FIGURE 15.1
Level 5 Leadership by Jim Collins.

A mental model is the complete set of assumptions about how the world works, and is based on our experience, education and temperament. This is a lens through which we look at the world and interpret the information we receive from the outside world. In effect, the lens is our filter that helps us to understand and make sense of what we experience. It therefore also disturbs our view of the world and creates our perceptions. Changing a mental model can be a disconcerting experience since it shakes the foundation of what we know and do. If something you have learned to be true turns out to work differently than you had been led to believe, the effect can be very unsettling and most people aim to avoid the pain of being disconcerted or unsettled. It can even have the effect of people saying things like: "So, up to now, we have been doing everything wrong!" Leaders, therefore, need to show the way, by adjusting their mental models through the application of the Lean and Lean leadership principles, and coaching and teaching people about the way forward. One important realization in this respect is that over the generations of past leaders, a system has been created in the IT organization based on the insights of the past 30 or more years; based on new insights, we are changing the system one step at a time. This does not mean that everything we have done to this point has been wrong, it is just that we are finding a better way.

What mental models are currently prominent in traditional IT organizations that need to be adjusted when using Lean principles? The following examples are not exhaustive and you can probably think of others, but they indicate how our world is shifting.

- We are changing from a paradigm in which specialization and coordination are the main drivers of organization towards one in which value and teams are the drivers.
- The move from the manager who knows best, to a leader who teaches and helps others closer to the problem to solve it.
- A manager who leads through meetings, to a leader who goes to the gemba and sees what is going on.
- Standards that are collected in binders, to simple instructions that are visible to all and used as the basis for further improvement.
- Workers who need to meet quota requiring production to run as much as possible, to empowering team members to stop the work if they find an error, and correct the error before moving the work forward in the process.

- Making sure you do not get blamed for a problem, to an environment in which problems are welcomed as part of daily work.
- Leaving problems to be identified and solved by management, to mobilizing the team members to get engaged in solving problems, possibly with support from experts in specific areas.

These are all subtle changes in the mental models of leaders wishing to move their organizations to a Lean principle-based environment. Some of these mental models are already visible in the ways of working found in IT organizations using Agile and DevOps.

One of the elements of being a Lean IT Expert is understanding and practicing leadership. It does not matter what your hierarchical position is; in a Lean IT organization, everyone is expected to show leadership. A technical expert needs to show leadership skills when helping to define the way forward with a service. This is just as important as a manager, a formal hierarchical leader, must demonstrate leadership skills to advance the performance of a team, a collection of teams or the entire IT organization. The interaction between IT and customers and suppliers also requires leadership behavior.

How do we develop leaders capable of leading in a Lean environment? In 2011, Liker and Convis published *The Toyota Way to Lean Leadership*. In this book, they described the Lean Leadership Development Model. It contains five key components: four steps for developing Lean leaders and a set of "True North Values." This model has proven to be highly applicable and relevant to leaders transitioning their IT organizations to a Lean (or Agile or DevOps) way of working (Figure 15.2).

A True North Value is a core value by which everyone within an organization lives. True North is what you should do, not what you could or can do. Liker and Convis identify five True North values based on their experiences at Toyota: Challenge, Kaizen Mind, Go and See, Teamwork and Respect. These True North Values represent an excellent starting point for any organization taking its first steps on the Lean journey. However, the leaders must develop their own True North Values using words that resonate with people in their own organization. When defining True North Values, they may be represented by individual words or short sentences, but it is important that there is a clear explanation supporting each value.

- **Challenge**: Challenges create pressure to improve and, therefore, must be welcomed rather than avoided. Maximum performance is when there is the right level of stress: neither too little nor too much.

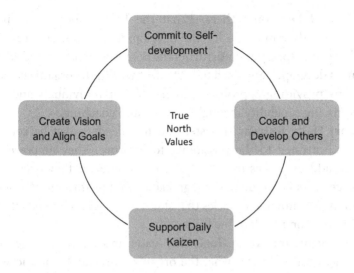

FIGURE 15.2
Lean leadership development model (Liker and Convis, 2011).

Learning and performance reduce if stress is too high. There is an equally important finding that if people are not challenged enough they will stagnate, decreasing performance and learning.

- **Kaizen Mind**: Improvement is a daily task. We achieve systematic and continual improvement through a structured process. We approach any challenge by following the right process.
- **Go and See**: We rely on first-hand observation and learning to understand situations. Being at the *gemba* will provide the greatest insight into problems and solutions.
- **Teamwork**: Teamwork and individual performance are two sides of the same coin. Great teams require highly developed individuals.
- **Respect**: Each individual has the right to contribute according to their strengths and capabilities, and is encouraged to improve through coaching and learning. Customers, society, team members, partners, communities in which you do business all deserve respect.

The development model itself describes four key steps:

Commit To Self-Development: The most important step for a Lean leader is to make the explicit commitment to develop. This means making a concerted effort to go through individual learning cycles focused on improving the ability of the leader to adhere to the True North Values and improve the ability to execute the other steps.

Coach and Develop Others: What the leader does for their own development, they must do for the development of others. This means identifying, mentoring and nurturing the potential in others and ensuring that this is developed and used to best effect within the organization. This is done by providing appropriate challenges for individuals and teams, and improving capability through training and coaching.

Support Daily Kaizen: This step means a leader must be constantly aware and attuned to the possibility to improve. They empower their people to address issues impacting customer value as they occur and at the source. This is not done through criticism, but through the ongoing dedication to removing obstacles that stand in the way of the people doing the daily work on behalf of the leader.

Create Vision and Align Goals: The leader must ensure that everyone in the organization knows what the organization stands for and what it is trying to achieve. Leadership establishes structures and processes to cascade "True North" values and principles throughout the organization. Leaders nurture a culture of personal accountability to ensure that supporting goals are defined and accomplished. They ensure that goals are shared and are consistent across the individual teams within the organization.

We will look at each of these steps in more detail, focusing on how to put them into practice in an IT organization. These steps are not difficult to understand, and I have found that discussing these steps without going into too much detail provides a basis for the first steps of self-development and reflection on the leader's individual situation.

At this point, I like to give leaders the following exercise.

> Take your calendar from the current week and decide what the *primary* reason is for your attendance of each meeting. Choose out of the four aspects of the Lean Leadership Development Model. The question to be answered is: Were you at the meeting to develop yourself, help someone else develop, encourage continuous improvement or to ensure that everyone was clear on the direction and goals?

There are many reactions to this exercise. Some leaders say that they, of course, need to do all four in each meeting, and they are right because meetings can develop in such a way that the primary reason for being there may be superseded by something that happens in the meeting. For example, you may be at the meeting to observe a person with who you aim to have a feedback meeting, but end up having to coach the team through problem-solving. The question remains: What is the *primary* reason you were at a meeting or are going to be at a future meeting? This generally triggers leaders to think about how they have prepared themselves for their meetings. Often, it uncovers the fact that IT leaders tend to prepare themselves from a content perspective (they feel they need to know all the technical details) but not from a coaching or improvement perspective. The result is that they get involved in the content (what they prepared), which is something that should be left primarily to the team.

The second part to this exercise is to understand what behaviors are necessary depending on the choice of primary reason. When you attend a meeting with the primary intent of self-development, what are the key behaviors that the attendees can expect from you? The majority of the responses revolve around "listening," "asking questions," "observing," "taking notes" and "thinking about what others say." Moving on to "helping others to develop," what behaviors are necessary? "Listening," "observing," asking questions" and "taking notes." And if you are present to encourage continuous improvement? "Listening," "observing," "asking questions/ challenging assumptions" and "guiding the problem-solving process." When we get to Create vision and align goals, there is a noticeable relief when the leaders say that this is the moment they can "talk," "tell people where we are going," "explain the rationale" and "answer questions."

This exercise based on a basic understanding of the Development Model provides insights into how conscious leaders are of the way they spend their time and whether they use meetings effectively to achieve their goals. It also links the intent to the behaviors that are effective in each situation. This exercise generally leads to hilarity as the leaders try to come up with the most inappropriate answer like "tell them what to do," "give them the solution" or worse.

On the subject of fun and hilarity, most leadership teams have a very high level of seriousness, solemnity and formality. One of the side effects of working with the Lean Leadership Development Model is that most leaders wake up to why they wanted to become leaders in the first place, and that was to help others to achieve great things. Re-learning the fun of leading is part of the transformation to Lean IT Leadership. Some people realize that this is not the kind of fun they are looking for and choose to step away from formal leadership positions.

The Lean Leadership Development Model clearly defines the starting point of the development journey at commitment to self-development.

However, in practice, IT managers and leaders will readily say they commit to self-development. The problem is that they have no concept, no idea of what this actually means. And this is understandable. If the IT organization does not have a culture of structured continuous improvement, coaching and team development, the chances of having leaders who understand the concept of self-development are slim.

In practice, the journey starts with an investigation into Create Vision and Align Goals. We have seen that IT does not entirely govern its own destiny; it exists within the context of a larger business ecosystem. This context has existing demands and requirements regarding its IT services. These demands and requirements mean that the IT leadership team (consisting of all levels of leadership within IT, but starting with senior leaders) must be aligned before each individual leader knows what they are committing to or where they need to focus their self-development. The process generally starts with the IT Management Team explicitly defining the vision they have regarding the IT organization. This vision must be consistent with the larger vision of the business organization within which the IT organization exists and which it serves. Initially, it will typically focus on the primary service categories and the larger scale developments that need to take place from a service or technology perspective. However, this does not provide the necessary constancy of purpose. The foremost addition to the vision is *how* the IT organization intends to operate; what kind of organization it will become. This is the context within which leaders must commit to self-development. It is in this vision that the IT management team must individually and collectively commit to applying Lean principles within the IT organization as an integral part of the vision. Having agreed as a team to the definition of "True North," this collective commitment means that managers will support each other in the application of Lean principles in the IT organization. From this preliminary commitment to each other, each manager can commit to their self-development with Lean IT being the core of that self-development. I have found that an open statement of commitment to the rest of the management team can be quite an awkward moment for leaders because, to be fair, it is still not totally clear what they are committing to. The aim is not to get a round of socially desirable answers. The idea is to understand under which conditions the leaders will commit to the transformation. There will be the leaders who say they will commit if they have "enough time"; others state they will commit if the management team are "in it together." These are all problems that can and need to be solved as a team.

We saw in the Starting Out part, that IT leaders are challenged to define their goals, translate them into KPIs and, then, to create both a plan and a change story for the transformation to Lean IT. This is the moment to revisit those change stories. In some cases, I will ask leaders to read out their current change story. Most of the senior leaders realize that their initial change story does not represent very well how they feel about the change at hand; the move to Lean IT.

This first session mostly ends with the leaders completing a Lean leadership assessment. This assessment covers their capabilities related to the Lean Leadership Development Model and serves as a baseline for the rest of the Leadership transformation. The assessment includes both a self-assessment and a peer assessment.

The "homework" from this workshop tends to focus on working on the change stories. The challenge is, of course, to practice the change story with people in the teams. Another piece of "homework" is to record the *primary* reason why a leader is at a particular meeting, and to describe what happened and how they acted based on this primary reason. The final part of the homework is to try to recognize the Lean principles (customer value – value stream – flow – pull – perfection) and Lean Leadership principles (respect every individual – lead with humility – constancy of purpose – think systemically) in daily work.

A relief descends over the participants … it has begun and it was not too bad after all.

A week later, Wednesday afternoon. The clock ticks 14:03 … 14:05. The leaders trickle into the meeting room. By 14:10, all the leaders are in place. Usually, the mood is more upbeat, less tentative than the previous session.

So, who's done the assignments?

The answer ranges from a full yes through a tentative yes to a silent no. The "homework" was not particularly challenging, as it did not require very much interaction or preparation, except telling some people the change story. Most of the leaders have attempted the assignments to a certain degree. Generally, the interaction with the team members will be something that they "didn't get round to doing. But I did rewrite my change story."

Most leaders respond positively to the insights they have gained, particularly describing the primary reason for the attendance of meetings. We revisit the exercise of the first workshop: What behaviors did you perceive in yourself? The results from the workshop tend to be confirmed and, sometimes, further specified.

The principles assignment turns out to be a lot more difficult, mainly because nobody remembered to write down the principles on a card or cheat sheet, to refer to during the week. The consequence is that, in fact, nobody did the assignment because nobody could remember the principles. This is an opportunity to practice the "chant": "customervaluevaluestreamflowpullperfection."

In the end, it turns out that the effort made with the assignments was average at best. This leads to the question: "Why did you not do the assignments?" This generally turns into the first encounter with the Five Whys method (which we will deal with in detail in a later workshop). Key elements of the root cause investigation of this question invariably uncover reasons like "no time," "didn't give it priority," "didn't create a reminder for myself" and "I forgot in the daily rush."

The discussion moves on based on the following question: "Based on your assertions last week that this transformation is important to you, why did you not allocate time or attention to the 'homework'? What was more important?" The silence that ensues is deafening, followed by the old chestnuts "Customer …", "Project …", "Critical incident …", "Sick employees/holidays/absences …" Fortunately, there is always someone who recognizes that these are excuses for not having done the work.

As leaders of organizations, we try to steer the organization in a particular direction. As a coach, we try to help steer people in the direction they want to go. But what is steering and how do we steer? In this context, steering is guiding the evolution of behaviors, and this is the essence of a Lean IT transformation. In order to understand the evolution of behaviors, we take a brief step outside Lean to Organizational Behavior Management (OBM). The two fields of study are very much related.

At the heart of OBM, there is a simple model that describes the relationship between behavior and its causes and effects. OBM says that our behavior is preceded by an antecedent and each behavior has a consequence. Antecedents are the things that managers are good at. Antecedents are policies, rules, structures, agreements, tools; in short anything that is intended to create an environment in which particular, desired, behavior can be exhibited. Behavior always has a consequence. The aim of each individual is for their own behavior to have a positive effect on themselves, even if this behavior has a negative effect on others (Figure 15.3).

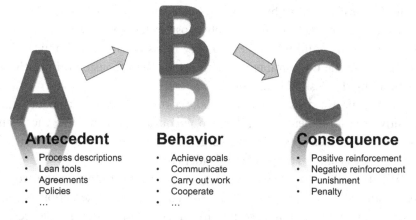

Antecedent
- Process descriptions
- Lean tools
- Agreements
- Policies
- ...

Behavior
- Achieve goals
- Communicate
- Carry out work
- Cooperate
- ...

Consequence
- Positive reinforcement
- Negative reinforcement
- Punishment
- Penalty

FIGURE 15.3
ABC model.

The OBM theory goes on to say that the best way to ensure that desired behaviors are encouraged, is meeting them with positive reinforcement. This means that a person receives something they want as a result of the behavior. This reward may be material, emotional or social in nature. The only criterion is that the person is particularly pleased to receive the reward. This effect is known as positive reinforcement and it increases the behavior it rewards. A classic example of positive reinforcement is the proverbial pat on the back. Most people are spurred on by regular (but unexpected) recognition of their effort and results (behavior). Another way of increasing behavior is through negative reinforcement. In this case, people avoid something they do not want by behaving in a particular way. In effect, negative reinforcement gives you exactly enough of the behavior. An example is studying for an exam. You want to avoid getting something you do not want (a fail), so you do just enough studying to pass. Bonuses work in the same way; people do exactly enough to achieve the bonus. A well-known effect is when sales people either rush to book sales in a particular quarter or, if the target has been met, delay on purpose so that the sale counts for the next quarter.

The best way to work with people is to encourage more of the desired behavior through positive reinforcement. On occasion, however, undesirable behavior needs to be decreased. There are two options: Punishment (getting something you do not want) and Penalty (losing something that you have).

The interesting aspect of the model is that leaders of organizations tend to focus heavily on the antecedents. The problem with this emphasis on antecedents is that most behavior is in fact caused by its consequences and not by the antecedents. Unfortunately, most leaders pay very little attention to consequences and when they do they focus on financial bonuses and on reducing the undesirable behavior rather than focusing on positively reinforcing the desired behavior.

Every time we discuss behavior, take a moment to think about what positive reinforcement would help to encourage and increase the Lean behavior you wish to see in your organization. This is vital for Lean IT experts, especially in their roles as leaders or coaches.

"What would you do with a team member who didn't do the work? And can we do the same to you?" The effect of this interaction is that the management team has a serious discussion about the consequences of not doing the homework. This leads to a fanciful enumeration of possible punishments and penalties, that fortunately lead to some hilarity. The question to be answered by the team is: "What positive consequences are necessary for you to do the 'homework' each time?"

The first responses are quite predictable: The "homework" must be interesting and it must have a positive effect on me as a person. We agree to evaluate each assignment upfront in such a way that everyone deems the assignment to be interesting and of value. But then comes the bombshell: "My colleagues in the management team should take interest in what I say when I explain what I did."

This is a major issue in many management teams. Mostly, leaders are not really interested in what the other does or says. This has much to do with the way in which responsibilities are distributed in the management team. We tend to organize IT management teams in such a way that the responsibilities are clear and do not overlap. The benefit is that it is clear who needs to take action if there is a problem in a specific area. The key problem is that leaders do not really care about what others do as long as their own "house" is in order. The consequence is that most IT management teams are not teams at all; they are at best groups, at worst a collection of individuals doing their own thing. This realization can lead to moving the High Performance Team Workshop up. For now, we will leave it where it is in the sequence of workshops.

16

Fulfilling the Commitment

Commitment is a word that will appear regularly in this book. Commitment is the state or quality of being dedicated to a cause or activity; it is a willingness to give your time and energy to something that you believe in, or a promise or firm decision to do something. The effect is that giving commitment raises an expectation regarding the steps to be taken. As Deming states in his book *Out of the Crisis* (2000): "It is not enough that top management commit themselves for life to quality and productivity. They must know what it is that they are committed to – that is, what they must do. These obligations cannot be delegated. Support is not enough: action is required."

The question that you need to answer is: Are you committed to helping your IT organization make the transition from Mass Production to Lean Production? As a prospective Lean IT Expert, you will – hopefully – answer affirmatively, but not blindly. Understanding what you are committing to is vital. Probably the most important thing you are committing to is allocation of time. And we saw that this was a theme that returned in the first two sessions. I sometimes refer to this second workshop as the "Finding Time" session.

One of my first questions to IT leaders wishing to develop to a Lean IT leader is: Can you describe how you will do your current work in three days per week (assuming they work five days a week)? Take a moment to think how you would answer this question.

This question has a purpose. First, you are about to make a commitment; will you be able to live up to your commitment? The second reason is to challenge the current status quo that is your calendar. Most leaders' calendars are not under their control and I do not mean you have a secretary. The environment causes your calendar to fill up with (seemingly) important meetings and activities. Leaders need to take personal control of their calendars. Third, it is about discriminating between time usage that helps you achieve your goals and those that do not. Leaders are very easily sucked into spending time on other people's goals under the pretext that the leader holds final responsibility for those goals. Finally, there is a fairly high level of inefficiency in the work of leaders. Accepting the task of taking control of your calendar is challenging yourself to do your work more efficiently. In essence, this is the first exercise towards defining Leader Standard Work.

Before we look more deeply at Leader Standard Work, we must look at Lean's relationship with standards. In common parlance, the word "standard" tends to be regarded as the lowest common denominator or at best the average. Lean defines the standard as "the best known way of doing something." The implication of this statement is that there *is* a better way only we do not know it yet. That is why we continuously improve, to find that better way.

Interestingly, asking people (leaders and technical people) how work can be done better tends to draw blank faces. I have found that leaders have a particularly difficult time identifying how they can do their work more efficiently or at a higher level of quality in the same time. One way is to frame the challenge as a problem, for example: "How will you find 30 minutes within work time every day to reflect on the application of Lean principles? Solve the problem."

We now know what a standard is. "Standard work" is defined as "The repetitive pattern of activities that represent the current, least wasteful method of planning and controlling normal business processes." (Liker, 2014). Standard work answers the 5W+1H of a process – the who, what, when, where, why and how. That being said, standard work is not necessarily hard and fast. It is certainly not perfect but is the best we can do at this point in time. Standard work is a collection and implementation of the best practices known at that point. It incorporates what is needed to start the process and the finished state of the process, and includes the necessary resources, how often work is delivered and where the work is done for optimal flow. Standard work is not the goal; optimized productivity, customer satisfaction, safety and quality are the goals. Standardizing is merely a tool to ensure that those real goals are met. Standard work is more than a work instruction document. It is created by the process users, based on customer requirements and functions as the stepping stone for further improvements. In the same way, standard work should always be questioned and improvements sought. Expect standardized processes to change as a result of advancements in technology and as opportunities for improvement arise from kaizen.

In a meeting with two technical experts and their manager working in an Agile environment, I was party to a seemingly flippant exchange. One of the experts was asked how long it would take to carry out a certain task allocated to him. He responded "Three hours," at which his colleague expert snorted and said: "I can do it in one hour." I waited to see whether the manager would react. The manager said "OK" and moved on to the next order of business. As their coach, I stopped the conversation and asked whether anyone had understood what had just happened. Blank faces ... until one of the experts said, "what's the standard?"

This was not the first time I had witnessed this kind of exchange and I am sure that this type of interaction happens in every IT organization every single day. There are people who know how to do work more quickly than others, only nobody is taking responsibility for sharing the "best known way of doing something." Without intervention, the work would have been the first technician costing the organization two precious hours more than it should have done and there would have been no learning. Leaders need to be acutely tuned to this kind of signals that time can be saved and ensure that the standards are defined and used.

The section about standards begs a question among the leaders: "What are our standards and do we adhere to them?" The response is that many standards are available on the intranets of IT organizations. Does anyone know where to find them and if they do, do they actually use them? The follow-up question is "What about standards in our leadership work?" This is the subject of an exercise later in the session.

We must first introduce the term "kata." This Japanese term literally means "form" and comes from the martial arts in which detailed movement patterns are practiced. Kata is the defined routine for thinking and acting in a particular situation, and is the starting point for all learning. Kata is the way in which standard work is carried out. Within IT, examples of kata are standard changes, investigating and solving a problem using a structured method, or work instructions for configuring an application or piece of hardware. So we have standard work with a form, kata. But how does the kata come about, and how is it improved? In Lean, there is a model of learning based on kata, Shu-Ha-Ri. This model is at the core of self-development.

Shu means "obey." Shu is about learning the traditional wisdom; learning fundamentals, techniques and proverbs. The student must learn the defined routine ("kata") exactly. Teaching is focused on ensuring that the student understands the need to follow the exact procedure. In this phase, deviation from the kata is not acceptable. This phase of learning is about "automating" routines. It is about ensuring that the activities become a routine, a habit.

Within IT, new engineers become familiar with the IT environment by starting on operational activities; simply ensuring that the systems are "cleaned up" on a daily basis so they continue to function correctly. A next step would be to carry out standard changes such as getting a new laptop ready for use. In both cases, the work will be accompanied by either a checklist or a set of steps to be followed in a specific sequence. Unfortunately, in many IT organizations checklists are seen as unnecessary documentation, because they appear to contain obvious statements that "everybody knows already." In *The Checklist Manifesto*, Atul Gawande (2011) explains that even highly experienced surgeons are prone to forgetting key pre-operative steps that may cause serious problems during an operation. Checklists and standard operating procedures are an integral part of ensuring the kata is defined and followed in IT.

One of the interesting practices within IT organizations is to put junior technicians at the Service Desk. This work tends to command the lowest pay, so the most junior people are allocated to the work. The problem is that the junior people do not know the kata, they do not know the standards yet, so it is very difficult for them to help the customer who has a problem. They end up becoming nothing more than a dispatcher of calls. From a Lean perspective, we are failing on three basic Lean principles: 1) We are not providing Customer Value which is that the call is solved, 2) we are not working in flow because the call needs to be routed to someone else with the chance of waiting time and 3) perfection is not being strived for because the service desk technician will still not be able to solve the problem next time it arises. Only people who know the kata of the most prevalent calls should be put at the service desk. The leader responsible for the service desk tends to chip in with the fact that this is what he/she has been saying for years, but nobody listened.

The second step in the learning process is Ha which means "detach," and is about breaking with tradition; diverging from the kata. The person carrying out the kata is permitted to improvise to a certain extent. The student has learned the routines; the basics are natural to him. He has turned the kata into habits and no longer needs to think about the routines but is able to execute them automatically. The student can now diverge from the rules and improvise within the confines of the kata.

Within IT, an engineer will have moved on from carrying out standard changes to executing a non-standard change. This will need to be carried out according to the agreed change process, whereby small variations will be acceptable between the key decision moments. The engineer will be able to identify small improvements to, for example, the checklists for operational activities. One of the most common Ha activities is the automation of manual tasks, thereby improving the standard and adjusting the kata.

The last step is Ri, meaning "separate." In effect, the kata is adopted and adapted to the individual, since the form has been completely mastered. The student now focuses on deepening their understanding and skills, and is truly free to learn the art of performance. What has been learned of the kata is now so natural they do not have to think about it.

Executing a project is an IT form of Ri. The engineer is so well versed with the execution of both standard and non-standard changes (which together make up the project) that she can improvise with both forms of change in the aim of achieving the project results. At the same time, the kata of executing a project must be respected. Depending on how experienced the project manager is, she may even be at the Ri level in managing the project. It should be noted that Ri is not the same as "winging it," although it may appear so for an untrained eye. Ri requires such a deep understanding of the important aspects of the kata that these are done automatically.

As a young interim manager, I once witnessed an experienced IT project manager. This project manager had a routine for keeping stakeholders informed of progress, which had become second nature as a result of having followed a method (Prince2) for many years. He would use the product breakdown structure and the product-based plan at every meeting with the stakeholders. His ability to keep his environment up to speed on the status of the project appeared effortless. Less experienced IT project managers would try to copy his way of working without understanding the rules – create an extremely good product breakdown structure and associated product-based plan – embedded his way of working. The less experienced project managers only saw that he had a plan, but they were not aware of how the plan had been built and how much time went into ensuring that it was correct and updated every time a new product was identified. This is a clear example of what happens when someone becomes excellent at the kata.

This explanation of shu-ha-ri raises the question: "Where would you place yourself on the shu-ha-ri scale when it comes to Lean IT leadership?"

It is somewhat humbling to see experienced managers realize that they are starting a new learning curve and the fact that they do not know the principles according to which they wish to lead the IT organization means that they are mostly in the Shu phase. This fortunately opens the door to the possibility of publicizing the fact that the management team is going through a learning process. When the leaders are open about their own learning experiences, they are leading by example, which has a positive effect on the rest of the organization's attitude to the Lean IT transformation and learning new ways of looking at the work.

As you develop as a Lean IT expert, you can use shu-ha-ri to understand how you are doing with the various tools, methods and routines that you need to learn to embed the knowledge and behavior you need to be effective. In essence, shu-ha-ri, kata and standard work are all about habits. Habits are a human's optimal form of standardization. Habits are the things we do automatically, without really thinking about them. We all develop habits, because thinking and deciding costs a huge amount of energy; our brains consume large amounts of energy when we learn or create new routines.

A certain cue is followed by a particular behavior, and the subsequent reward for this behavior reinforces the behavior itself. The more often the brain uses this sequence, the deeper the behavior becomes ingrained, to the point where the behavior itself becomes more and more automatic. Eventually, the cue ends up being so bound up with the reward that the cue itself will trigger a craving for the reward. When a particular cue triggers a craving directly, then the associated behavior truly becomes a habit. Only when your brain starts expecting the reward will the behavior become automatic.

For example, when learning to use an IT system that requires action from the user to save data, there will invariably be moments that the user forgets to save and loses data. In the beginning, the user needs to continuously remind himself of the need to save the data from time to time. Loss of data is a particularly strong reminder of the lack of a habit. Over time, saving data on a regular basis becomes an automatic action. The habit is thus created to ensure the user avoids the pain and frustration of rework.

Unfortunately, not all habits are productive or efficient, or a habit may start off being productive but as new methods are discovered, may become less efficient. The problem with these (now) inefficient routines, is that they feel efficient because we do them without needing to think about them. The leader is tasked with identifying when routines (or habits) are no longer efficient. An example of inefficient behavior is continuing to drag e-mails to their destination folders, because it seems too much of a time investment to learn how to set up rules that automatically sort your incoming e-mail into the correct folders.

Fortunately, Duhigg (2013) explains this in his book, *The Power of Habit*. The most effective way to alter your habits is to attack the habit loop directly and to replace an old routine that is associated with a certain cue and reward combination, with a new routine. If you want to change a habit, you must first identify the cue that is triggering the routine (this may be anything from a location, a time of day, an emotional state, the presence of certain people, or an immediately preceding action).

Second, identify the reward that the habit is bringing you. This can be tricky, as the reward is sometimes masked among other things. Given the sometimes obscure nature of the rewards that drive our habits, you may need to experiment with your routine a little, in order to identify precisely what the reward is that is behind your behavior. Avoiding discomfort in learning something new can be its own reward, as in the example of saving or losing data above.

Once you have identified the cue that triggers your routine, and the reward that it brings, it is time to come up with a plan to replace your current routine with a new one. If we keep the same cue and the same reward, a new routine can be inserted. "But that's not enough. For a habit to stay changed, people must believe change is possible. And most often, that belief only emerges with the help of a group" (Duhigg, 2013).

A classic case of changing a habit can be found in every Lean IT Transformation. Standard team meetings are changed from a traditional form to a Lean form in which visual management supports, for example, a one-hour week start and four fifteen-minute day starts. The agenda of the meetings and their form ("kata") changes. This is a learning process and every team goes through a Shu-Ha-Ri process of integrating both the meeting and the associated visual management into their standard way of working. Leaders must recognize and steer this process.

An important point when instilling new habits is to always give them 60 "times" to settle. Something will not become a routine if you only do it once a week; daily or more frequent repetition helps to create the habit. After this, the habit can be evaluated as a success or failure. Often people give up the routine after a handful of days or times, stating that it did not work. This does not mean the routine cannot be adjusted during the 60 days. It is recommended to adjust the routine if it ensures the same result is achieved more easily.

Having discussed kata, standards, shu-ha-ri and habits, we return to the earlier question: "What are the standards in leadership?"

Defining the kata for operational or technical tasks is relatively straightforward. Defining the kata of leadership is somewhat more challenging. The first step in the shu-ha-ri of Lean IT leadership is to define the kata of your own leadership as a Lean IT leader. This means building your Leader Standard Work. Leader Standard Work is a list of standard tasks, performed regularly by leaders to achieve strategy deployment and maintain continuous improvement momentum. It is a method to ensure daily progress which directs the leader to check on and support key metrics. It also ensures that the leader plans her presence on the gemba.

Research (Liker, 2014) has shown that the repetitive nature of leader's work decreases as the hierarchical level increases. This merely means that the nature of the leader's standard work may be different. Standardization may take on a different character, but there is always work that can be standardized.

Leader Standard Work is about identifying the vital tasks that contribute most to the two key Lean aspects of doing the work (i.e. delivering customer value) and driving continuous improvement, and ensuring that there is time to do this work, in precedence over other work. Leader Standard Work structures the work of the leader so that the leader can be proactive rather than reactive. It is a clear way of indicating the intent of the leader. Tasks for which the leader reserves time are obviously important. Effective Leader Standard Work is developed by the manager and checked with the team, since the leader is there to facilitate the work done by the team.

Leader Standard Work is beneficial in a number of ways. It makes work plannable and avoids the most basic problems such as non-execution as a result of time pressures or changed priorities. This is the result of knowing how tasks need to be carried out and how long they take, since this has already been defined, understood and tested. Fewer resources are needed to achieve the desired results as the work is carried out according to "the best way of doing the work." Since the standard work has been written out and it is thus known what should be done, standard work is (by definition) achievable. The ability of an IT organization to carry out the agreed Leader Standard Work is a mark of an IT organization that is in control.

Leader Standard Work contains work with varying frequency. It starts with the daily routine. Weekly, monthly and quarterly tasks are recorded so that they can be planned as and when required. Lastly, a Leader Standard Work list contains a space for reminders. These tend to be ad hoc activities that need to be carried out but are not yet standardized in such a way that they fit into the other categories (Figure 16.1).

Within IT organizations, leadership work can be standardized. There are routines identifiable at all frequencies (see Table 16.1). The routines include activities that may be new. We will discuss these activities in the following section.

Quarterly/annual activities appear to be special and one-off because they do not occur as often as daily or weekly activities. However, they do

Daily	
7:30	
8:00	
8:30	Check previous day's numbers
9:00	Day Start with team
9:30	
10:00	
10:30	
11:00	
11:30	
12:00	Check email
12:30	Lunch
13:00	
13:30	
14:00	
14:30	Problem-solving
15:00	Problem-solving
15:30	Review Resource planning
16:00	
16:30	
17:00	Check email / next day's planning
17:30	
18:00	

Weekly		
Mon		
	16:00	1-to-1 coaching
Tues		
	16:00	1-to-1 coaching
Wed	10:00	Gemba walk
	16:00	1-to-1 coaching
Thurs	10:00	Kaizen
	16:00	Metrics review for week start
Fri	13:00	Week start / review

Monthly		
Week 1	2 hours	Hoshin Review Meeting Preparation
	2 hours	Hoshin Review Meeting
	8 hours	Kaizen
Week 2	2 hours	Team communication
	4 hours	Customer meetings
Week 3	8 hours	Kaizen
Week 4	2 hours	Team communication
	4 hours	Customer meetings

Quarterly	
3 days	Suppliers

Issues / Follow-up

FIGURE 16.1
Example of Leader Standard Work.

TABLE 16.1
Examples of Leader Standard Work Tasks and Their Frequencies

Daily	Weekly	Monthly	Quarterly/Annual
• Attending day start(s) • Checking the previous day's performance reports • Gemba walk • Individual coaching sessions • Daily kaizen activities • Review resource planning	• Reviewing performance measures • Attending week start(s) • Team coaching sessions • Weekly improvement activities (e.g. processing issues on the improvement board) • Review week resource planning	• Activities to align longer-term goals • Supplier meetings • Customer meetings • Improvement kaizen • Update longer-term resource plan	• Annual budget cycle, with a quarterly review • Updating the service catalog • Setting up new service level agreements • Reviewing architectural roadmaps

contain routine elements, or can be turned into routine activities through planning and standardization. A leader could make the annual budget cycle much less arduous by turning the quarterly review into a monthly or even weekly review, which would allow the leader to gain more practice.

This aspect of increasing the frequency of tasks that are done irregularly is almost always a point of contention. The key argument is "What's the point? It only takes up even more time." A classic example is "checking the numbers." Leaders contend that the numbers do not change so why look at them more frequently. This is an example of a change in the way of thinking and acting. Firstly, many IT managers are not used to looking at the "numbers" of their organization. This means that they are unaccustomed to carrying out this task. Often reporting is monthly and shows data that is already old, meaning it is no longer of any interest for steering the organization. Secondly, when managers do look at the numbers they take a cursory glance and do not always understand what the numbers are trying to tell them. The change in thinking is that managers need to believe that they need to see updated numbers more regularly. On top of this, they must learn that whatever the change from one day or week to the next, it is significant enough to try to understand why the numbers changed (or not). This leads to "acting" differently. Managers start to require updated reports on a more regular basis (every day or, at worst, once a week) and they spend more time understanding what the numbers are trying to tell them.

Leadership work contains many meetings. Meetings are a source of a huge amount of potential waste if they are not managed correctly. Waste is possible on two levels: running of the meeting itself and the connection between the various meetings.

Meetings that are not standardized fail to reach their intended goal, because distractions cause the participants to deviate from the purpose of the meeting. Routine meetings should be performed in a standard way to increase the efficiency of time spent on addressing the agenda of the meeting, thus reaching its goal. The standardization of the meeting increases the ability of the attendees to focus on the important aspects of the meeting, such as decision-making, communicating decisions, or agreeing on distribution of work.

There are inherent links between many of the meetings within an IT organization, especially between the routine meetings. Thus, it is vital to synchronize these meetings throughout the organization. Synchronizing increases predictability and efficiency of time spent on coordination.

Standardizing routine meetings means fundamentally aligning the agendas of the various levels of management and the teams. This is done by analyzing the calendar of all leaders (known as a "day-in-a-life-of" or DILO-analysis) and identifying recurring meetings, time-frames, involved roles and required decisions. The key to successfully aligning agendas is to start with the needs of the teams, thus placing emphasis on the operational work. After this, align the various leadership levels with the meetings in the teams.

And so we come to the assignments:

- Create your own Leader Standard Work. Discuss it with more than one team member.
- Do an analysis of your own calendar and discuss it with a colleague. Challenge each other to identify where you can find time and to do your current work in three days.
- Identify three work habits that you have that have a positive effect. Identify three habits that are probably causing more harm than the benefits they deliver.

We come to session four of the leadership track. It is 14:00. Two of the leaders enter the room. In the next ten minutes, the rest of the management team arrives.

Before we start with the experiences, we investigate a habit. It starts with a question: "Did you realize that every one of the meetings we have had together has started ten or more minutes late?" This question can be interpreted as criticism and leads to a defensive response, with all sorts of reasons as to why people are late. The question is simply a Yes/No question, either you realize or you do not. The follow-up question is: "Are you late for other meetings? Or can you identify meetings that you are on time for and others that you are late for?" The pattern that emerges is that most IT leaders are late for a lot of meetings. The only ones that they are on time for are the ones that involve top-level business executives.

We can conclude that being late for meetings is a habit, with a limited number of exceptions.

There is a useful exercise for investigating this and other habits. The first step is to identify why the behavior is successful. In this case, answers include not having to wait for others, you can finish a job before the meeting, you can "make an entrance," it gives you status especially if you can say you were late because you were in a meeting with an important person ("name dropping") and, lastly, you can get away with it because no one ever complains. The second step is to investigate why the behavior is not acceptable. The responses include lack of respect for colleagues, preparing and being on time feels good, it demonstrates a lack of commitment, we lose time and the meeting is disrupted as topics need to be summarized for the late arrival. By applying the Lean leadership principles, we see that the behavior is not consistent with Lean. All in all, the habit may have a positive consequence for the individual, but always a negative one for the group. The idea is to turn this around so that the positive consequence for the group is aligned with a positive consequence for the individual. The third step is to uncover the assumptions that people make about the meeting. The assumptions were that there were no benefits to arriving on time, no decisions are made early on in the meeting anyway and I won't miss anything because someone will give me a summary. The final step is to identify alternatives and choose which one(s) will be used in this setting. The chosen alternative is then described in terms of desirable behavior. This behavior is observable and the other team members can give feedback on what they see. The alternatives may include ensuring the meeting starts and ends on time, ensuring that the meeting has a clear agenda and set of decisions to be made and ensuring that the topics in the meeting are important.

One such discussion revealed that people were late for their own management team meeting because time and again the meeting was unsuccessful in terms of decision-making, discussion of the key topics, clarity and structure of the meeting and particularly, too many topics meaning that each was only dealt with in a cursory fashion, leading to decision-making outside the meeting. Once this became clear, the meeting was re-organized to meet the criteria for an interesting meeting, and all participants arrived on time.

The Leader Standard Work assignment is all about finding time. The challenge is to identify the work that truly adds value from the perspective of the teams and the individuals who need to be developed to Lean IT leaders. The exercise is remarkably easy. With the four aspects of the Lean Leadership Development Model at hand, leaders are very capable of defining their most critical activities on a daily, weekly and monthly basis. Add this to the DILO-analysis and most leaders realize that they have filled their calendars with the wrong activities. The problem with this exercise is that many leaders feel like they are failing because they are not living their work lives as they feel they should. The most important step to take is to start working towards the desired situation, day by day, week by week.

One of the great things about calendars is that if you look three months into the future, you tend to see a pretty clean slate, and if you do not, most of the meetings that are there can be rescheduled relatively easily to fit a new configuration of meetings.

But again, changing the way meetings are planned requires commitment. In this case, it is about the commitment to self-development. Self-development is an activity that requires both individual reflection and feedback from outside; it is the act of reflecting honestly on one's own actions, thoughts, behavior and attitude with the aim of making these more effective. This is why committing to self-development is more difficult than it may seem. Committing to self-development does not mean, for example, that you commit to reading a book about how to be a better leader and then do your best to implement some of the ideas or suggestions; it means taking steps to change your behavior. It is an activity that needs to be planned and carried out on a regular basis. The commitment to self-development is the pre-requisite for the success of Lean within any organization, and it is no different for IT organizations.

Toyota believes that the key trait that distinguishes potential leaders from everyone else is self-development (Liker and Convis, 2011). Leaders actively seek to improve themselves and their skills. Potential leaders need to be given the opportunity to self-develop and they need to be supported along the way of their development. Leaders do not self-develop on their own. This means finding the right challenges for self-development, allowing space for self-development, and coaching at the right times in the process. At a high level, self-development is about obtaining Lean IT leadership capabilities and acquiring a certain set of skills.

Understanding the True North values, with the aim of ensuring that these values become the way you are and the way you think ("Know Why"), leaders must deliberately learn and practice to self-develop their leadership abilities to fit into a continuous improvement environment. Learning to manage from the *gemba*, relying on truly understanding what is happening in the teams to ensure that decisions and developments are based on reality, leaders must become experts in observation and process improvement. Being able to see and then respond in a way that moves the team forward through coaching and the removal of barriers, instead of stopping the team in their tracks, you must be able to facilitate a structured problem-solving process. However, this does not mean solving your team's problems for them; rather it means mentoring and coaching other people to think about what the problem is, and find solutions using a logical process. The leader must help to develop these skills in others through deliberate learning and on-the-job development. Once these capabilities have been mastered, the leader can teach others through on-the-job development.

What are the key skills that need to be acquired to become a proficient Lean IT Leader?

- Have an active and open mind while observing the work of the organization;
- Practice active listening to hear what people are really saying, followed by investigation through unbiased questioning;
- Apply systemic thinking, which means understanding how different variables affect the work done by the organization;
- Understand the actual strengths and weaknesses of each person;
- Define problems clearly and identify the root cause;
- Plan the execution of work and the allocation of resources to that work;
- Identify countermeasures to the true root causes;
- Translate plans into action with clear accountability;
- Motivate and influence people across the organization (with no direct authority) toward common objectives;
- Be able to teach others all of the above.

If self-development was easy, everybody would be doing it. Self-development is not something that comes naturally to most people. For self-development to be successful, the individual leader must make the commitment, must ensure there is a "support system" in the form of coaching and must create time to practice.

Self-development has two aspects: developing yourself to become a Lean IT leader and developing team members to become Lean IT leaders themselves. The first step is to find people who are willing to commit to self-development, who wish to commit to learning the True North values of the IT organization, and who wish to *live* by these values. You cannot teach someone who does not want to learn. Self-development takes time, and dedication to understanding one's behavior and changing it where necessary. Becoming a Lean IT leader does not happen overnight; learning is a process that goes in small steps. Start with learning basic routine patterns of behavior followed by more detailed and extensive learning. Learning cannot be rushed. The learning process can, however, be facilitated by engaging others in the process.

Leaders, possibly by nature, have a certain impatience, also with themselves. Understanding Lean is not a problem, however, committing the time and attention—put that mobile device away—to truly know what it means to be Lean is more difficult. This can only be done by practicing what you learn, trying things out. In the Western style of management, leaders are expected to be infallible; they do not make mistakes and they know everything they need to know. Practicing leadership implies that the leader does not know everything and is likely to make mistakes. I have found that leaders start their leadership program enthusiastically but when confronted with the need to practice, the excuses start to come.

There are two parts to the "support system." The first and most important is the coach. Ensuring you have a person who regularly observes what you do and gives feedback on your behavior, means you will make an effort because you really do not want to get the same feedback twice. Learning requires reflection and reflection means getting feedback from others. The coach collaborates intensely with the leader to turn problems into learning moments through the application of the values, principles and techniques of Lean together. You need a coach to develop yourself and you need to be or to become a coach to develop other Lean leaders. A coach helps to uncover blind spots and helps to maintain the commitment to self-development, simply by being there. The second part of the "support system" is the rest of the management team. I have found that many management teams have a "live and let live" attitude, i.e. there is an implicit agreement "If I don't criticize you, you won't criticize me." This is not very helpful in a Lean IT transformation because the leaders do not help each other to get better. This means that when a member of the team has not practiced, the others should spur them on and provide help.

In Lean, every leader is expected to figure out what they have to learn. Leaders need to identify their personal challenge to better align their people's work with customer value and, in so doing, align sustainable, profitable growth with employee satisfaction. This is a combination of gaining new insights, i.e. acquiring knowledge combined with learning through observation. This learning style is fundamental to Lean. The leader's learning evolves from providing support for team-level learning activities. As the teams solve their problems or show initiative, the manager is expected to interpret their conclusions in the wider context of the business, as well as support further learning activities in the workplace (systemic thinking). In other terms, if they learn, you learn.

Lastly, every leader must create a learning environment for their team members. Learning on the job is never easy, particularly not with the pressures of today's IT environments. Consequently, one of the key roles of a Lean IT leader is to create a visual environment together with team members in which the abnormal is easily distinguishable from the normal and where opportunities for small-step continuous improvement are clearly visible to all. A learning environment also means an environment in which mistakes are not punished but seen as sources of learning, and where employees feel they can thrive without fearing arbitrary, sudden changes. This is also the environment that needs to be created within a management team.

17

Go See

The previous sessions have given the leaders the opportunity to investigate basic aspects of leading in a Lean environment. The awareness of the principles, understanding the effect of habits and foremost the step towards taking control of their own time usage give leaders the foundations for further steps. This workshop is an extremely important one: Doing a gemba walk is a skill that all Lean IT leaders need to master. One of the greatest showcases for gemba walks is the TV program, *Undercover Boss*. This program is popular in all cultures, evidenced by the fact that it has been syndicated in sixteen countries with five others working on their own versions, and many other countries showing other countries' versions. This program features the owner, CEO or senior managers of an organization joining their own organization as an entry-level employee. The accompanying camera crew is explained by the fact that the new employee is taking part in a documentary. Based on the success and broad adoption of the format, we can conclude that people love to see leaders confronted with the reality of their own organizations. The leaders seem to enjoy it as well, since they see the hard reality of their organizations. They always seem grateful for the direct feedback they get, even though it essentially uncovers their own failures as leaders. The end of every episode begs the question: Why did it take a TV show for you [senior leader] to go to the gemba? If going to the gemba is so effective and provides so much insight, why is it not done everywhere, all the time? The point, of course, is that if people see the "boss" they will act in a different way. Taking a deeper look at gemba walks can help to understand how they can be done without having to don a disguise every time.

Lean IT leaders must create and maintain environments in which future leaders can sustainably learn and practice what it means to be a leader. This means ensuring that the environment challenges, but also nurtures, these potential leaders. When coaching leaders to create a learning environment, it is important to be aware of whether team members are actually learning. A simple model that can be used to gauge learning is the following model (Figure 17.1):

The first point to this model is that you can apply it to yourself. For each situation, you encounter you can check for yourself what zone you are in. The comfort zone is a zone in which all activities that you do regularly and are good at reside. The fear zone is where you are not confident of what is going to happen, you are wary and possibly in a defensive state of mind. In the fear zone, you do not learn; you are just hoping you survive. In between the comfort zone and the fear zone, is where you actually learn. There will be some tension since you are not completely clear on what will happen but you are excited about the experience.

When a Lean IT transformation starts, I have found that, for many people, the move from comfort zone to fear zone is very quick. This means that it often takes a while to get people into their learning zone. In the learning zone, people feel comfortable about questioning current practices and thinking up new ways of doing work. When we first start talking about improving, many team members will defend the current way of working (comfort zone) and as the possibility of change becomes greater, they attack the possible change as not being any better than the old way of working (fear zone). The aim is not to push forward regardless, but rather to help team members to envisage the new of working by, for example, doing a dry-run to see how it works and potentially iron out perceived problems.

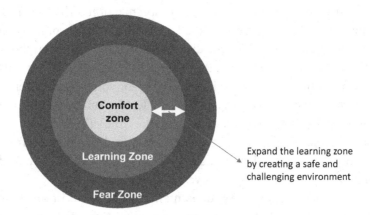

FIGURE 17.1
Learning zone model.

If you apply this model to yourself, you will be able to relate to what team members may be experiencing. Use it to discuss with your coach whether a new challenge is too easy (you remain in your comfort zone) or too difficult (the thought of the challenge turns your stomach and puts you in your fear zone).

As we have seen, each potential leader must follow the development path, starting with a commitment to self-development, and we saw the activities that need to be carried out in the "steady state." But the whole point is to develop new leaders and promote them to new levels of authority and accountability. PDCA is also applied in this situation, only the cycle starts at a different point and the A takes on a different meaning; we start with the A. Advance a job is selected that fits the leader's next development step to advance learning and growth. The next step is to Prepare. The new leader must understand the gaps between the current situation and True North vision by going to the *gemba* of the new situation and gaining a deep understanding of what is actually happening there. Also, the leader must build relationships with people in the team. The leader then leads and develops others to achieve challenging goals (Do). This is where the practical experience of leading is tested. Then, the leader discusses their leadership experiences with the coach (Check). This is often done during the "doing" so that the leader can reflect, learn and apply the lessons learned.

So far, I believe it is clear that the skill of observing what is going on is a very important one for the Lean IT leader. Taiichi Ohno had a novel way to get leaders to observe. He would draw a circle on the factory floor and get the leader to stand in the circle. He would then go off, returning later with the simple question: "What did you see?" If the answer was insufficiently insightful, Ohno would ask the leader to continue observing and he would come back later with the same question. The aim was to get the leader to observe what was happening, apply Lean principles to what he saw and describe what problems he saw. This exercise is somewhat more difficult in IT organizations because much of the work is done based on working on a computer. The steps that you as a Lean IT leader must follow remain the same. Observe. Apply Lean principles. Uncover problems. Challenge the team to solve the problem.

One of the most succinct descriptions of what a Lean leader does when helping others to develop are the six words of Fujio Cho, Chairman of Toyota: "Go See, Ask Why, Show Respect" (Shook, 2011). We go to the gemba to observe what is really happening. We need to ask questions to truly understand what we are seeing. This should all be done in a way that respects the efforts of the people delivering value on a daily basis. We are, after all, trying to encourage Lean IT leaders to exhibit behavior that supports individuals and teams in the delivery of value to customers. If we structure the interaction at the gemba according to the "Go See, Ask Why, Show Respect" adage, we can bring together a number of Lean aspects into the way leaders approach their interaction with the teams in order to help others to develop.

Genchi genbutsu is the Toyota principle of "Go and see" or seeing reality. It means going to the source and truly seeing what is happening there. This is where a huge problem lurks. What is reality? We all see the world through our own mental filters. We all interpret what we see. The aim of genchi genbutsu is to go to the gemba and observe what is happening without judging. That is, objectively noticing what happens without second-guessing the reason why things happen the way they do or deciding whether this is the right or wrong way to do it.

When Lean IT leaders go to the gemba, they do what is called a gemba walk. This is in marked contrast to a gallery walk. The latter is a walk-around on the work floor that is more about the leaders being seen. The leaders give cursory attention to what is going on and are principally there for their own benefit. In comparison, a gemba walk is about increasing understanding. The gemba walk takes time. It is important that the leader encourages teams to use visual management so that the leader can rapidly assimilate the information. This makes the step to understanding the situation much smaller. It is better for the Lean IT leader to do a gemba walk every day to ensure that the team does not need to give long (historical) explanations before tackling the problems at hand.

During the gemba walk, the leader must have time to ask questions and truly absorb the answers. An answer will usually lead to further questions to help the leader to grasp the challenges facing the people on the work floor. A gemba walk will only be successful if the leader is truly interested in understanding what is going on. This sincere desire is part of the leader's own self-development.

The gemba walk is used by the Lean IT Leader as a method to observe behaviors and coach, to challenge people to improve, to communicate strategy and to develop the engagement of people with the goals. There are basically three aims when doing a gemba walk: support, teach and promote. Leaders support the teams by removing roadblocks and providing necessary resources. If there is uncertainty in the teams regarding the strategy, Lean tool usage, controls such as quality, policies or required skills, the leader should take the time to teach. The key is to explain why a certain policy, quality control or KPI is in place. Lastly, the leader can use the gemba walk to promote the True North values, continuous improvement, safety, security, learning organization, teamwork and so on. Remember: The best method of promoting is being the role model, leading by example.

Doing gemba walks has a number of very concrete benefits for the organization. It helps you as a leader to build relationships with the team members. This in turn helps to break down barriers between leaders and the teams for which they are responsible. When you see people doing work, you know that they are actually working and you can also catch them doing something good. Presence at the gemba, thus, provides the opportunity to praise people or otherwise positively reinforce behaviors. It also means you can find out about problems that may exist. Being visible as a leader helps to remind team members of the agreements they made with you, and the discipline to maintain those agreements is increased.

Defining what a gemba walk is can help to increase its effectiveness. A gemba walk is not MBWA, Management By Wandering Around. A leader on a gemba walk has a purpose: to learn something about the IT organization. Otherwise the gemba walk becomes MBWA, Management By Wondering Around. A gemba walk is not an opportunity to point out mistakes or things that should be done differently.

A gemba walk has a before, during and after. In each phase of the gemba walk, the leader must take action.

Before going on the gemba walk, the leader must ask herself whether she is truly interested in what is going on. Assuming the answer is affirmative, the leader must identify the purpose of the gemba walk. Why are you going to the gemba? It is advisable to prepare the gemba walk with a coach. The coach will help to ensure the gemba walk has a valid purpose. Going to the gemba because there is a crisis is a reason to go, but the coach should agree with the leader to set aside time in the schedule to do gemba walks at least once a day. When coaching the preparation of a gemba walk the coach may use a gemba walk checklist. Alternatively, the five questions from the Coaching kata (Rother, 2009) may form the basis for the discussions at the gemba (Figure 17.2).

It is also important for the leader to agree with the coach, whether the leader will receive coaching during the gemba walk or afterwards, in the review of the gemba walk. The last thing to do before embarking

Coaching Kata

1. What is the target condition? (The challenge)

2. What is the actual condition now?

3. What obstacles are now preventing you from reaching the target condition?

4. Which one are you addressing now?

5. When can we go and see what we have learned from taking that step?

FIGURE 17.2

Coaching kata: The 5 questions.

☐ Has the agreed target been met?

☐ If the target was not met, what was the reason? Use 5 Why.

☐ Is there any inventory or overdue items? If so, why?

☐ Was there Rework and/or Defects? If so, why?

☐ Is the process in flow?

☐ Which improvements have been identified?

☐ What needs to be done to ensure improvements are implemented?

FIGURE 17.3

Example of a gemba walk checklist.

on the gemba walk is to leave all assumptions and opinions in the office (Figure 17.3).

But what happens when a senior manager does a gemba walk? The first time this happens the teams are usually flabbergasted. They are simply not used to seeing senior managers in the teams. The funny thing is that usually the senior leaders are as nervous about going to the gemba as the teams are to see the leader. It is vital that the gemba walk is well prepared so that it is neither intrusive nor banal. This is where visual management is very useful. A senior leader showing real interest in the content of a visual management board is a great way to break the ice. A question to a team member like: "I know you are doing a great job in this team, but can you show me how I can see this on your boards?" Remember the words of Deming (2000), the team is always doing a good job. If they are not then there is something wrong with the system. The question tends to lead to a lively explanation of what can be seen on the board. The effect is that the senior leader now knows what to look for on the board and encourages the team to keep the information on the board up-to-date. My experience is that many teams will also explain what problems they face with little prompting. If they appear to be sugar-coating the message, the senior leader can always ask what needs to be done for the team to do an even better job.

A useful technique to have when carrying out a gemba walk is the performance dialog. This is a specific way of discussing performance. Lean IT leaders need to master this technique to be effective. The performance dialog brings together a number of Lean behaviors: goal-setting based on an integral and factual view of the work, providing support, giving feedback, showing respect.

New and ongoing objectives are discussed between leader and team member. What are the mutual expectations and how have these been defined? Unclear expectations are the most common cause for disagreement between leader and team member. In the performance dialog, specifically defined objectives are discussed and agreed. These objectives should be SMART. To ensure valid criteria, the leader should be knowledgeable about the daily operation of the team. That is one of the reasons that a team leader should spend 50% of the time with the team in the workplace.

As a leader, you must facilitate the team members in achieving the objectives by offering support. What does the team need to achieve these objectives? How can the leader facilitate this? In this situation, you play the role of a coach to help the team members express their needs and discuss how they can achieve the objectives.

Leaders must give constructive feedback and suggestions for improvement, principally by asking questions. The leader has observed the team member while working, and gives feedback on how the team member performs or behaves, with the intention of developing the team member. This only works (and ends) well in a climate of trust and respect. Although trust and respect can be difficult to achieve, they are essential for building a high performance organization.

A performance dialog can take the form of a one-to-one discussion, but carrying out a day start or a week start is also a form of performance dialog. The ability to effectively hold performance dialogs is a key skill of *anyone* working in a Lean environment, but especially of leaders.

One question I am regularly asked is: When should I do a gemba walk? The answer is daily. But it depends on what you are trying to understand. Attending a week start or a day start is a useful gemba walk. Often the morning is effective because people are working and helping to solve issues that can make the rest of the day more productive. Mostly, it is best to pick different times so that people do not know when to expect you. Your presence at the gemba should not lead to disruptions; it should become a natural and regular occurrence.

Once you have left the office and are on your gemba walk, what should you be doing? Your aim is to understand the behavior at the gemba and how it relates to the specific situation. This means you will need to interact with the team, not just talking to a team leader or a senior technician. By interacting with all (or many) of the team members, you are showing them respect. Make sure you check whether you are disrupting their work. If so, come back later. Knowing that you need to teach, support and promote, you can seek out opportunities to reinforce the Lean (or Agile or DevOps) message.

If you are coaching someone doing a gemba walk, it is important to observe how they act as they interact with the team, and only intervene with coaching if that has been agreed upfront. With respect to the amount of time you spend, the gemba walk can last as long as is necessary for you to understand the situation. Generally, it is up to an hour, usually between 15 and 30 minutes. If you need to spend much more time, then it is possible that your goals were too ambitious. Remember, the aim is to do gemba walks every day.

When going to the gemba, you may use a checklist. However, you can also choose to use a view of the world. There are five views each of which can help to look at what is happening in a different way. Deciding on which view to use is part of the preparation, and helps to focus the mind. The tendency is for leaders to be on the lookout for waste, but there are other views. The idea is to switch between the different views over a number of gemba walks. Let us look at the views.

The Potential view is the people-focused gemba walk. In this gemba walk, the leader is challenged to look for the true potential in others. By objectively observing people at work, the leader can identify skills, knowledge and capabilities within people that have not yet been (fully) recognized. By taking this view on your gemba walk, you may see leadership potential in the interaction between two engineers, presentation capabilities that can help to translate strategy to the work floor or a desire to further develop technical skills that have not been tapped.

This waste view is the most used view on gemba walks. Leaders look for waste. The gemba walk is principally about encouraging team members to remove the waste. This means that "you should do something about that" must be replaced by "let's look at what we can do now to improve the situation." The leader should, together with the people, investigate the waste, measure it on the spot and help to decide how to eliminate it. This way of working demonstrates the leader's commitment to removing obstacles to the delivery of value. Leaders must be particularly vigilant of muri (overburden) and mura (variability). These are forms of quality loss that directly result from choices made by leaders in the IT organization. These are forms of waste over which a leader has control themselves. For example, long lead times to implement changes may be caused by the policy to have a Change Advisory Board (CAB) meeting once a week, for which changes must be submitted three working days in advance in order to be considered. In effect, this can cause waiting times of between three and eight days. This waste is based on two policy statements: a weekly CAB and a three-day minimum submission period. The challenge is how to reduce or even remove these delays.

The kaizen view is about looking for patterns, forms, habits and routines; in short, being attuned to the kata and how it varies from defined standard work or the lack thereof. The leader must observe work being done and help identify where work can be standardized to improve the quality of the outcome of the process. This will generally mean looking at the value stream map (VSM) together with the team members. From the VSM, both daily kaizen and improvement kaizen can be identified. The leader must encourage the team to pick up daily kaizen activities and implement small improvements to the process. Within IT, one of the areas that need constant attention is describing standard changes or updating descriptions of standard changes (define and improve the kata). In paying attention to this form of standardization, the leader can get engineers to further improve the ability to rapidly deliver value to customers.

The benefit is also that work done by experienced engineers can now be carried out by less experienced engineers without loss of quality.

The leader who goes to the gemba with the problem view tends to be looking for the reason something went wrong. As we would expect from someone with a kaizen mindset, the focus should be on problem-solving, not on "finding the culprit," even when the latter has become a habit in this view. The problem view should start with confirming the goals and objectives of the work being done. The leader's key question is "What are you trying to achieve?" Assuming that people at the gemba can answer this question, the leader can then ask "What is getting in the way of achieving this goal?" If the people are unable to state the goal, then this becomes an opportunity to teach and promote. A useful set of topics to use within the Problem view is the branches of an IT Ishikawa diagram: Policy, People, Process and Technology.

Questions you may ask as part of this view include:

Policy: Which policies prevent the team from achieving the goals? Which policies cause additional work?

People: Are there morale issues? Are there problems with availability of skills or knowledge? Are there sufficient or too many resources?

Process: Is the process too complicated? Are there too many different roles involved? Are there too many handovers? Does the process discriminate sufficiently between various types of units of work? Where can the process be further standardized and simplified?

Technology: Does the team have the tools to do their work to the best of their ability? Are there possibilities to further standardize work through automation? Are the available tools used to maximum effect?

The last view, the Solution view, is not very Lean at all. It is, however, one of the views most used by IT leaders and this explanation serves more as a warning than a recommendation. The Solution view is the view where IT leaders go to the gemba to recommend solutions to problems they see. Everybody within a Lean IT organization is allowed to suggest improvements or solutions to problems, and this also applies to Lean IT leaders. The main issue is that leaders do not spend sufficient time on the gemba to actually know what the best solution is. The danger is that they jump to conclusions and strongly suggest a particular solution, when the people know that this is probably not the right solution. It is important for the Lean IT leader to help the team to come to their own solution. Where the Lean IT leader can provide a solution is in recommending and explaining the application of Lean tools. The aim of applying Lean tools is to help people gain deeper insights into where there is waste (muda), variability (mura) or overburden (muri). In this respect, the Lean IT leader takes the opportunity to teach and support, rather than tell.

Having observed activities at the gemba, a Lean IT leader must seek to understand why things are done the way they are. This questioning is not necessarily only for the benefit of the leader. In searching for the underlying details of a particular situation, the Lean IT leader helps the engineers to better understand the situation, to challenge the current way of doing things, to look for root causes to problems and to find ways around impediments. One of the best ways to do this during a gemba walk is to use the Five Whys technique.

The Five Whys analysis is a simple root cause analysis that aims to question a situation through sequential causes. "Why" is asked to find each preceding trigger until we arrive at the root cause of a problem. When using Five Whys during a gemba walk, it is useful to ask the question "Where?" three times before starting the five whys. The where questions allow the team and the leader to pinpoint the specific location of the problem so that they can go and observe what is actually going on. It is vital *not* to ask "Who?" This implies that a person is to blame. The Lean IT leader must always assume that the error or lack of quality is the result of an error in the organizational system (policy, process and technology). Even if it turns out that someone has not followed an agreed procedure, the Lean IT leader must understand what issue in the "system" allowed this to happen; which oversight caused a person to not use the agreed procedure? Each answer to a "why" must be supported by evidence that proves the answer is right. Failure to do this may send the team on a wrong failure path (Table 17.1).

An aspect to keep in mind when asking why is one of communication. "Why" is a word that, depending on intonation, can have an inspiring and investigative character or a threatening character. Leaders should, of course, try to be inspiring and investigative.

As one of the core values of Lean, showing respect is something that Lean IT leaders need to make concrete and tangible. What can you do to show respect? Respect is a way of treating others and thinking about others that shows that you regard them highly. We show respect by being kind and polite to people, by showing empathy and by abstaining from

TABLE 17.1

Five Steps to Perform a Five Times Why Analysis

Step	Activity
Step 1	Determine the exact location of the problem by asking "Where?" three times to identify the location of the problem.
Step 2	Make a table with two columns and five rows and write the question from the problem statement at the top of the table
Step 3	Ask the question: "Why did this happen?" Find the answer, supported by evidence, and write the answer in the left-hand column of the top row.
Step 4	Repeat this question and answer cycle, four more times. List the answers in the left-hand column of the table.
Step 5	Determine a solution for each of the answers and record these in the right-hand column.

discriminating in any way. Other ways to show respect include showing gratitude for what others do, respecting their abilities and complimenting their achievements. It is important to be sincere, to genuinely believe what you are saying. As a leader with many demands on your time, it is also respectful to others to say what you will do, to do what you say you will do, and also to offer help.

When you go to the gemba, you will undoubtedly hear others' opinions. Listen to what is being said, ask questions and try to understand the other's perspectives. You should also investigate why the other person holds to their opinion. If you disagree, then you should voice your reasons for doing so. Respect also means avoiding unnecessary arguments and apologizing if you were wrong. However, you should not shy away from a discussion of ideas. The key to respecting people is to refrain from judging them; give people the benefit of the doubt. There are very few people who come to their work with the express intention of doing things wrong or delivering poor quality. Work from the premise that intentions are good. Lastly, a leader has a position of power that can easily be abused; this should be avoided at all cost.

Having completed the gemba walk, you will need to review what you have seen and learned. When you get back to your office take your notes and follow-up on them. Write down any additional items you want to remember or that need to be done. Take care of any problems you found right away. If someone had a problem and you are the person who needs to solve it, let them know when it has been taken care of. As a coach, you will provide your observations on the gemba walk and help the leader to decide on actions or improvements.

The "homework" related to this session is obvious: Go and do one or, preferably, more gemba walks.

The following session is one of my favorite experience sessions. This is the moment that leaders have carried out their first gemba walks and share their findings with one another. The experiences range, not surprisingly, from very positive to quite negative. The experiences are generally a function of the existing relationship between leader and team, the preparation of the gemba walk and, of course, its execution.

One leader did a gemba walk at a location that he had not been to for a long time. The reaction of the team was so positive to his presence that he was able to focus on carrying out the gemba walk as he had planned. The team members were open about their successes, challenges, problems and failures. He was able to identify a number of improvements that he personally had to organize (removing muri). The leader had embarked on his gemba walk with a healthy dose of trepidation, and had been pleasantly surprised by the response. This gave him the energy boost to keep doing gemba walks. Later experiences were not always so positive, but that first experience demonstrated the value of doing the gemba walk.

Unfortunately, not everyone has the same experience on their first gemba walk. In fact, the general response from the teams is cool to lukewarm, at best.

At the other end of the spectrum, one leader walked into the team room and the first comment he heard was "What's he doing here?" An auspicious start ... not. The gemba walk went downhill from there. He recounted how the team leader had shadowed his every move, making sure that the story he was presented with was positive, and if it was negative the bad bit was due to other teams not doing their work properly. Admittedly, he made the mistake of stepping into the team leader's shoes and telling a team member what he should be doing. It took a concerted effort, and some coaching, over the following weeks to redress the situation.

Generally, teams are quite pleased to get attention from higher levels of leadership. The initial effect is to disrupt the team's work. This has two components. The first part is the disruption of the leader actually being there. During the first gemba walks, this is almost unavoidable because it is such a novelty to see these leaders at the gemba. The second part of the disruption comes when the leader has left. Team members stop working to discuss what just happened. Both effects reduce dramatically as the leader does regular and frequent gemba walks. On a side note, the negative effect of a gallery walk is much greater. Teams spend a lot of time prior to the announced (because gallery walks are always announced for maximum publicity purposes) attendance cleaning up the team environment for maximum impression. The presence of the leader and entourage is so stressful that team members are drained by the time the gallery walk is completed, leaving them incapable of picking up work effectively for the rest of the day.

The effect of gemba walks on the leaders is, despite a poor start, almost unanimously positive. Being close to the real work has a hugely positive effect on leaders. Most IT leaders have risen through the ranks of IT organizations and are reminded of their operational work when they go to the gemba. They see how much has changed in a short time and what cool things are being done in the teams. There are also things that may not have changed very much and these are areas in which the leader can encourage improvement, offering help in how potential obstacles can be removed.

18

Control

One of the greatest leadership fears when moving to Lean production is the fear of losing control. Leaders are used to a particular style of control, based on reading reports, having steering committee meetings in which project updates are given, telling people what to do and other such behaviors. These behaviors give the illusion of control, but mostly they occur too long after the associated behavior has taken place. The organization has moved on. I strongly believe that Lean structures, particularly visual management, provide a much higher degree of control in a much less threatening way. However, until leaders have learned to rely on the information on visual management, they find it very challenging to let go of the traditional "control" structures.

An important success factor of gemba walks is the presence of visual management to support the leader in asking the right questions. As we saw, when IT organizations start out, one of the approaches is to introduce visual management with the associated meetings in the teams. At this phase of the Lean IT transformation, it is distinctly possible that a leader goes to a team that does not have visual management in place. In these case, the leader will find doing a gemba walk challenging as they will need to gain *all* information through talking to people, which is a highly disruptive process. So far, we have talked about using visual management in the teams but, as we said earlier, the management team is also a team. This team needs to be supported by visual management as well. The most effective use of visual management for a management team is in a so-called obeya (Japanese for "big room" or war-room). The obeya must contain all information necessary for the IT management team to know what is going on in the IT organization. Before we discuss the obeya in more detail, we must take a step back. The step back is about the creation and communication of the vision and goals of the IT organization.

The IT organization exists in a context, and broadly speaking this context provides the fundamentals for the vision of the IT organization. There are basically two types of IT organizations: The IT organization operating within an enterprise, providing a wide range of IT services to that enterprise and the IT organization as its own enterprise providing specific services to a variety of customers. In relation to the activity of creating a vision, we shall refer to the former as an internal IT organization and the latter as an external IT organization.

For an internal IT organization, the vision will necessarily be intricately related to the vision of the entire enterprise. Somewhere in the vision statement will be the sentence "our vision is to provide excellent IT services to [insert name of your own company]" or something similar. Many of the subsequent choices and goals will be dictated by the vision and strategy of the enterprise. The one area where the IT organization should be free to make choices is in the technology used to provide the IT services and the way in which it will serve its customers (the True North Values).

For an external IT organization, the vision contains more degrees of freedom. The external IT organization can define its preferred customer segment, the services it wishes to provide and the way in which it aims to deliver the services. In the market, we can identify IT organizations that provide software, with or without direct support (i.e. some deliver support through partners or through the internal IT organizations), those providing hardware, again with or without direct supporting services, those that act as integrators of services provided by hardware and software providers and IT organizations that provide services and support to help make better use of software and hardware. Each of these types of IT organizations will develop a different type of vision.

Interestingly, Lean always stresses the focus on long-term goals. Long term means 5 to 10 years, sometimes longer. Here, we meet a perceived difficulty within IT. The sector and its capabilities have changed (evolved and revolved) so quickly over the past 25 years that predicting where an IT organization will be in ten years is almost impossible. Especially for the commercial IT organizations, a revolution in IT may signal their demise or an almost inconceivable growth. For the internal IT organizations, the vision is somewhat more predictable, given that the enterprise itself continues to thrive. The key is not to focus on the technological aspects of the IT organization, rather base the vision on our own True North values and principles. We can turn this into a vision of how the IT organization aims to operate in ten years' time. From this overall vision, we derive a medium to long-term plan, which, for an IT organization, will cover at most the next three years. The aim is to create a consistent and aligned set of goals that will help the IT organization to move towards its longer-term vision. These goals must be brought into a timeframe that is more manageable for employees and leaders, at a day-by-day level. The mechanism used within Lean to translate longer-term goals to the more immediate future is called Hoshin Kanri. Literally, Hoshin means "pointing device" or "direction" and Kanri means "management." Hoshin Kanri tends to be translated as policy deployment.

Hoshin Kanri is a cyclic planning and management concept applied at the strategic level to achieve breakthrough objectives, and at the day-to-day level to manage the operation to keep the business running. It supports the activity of creating a vision and aligning goals across the organization. Hoshin Kanri sets high-level objectives which are translated into specific actions through daily management. It has a long-term focus, with a strong link to guiding principles and/or True North Values and is concerned with results. The accompanying process focuses on achieving the results through people development. It has both top-down and bottom-up components. The top-down aspect is all about setting the overall direction. The bottom-up aspect is a flow of information so that decisions can be made at the right level concerning the achievement of the result. It is primarily oriented towards ensuring and using the correct responsibilities and accountabilities set throughout the organization. Hoshin Kanri is a participative process, in which all levels of the organization are involved through consultation and decision-making, a concept known as nemawashi.

Kaoru Ishikawa described the working of Hoshin Kanri as follows:

> Top managers and middle managers must be bold enough to delegate as much authority as possible. That is the way to establish respect for humanity as your management philosophy. It is a management system in which all employees participate, from the top down and from the bottom up, and humanity is fully respected.

(Ishikawa, 1985)

Policy deployment starts with top management setting the overall vision and the annual high-level policies and targets for the IT organization. These targets must include objectives that will take the IT organization closer to its long-term (True North) vision. At each level moving through the hierarchy, managers and employees participate in the definition of the strategy and a detailed action plan, which they will use to attain their targets. They also define the measures that will be used to demonstrate that they have successfully achieved their targets. Then, targets are passed on to the next level down. Each level under top management is, in turn, involved with the level above it to make sure that its proposed strategy corresponds to requirements. Regular reviews take place to identify progress and problems, and to initiate corrective action.

Hoshin Kanri used in IT is a method for translating IT strategy to IT operations and ensuring alignment across the various aspects of IT development and operations. It works in two ways. Hoshin Kanri aligns both *vertically* and *horizontally (or cross-functionally)*. Vertical alignment ensures that all stakeholders, from the boardroom to operations, are aligned. Through the layers of management interaction, goal setting and review, goals are set and adjusted so that they continue to fit. The vertical alignment enables anyone to trace activities and objectives back to the strategic goals of the IT organization and the enterprise (in the case of an internal IT organization). This means that individuals and teams can quite easily see how they contribute to the achievement of the goals. Cross-functional (horizontal) alignment ensures that cross-functional stakeholders of each value stream have aligned goals that lead to the delivery of value to customers. Supporting processes, projects and kaizen initiatives are all included in the horizontal alignment. The key is to share common objectives, make appropriate prioritization and resource allocation decisions that add value to the customer. Both types of alignment are absolutely vital within IT organizations. Cross-functional alignment is especially important in traditionally organized IT organizations in which the cooperation of various functional departments is necessary to deliver an IT service to the customer.

In traditionally organized IT organizations, the alignment of goals is an arduous affair. The problem is that a goal is split over the technical silos. The individual components of the goal must be carried out at exactly the right time and sequence to avoid delays. This has given rise to the huge importance given to portfolio and program management. As IT organizations have become organized in a more customer-centric manner (DevOps), the alignment of goals takes on a different, much less laborious character. Most developments are discussed directly between the customer and the team carrying out the goal. Alignment between teams is now only necessary where there are dependencies, and these are strongly reduced as compared to traditional IT organizations.

One way that leaders show respect within a Lean organization is through the process of participative decision-making, or nemawashi. This is the informal process of laying the foundation for a decision, change or project. Nemawashi is not a democratic or consensus-building process, since not everyone needs to agree. However, seeking the opinions of others is a mark of respect even if the person does not agree. The important thing is that people are informed and aware of what is coming. Nemawashi is about consulting, discussing and adjusting proposals, and it also means taking action.

The communication of goals through the hierarchy is done using a technique called catch-ball communication. Catch-ball is a method of idea generation and sharing. The key principle behind the method is *respect* for the ideas and abilities of others. Catch-ball is used any time when a higher-level planning team needs to ask others to implement their plans. It works like this. The "need" (a proposed vision or direction) is expressed by the leader, and the subordinate responds with an interpretation of what that direction will mean within the subordinate's realm of responsibility. The leader then reviews the response with humility, open to proposals or ideas previously not considered by the leader. As the ball (idea) is passed back and forth, new ideas emerge, as does a decision on the right course of action. This process exemplifies the principle-based thinking that is a hallmark of excellence and is a practical example of nemawashi. Catch-ball communication is essential for the success of Lean as a systematized, teachable, repeatable way to confirm the practicality of proposed plans (and their probability of success) and actively solicit (and act upon) feedback and ideas from the "lower" level people that are responsible for actually implementing the plans. Catch-ball communication greatly improves widespread understanding of what needs to be done, why and how. It also emphasizes ownership and buy-in from the people responsible for results. And leaders at all levels are dissuaded from demonstrating dictatorial leadership traits.

So far it may seem as though Lean IT leaders must focus on what are commonly known as "soft skills," the development of people. Leaders within a Lean IT environment must know where they stand in relation to their goals. This must be based on facts derived from the reality of the situation. These facts are referred to as performance indicators. They give a representation of the current state of the performance of the IT organization in relation to its goals and vision. The challenge for the Lean IT Leader is ensuring that KPIs are clearly linked to the strategic goals and that metrics used within the IT organization lead to consistent behavior towards achieving the goals. What does this mean in practice? Lean IT leaders create a vision of where their organization needs to be. This vision tends to be described in a qualitative way. It is vital for the leadership team to explain what the organization looks like when the vision is put into practice. These are the areas in which performance is required. The concrete descriptions of the performance areas that constitute the vision provide the input for the definition of the KPIs. They also provide input for the change story of the IT management team.

The teams within IT must define their own contribution to the achievement of the organization's KPIs. This can take one of two forms. Either the team uses the KPI to measure their specific team performance or the team chooses a metric that provides a positive impulse to the achievement of the KPI.

An example may be that the IT management team wishes to measure the reduction of the impact of incidents on customers, for example by measuring and managing the reduction of lost production time in the business. A team may wish to measure—and reduce—the number of incidents that the team needs to process. Alternatively, a team may choose to measure—and increase—the number of problems solved to remove the sources of incidents. Both metrics help to achieve the strategic goal of reducing the amount of production time lost in the business. This is one of the most powerful ways that leaders can align the goals within the organization (Figure 18.1).

The main question to be answered at this point is: How does the leadership know whether they are getting closer to their goals or not? We have seen a number of components so far: the vision, the goals, the KPIs. And we have a principle: jidoka. Jidoka is the principle concerned with ensuring that leaders create an environment in which problems cannot remain unseen. Jidoka also means giving the *accountability to the work floor* to stop errors from going forwards in the process. Applying jidoka makes doing a gemba walk substantially more effective. As we saw earlier, work and issues are clearly visible on the basic set of visual management boards: the day board, week board and improvement board. The Go-See principle is one of the most powerful reminders of the need for jidoka and the associated visual management. On top of these boards, the key processes should be visible in the form of Value Stream Maps posted on the walls. Jidoka goes beyond "just" ensuring that problems are uncovered. It also gives employees the authority to *stop the production line* as soon

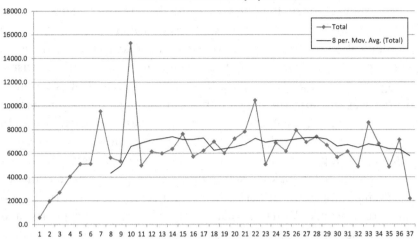

FIGURE 18.1
Lost production days.

as a problem is identified. A key question for the Lean IT leader to ask a team during the gemba walk is: "What is your andon cord?" Which translates to: How do you ensure that errors do not get passed forward in the process? How have you constructed your processes so that we do not need additional controls, but still ensure quality at the source? These are difficult questions to answer within an IT context, specifically as a result of the intangibility of IT work and the regular need for multiple teams to be involved in solving an incident or carrying out a change. Examples of solutions include the standardization of changes, programming in pairs, solving technical problems in teams, (automated) testing and creating automated checks of changes.

Open, transparent communication lies at the heart of the Lean way of working. There are many sides to communication. In Lean IT leadership, there are five tools and techniques that enhance the quality and openness of communication throughout an IT organization: performance dialog, cascade, change story, a structure for building communication and visual management. Lean IT leaders must be proficient in each of these methods. We have already looked at the change story and the performance dialog. We will look at the structure for building communication in Part V. We now need to look at the way leadership makes use of visual management in the communication of the vision and the alignment of goals.

Visual management is the tool that embodies the need to make the current state clear so that problems can be identified. Furthermore, humans are highly visually-oriented beings. Much of our (inter-personal) communication is based on what we see. Visual management is therefore vital for ensuring, enhancing and facilitating communication. Thus, visual management is an *absolute necessity* for Lean IT leaders. It is the most effective way to know where the IT organization stands at any moment in time. Visual management ensures that a gemba walk can be carried out in a short time but is still highly effective. Use the visual management tryptic, as described in part II, in the teams. *All of these* are necessary to deliver the information for making key daily decisions regarding continuous improvement, operational performance and balancing workload within and across teams. Visual management infrastructure supports and aligns teams in their effort of creating value for customers and enables continuous improvement.

We have discussed the role of visual management in the teams and indicated that the visual management of management teams is found in an obeya. What are the typical topics to be found in an obeya?

- Overall strategy of the organization accompanied by the vision and strategy of the IT organization. Through the process of Hoshin Kanri, the vision and goals have been created. These need to be visible as support for the constancy of purpose principle. The overall strategy of the organization helps to ensure that choices can be related back to the goals of the customer.
- Project portfolio. In IT organizations, we still tend to work with projects although their importance is reducing with the growing influence of DevOps and Agile ways of working. Most IT management teams need to have an up-to-date view of which projects are running and which are in the pipeline.
- Goals for the next four quarters, the next month, the next week. One of the most important parts of the obeya is the goals section. Goals are broken down on the boards. They start as high-level goals posted in the quarters when they are expected to be achieved. These goals are broken down into goals for the current month, and then into goals for the week, for the management team members.
- Performance numbers. The management team must have a comprehensive view of how the IT organization is performing. We

can expect to find a graph demonstrating the trend of each of the KPIs chosen earlier in the Lean IT transformation.
- Problems and improvements. The management team must have its own Improvement board on which both problems and potential improvements can be posted.
- Customer satisfaction. The leadership must have a view of what the customer thinks of the products and services delivered by the IT organization.
- Employee satisfaction. Maybe most importantly, the IT leadership must have a clear and up-to-date view of how the team members feel about working in the IT organization (Figure 18.2).

The information in the obeya must be at the level that is relevant to the management team. When IT management teams start with visual management, they have a tendency to want to know everything to the greatest detail. The result is an overfilled obeya, including information that can also be found on the team boards. As time goes by, leaders learn that this information is not directly relevant to them and that if needed it is available on the team boards. Step by step, the obeya becomes more focused on the information and problems that need to be tackled by the leadership (Figure 18.3).

The obeya, the visual management in the teams and any intermediate levels of visual management (obeyas for lower-level management teams in large organizations) are all part of a larger construct within the IT organization. This is the cascade. Visual management ensures information is available at the place it needs to be. The cascade ensures that information flows through the IT organization to the place where it is needed. The cascade is where Leader Standard Work, the aligned meeting structure,

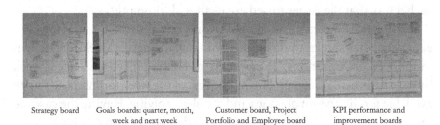

Strategy board   Goals boards: quarter, month, week and next week   Customer board, Project Portfolio and Employee board   KPI performance and improvement boards

FIGURE 18.2
Initial versions of obeya boards for an IT management team.

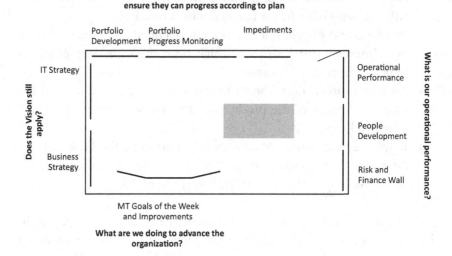

FIGURE 18.3

Example of layout of an obeya.

visual management and gemba walks come together to create an effective and quick method for moving information through the hierarchy to where it needs to be. The key to getting the cascade to work is to align the agendas of the various levels of management. It is important to ensure that the upward and downward flow of information is optimized.

This means, for example, setting the time when all teams have their day starts. Most teams will have their day start between 08:00 and 10:00 in the morning. The team leaders will come together with their manager at 11:00, and the management team may meet early in the afternoon. In this way, issues from the work floor are transferred through the hierarchy of meetings as quickly as possible. This means that information is communicated to the right level quickly. The meetings must be run in such a way that the issues raised are dealt with promptly.

Ideally, this mechanism should work on a daily basis. However, experience has shown that running this cascade once a week is sufficient in most IT organizations. The benefits of holding meetings once a week include time being freed up during the rest of the week for managers to be available for discussion of issues and problem-solving. Having the cascade in place reduces the time spent on chasing decisions dramatically, because the flow of information is clear; everyone knows when they can expect an answer. Issues and requests for help no longer get passed into (or stuck in) a black box. They are passed up the cascade and there is a clear expectation that the leaders will do the work for which they are employed: to facilitate the work floor, particularly by removing mura and muri.

The greatest challenge to getting the cascade to work is actually emptying agendas and re-planning the meeting structure. However, most agendas are relatively empty a number of weeks in the future. By ensuring that the meeting structure is changed in the electronic agendas a number of weeks in advance, people will have room for particular meetings taking place at different times (Figure 18.4).

When the cascade in an organization works effectively, there is notably less stress and fewer problems are escalated up the chain of command, largely because leaders go to the gemba (team visual management) to collect detailed information that they need for their discussions at the obeya.

The assignment is, as it is for all of the later experience sessions, go to the gemba! Each leader must choose their own focus, however, they are usually assigned to observe what visual management is present and how it is used, and whether there is evidence of a cascade. One extra piece of homework is to determine what information needs to be seen in the obeya.

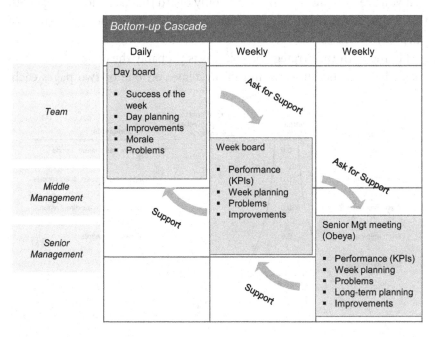

FIGURE 18.4
Example of cascade.

As the cascade is designed and built, it is quite normal to find anomalies in the way the organization is set up. To gain insight into the communication requirements of each leader, we may carry out a span of control analysis. This analysis helps to provide understanding of the effectiveness of the management structure of IT and delivers insight into the current structure of the IT organization. In many IT organizations, costs have been cut by creating excessive spans of control, particularly at team manager level. At higher levels, the span of control tends to be too low. This tool helps to identify where management is over- or underextended and helps to provide understanding of where managers may truly be extremely busy and where leaders can be helped using Leader Standard Work to regain control of their calendars (Figure 18.5).

The experience session associated with this deep dive is about building the obeya. We saw that the obeya is made up of a diversity of boards together providing all of the information a management team needs to understand where things are going well and where they need to be improved (think systemically). When deciding what information needs to be on the boards, it is important to take into account that you need to update this information on a daily or, at worst, a weekly basis to ensure that you are looking at "reality." The only board that does not change with this frequency is obviously the Strategy Board (remember: constancy of purpose).

Starting with the Strategy board, this is probably the easiest to fill. You basically need the business and IT strategies on one or two pages each.

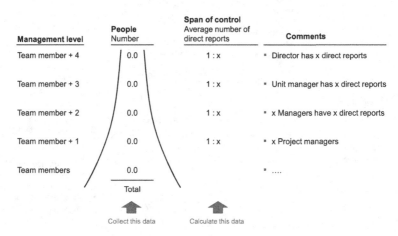

FIGURE 18.5
Span of control analysis.

They need to be high level and readable at a distance, i.e. no huge swathes of text. We are looking for graphics and short lists that act as a trigger for constancy of purpose. Often, in the first pass, the team will try to be too complete leading to an overload of information.

The Goals boards are the first boards that need to be activated. These are the boards that drive the activity of the management team. The Quarters board should contain sticky notes with the high-level deliverables that need to be created per quarter. They will include key *management* deliverables. These may include the initiation of a variety of technological projects. It does not include the intermediate or end products of a project since these should be on the visual management run by the project manager of that particular project. A summary of progress of the project can be found on the Project portfolio board. Management deliverables include the budget, bi-annual people reviews, annual customer satisfaction surveys, specified organizational improvements and so on. The Month Goal board is derived from the Quarters board, i.e. what are the most important deliverables from our quarterly plan that we are going to complete this month. The Week and Next Week Goals boards work in two ways. They reflect the need for short-term deliverables that may not be derived from the longer-term plan and, of course there will be the goals as abstracted from the Month board. One of the behaviors that is not self-evident is managing the flow of work from an annual plan to a weekly set of deliverables. Experience has shown that managers have the same difficulty of turning their activities into deliverables, as is evidenced in the teams.

The Project Portfolio board is a strange part of the obeya. Traditional logic would dictate that this is a board on which the management team spends a large amount of time. The project portfolio is always a major topic, especially its complexity, the interrelatedness of projects, the pressure of customers. The reality is that it usually warrants a cursory glance and then only to check whether projects are on track. This is the effect of having a clear overview of the status of projects available visually. With a single look, leaders are reminded of the status. Even when one or more projects are disastrously off-track, the time spent on discussing projects is relatively low, since usually the main discussion has already taken place at the board where the project's details are discussed. There is no need to regurgitate a discussion that has already taken place, aside from discussing the problems that need to be solved to get the project, as much as possible, back on track.

Gathering and presenting up-to-date information regarding the customer is more challenging than it sounds. Some IT organizations have automated satisfaction surveys as a result of calls to the service desk. These surveys can provide weekly input for the obeya. However, this survey information tends to be most relevant on the visual management of the service desk. In order to sharpen the senses of the leaders, my favorite way to fill the Customer board at the obeya is by ensuring that the leaders talk to customers and bring back actual quotes. There is nothing that brings home the need for action than real customers saying real things about your services. Leaders (generally) talk to leaders and the information they bring back to the obeya tends to indicate the general mood of the customer organization towards the IT organization. The need to fill this part of the obeya with relevant information makes IT leaders realize how often (or not) they actually talk to their customers. The ongoing assignment in these discussions is "listen carefully to what the customer says" (respect every individual). Then bring back one or two choice quotes, write them on a sticky note and put them on the board. Discuss each new quote at the obeya meeting.

On the Employee board is where leaders react with the most incredility. The aim is to post new information on employee satisfaction *every week*. Most management teams tell me that this is not possible. The question is: Do you think it is important to understand how the teams or team members are doing on an ongoing basis? The answer is mostly yes, as leaders realize that answering no is just not an option. So, we now have a problem (getting frequent feedback from employees). Solve it. The most heard argument is that people get tired of surveys. This is true … if you do nothing with the results or appear to do nothing with results. The trick is to take the results of a survey seriously, give feedback quickly and act on the insights gained. We will look at one mechanism for collecting this information in Part IV. Most IT organizations do an employee satisfaction survey once a year. It takes so long to get the results together that they are a historical artifact and close to useless by the time they are posted. Another interesting phenomenon regarding the annual employee satisfaction survey is that the management team needs to discuss the results before they are distributed, as if this would change the results in any way. The argument for this delay is that the management team needs to study the results to determine their response. Lead with humility: Share the results as quickly as possible and discuss them openly.

The KPI performance board shows operational performance. Most IT organizations will initially post a trend graph of numbers of calls and changes opened and closed per week, maybe split by department or team. Also, there will be a graph of whether SLA targets were met for calls. Then it turns out that these are not the KPIs that will help to determine whether the management team is achieving its strategy, they were just easy metrics to post and ones that the organization has been using for a long time. The leaders need to go back to the KPIs they defined (see Part II). In the KPI cards, the calculation and data collection methods have been defined. They may need to be revisited but, mostly, the KPIs are more relevant than the data that gets posted initially. The problem is that it turns out to be some work to get the KPIs measured, recorded, programmed into a reporting tool and presented in a way that provides the data with meaning. So, solve the problem. Usually, there is help at hand in terms of data analysts and business intelligence experts to ensure that the KPIs can be delivered on a weekly (often on a real-time) basis. But then comes the real issue, the leaders do not know how to interpret the information they are presented with. Again, the resolve of the leaders is tested: Either they complain about the graph or they take the time to truly understand what the graph is trying to tell them. This takes time and is the reason why leaders must have half an hour set aside every morning in their Leader Standard Work to look at the data and understand what it is telling them. Learn.

The subject of learning brings us to the last part of the obeya: the Improvement board. This is the place where problems and improvements that need to be actioned at the management team level should be posted. Here lies another huge learning opportunity for the leaders. Experience has shown that leaders find it very difficult to state their problems. They are excellent at pointing out somebody else's problem, mainly where the teams need to improve, but identifying and posting their own problems is a learning process. To kick-off the improvement board, the coach can challenge the leaders to identify problems. This is duly done. And then something surprising happens. Despite reminders, nothing is done about the problems. Nobody has "stomach ache" from these problems. Mostly, the leaders just work around them (hugely non-Lean behavior). In short: These are not the right problems. It can take many sessions at the obeya before managers start to de-immunize themselves from the problems around them and develop a fire inside themselves to actually tackle the organization's systemic problems. One classic problem that is present in every traditionally organized IT organization is the unsatisfactory communication between development and operations teams. This is a management problem. So, solve it. However, this is a problem that is so engrained in the fabric of IT organizations that many leaders do not register that it is a problem. And there are many more like it. My people are too busy to pick up new requests. It's a problem. Solve it. People leave incidents open for too long without working on them. It's a problem. Solve it. Communication with customers is terrible. It's a problem. Solve it. The lack of problems at the obeya improvement board drives leaders to the other end of the spectrum. They open their improvement board up to the whole IT organization. This leads to a host of problems at the obeya that need to be solved in the teams, not at the management team level. This is the non-Lean behavior of getting leaders to solve the problems and it is vital that this practice is stopped very quickly. The rule is that problems from the team must go through the cascade, i.e. a member of the management team must bring the problem to the obeya. This ensures that the problem is in fact one that needs to be solved by the leaders.

The first versions of the obeya boards are purposely unprofessional because they beg to be improved. Also, the management team needs to improve. There is considerable trepidation to adjust the boards. Managers are not used to "getting their hands dirty; they need to get stuck into solving the organization's problems. They do not seem to realize that it is *their* visual management and, if it needs to be different, they should take the step to change it. As a coach, I set up a "best practice" version that is there to be changed, altered, adjusted, improved. Management teams are remarkably hesitant to take matters into their own hands. Another humorous aspect of obeyas is that leaders must create their own sticky notes. The general behavior is that they expect someone else to write down their points. One of the main behavioral changes is that leaders start coming to the obeya with their own set of sticky notes, ready to write actions, problems or other points. It has been known for some management teams to take months to reach this point.

Despite the extensive attention to the obeya, leaders also need to spend time on sharing their experiences at the gemba. This is about the time that leaders start to skimp on their assignments from leadership deep dives. Only half will have done the gemba walk as agreed. Sharing experiences is important, but not as important as ensuring that all of the leaders actually have an experience to share. If only half have done the work, we are back at the discussion we saw earlier about coming to meetings on time. Fundamentally, it is about the commitment to Self-Development, the *first* step in the Lean Leadership Development Model. The attention to the gemba walk (helping others to develop) and the obeya (create vision and align goals, continuous improvement) brings us around and back to the starting point, the commitment to take Lean leadership one step further. This means re-confirming the commitment.

This section is about leaders having control through the mechanism of visual management. One of the best ways to gain control is, paradoxically, to speed up. Most leaders were brought up in the "monthly-quarterly" cycle of reporting. If you as a leader truly wish to gain control, then decreasing the length of time between reporting moments is an absolute prerequisite. Here we encounter two problems. First, managers complain that they cannot get information reported more frequently. It's a problem; solve it. In the end, most operational data can be reported on a real-time basis. The challenge is to gain insights into customer and employee satisfaction on a regular basis. These are performance indicators that are often more difficult to refresh on a weekly basis because they involve surveying the two populations, and people get tired of filling out surveys. A possible solution is to find a surrogate measure that we know is correlated to customer or employee satisfaction. The second problem has to do with managers who do not see the value in receiving information more frequently. This is like saying that the fuel gauge is not important in a car because it barely moves as you drive. Finding the value in frequent reporting is one of the lessons that managers need to learn. The lesson is that you never know when trends will turn or when there may be a large swing. You need to be able to catch the change as quickly as possible. The only way to do this is to follow the movement of performance indicators closely and frequently.

19

Organizing for Flow

We ended the last experience session talking about speeding up the frequency of measuring and analyzing performance indicators. This chapter is all about speeding up. The workshop on flow and capacity tends to be a landmark session. The topic of flow is a hugely important one and is underestimated by leaders, especially regarding its effect on behavior both in the teams and from the leaders. Leaders *must* understand the concept and effect of flow. They must do everything in their power to create an organizational system in which work flows unimpeded through the organization. Improving flow through the IT organization involves everyone in the organization, since every unit of work needs to flow from the customer through the IT organization, back to the customer as quickly as possible, irrespective of which teams the unit of work needs to go through. Until now the leaders have been largely on an individual learning journey with a growing orientation towards their teams. The last workshop brought the management team together based on the obeya. Flow is the topic that shows the interconnection of all things IT.

Just a reminder: Flow is about ensuring that all activities in a process are carried out one after the other so as to remove the need for intermediate inventories and waiting times. On top of this, all other forms of waste must be removed and necessary Non-Value-Add activities must be minimized (Figure 19.1).

IT organizations have traditionally been seen largely as cost centers. The consequence of this way of thinking, is that enterprises have a primary aim to use this resource as efficiently as possible, which usually translates to: Ensure that the "expensive" IT people are filled with work, since not working on something equates to waste in this way of thinking. This way of thinking has caused non-Lean IT leaders to steer the IT organization on maximum resource usage (resource efficiency). In turn, the IT leaders

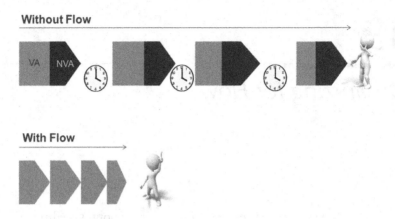

FIGURE 19.1
Flow.

have embedded this way of thinking in their management behavior. In "resource efficient" environments, inventory is welcomed because with inventory we know that nobody will ever run out of things to do. However, this causes team members to become overburdened (muri), thus creating a highly stressful environment in which relatively little work actually gets done, and little of it on time. Team members who have too much work in progress (WIP), will spend little to no time focused on improvement or innovation. The result is that there is less focus on getting work done, rather it is all about being "busy." Consequently, there is a lack of attention to the needs of the customer, which leads to much lower customer value on a long-term basis.

Lean thinking challenges IT leaders to look at the ability of the IT organization to deliver the required customer value as efficiently as possible. Efficiency, in this case, is not that the IT employee is optimally filled with work, but that the unit of work representing the value is processed through the IT organization in the most efficient way. This is called *flow efficiency* (Modig and Ahlstrom, 2012). The challenge to optimize flow efficiency is the high-level problem that IT leaders must resolve together. Once this problem has been solved, then (and only then) the focus can return to optimizing resource usage within a flow-efficient context. One of the main barriers to moving to flow efficiency is the almost unshakeable perception of IT leaders that changing to flow efficiency will "destroy productivity" and cause "customers to get extremely irate" because their work is not getting done. The fact that experience proves this to be untrue appears to be of no consequence ... until you have experienced it. And if you do not try to achieve flow efficiency, you will not gain the experience, leaving both the mental model and the mental anguish of the team members in place.

Getting IT leaders to first truly understand flow and then make it the focus of their attention as they do gemba walks or interact with teams, is one of the most difficult coaching activities. Cognitively, flow is not so difficult to comprehend but turning this comprehension into daily behavior is not self-evident. It requires an intimate understanding of lead times and process times for each process. But as we have seen, many IT managers simply do not take the time on a daily basis to "understand the numbers."

Take an example from a kaizen. There was a team of four people, a team leader together with three team members, accompanied by their manager, who was the sponsor of the kaizen. We investigated a process that was fraught with errors and problems. The problem was that the data from applications of national business units needed to be linked to or brought into a data lake, so that it was possible to report all national and international data from a standard platform. The process was highly manual and error-prone, and it took 18 weeks on average. The team members drew out the process in the form of a Value Stream Map, explaining how long each step took to execute (process time) and how long the entire process took (lead time). The result of this exercise was that the time worked (process time) amounted to 42 hours. This included work on both the national side and within the central IT organization. We investigated the various steps to uncover the cause of errors and problems. I waited to see whether anyone would comment on the time data. No-one batted an eyelid regarding the relationship between the 42 hours and the 18-week lead time, least of all the manager who regarded the time aspects as a given. The significance of this relationship was on *nobody's* radar screen. In an IT organization that seriously works with Lean principles, it should have everyone's attention, particularly that of the leaders.

Flow has a very useful characteristic. As you increase the rate of flow, the chance of making mistakes increases and their perceived severity is higher. In a traditional IT organization this is something we aim to avoid at all costs, so we do things "slowly" because it gives us a chance to cover up or recover from mistakes before the customer notices. The effect is that we do not uncover the root causes of errors. If we increase the flow, the problems come flying at us and we need to stop the process to investigate and structurally correct the cause. But that causes delays in the delivery to customers, I hear you say. Yes, for this particular delivery. Subsequent deliveries will all go much more quickly.

What should have happened (and did) in the kaizen? With a bit of prompting, the five participants agreed that 18 weeks was really excessive. Averaging about 2.5 hours of work per week was agreed to be really inefficient. The team set about looking at how the lead time could be halved, initially. With further improvements planned for later. This is where leaders need to step in and challenge the status quo, by focusing on flow. In this case, it turned out that 15–20 applications per year could be integrated into the data lake by the team with the existing process. The key problem was that the team had 6–7 applications "on the go" at any one time. This caused many of the technical and planning problems that were experienced during the process. By reducing the lead time, they were able to reduce the number of applications being worked on concurrently, thereby reducing the number of errors. This led to less time spent which led to further shortening of the lead time and an increase in the capacity to process application data. This effect has been demonstrated time and time again both within and outside IT. And, still, leaders do not take the step to take flow and its consequences seriously.

On the topic of efficiency: To be frank, efficiency in the world of IT essentially means doing the same (or more) work with fewer people. This has always been the case, and it is a natural state of affairs that leaders need to manage and encourage. As has been stated a number of times, standardization is something that is *absolutely vital* for IT organizations and teams. There is a well-known series of developmental steps regarding changes within IT: The first time we do something, it is a project. With some experience, it becomes a non-standard change. As capabilities (both technical and human) improve, it is turned into a standard change. Finally, we automate it. This series of steps is all about improving flow and the efficiency in the delivery of value. Mostly, this process is more or less accidental or haphazard. As a Lean IT leader, you must encourage this process purposefully to ensure that the amount of time spent on each and every activity is reduced to a minimum, by removing Non-Value-Adding activities, minimizing Necessary Non-Value-Adding activities and optimizing Value-Adding work. The day-to-day activities of going through this process are all part of continuously improving the flow of value to customers. The implicit consequence is: We (appear to) need fewer people.

In his books (1988, 2012), Taiichi Ohno regularly refers to the fact that work should continuously be improved so that it can be done with fewer people. He emphasizes the fact that people should be removed from the team when the work can be done by fewer people, so that the savings are actually effectuated. Often, savings are fictitious because an improvement may save time but it does not result in having fewer people on the team. The interesting aspect of Ohno's drive for efficiency and fewer people is that he does not state what needs to happen with the people. The traditional Western action would be to remove people from the organization altogether (i.e. fire them). What Ohno actually did was remove one person from the team and put this person on improvement activities so as to accelerate the rate of improvement (Harada, 2015). In the Western world, we would identify and remove the lowest performer; Ohno always removed the *best* performer, since this is a person who best understands the work and is best able to take the standard and improve it. The fact is, in today's world, getting hold of IT people is a challenge. Why would you then want to fire them?

Flow within an IT organization is a mark of how we use time. Time is an absolutely vital part of the equation of delivering value to our customers because most of the value is created by people spending their time on creating new capabilities for customers. However, as a result of the way we have spent our time in the past and how we are currently spending it, the amount of time we have to create new capabilities is, sometimes severely, restricted.

Within an IT organization, the key component for delivering the performance that customers require is people. It is people who decide which technology choices to make. It is people who design, deliver and manage IT services. Breaking down the "people" component, we find that it is all about ensuring the availability of the right amount and allocation of knowledge (and behavior) at the right time.

The aspect of people can be subdivided into two key components. When we hire a person, we are in essence "buying" behavior and knowledge for a specific amount of time. Time is, therefore, the key production factor within IT, since it is only through people applying their skills and knowledge for a period of time that the money spent on technology (hardware and software) can be put to good use.

There are two characteristics of time that make it useful as a performance indicator: control and immediacy. We have direct control of cost through time usage. It is more difficult to control cost based on managing salaries since contractual agreements are not easy to change in many countries. We have immediate influence on time. We can almost instantaneously change what somebody is doing with their time. If someone is working on a change and an incident comes in, we can ask the person to stop working on the change and pick up the incident in a matter of seconds. This obviously has a downside: Too much chopping and changing will lead to a "fire-fighting" environment within the IT organization.

Lean IT requires an intimate knowledge of time usage within the IT organization. We need to understand how time is used, particularly related to the delivery of value. We can define time based on the activity that is being carried out: Value-Add, Necessary Non-Value-Add and Non-Value-Add. Achieving flow in processes is one of the ways in which Lean changes the way time is used. The question we must answer is: How should we use free time? Lean recommends using it to carry out improvement initiatives or respond to changes in customers' requirements. One of the most useful Lean IT tools for understanding time usage at a leadership level is Earning Capacity Analysis.

The primary process of an IT organization is delivering IT services. But what are these services? To define the services of an IT organization, let's look at what the customers of an IT organization actually want. In essence, they want three things: They want their existing IT stuff (or functionality) to work properly, i.e. no disruptions, they want new stuff (new or additional functionality), preferably as soon as possible, and they want advice on how best to use their existing and new stuff.

These are the three basic services of IT for which a customer is willing to pay, i.e. they represent value for the customer. And the customer is actually willing to pay for these activities. These are the activities that make up the Earning Capacity of the IT organization, they broadly equate to Value-Adding activities.

It is very important to distinguish between what a customer wants to pay for and what we actually make them pay for. A rather distressing example is the contract in which the customer gets to pay for having an incident solved. This really should be in the warranty of the service and not a money-generator for the service provider.

What are the components of Earning Capacity? From the three basic services, we know that the elements of Earning Capacity are 1) customer-initiated business improvement projects: these are changes and projects requested by the customer; 2) running the IT operations: all activities associated with ensuring that the IT service works without incidents on a daily basis; and 3) providing advice: the advice customers are looking for from their IT organization is basically the result of the analysis required for availability and capacity plans and market research on technology applicable to the business of the customer. If we translate this into basic IT processes, we are talking about the activities in Development/Change/ Release/Configuration Management, Request Fulfillment, Availability/ Capacity Management and IT Operations Management.

The aim is to increase the proportion of time spent on these activities. All other activities are secondary in nature. These activities are collectively called Burning Capacity. For many IT organizations, the activities (and processes) that make up Burning Capacity may be counterintuitive for the simple reason that the IT organization charges the customer for these activities. Remember, there is a major difference between what a customer *wishes* to pay for and what we *make* them pay for.

Burning Capacity activities are Incident Management, Problem Management, Service Level Management and other coordinating activities, strategic activities and any tactical activities that do not lead to advice for the customer, to better guarantee and manage their own services and products. The aim for an IT organization is to reduce the amount of time spent on these activities as much as possible (Figure 19.2).

How can managing Earning Capacity help you improve the financials of your IT organization? As we have seen, gaining insight into the aspects of IT that earn and burn money is the first step. It is now up to the IT management to improve the ratio of Earning Capacity to Burning Capacity.

To illustrate the financial effect, let's take a fictitious IT organization. The example may appear to focus on commercial IT organizations, but the phenomenon works for internal IT organizations as well. This organization is able to charge its customers on average $100 per hour. Its internal costs for an employee are on average $50 per hour. If the IT organization has an EC:BC ratio of 50%, it will break even, since each paid (EC) hour needs to cover the cost of 2 hours (1 EC hour and 1 BC hour). If we improve the EC:BC ratio substantially to 66%, we see that each BC hour is supported by 2 EC hours. This means that the cost of an EC hour changes from $100 to $75. If the IT organization can sell its EC hours for an average of $100 to customers, it will be making a $25 profit per hour. The organization obviously has a choice. It can either pocket the margin or give some of it back to its customers in the form of a cheaper price per hour. The effect will probably be an increase in demand. An IT organization with an EC:BC ratio of 33% will need to cover 2 BC hours with 1 EC hour, i.e. in

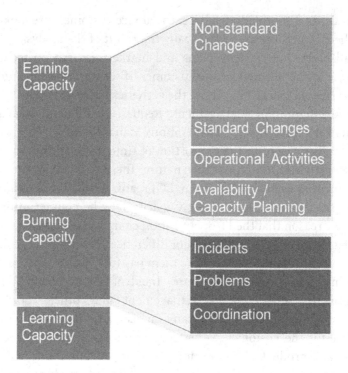

FIGURE 19.2
Overview of Earning, Burning and Learning Capacity.

this example, it will need to recuperate $150 per hour from its customers to break even. Its chances of success are strongly reduced. The assumption in the above example is that the net financial effect of technology is zero, i.e. the customer effectively pays for all hardware, software and communications.

The third component of the Earning Capacity Analysis, next to Earning and Burning capacity, is the alliteratively responsible Learning capacity. Learning capacity is the time spent on learning activities. This may be knowledge sharing sessions, (internal or external) seminars, peer-to-peer learning and, obviously, training. Generally, 5-10% of all time should be identifiably spent on learning activities.

Bringing together the three components, leaders can create an overview of how time is currently spent and make a plan for shifting the way time is spent across the entire organization. Looking at an average IT organization, it is rare to find that they spend more than 50% of time on Earning Capacity activities. In part IV, we will look at capacity planning from a team perspective.

The assignments for the next experience session are fairly obvious: Go to the gemba and find flow, and work out what the earning capacity of the IT organization is.

The flow gemba walk is a real eye-opener for most leaders. Investigating the lead times and process times of a variety of units of work in different teams provides, sometimes shocking, insights. The challenge for the leader is not to triumphantly have an opinion on how poor the flow is but to help the teams to identify the root causes for why work does not flow readily through the IT organization. Leaders find that there is no silver bullet here; there is a multitude of small to large occurrences that cause work to stagnate. The key question is: Is somebody paying attention and identifying these units of work? The key lesson learned here is that progress monitoring is one of the principal management activities that need to be carried out in the teams, not by leaders but as the responsibility of the team. This obviously means that they need access to the right information. Generally speaking, the information is available in the service management (or other) tool in which the units of work are recorded.

The other eye-opener is measuring the Earning Capacity for teams and departments. There are a few ways to measure Earning Capacity. One is based on estimates of time spent from the team members. Based on the list of units of work, team members fill in the percentages of time they spend on each per week. This usually gives a reasonable impression although the percentages usually represent the most recent week. Other possible errors come from the fact that team members may wish to "make a statement," by overestimating the time spent on solving incidents or stating that all time is spent on projects thereby ignoring the interruptions caused by incidents, service requests and other such activities.

A more accurate way of calculating Earning Capacity is by analyzing the units of work processed by the team over the past three months. This requires assigning a time value to each unit of work and collating the data into the Earning, Burning and Learning categories, followed by a calculation of the percentages. We will look into the time value of units of work in the Team Transformation. A third way to calculate Earning Capacity is to collect actual time data over a period of two weeks. See the Team Transformation for how to do this.

Whichever way is chosen to calculate Earning Capacity, leaders tend to be surprised by the low percentage of time spent on Earning Capacity activities. The manager of a team of developers had jested with his colleagues that his team would be the one to increase the Earning

Capacity because of all the changes, whereas the Service Desk would be full of Burning Capacity. During the feedback in the Experience session, it transpired that the numbers were not as pronounced as one would expect. As a result of the large number of standard changes carried out at the Service Desk, their Earning Capacity was at 38%, while the Earning Capacity of the developers lingered at 69%, when the expectation had been over 80%. It turned out that a lot of time was lost on investigating problems together with the application teams and the coordination of work ("project management").

By this time, leaders start to send mixed messages. The first is based on the fact that they are starting to get impatient. The leadership track has been going for some ten weeks, teams may have started their transformation, and the general mood is that we should be seeing some improvements by now. This "faster, faster, faster" message is accompanied by a "things take time, especially organizational change" message. The experience session is used to list the personal and collective changes that are visible. Based on the observations during gemba walks and other personal actions taken by the leaders, the list ends up being quite long. The leaders feel a sense of relief that things are going in the right direction. This is a moment to review the OBM behavior model. Leaders have become more observant when it comes to behavior and are better able to identify triggers and consequences, and they realize that to actually observe the behavior you need to be there where it happens, when it happens. This is another reason to continue doing gemba walks.

20

Leadership Kaizen

Not to labor the point too much but in case you had not noticed, Lean is about improving. When talking about improvement, IT leaders have a tendency to look at what is going on in the teams, particularly between teams, and then make an effort to improve the performance of the teams by finding the waste and problems in their work. Whether the problem concerns processes or technology, IT leaders get stuck in. This detracts from the real problems that leaders should be solving. Earlier we talked about policy-based waste (muri). This is the waste that leaders should be looking for and work hard to remove. When an IT organization is starting out with Lean, the leaders do not tend to get involved sufficiently in the process of problem-solving. This comes from insufficient attention to the self-development of the leader and, subsequently, to the resolution of management problems. Not all problems are problems at the gemba or in operational processes. There are also problems to be solved at upper and middle management levels. These problems cannot be delegated to others to be solved; the leadership team must solve them together. This is why Lean IT leaders must be proficient in structured problem-solving.

In fact, IT leaders appear to have some difficulty actually defining the problems they need to have solved. It is not that they do not see what is going on; they do not connect the fact that there is a problem and it needs to be solved. Generally, the comment is "we're working on it." On further questioning regarding when the issue will be solved, the average answer amounts to "Well, it's already much better than it was. So, in fact, it's not a really important problem." The follow-up question, then, is: "Well, if that's not important. What *is* an important problem that you need to solve?" A quiet descends over the meeting. We saw this phenomenon at the obeya.

In my experience, IT leaders always have three specific problems they need to solve for themselves before focusing on the work of others:

embedding the kaizen mindset into their own work, getting teams to work effectively together and achieving flow in the organization.

In Part II, we saw how teams were activated to solve problems, using the DMAIC problem-solving method as part of improvement cycles. The Lean IT Association refers to this type of kaizen as improvement kaizen. There is a second type of kaizen called daily kaizen. And this is where leaders need to be alert. Organizing improvement kaizen is important. However, to build the learning habit, leaders must ensure that both they and the teams engage in daily kaizen ... every day. Daily kaizen is the routine of tackling small problems on a daily basis. Its effect is to make doing the work easier. This is the first ongoing problem for leaders to solve.

What does this mean for the daily practice of the Lean IT leader? Daily kaizen means being alert and observant. It means knowing the standards and understanding when they are not being met. The aim of the Lean IT leader is to ensure action is taken to meet the standard, or better still: to improve it. Daily kaizen is more closely related to the kaizen mindset, because it means continuously looking at the environment in which we operate and changing things to make it easier for the people in this environment to deliver more customer value, more quickly and more consistently. In this respect, daily kaizen is about learning proactively because the team is encouraged to improve their environment based not on fire-fighting but on a desire to make things better. Daily kaizen is where the Lean IT leader must prove their value. In fact, the leadership of a Lean IT organization can be described as the improvement engine of the whole organization. Where teams tend to focus on delivering work, leaders should help to ensure that improvement remains on the agenda of the team.

There is a paradoxical relationship between improvement and standard work. Standard work ensures that routines and habits are created. By definition, a habit maintains the status quo. A team must create a habit of doing improvement work. Leaders must help teams to ensure this happens by challenging what they see in the teams and supporting the teams when they need to allocate (more) time to improvement. In most IT organizations, time is not structurally set aside for improvement. This is one of the pain points in all transformations. It is the leaders who must ensure teams know that it is alright to spend time on improving work. This may seem to happen at the expense of delivering customer value. However, in the long run, reserving time for improvement is actually not an option at all. This is generally where leaders are handed a choice: "Either we do work or we do Lean." Remember, Lean thrives on scarcity. Leaders must challenge teams to solve the problem: How can we do more work in the same time so that there is time to learn and improve? It's a problem. Solve it. And, by the way, adding more people is not the solution, it only ever ensures that people maintain the current way of working at a higher cost.

In the Leader Standard Work of a Lean IT leader, we may find on an average day that the leader attends two day starts, has reserved an hour for a gemba walk and an hour for specific team coaching of, perhaps, a project team. Each of these planned activities provides the Lean IT leader with the opportunity to observe how work is being done. Experience has shown that in each of these occurrences, people will voice concerns or highlight issues. The Lean IT leader must listen carefully to understand the problems, and ask how these problems could be solved in a "small" and simple way. Solutions like making a checklist, creating a written definition or sketching out a process may help to alleviate the problem for all involved. Now, here comes the real point of all this: The Lean IT Leader must ensure that the proposed action is carried out *that day*, mainly because there will be another bit of daily kaizen tomorrow. The team must become accustomed to tackling small problems instantly. This is the essence of daily kaizen. The other part of daily kaizen is the improvement of the leader's own work. Leader Standard Work should also be questioned on a daily basis as to its effectiveness and, where possible, improved.

In the course of doing daily kaizen, a team may come across a problem for which no one really knows the best solution, even a small step to alleviate the problem. The Lean IT leader must then facilitate the resolution of the problem through a kaizen event, or improvement kaizen. Both types of kaizen (daily and improvement) must be present in an IT organization to be able for it to say it is continuously improving. One of the most heard complaints about IT from both customers and employees is that IT only focuses on fire-fighting. This is the best reason to shift the focus to integrating continuous improvement into the way of working for the leadership of the IT organization. Fire-fighting essentially means that symptoms are addressed and mitigated on a temporary or one-off basis. However, time is not spent on establishing the root cause and implementing a permanent solution with controls to ensure that the benefit continues to be realized. This means that there is a high risk of repeating the error, which leads to more short-term time investment in fire-fighting. In short, there is no evidence of long-term improvement. In fact, it is highly likely that all fire-fighting time added up exceeds the time that would have been spent fixing the root causes. Lean IT leaders must consciously choose to direct team effort towards solving problems through both daily and improvement kaizen.

Another example in which the Lean IT leader can apply daily kaizen is by helping teams to unclutter their work environments, both physical and digital. Clean desk policies and flexible workplaces have had their effect on keeping the physical environment neat. The problem is with the digital work environment, because it is an "invisible" problem. However, the digital work environment concerns all the units of work recorded in the IT service management tooling. Using the 5S technique in the digital environment offers a unique challenge, simply because everything looks neatly sorted in computer systems. Finding a document on the intranet site is a good example. These improvements are part of daily kaizen.

The Lean IT leader's responsibility to encourage continuous improvement on a daily basis can be summarized by the following activities:

- Understand daily kaizen in the context of IT. Develop the kaizen mindset and develop deep understanding of how to encourage improvements, by knowing the reasons for and sources of improvement, for example, building team capabilities and especially increasing flow efficiency.
- Help teams to develop by instituting routines based on standard work which enable the Shu-Ha-Ri principle and the use of kata. Ensure that standards are created, monitor whether the standards are met, identify improvements in the standards and ensure daily and improvement kaizen to resolve problems.
- Ensure that routines become habits. Create positive reinforcement feedback loops that encourage people to carry out daily kaizen as part of their daily routine. Turn this action into a habit by reviewing performance at each day start
- Support daily kaizen. The Lean IT leader is responsible for injecting new energy into the team. Without additional energy, the team will eventually fall into a state in which improvements are not continuously sought.

The homework is simple: Engage in daily kaizen with the teams. Where necessary, the leaders may need to do improvement kaizen. This means that they need to be ready to explain DMAIC and use the 5-Why technique.

The feedback during the experience session shows that leaders generally find it challenging to use the DMAIC method, despite its intuitive nature. On questioning this reticence, there is still some insecurity about trying something that is unfamiliar. The DMAIC method has been explained and understood, at least that was the feedback. Yet, going out into the organization and attempting to help teams solve problems with the structured problem-solving method is a bridge too far.

A representative exchange during the session:

Q: What would you have needed to try using DMAIC?

A: A bit of coaching would have helped.

Q: Did you seek out a coach?

A: … No.

Q: Why not?

A: Because I decided on the spur of the moment that I wanted to use the method.

Q: Did you prepare the gemba walk, knowing you were asked to engage in daily and/or improvement kaizen?

A: No

Q: Why not?

A: I just didn't think it was necessary.

Even leaders forget how to help themselves improve.

There is more success with daily kaizen and often one or more leaders will have practiced five why. The response is a mixed bag, but generally positive. Daily kaizen usually provides a good feeling as leaders help to encourage teams to make time to carry out small improvements.

Five why turns out to be a bit more difficult. Helping teams to investigate what the answers are to the successive why questions is quite a challenge.

The first part of the challenge is actually defining the issue to be investigated, not going for the first thing someone says. Just taking the time to generate a number of possibilities and then let the team choose one, is something that leaders must be prepared for. If you are in a hurry, it is best not to try and do a 5 Why.

The next difficulty is determining whether the answer that is given to the Why question is the right one. As we saw, ideally there is clear evidence that the answer is correct. However, that evidence is not always available.

The leader and the team may need to make assumptions that will need to be validated at a later moment in time.

"Leading the witness, your honor" is the third and probably the hardest challenge to address. As a result of time pressure or a perceived pressure to get the team to the root cause, leaders are known to project their own perceptions onto the team, thereby unduly influencing the team's process towards its own answers. Leaders must remind themselves to listen, observe and ask questions, rather than focus solely on getting to a result.

21

High Performance Team

In the 1920's, Otto Köhler, head of the Psychology Institute of Berlin University, investigated the effect of teamwork on people. Amongst others, he did performance experiments together with the university's rowing club. He looked at how rowers performed on their own and in teams. The resulting phenomenon became known as the "Köhler effect." Köhler demonstrated that teamwork could produce significant gains in motivation. He also found that individuals perform better when working with a more capable partner. The individual felt that they were an indispensable part of the team and that their performance was crucial to collective performance. This leads to higher motivation and performance than if a person were working alone. The interesting facet is that this effect is most pronounced when it concerns a conjunctive task, a task that requires coordination between team members. If we look at the units of work carried out by IT organizations, we find that the smaller units of work will generally be individual tasks, but as work gets more complicated (difficult incidents, larger non-standard changes, complex problems), IT work increasingly gains a conjunctive character. It seems obvious that a rower in a four or an eight will be spurred on by team mates to reach greater performance levels.

The interesting aspect of the Kohler effect is that it also works in situations where you would not expect it to work. Looking at a relay team, we see four people doing what is essentially an individual race per person. However, successful relay teams also act as a team. A great example is the US 4×100m swimming team at the 2008 Beijing Olympics. Each of the swimmers in that team (Michael Phelps, Garrett Weber-Gale, Cullen Jones and Jason Lezak) swam the 100 meters faster than they ever did during their entire careers, with Jason Lezak undercutting his career individual personal best time by more than 1.5 seconds (Table 21.1).

TABLE 21.1

Relay Team Results

Name	Career Personal Best Time 100m Freestyle (seconds)	Beijing 2008 4 × 100m Freestyle Relay Time (seconds)	Difference (seconds)
Michael Phelps	47.51	47.51	0.0*
Garrett Weber-Gale	47.78	47.02	−0.76
Cullen Jones	48.31	47.65	−0.66
Jason Lezak	47.58	46.06	−1.02

* Michael Phelps never competitively swam the individual 100m freestyle. This was his best 100m time in relays.

One of the key characteristics of IT is that it is a team "sport." Individuals do great things, but customers get great IT services through the cooperation of people in teams to deliver the required IT services. Continuous improvement starts at the team level, where the value-added work is done. It is possible only if people across the organization continually check their progress relative to goals and take corrective actions to address problems they come across while trying to achieve these goals. This is an ongoing problem for leaders to solve (if they cannot come up with a more pressing management problem).

It is, thus, hugely important to cultivate strong team leaders and allow them, and their teams, to have ownership of their area with its strengths and problems. In fact, experience has shown that insufficient attention to the first level of management and leadership in the IT organization can be the cause of poor service delivery. Team leaders represent the most critical coordination layer within the IT organization. We must therefore pay attention to their team-building and team-leading abilities.

As we saw earlier, the traditional form of IT organizations is a set of technically-oriented "teams" doing their part of delivering the IT services. The word "team" is used quite easily to define a group of technical people working together. In their 1993 article, Katzenbach and Smith clearly define a team as: "a team is a small number of people with complementary skills who are committed to a common purpose, set of performance goals, and approach for which they hold themselves mutually accountable."

Table 21.2 shows how Katzenbach and Smith propose to identify the difference between a team and a group.

Teams and groups are very recognizable within IT organizations. For example, in a large IT organization, there is a team of ABAP developers.

TABLE 21.2

Team v. Group

Group	Team
Strong clearly focused leader	Shared leadership roles
Individual accountability	Individual and mutual accountability
Purpose is the same as the broader organization mission	Specific team purpose that the team itself delivers
Individual work products	Collective work products
Run efficient meetings	Encourages open-ended discussion and active problem-solving meetings
Measures its effectiveness indirectly by its influence on others	Measures performance directly by assessing collective work products
Discusses, decides and delegates	Discusses, decides and does real work together

Based on Katzenbach and Smith (1993).

These engineers ensure that all adjustments to the SAP ERP system are carried out in a consistent manner. This set of developers is referred to as the "ABAP Team." At closer quarters, we see that this so-called team is, at best, a group; at worst, a collection of technical experts who happen to work on similar technology and happen to have their desks in the same space. SAP is made up of a multitude of modules. The twelve developers have been allocated to the different modules and there is some overlap. The modules have such different functionality at a detailed level that generic SAP knowledge will only take an ABAP developer unfamiliar with a certain module so far. On a daily basis, most of the developers are at meetings with project teams or other teams supporting the various modules for the customer. Referring to Table 21.2, we see that the ABAP "team" fails to meet almost all of the team criteria. Some effort has been made by the manager of the group to introduce individual and mutual accountability, to define some collective work products and to introduce collective problem-solving. These actions were met with skepticism by the developers, as they realized that they were not a team. In fact, most of them felt more attached to the application support teams they worked with. And this is logical because together with the application specialists, the developers had a collective work product, a working application that gets changed when the customer deems it necessary. They also had better problem-solving sessions with their "surrogate" teams and found a clear and specific purpose for their expertise.

The average IT employee may work in a number of teams on a daily basis. It is therefore vital that every leader develops the skills to help team-building. Within IT organizations, teams are formed along four lines:

- **Technical team**: This is the traditional form of team within IT. These are, in fact, groups as described in the example above. The people in the team are all responsible for a similar part of the software or hardware
- **Project team**: This is another form of team that has existed for a long time within IT. Project teams are assembled to create new products and services, or simply to carry out large chunks of work. This is usually a virtual team with people drawn in from throughout the IT organization.
- **Service-oriented team**: This may be a virtual or an actual team. This type of team is responsible for ensuring that one or more IT services are delivered seamlessly. All of the skills required to deliver the service are represented in the team.
- **Customer-oriented team**: Like the service-oriented team, this team may be virtual or actual. This team is focused on managing and/or delivering the services for a specific customer.

In general, the last three may be teams complying with the definition of teams presented earlier. The first is generally not a team.

With the rise to prominence of DevOps as a way of organizing IT organizations, experts who are required to manage the full lifecycle of a customer's IT service(s) are purposely put in a team. In essence, this means bringing together IT operations experts, developers, some of the supporting roles and, in some cases, even the service desk capability. In this way of working, we see that a concerted effort has been made to create a true team that complies with the definition above. Where DevOps has been implemented with this team-based thinking in mind, we find substantial improvements in performance. As Katzenbach and Smith say: "Performance is the cause and effect of teams."

IT teams, facilitated by Lean IT leaders using Lean tools, can create a huge difference to customers. We saw that one of the units of work within IT is the non-standard change or project. This unit of work invariably requires multiple disciplines. IT organizations understand intuitively that the multi-disciplinary team is the best way to achieve success.

A (Lean) team is more than just a collection of individuals. A few prerequisites have to be in place in order for individuals to function as a

Lean team. First, the team leader plays a crucial role. The team leader is of vital importance in enabling effective teamwork. Team leaders can have a positive influence on behavior and a team's social climate, they can create a safe environment. One of the key skills of a team leader is, therefore, helping to create a functioning team, preferably a high performance team. This is an integral part of Lean IT Leadership.

A word on autonomous teams is useful at this point. Trends in the IT industry emphasize the removal of the leadership hierarchy at the expense of the creation of autonomous teams. Autonomous teams hold integral responsibility of the lifecycle of an information product and associated services for a particular customer. The ultimate form of autonomy is that the customer also has a delegate in the team. The team then decides together with the customer what needs to be done based on customer value. There is no team leader. The problem with this scenario is that at a micro-level (week by week) this may work, but in the longer term, problematic situations arise. For example, who decides who gets a pay raise? The answer, of course, is "the team." This argumentation ignores the fact that within a team, there is *always* a leader. If no formal leader is appointed, a leader will emerge from within. This leader has no authority, but people look to this person for direction. At the same time, the person has a content role within the team, so does not actually have the time to "lead" the team. The Agile world has a solution: From the content perspective, the Product Owner is the leader; from the "process" perspective, the Scrum Master is the leader. In many Agile environments, there is also space for leadership from an Agile coach. So, now there are two or three leaders. Once again, who decides whether I get a pay raise? We must first look at what the function is of leadership before we remove leadership positions. Lean IT has a clear vision of what leadership needs to do. The Lean IT leader helps others to develop, ensures continuous improvement and creates a vision and aligns goals; in short: The leader adds energy to the organizational system. We just need to identify how much time needs to be spent on these activities (not to forget working on self-development). This will decide how much leadership "overhead" is needed. I have not done research on this topic but most IT organizations I have seen work perfectly well with a leader to team member ratio of between 1:8 and 1:10, with this ratio shortening to between 1:3 and 1:5 going up the hierarchy. We now need to ensure that these people who do not produce any value for the customer actually do something that is of value; that is, lead in a Lean way.

One of the most important tasks of a leader is to ensure a team works well together. In his book *The Five Dysfunctions of a Team: A Leadership Fable*, Lencioni (2002) describes a number of characteristics of highly functional teams. These are compatible with the team definition as created by Katzenbach and Smith. Highly functional teams contain individuals who have a high level of *trust* in one another. They operate in a safe environment, meaning that they are free to speak their mind without fear of reprisals. Trust starts with the fact that people feel safe to show their vulnerability. A Lean IT leader can encourage this behavior by being an example. Showing vulnerability means being open about aspects of work that the leader finds difficult or challenging. An important aspect of vulnerability is admitting to making mistakes. It does not mean that the leader must burden the team with all of the doubts, fears and emotions that the leader may have; it just means not covering up issues that occur. Trust is the starting point of learning to develop; it ensures that the gap between comfort zone and fear zone widens. If there is trust and safety, team members will be more likely to be prepared to take calculated risks. Taking risks is what helps the team to take improvement steps beyond what is known.

The team members engage in discussions regarding their ideas with the aim of improving the quality of these ideas. In this respect, they seek *conflict* with one another as a way to sharpen the thought process and its results. The next step seems paradoxical: Lean IT leaders encourage conflict. The type of conflict they encourage is the positive exchange and discussion of ideas in order to make the ideas better. Many IT leaders are reluctant to let team members have conflicts, because they feel that it destroys harmony within the team. The leader's role is to ensure that the conflict remains constructive. One of the behaviors most seen at the start of a Lean IT transformation is that team members look to the team leader to solve these conflicts. Leaders must refrain from intervening, even when the team's first reaction may be to look to the leader for the answer. Rather, the leader should lead the process of resolving the conflict. Lean IT leaders encourage team members to have faith that solutions will come during the process; show trust even when the conflict is heated. The Lean IT leader leads by example and must be able to show constructive behavior in showing team members how to rebound from the challenges and conflicts.

Team members *commit* to decisions and plans of action. A team that shows commitment is clear on the goals, targets and priorities of the team. Commitment is not a democratic process to achieve consensus: Commitment is a choice. The team knows that seeking consensus does not help them; they seek constructive conflict to get to a point where each team member understands the goals and chooses to help the others in the team to achieve these goals. The Lean IT leader creates a trusting environment by being transparent about decisions and actions; visual management helps to achieve this transparency. A good example of where the Lean IT Leader can practice the first three characteristics of the team is in problem-solving. There needs to be openness about the existence of problems. Then the leader encourages team members to engage in a constructive conflict about how to solve it. The discussion should end with a solution to which the team commits. Not everyone needs to agree with the solution. However, the team members commit to implementing the solution. If a team member subsequently "sabotages" the chosen solution, then it is clear that the team has not yet reached this level of teamwork.

In a high-functioning team, team members hold each other *accountable* for achieving the goals. This means that once choices have been made, even if a team member was not completely convinced of the choice, they still commit to helping the team to achieve the goals. Team members motivate each other to excel in their tasks by setting standards (best known way) and working every day to achieve them. This happens with the guidance and encouragement of the leader, who observes the team and helps to ensure the behavior evolves in such a way that the team is able to work well together. The leader gives frequent feedback based on observations. The team is also able to sustain this behavior even without the constant presence of the leader. The team is able to address non-performance. Addressing non-performance within the team is one of the forms of conflict that may take place. In the aspects of team behavior, the team has learned how to discuss this kind of issue. There is trust that team members do not cause damage to one another, they have learned to manage conflict, and they have committed to each other and to the common goals. The Lean IT leader ensures progress meetings, fully supported by visual management, are held and that the necessary discussions take place.

Lastly, the team members focus on the *collective results* of the team, rather than the results of individuals. When teams have mastered the previous levels, the Lean IT leader encourages the team to present and communicate their desired results. The focus shifts from the results to the appreciation of the behavior that contributes to the team targets and results. The leader must become more severe with team members who demonstrate non-Lean behaviors, like pursuing self-status or individual advancement, because this behavior hinders the entire team. Up to this level, there is still a focus on the individual contributions to the team and that these are aligned to the team goals. A good leader recognizes the individual contributions, so that they can effectively praise and encourage Lean behavior of each team member. With goal-sharing, the leader challenges the team by focusing on the collective goals and letting the team determine how these goals will be achieved and who will do what work. The Lean IT leader focuses on creating positive reinforcement for the team. A reward system supports the creation of a spirit of team responsibility, rewarding the team's results with team rewards.

Around this time, the leaders have gained significant insight and experience into what is required of them as Lean IT leaders and are ready to "go it alone." By this time, there is usually an embedded routine at the obeya. Most leadership teams tend to meet twice a week at the obeya: once for a longer session (week start) and once for a shorter update (day start). The challenge is to keep practicing the behaviors learned over the previous thirteen weeks. With the help of an embedded cascade and leader standard work, the structures are in place to ensure that there is space in the calendars to practice on a daily basis. The additional structure is to ensure that discussing experiences as a fixed part of the obeya discussion ensures that leaders continue to turn the behaviors into habits. Here, we see that regular positive reinforcement, interspersed with some less positive reinforcement experiences, supports this process of embedding the behaviors.

After a series of deep dives and experience sessions, the character and length of the sessions generally change. The session is used to spend time at the obeya discussing the progress of the organization in terms of developments, performance and improvements. The learning is now based on practice followed by feedback from both coaches and teams.

The challenge for the senior leadership team, who have been through the deep dives and experience sessions, is translating the lessons learned to the rest of the leadership hierarchy. Will the mid-level and team management go through a similar process and, if so, how will the senior leaders fulfill their role as Lean IT leaders towards their mid-level and team leaders? It is about building the Lean Management System, comprised of the components discussed during the deep dives.

Part IV

Team Transformation

"The price of doing the same old thing is far higher than the price of change."

Bill Clinton

22

Getting Teams Prepared

Teams within IT represent 80–90% of all of the people working in the IT organization. It is therefore here that the bulk of the transformation effort must be directed. However, the transformation of Leadership and teams bear equal weight; both aspects must be given similar attention. We saw in the Starting Out phase that the activities are very much focused on getting the teams to work more effectively. The Starting Out phase generates some momentum and enthusiasm. Many team members see the potential and want everything to go faster (where have we seen that before?). As with the leaders, the first insights and successes beg for more. The problem is that "more" can only be achieved through the repetition of behaviors so as to create habits, also in the teams.

Looking at the transformation I have been involved in, I have always found the teams to be the most inspiring places to work. They can also be very frustrating, but the most fun. The best results and the greatest level of learning are to be found in teams that are given the space and support to learn. It is in this process of helping teams and individual experts to understand what is happening and what it means to them personally, and as a team, that amazing things occur.

The key to success is being clear on what is going to happen. This means having a detailed plan that will be used for helping the teams to integrate Lean thinking and acting into their daily lives. We saw that a plan needs to be created at the end of the Starting Out phase in order to provide the insight to the organization as to what is going to happen. The team transformation can rarely be done in one go and is therefore subdivided into waves. Each wave is made up of Analyze and Implement steps preceded by some form of preparation. At the beginning of the transformation, the preparation step will be longer than when the Lean IT transformation is in full swing (Figure 22.1).

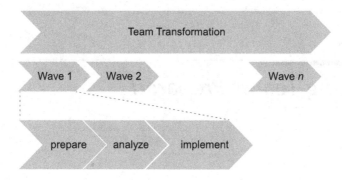

FIGURE 22.1
Overview of the team transformation plan.

Experience has shown that a period of twelve weeks is necessary to take the first steps. This usually gets the team deep into the "Know What" phase. You may need two more of such twelve-week cycles to help the team move from Know How to Know Why, with extensive practicing and coaching in the meantime (Figure 22.2).

When IT organizations start out with Lean IT, the whole exercise tends to come as a bit of a surprise for the rest of the organization. Often, leaders have been talking about Lean IT for some time without informing the rest of the organization. Once the leadership team has made the decision, they want to get up and running as quickly as possible. This causes unnecessary resistance in the teams. Getting teams ready for the Lean IT transformation is therefore an important, often overlooked, activity.

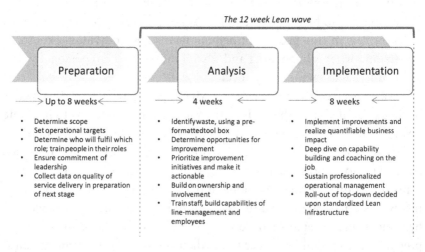

FIGURE 22.2
Team transformational model.

What needs to happen?

Leaders must be clear on the scope of the transformation. This may seem obvious but time and again transformations are announced only to bring up all manner of reasons why a particular team should be "left alone" for a while. These teams then get moved to "later in the transformation" or worse they are exempted from the transformation until a much later date. Let us reiterate one key aspect of a Lean IT transformation: It concerns and affects *everyone* in the IT organization. No-one is exempt. Everyone can explain why they are too busy, have a critical project to deliver and so on. However, if leaders are serious about the transformation, they must find a way to make it happen ... for everyone. In fact, as we saw earlier, Lean is most needed where there is scarcity, and a team with no time to do the Lean IT transformation is precisely the team that needs it most.

Leaders must analyze the IT organization at a high level and determine operational targets based on the KPIs they have created. These targets must be formulated as a milestone in the trend that needs to be created. The targets must be relevant to the operational teams. This means collecting data on the overall quality and performance of service delivery, both the operational and development aspects.

As we saw in the Leadership transformation, leaders must commit not only to their own self-development but to the Lean IT transformation as a whole. This commitment must be apparent and clear prior to starting the transformation of the teams.

Lastly, as we saw, there are different roles in a Lean IT transformation: leader, kaizen lead, coach and team member. The leadership team must be clear who will play which roles and initial training must have taken place before the transformation is started. The leaders are essentially everyone in a hierarchical role, responsible for one or more teams. When starting a Lean IT transformation, you will need at least one person per team to be trained as a kaizen lead, but preferably two. Embedding the kaizen mindset and ensuring that problem-solving is done in a structured way is essential to the success of the organization. These are skills that must be acquired and sustained by the IT organization. Initial coaching in this area may be acquired from outside the IT organization, but in the end, everyone must master the skill. The role of coach is more difficult.

Many IT organizations get coaching from outside based on the idea that coaching is a temporary role that will no longer be necessary after the transformation. This is simply not true. The role of Lean IT coach is an absolutely vital role for every IT organization. The coaches supplement the leaders in showing leadership towards colleagues, and the significant need of the coach to embed Lean IT knowledge and skills is most acute. And, if your IT organization is to become sufficiently endowed with Lean IT Experts, you will definitely need people to fulfill the coach role.

The coach is probably the most challenging of roles. The coach needs to help leaders to drive the change to a high-performance organization. This may mean taking the lead in an effort to develop and implement new or revised processes and procedures within or across teams. Key capabilities include an ability to understand the overall strengths and weaknesses of a team or collection of teams (covering a value stream), the ability to bring structure and knowledge of Lean IT principles, tools and techniques to guarantee the rigor of the transformation, the ability to train team members in Lean IT and to resolve inquiries related to the Lean IT transformation. The coach also helps leaders to set challenging, ambitious but achievable goals for the organization as a whole and for individual teams. During a "wave," coaches will also be required to carry out operational tasks such as observing the gemba and conducting analyses. Also, they will plan improvement activities, prepare and facilitate workshops on a variety of Lean topics and will coach leaders on *their* ability to adhere to the Lean principles and help teams to develop.

The big question for many IT organizations is: How many coaches do I need? This will depend very much on how many teams need go through the transformation and how quickly the leadership intends to make this happen. A rule of thumb is that a practiced coach can coach two teams through the twelve-week analysis and implementation phases at a time. More teams mean that the coach has insufficient time in the team to observe what is going on and help the team where necessary; less teams mean that the team does not have a chance to show what they can do without help, since the coach is there permanently (Figure 22.3).

| | Preparation | Wave | | | | | |
		I	II	III	IV	V	Total
FTE educated		80	160	240	320	320	~1050
Total Lean IT coaches available		4	8	12	16	16	16
Number of Lean IT coaches to train	4	4	4	4	0	0	16

FIGURE 22.3
Example of calculation of scaling up of coaching capability.

Some of the preparatory activities are one-off at the beginning of the transformation, for example overall goal-setting and determining the sequence of transformation; some need to be done every time. One of the most vital preparatory activities is training. In the case of team members, this means basic Lean IT training (e.g. Lean IT Foundation). The timing of training is critical, too early and teams will no longer remember what they learned, too late and people will feel ambushed. Experience has shown that training should be between two and four weeks before the start of the Analysis step. Team leaders should be encouraged to enter into discussion with team members about what they learned in the training, to keep the knowledge active.

23

Analyzing a Team

If you want to know what improvements are possible, you need to analyze the situation. And so it is with the teams. A series of tools are used to objectivize the problems faced by the team. Many problems are known but their definition is not based on a structured analysis of the situation. This is what the Lean tools are for. To be clear: Not everyone is eagerly anticipating the outcomes. Some people are decidedly not happy with the fact that aspects like the workloads processed by each team member, the knowledge contribution or the involvement in solving problems, becomes highly visible.

This period of four weeks is intensive although it seems more demanding than it turns out to be in practice. Having said that, it is important that, while preparing, a concerted effort is made to reduce the operational workload of the team so that the team members can pay sufficient attention to the Lean analyses. The eight implementation weeks are used to revisit a number of analyses, so do not worry if someone misses out on a particular aspect. All aspects need to be embedded in the team's rituals so there will be ample opportunity to help those who missed out to understand what they need to do and think (Figure 23.1).

WEEK 1

The first step for the team is to define their purpose. On many occasions, I have decided to skip this step based on the argument that it is obvious what the team does and the team members have been together for so long that defining their purpose is completely superfluous. Each time, I have found myself being forced to revisit my decision. The assumption is that

	Week 1	Week 2	Week 3	Week 4	Week 1 Implementation
General	☐ Dummy commitment document discussed with management; management takes responsibility of this document ☐ Plan commitment meeting in week 4 on team level ☐ Already recognised improvements added on general improvement list	☐ First analysis results added to commitment document ☐ General improvement list added with recognised improvements from the analysis	☐ Further analysis results added to commitment document ☐ Improvements prioritized ☐ Causes and improvement points identified ☐ General improvement list added with recognised improvements from the analysis	☐ Improvements prioritised on impact and feasibility ☐ Kaizens determined and planned ☐ Commitment document finished ☐ Commitment meetings held on team and unit level ☐ Commitment given	
Customer	☐ Team purpose defined ☐ Customer interaction initiated based on VoC questions	☐ Customer goals decided ☐ Commitment on customer specific KPI given ☐ Results VoC (perception) checked with facts (issues) ☐ Initial CtQs built based on VoC information	☐ CtQs reviewed and improved based on VoC information ☐ Team purpose reviewed and confirmed	☐ Team purpose poster on the wall, signed by all team members ☐ Customer compass implemented ☐ Customer goals (CTO) discussed with customer	
Process	☐ Units of work analysis ☐ High level value stream of unit/teams / process made (SIPOC) ☐ Waste analysis ☐ PCE time measurements started	☐ High level VSM made in more detail for the major process steps including identifying waste and issues (quantified) ☐ Time writing started	☐ Optional: process check with best practices ☐ Finish writing time and summarized in PCE ☐ Waste identified and quantified	☐ PCE time write results discussed with team	
Performance	☐ Cascade explained ☐ List of PIs in unit/team compared with general KPI set ☐ Gaps identified ☐ Regular meetings and issues identified ☐ ECA time writing communicated	☐ Collect KPI baseline data started ☐ Additional team PIs identified based on CtQ ☐ Progress visualised	☐ KPI baseline data collect on team and process level and compared with ITSM standard KPI's and customer wishes ☐ Finish writing time and summarised in ECA ☐ Progress visualised	☐ Impact from commitment of KPI's identified (hard goals) and checked with program / organization goals ☐ Week board and day boards introduced on the wall ☐ ECA time write results discussed with team ☐ Progress visualised	
Attitude and behavior	☐ Lean leadership self assessment executed by management ☐ Lean Leadership assessment sent to employees and manager (360 assessment)	☐ Agenda analyzed of team leader and coaching time planned ☐ Lean leadership assessment results analyzed ☐ First weekly coaching meeting held and lean leadership assessment results discussed	☐ Decided on new team and personal agenda / rhythm ☐ Weekly coaching meeting held between Lean IT coach and management ☐ Weekly coaching plan made between Lean IT coach and management based on gaps / issues from team leadership assessment	☐ Weekly coaching meeting between Lean IT coach and management based on coaching plan	
Organization	☐ Team barometer introduced and team questions defined ☐ Management reporting introduced	☐ First Team barometer assessment as baseline defined and held ☐ Skill & knowledge matrix defined and held ☐ First week start with week board	☐ Team barometer visualized and discussed with team ☐ Establish Visual Management boards and use ☐ Introduction of improvement board	☐ Visual Management in place ☐ Skill & knowledge matrix filled and improvement plan defined	☐ Kaizen Training (week 1 implementation)

FIGURE 23.1

Example of plan for the 4-week analysis phase (2-page spread).

the team is clear on its purpose and high-level goals. More often than not, this is a false assumption. The reality is that IT teams get so caught up in doing their changes, solving their incidents, answering service requests and contributing to projects that they have not taken a step back to consider why the team exists. Defining the purpose of the team gives it a second wind. It energizes the team members and helps to refocus their efforts on the work that has value.

When defining the purpose of the team, there are two aspects that feature prominently: the products and services delivered by the team and the customer to which these are delivered. Together these form the basis for the discussion of value and, essentially, the team's Why.

Bicheno (2008) sums up the various definitions of value in his book *The Lean Toolbox for Service Systems* from an economic definition of value to qualitative definitions. This shows how illusive the concept of value can be. In order to make value more concrete and usable, it is useful to understand the different types of customer value. Value tends to be described by adjectives that indicate the importance of particular attributes of a product or service. In many cases, these are measurable. However, the customer will perceive each attribute with a different level of importance. As an example, let us look at the value requirement "cheap." This word alone begs a whole host of questions: What is the product or service? What does the product or service mean to the customer? Does it help the customer to generate more business? What is the market price for similar products or services? What is the customer's perception of "cheap"? And so on. "Cheap" can be replaced by any number of characteristics for products and services. For products, examples of characteristics are performance, timeliness, reliability, serviceability, durability and aesthetics. These come on top of the specific features that define the product itself. Similarly for services, a customer may define the following types of value: competence, accuracy, responsiveness, access, communication and credibility. Some of the types of value of services and products may be the same but there are also differences. Understanding and defining the value required by the customer is not as easy as it may seem, especially when it comes to working out exactly what the customer is looking for when they say (for example): "It's got to be responsive."

The customer may define any number of characteristics for the product or service. It is up to the team delivering the value to determine which of the characteristics are requirements, i.e. the customer will not buy the product or service without these characteristics, and which are wishes, the characteristics that have the potential to delight or excite the customer. The aim is to create a product or service that meets the expectations of the customer. The goal is that this will lead to a higher level of customer satisfaction with the products and services delivered by the IT organization. The only way to determine the value characteristics of a product or service is through direct interaction with the customer. Which brings us neatly to the core of the team's challenge: Who is our customer?

The customer features prominently throughout this book but who is the customer? In a generic sense, we can identify two types of customers: the customer who uses or derives value from the product or service, and the person next-in-line in the process.

The second type of customer is relatively easy to identify since we generally know who receives work from whom. The first type of customer can be quite confusing. In the case of an IT team, who is the customer? Is it a person who uses the IT service or the person who buys a product or service from the organization that IT is serving? Both of these may be within or outside of your own organization. Take, for example, the employee of an insurance company using an IT service in order to record a sales order and start an insurance policy for a customer. In this case, the employee can be seen as a customer of IT. It is also possible that the person buying the insurance policy accessed a website and committed to the insurance through a web-based application without the intervention of an employee of the insurance company. In this case, the person buying the insurance is the customer. We thus have two distinct customers for essentially the same service: the employee and the insurance buyer.

In Lean, it is only the customer who can define the value. But always remember, the perception of value is subjective per customer and consists of a collection of requirements and wishes. These requirements and wishes change over time with new insights and expectations. On top of this, not all customers are the same. It is therefore important to understand which customer segments there are, since each segment may have different needs and spending capability, for example high-intensity users, users who use their IT services infrequently or specialist users.

Fortunately, we have a generic starting point for determining value within IT since customers, especially the internal kind, want three basic forms of value:

1. Ensure that any existing service I use works and when it stops working, please restore it as quickly as possible.

2. I regularly need new functionality to match the way my business is evolving, please give me new functionality as quickly as possible so that I can meet the needs of *my* customers.
3. Assuming that everything else is going well enough, I may require advice about how I can use IT to improve my business processes (Figure 23.2).

These are the three generic pieces of value that IT must deliver, at reasonable cost. The external customers who bought through web-based services have needs that particularly focus on the first two pieces of value. Their needs may however diverge from those of the employee in the area of ease of use or level of functionality. Embedded in the three basic forms of value is a catch. It appears that restoring a service that has stopped working represents value to a customer. This is most emphatically not the case. A service that no longer works based on a defect is, according to the last letter in the TIMWOOD acronym, waste. We need to distinguish between two types of customer demand. Value demand is the demand that a customer is prepared to pay for because it delivers something of value to the customer. In the case of our IT team, this is a working product or service and the related operational tasks needed to keep the product or service "healthy," the new functionality and the advice. Failure demand is when a customer needs to contact the IT team based on the fact that the product or service does not work or appears not to work properly.

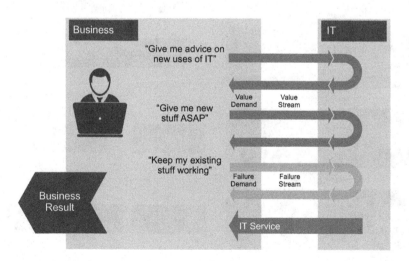

FIGURE 23.2
Generic IT customer value.

This is known as failure demand and is fulfilled through a failure stream. Incident Management is a failure stream. From a Lean perspective, it is very dubious to ask someone to pay for the resolution of an incident, i.e. a technical malfunction of the IT product or service, even though this is common industry practice in many contracts between IT organizations and external suppliers.

Value consists of requirements and wishes, also known as the Voice of the Customer (VoC). From the VoC, the IT organization delivering the value must distill and prioritize the requirements and wishes that are most important for the customer, the aspects that are Critical-to-Quality (CTQ). Having defined the CTQs, the organization must define their key internal attributes. The attributes must be measurable. In this way, customer expectations are translated into measurable internal objectives and activities. The CTQs and attributes related to the Voice of the Customer are referred to as the CTQ Tree (Figure 23.3).

The objective of investigating and understanding the Voice of the Customer and using the CTQ structure is to examine and understand the end-to-end customer experience, in relation to the value that the customer expects to receive.

Let us briefly look at a classic situation facing an IT team. Customers indicate that the delivery time of changes needs to be shorter. From

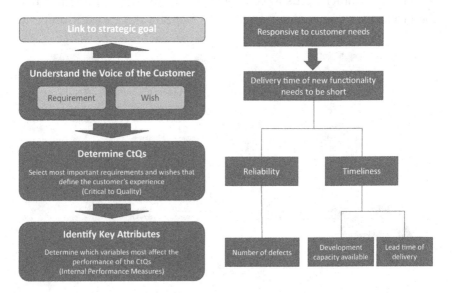

FIGURE 23.3
Steps for carrying out a critical to quality analysis.

discussions with the customer, it has become clear that there are two important drivers for achieving this requirement: reliability and timeliness. It is important to clearly define what is meant by these two terms. Reliability could be explained as the ability to deliver on time. The attributes would show a measure such as percentage of changes delivered on or before the agreed delivery date. Alternatively, reliability could be described as the ability of the customer to work with bug-free software. An attribute would be the number of defects related to changes. Timeliness may also be described by more than one attribute: the availability of development capacity and the lead time of the change process. The attributes are generally process performance indicators (or metrics). At the Voice of the Customer level, the indicators tend to be economic in nature.

The first question the team must ask is: Are we meeting the requirement(s) from the Voice of the Customer? There are three possible outcomes of this question:

1. We are meeting the requirement. We need to investigate the Voice of the Customer further to see whether there are other requirements or wishes that are not being fulfilled.
2. We are not meeting the requirement. We have a problem that needs to be solved.
3. We are not sure whether we are meeting the requirement. We must measure the attributes and ask the customer whether the performance is good enough.

A final step in getting the CTQ to provide insights is to link the Voice of the Customer requirements to a strategic goal. In this way, operational improvements within the team can be directly associated with a clear business benefit. It is surprising how often teams indicate in purpose sessions that they feel detached from the strategic direction of both the IT organization and the business as a whole. Explicitly creating the link between the CTQ and the strategic business goals helps to restore the connection and increase the engagement of the team members.

The question is: How can the team collect the Voice of the Customer? There are a number of ways. Observation is a preferred method within Lean. Go and watch your customers using your product or service at their location or the point where they interact with your company. See what it is like to be a customer (user) of your product or service. You may wish to interview customers, using focus groups, face-to-face or telephone interviews. The aim is to get feedback on current functionality and performance, and to identify new product requirements. Surveys can also be used to collect data from a larger sample of the customer base. Increasingly, social media can provide brutally honest feedback about how the IT organization is doing.

We saw in the Starting Out part that it is important to collect customer satisfaction information regularly and present it on the week board. One of the best ways of doing this is to simply ask the customer three questions in the course of the regular interaction between team members and customers. The idea is to then bring back this information in the form of quotes that can be posted on the week board. The three questions to be asked are: What do we do for you that has value for you? What do we do well? What could we do better? These questions take all of three minutes to ask and answer. In general, I have found that the "value" question is quite difficult for customers to answer initially. They are not used to being asked about the value they place on their IT services. My experience is that it does set the customers thinking and often they come up with insightful comments when the question is asked again at a later date. It is important to get the team members asking these questions as quickly as possible so that VoC information starts becoming available to drive improvement. However, team members tend to be reticent when it comes to asking customers the three questions. They are concerned that they will either have to deal with an angry customer or that the customer will expect direct improvement on things that should be done better. Only experience will allay the fears they have, meaning: Get out there and ask customers for their feedback. Most responses from customers are actually quite positive, especially when the questions are asked in person.

During the discussion of the team's purpose, there are some aspects that tend to crop up, which identify three other sources of improvement on top of the Voice of the Customer. The Voice of the Process (VoP) is about processes not working correctly. This is the second most important source of improvement information. The VoC may indicate that the results of the process may be satisfactory. However, the process may indicate that, for example, even though changes are delivered on time and with few incidents, the variability of the process gives cause for concern.

Increasingly, regulators have influence on industry sectors, notably finance, healthcare and utilities, and this influence finds its way into information systems. The Sarbanes-Oxley Act (2002) specifically stipulates how IT must create an audit trail of changes. As IT becomes more entwined with the primary processes of business, or even replaces these primary processes with systems that only require humans to see the exceptions, IT will find itself more directly affected by the regulator. This means taking the Voice of the Regulator (VoR) into account.

Lastly, there is the Voice of the Business (VoB). For IT, this concerns the "business" of the IT organization itself; not to be confused with the fact that the customer of IT is regularly referred to as "the business." Even if the VoC does not identify any problems, the VoB may well find problems to be solved. An example could be that the customer is very happy with the quality of the IT services, but the Voice of the Business tells us that cost levels are too high and that budgets will be exceeded before the end of the year. The VoB would indicate that the IT organization needs to carry out a kaizen to understand where cost is excessive, why this is the case and to create solutions for how cost can be reduced.

The team can combine three components to create a powerful purpose statement for the team to adhere to and on which to model their behavior: 1) clear understanding of the customers to be served, 2) the way the team wishes to be perceived by the outside world, 3) the product or service and the way the team wishes to deliver it.

The next step in understanding where the team can improve is to look at the Process dimension. The first analysis that needs to be done is the Units of Work analysis. This helps the team to understand what types of work enter the team. These are the inputs for further process analysis, as we shall see later on (Figure 23.4).

Gaining a full understanding of the average volume of each unit of work per week helps the team to understand the demand. It should be possible to construct a historical picture of how most of these units of work have developed over time based on a dump from the service management tool, or other repositories where work is recorded. Where this is not possible or incomplete, the team will need to start recording volumes directly so that a representative view of units of work volumes can be gained by the end of the four-week analysis phase.

The units of work are the starting point for some high-level value stream analysis. Value streams are the "vehicle" for delivering value to customers. A value stream is a chain of specific and identifiable actions that lead to the creation of a product or service that has value for the recipient of the product or service. It consists of steps that add value to the unit of work being processed. The actions must be performed correctly in the right sequence at

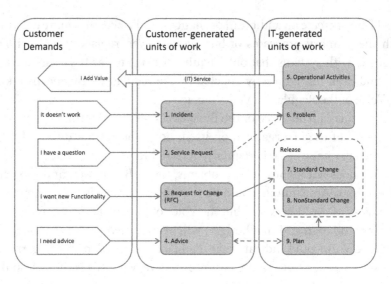

FIGURE 23.4
Units of work.

the correct time for value to be created and delivered. The actions must also be executed in succession so that delays between steps are minimal. In this case, the value stream has the characteristic of flow, the third Lean principle. Our aim is also to start the value stream when a customer provides the trigger, also known as the fourth Lean principle of pull. Each of these steps is executed in a certain way. Lean aims to continuously improve, the fifth Lean principle, the way each of the steps is carried out, both individually and particularly as a chain of steps to be optimized. When work is not carried out correctly, or when the required value is not delivered, the first place we look to find the cause is in the value stream. In Lean, we find that every problem is a process problem in some shape or form. The assumption is that the way the process was designed or carried out is the cause of the issue, and often is, especially in service industries like IT. The beauty of investigating the process is that it is the central entity that will almost inevitably lead us to the cause of the problem at hand.

At any given moment in time, there is a best way to carry out the step or process as a whole. This process should be documented to create a standard which in turn ensures a consistent level of quality of the performance, the output and the way the output is created. The document describing this standardized way of working is known as a Standard Operating Procedure (SOP). The SOP helps to improve the value delivered to customers through standardization.

As we saw in the Lean principles, value stream was the second principle, after customer value. This underscores the importance of value streams, or processes, in the world of Lean. IT has been concerned with processes since the advent of ITIL in the 1980's. Lean IT takes a different approach to processes than the standard IT process frameworks. Lean challenges us to look at processes from customer triggers to delivery of value. This means that some processes as defined by ITIL are in fact not value streams. These are particularly the processes that are internally triggered by the IT organization itself, for example Problem Management. Sometimes, it is simply impractical to consider the entire chain of actions. We therefore need to be aware of the links between processes. This is done by being aware of the output of one process or action, which is then the input of the next process or action. A classic example is the combination Incident-Problem-Change. From the customer's perspective, this is a single value stream: The customer submits an incident and can expect it to be resolved completely so that it never returns. In the world of IT, this is not always possible and so we cut the process up into three parts. A key skill here is to be able to define products or intermediate products rather than focus on the activities. Experience has shown that within IT, people tend to talk about what needs to be done, rather than what needs to be created.

Before we dive into the details of Lean process analysis, let us acquaint ourselves with the most important elements of a process. Fundamentally, a process consists of input that is transformed to output through a series of actions. Input can be information, machinery, materials and labor or a combination of these inputs. Work is then done to create the desired output, being a product, service or information. The output is always created for a clearly definable customer. If we cannot identify at least one customer, preferably by name, it is questionable as to whether we should carry out the process at all. Every process has a goal and a predefined result. In order to ensure the process works correctly, we need to have people taking care of the activities. These people have roles and responsibilities. One of the responsibilities is to ensure the process works correctly. This is done by having process measures and controls to check how units of work are progressing through the process. It is important to understand each of these aspects of a process to ensure that when we aim to improve it, we do the right things.

At an abstract level, each organization has three processes: Design, Delivery and Support. The Design Process takes an idea from concept to the launch of a product or service. This product or service must then be delivered to customers. The Delivery Process covers the activities from order intake to the delivery of the product to the customer. During the lifecycle of the product or service use by the customer, the Support Process ensures that the customer continues to benefit from the value of the product or service. IT organizations obviously also have three similar processes: Product and Service Development, Production and Delivery and Service and Support: The Product and Service Development Process is concerned with the design of an IT service. The Production and Delivery Process is about ensuring the IT service is created and deployed. The Service and Support Process is concerned with operating and supporting the deployed IT service. It is important to understand these different processes because within IT they can become intertwined. If we look at the process of delivering a change, often the production and delivery actions follow the development steps seamlessly, leading to a deployed service for which support may be required the moment it is in production. This is where understanding the links between processes is vital.

Achieving the improvement of a value stream is done in two phases. In the first phase, we define the scope of the value stream we are aiming to improve. The second phase is all about detailing the value stream with the goal of implementing improvements. Scoping a value stream starts with the unit of work being processed. We can collect Voice of the Customer information regarding the performance of this unit of work and create the related Critical to Quality tree. Then we can identify an area where the organization is not delivering the value required and analyze the value stream to identify which waste needs to be removed. The next step is to define the boundaries of the value stream. We do this with the Supplier, Input, Process, Output and Customer (SIPOC) tool, which is a method for scoping a value stream to be improved. SIPOC is a method for scoping a value stream that needs to be improved. We must then discuss the scope of the value stream with stakeholders since process boundaries are not always obvious. What will form part of the analysis, and what is explicitly not part of the analysis, should be confirmed with the stakeholders. Each of the SIPOC entities may be adjusted as the value stream is analyzed. For example, the request fulfillment process that starts with a request will have a different SIPOC from one that starts with an *authorized* request especially if, in both cases, the request needs to be authorized before it can be fulfilled. Assuming the team aiming to improve the process has been able to identify the SIPOC components, the process steps can then be described. Generally, the aim is to describe the process in three to five high-level steps. A guide for defining the steps is to identify handover moments or moments that intermediate products are delivered (Figure 23.5).

The exercise of analyzing the team's processes is a relatively simple exercise since the process within a team is often quite short. The intent of the exercise is to draw the team's attention to the fact that most processes actually start outside the team or continue outside the team after their work is completed. It also highlights the waste that happens when work is handed over from one team to the next. This challenges the team to look at the quality they deliver. As part of this exercise, teams are challenged to think about the effectiveness of the processes by carrying out a rudimentary Process Cycle Efficiency (PCE) calculation. This basically means understanding the average lead time per unit of work and making an educated guess, that will be made more accurate later on, of the actual average amount of time spent working on each type of unit of work.

The question for the team is: Which process or processes do they need analyze? It is not possible to look at all of the processes running through the team and, generally, analyzing one or two processes will uncover the behaviors that affect the other processes. The process in which most time is spent is generally a good candidate and/or the process with which the team feels it has the most problems. Teams most often choose the incident process, the change process, the process of releasing to production or the development process (from development to release). These are the processes that tend to provide the greatest problems for teams, because when things go wrong in these processes, customers complain the most. Some teams identify Problem Management as the process to analyze because they feel guilty about not spending enough time on solving problems. The team's coach should reassure the team that the topic of Problem Management will come back with a vengeance at a later stage. Do not spend too much time on Problem Management at this stage. The aim is to identify the key issues in the main customer-facing

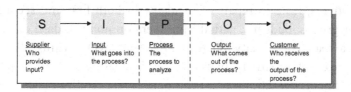

FIGURE 23.5
SIPOC.

processes. It is true that removing the root causes of incidents will end up creating more time for the team. However, although teams may wish to work on structural solutions to incidents, at this stage, the team is not ready to reserve time for problems. Early in the transformation, this time often gets sacrificed in favor of other units of work (mainly changes and projects). To avoid increasing the frustration of the team, the coach should ensure that solving problems is put on the list of improvements to be made in the Implementation phase.

Taiichi Ohno was a great driver of process improvement in a specific way. He challenged each team to understand the next steps in the process after the unit of work left the team. There are two reasons for this. The first is by understanding the next step in the process, a team is better able to deliver the required quality; the second is that the team can then be challenged to incorporate the next step in the process into their own work, thereby shortening the process, removing waiting time and handover moments, reducing the opportunity for mistakes and improving the quality of the product (Harada, 2015). Together, these lead to a reduction in the lead time of a process, meaning that the customer receives the requested value more quickly and with a higher quality, a fundamental aim of Lean.

The logical step after looking at the team's processes is to look at the performance. When starting out with Lean, senior leaders are challenged to identify the overall strategy and goals of the IT organization, in relation to the business strategy. As part of this, they develop Key Performance Indicators. With these KPIs as a guide, the team identifies the performance indicators that will show that the team is doing a good job in supporting the overall KPIs. They do not necessarily have to be the same but the team must clearly explain how their performance indicators relate to the overall KPIs. To do this the team uses the same KPI card to specify their team performance indicators. Generally, we see indicators that form part of the entire value stream. Examples include on-time delivery of design documents in the case of a team of architects, hours of rework in a team of developers, time to repair of incidents in both first and second line resolver groups, budget v. actual time spent on non-standard changes in technical teams or velocity in agile teams. For DevOps teams, all of these may be relevant, or simply focus on a single measure such as the number of deployments per day. Each of these performance indicators can be used to describe how well a team is doing in a particular area and can be related to the overall goals of the IT organization in relation to the business. In the end, it does not really matter what performance indicators are chosen as long as they meet the simple criteria of being meaningful and motivating to the team, and being linked to the overall strategy.

Having said that, one of the most critical indicators that must be measured is time usage. Understanding the way time is spent within the team is absolutely vital for helping the team to become more productive. During the first week of the Analysis, substantial effort is spent discussing the importance of time. Having explained the concept of Value-Adding activities as opposed to NNVA and NVA, interest is created in the team for how they are doing in this area. Fortunately, most teams recognize their own "busyness" and their own lack of understanding of where time goes in their team. Although time tends to be a very sensitive issue, the step to carrying out a time-writing exercise is small and is usually accepted quite readily by the team.

In the past, many IT organizations required team members to record how they spent their time. Mostly this was focused on time spent on projects with the support and maintenance work being bundled into a single category. Most people just ended up recording 40 hours on projects or 40 hours on support and maintenance with a few conscientious folks accurately recording their time use, principally because they were interested. The biggest problem with time-writing is the behavior of managers: They do nothing with the data; they just blindly approve the hours entered and never give feedback to the teams on how they are doing, nor do they attach improvement goals to the way time is spent. The way time is spent is seen as a result and not something that can be steered and improved. Providing feedback is the best way to emphasize the relevance of a particular aspect of the work. As a result of the behavior of managers, time data from a time registration tool is somewhat reliable at the organizational level but it is generally unreliable at a team level. Another drawback of time registration tools is that people tend to fill in the data after a, sometimes long, delay, for example at the end of a month. The way time was spent then needs to be reconstructed based on calendars which adds a level of inaccuracy to the data. Again, this is a result of a lack of understanding of what can (or should) be done with the data or, more often, an understanding that nothing is done with the data.

We saw earlier how Earning Capacity can be analyzed at an organizational level to provide leaders with insight into how time is spent in the organization as a whole. Earning Capacity Analysis is something that can be done in the teams. Generally, it is done once per half year or once per quarter. It is a simple spreadsheet-based tool that can be tailored to the team. This tailoring enhances its relevance.

First, the team determines which activities are most common within the team. The activities must be defined in a Mutually Exclusive, Collectively Exhaustive (MECE) way. This means that there should be no overlap between the activities and no grey areas, and team members should be able to record all of the time they spend. This may mean having a category Other, which is always Burning capacity. Each type of activity must be allocated to an Earning, Burning or Learning category (Table 23.1).

The team members are asked to record the date on which the activity took place, the start and end time for each activity to be recorded in chunks

TABLE 23.1

Example of Earning Capacity Analysis Categories

Activity	Earning-Burning	Definition
Incident	Burning	Resolving incidents
Problem	Burning	Working on problems
Change	Earning	Carrying out both standard and non-standard changes
Project	Earning	Executing projects
Operational activities	Earning	Activities that ensure the health of the systems
Management	Burning	Time spent on informing manager (employee) or on supporting employees (manager)
Coaching and training	Learning	One-on-one coaching, note who the coaching was with
Waiting time	Burning	Time spent waiting to carry out a task
Administration	Burning	Administrative work, such as time registration, submitting expenses, etc.
Knowledge Sharing	Learning	Ensuring knowledge is shared with team members
Lean	Learning	All time spent on activities to do with the introduction of Lean in the organization
Planning and co-ordination	Burning	All time spent on coordinating the work of others
Meetings	Burning	All meetings that do not fall under other categories
Rework	Burning	Work that had to be done again because it was incorrect or insufficient; repeats of discussions already held in which the same information is shared,

of 15 minutes. For example, if a team member works on an incident for 40 minutes, she would record 45 minutes in the spreadsheet. Any comments regarding the activity (e.g. change number) and whether the activity was planned or unplanned. The team members are asked to describe any frustrations or time wasters involved with the activity (Figure 23.6).

Collect two weeks' (ten consecutive working days) worth of data per team. Two weeks has been found to be a fairly representative timeframe. Obviously, it is important to understand whether this is the case. If the team is in the middle of working on an annual activity such as an audit or budget cycle, it may be worthwhile postponing until this activity is completed to gain a more representative view of time usage. It is important to collect the first weeks' worth of data and process it so that an initial analysis can be done, and team members can receive feedback on the time data. Usually, time writing will start halfway through the first week, so the initial feedback will be based on two or three days' worth of data. This is sufficient to determine whether the team is recording accurately enough. The data needs to be collated and using pivot tables, the team can be shown their time usage. Feedback is given at the end of the second week and when the ten days of time writing has ended. The data collected helps to make the PCE calculation more accurate.

So far the analysis has been focused on understanding the performance of the team in a variety of ways. It is important to turn our attention to the people aspect. It is very important for the team members to reflect on how the team is working. In the Agile world, the Retrospective is the event in which this is done. The aim is to get the team members and the team leader to start giving each other feedback in a constructive way. It is vital

Team							ECA Timesheet
Role							
Name							
Date	Start time (hh:mm)	End time (hh:mm)	Time (min.)	Activity	Comments	Is this activity a disruption?	Time wasters and frustrations
			0				
			0				
			0				
			0				
			0				
			0				
			0				
			0				
			0				
			0				
			0				
			0				
			0				
			0				
			0				
			0				
			0				

FIGURE 23.6
Example of earning capacity analysis timesheet.

that this behavior becomes embedded in the team. A tool that can aid the process of giving each other feedback on how things are going in the team, is the Team Barometer.

The team barometer is a very simple survey usually consisting of five or six statements that are used throughout the IT organization. In addition to these statements, a team may choose to add up to four of their own statements. The team members score each statement on a ten-point scale (Figure 23.7).

The surveys are collected by the team leader and the scores are collated so that it is clear what the highest, lowest and average scores are. The scores are then discussed in the next week start or retrospective. The aim is to identify and agree on the areas that need to be improved, and to identify one or two improvement actions to improve the area (Figure 23.8).

In the case of the team barometer results shown above, "decision-making" is rated poorly and will need an action to improve the score. The team chooses for which of the areas they wish to carry out improvements. Since this survey is done every two weeks, it is not necessary to create a list of improvements; carrying one area in which to improve is sufficient.

One important note: The scores and results of the team barometer are private to the team. On more than one occasion, IT organizations have "for the sake of efficiency" and "because spreadsheets are such ad hoc tools" built centralized systems to capture the data so that the results can be combined to an organizational level. The response rate plummeted for one simple reason: lack of trust. The leaders have not earned the trust of the team members yet. At the outset, the results of team barometers must be kept within the team. A team leader can communicate the actions being taken through the cascade, but it may take many months before the data is shared outside the team. Returning to the use of the spreadsheet within the team is enough to increase the response rate.

Please score the following elements	Very poor	poor	strongly unsatisfactory	unsatisfactory	mildly unsatisfactory	satisfactory	very satisfactory	good	very good	excellent	
	1	2	3	4	5	6	7	8	9	10	no answer
Direction - I know which goals this team needs to meet and which products to deliver											
Personal enthusiasm - I like working in this team											
Personal Development - I feel that I have enough opportunity to develop myself											
Team Atmosphere - I feel that I work in a safe environment (in which I can speak my mind											
Decision-making - I experience that decisions are taken quickly enough so that my work is not impeded											
Empowerment - I feel empowered to do what needs to be done											
Team-specific - I have a good work life balance											
[Team-specific question 2]											
[Team-specific question 3]											
[Team-specific question 4]											

FIGURE 23.7
Example of team barometer.

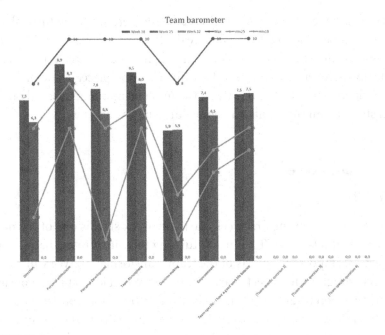

FIGURE 23.8
Example of results of team barometer.

The team leader completes the Lean Leadership assessment as was previously done by leaders in the leadership transformation. This time the assessment includes not only a self-assessment but also an assessment from the team members. The assumption is that the team leader will have been exposed to the leadership transformation to a certain extent, otherwise the assessment will have limited relevance.

In the first week, it is important to plan the week start meeting with the team. This will become an important moment in the week, a moment for sharing the results of the various analyses. Usually, a week start is one hour. In this phase of the transformation, it is useful to plan one and a half or even two hours. In the end, reserving two hours a week for the team to discuss performance, analyses and the coordination of work is time well spent.

The first week of the Analysis phase usually happens without too much resistance from team members. The main complaints are that a substantial amount of time is taken up learning the Lean "stuff" which may have been put to better use providing new functionality to customers. Here, the old adage of the woodcutter who never stops to sharpen a blunt ax works wonders. The lesson being that everyone needs to take time out to improve their tools so that they can do their work more effectively.

232 • *The Lean IT Expert*

In the Parker and Lewis curve, the team members are going through the first dip and are moving to the first peak. There is a realization that some things are different and that a bit of learning may be necessary, but overall the team members feel the world is still the same place. The real dip of despondency comes later, mostly in the implementation phase, when the team starts changing habits and embedding new ways of working.

WEEK 2

Monday starts with the first week start. The week start is one of the most important rituals in an IT team and turning this ritual into a habit is one of the most important aspects of the team transformation. We will follow a team through its first week start. The team we will look at is responsible for the functional support of the website of a utility and consists of seven team members. They have a relationship with a small team of five web developers and a team of three technical engineers responsible for the web servers, network connections and databases. On a daily basis, they have a wide variety of tasks to do. They are the primary contact point for the Service Desk regarding all aspects of the web services, solving incidents and service requests regarding the content management system (CMS). They carry out a fair number of standard and non-standard changes, although most of the latter are passed through to the two other teams. The functional support team does, however, carry out the impact analysis, manage the change and act as contact point for the customer. There are usually a few projects throughout the business that involve web services. From the technical and development teams, they receive information regarding updates, patches and other improvements to the web platform and CMS.

The team and their team leader gather around the sketchy week board. Their coach takes them through the procedure.

The first step is to agree on the goals of the week. Second, the team will discuss interaction with the customer, Then, the results of the team barometer will be addressed. Lastly, a couple of performance indicators will be dealt with.

Each team member takes a set of sticky notes and writes down their goals of the week. Most actually write what they will be doing this week. After about 7–8 minutes everyone is ready. They stick the sticky notes on the board, and linger at the board as they read what others have written. Some team members stick three notes, others may have up to twenty chronicling their entire week in minute detail. The sticky notes are rudimentary and are a combination of activities and deliverables. The first improvement is to review each of the sticky notes and turn it into a deliverable that will be tangible at the end of the week. For example, the team member with 20 sticky notes consolidates three "meeting" tickets, two "writing" tickets and two "review" tickets into a single "create user document for [new functionality]" ticket. This takes about 20 minutes as team members ask each other whether they have described a product or not. The number of tickets is reduced by half. It is agreed that solving incidents, service requests and standard changes do not constitute goals of the week since they are ongoing activities that return every week. This further reduces the number of deliverables.

After about 45 minutes, the team is satisfied with their "plan" for the week. The question is: Is it achievable? A new round of checking the sticky notes follows. Each person puts the expected time per deliverable. One team member has posted a ticket concerning an impact analysis for a change and has set aside two hours. It turns out that the impact analysis has to be reviewed by another team member. This was not taken into account in the original estimation. The budgeted time is increased to four hours to account for the review and any possible rework or improvements. It takes a further 10 minutes to estimate all of the tickets, with the necessary discussion. The discussion often involves team members telling each other that a particular product will take shorter (or longer) than planned.

The now complete set of goals of the week is evaluated and the coach asks both the team and the team leader whether they commit to delivering the agreed deliverables. An unease descends over the team, followed by a series of provisos. If the customer changes their mind. If nothing else comes along. If nobody gets sick. If … If … If … The coach challenges them to start at the beginning: Is the amount of work achievable in the coming five working days? Some team members react positively, others do not know. For those who react positively: How do you know you can complete the work? One of the team members has quietly added up the numbers on the tickets and triumphantly says that it adds up to 132 hours. "There are seven of us. That means we have 280 hours. No problem."

This leads to one of the most powerful aspects of the week start: the capacity plan. This is about understanding whether the team is committing to something that is achievable or whether they are setting themselves up to fail. Here, the work done in the first week comes in handy. The Units of Work Analysis gives insight into the volume of the team's work. On top of that, it turns out that two of the team members work part-time, four days a week. The work is divided into two categories: The ongoing work that needs to be done every week for which the team needs to reserve time and the goals of the week. The ongoing work is absolutely non-negotiable, customers expect their incidents to be solved and their questions to be answered promptly. Also the operational work of keeping the CMS running needs to be done. The team is somewhat ambivalent about solving a problem once a week. The team decides that it is something they should reserve time for but they do not do it at the moment.

The capacity plan for the week is shown in Figure 23.9.

Planning the capacity of the team must take into account the fact that about 10% of the available time is lost as a result of minor breaks, bathroom visits and so forth. The team effectively has 238 hours available to do work. It turns out that the team needs 84 hours a week to keep the team "ticking

Resource Planning for the Team						Standard norm times
Total time available					352	
		Flextime (Percentage)	Flextime (Hours)			
Flextime		10%	35		317	
Reservations						
	Average number per week	Norm time (minutes)	Time reserved (hours)	Time available		
Incidents	40	45	30	287		45 minutes per unit of work
Service Requests	36	30	18	269		30 minutes per unit of work
Standard Changes	25	60	25	244		60 minutes per unit of work
Problems	1	480	8	236		480 minutes per unit of work
Team Meetings	10	120	20	216		
	Number of hours per week	Norm time (minutes)	Time reserved (hours)	Time available		
Operational activities	65	60	65	151		60 minutes per employee per day
Minimum Team time				166		
Time available for Goals of the Week				151		
Goals of the Week						
			Hours planned			
Changes			24	127		
Projects			24	103		
Plans/Advice			12	91		
Training			48	43		
Old calls			12	31		
[unit of work]			0	31		
Time available			31			

FIGURE 23.9
Team capacity plan.

over." This leaves 154 hours for goals of the week. This week, the goals for the team leave a total of 22 hours unallocated. It is agreed that these hours are discretionary for the team leader. They are available to pick up any emergency ad hoc work or unforeseen absence of a team member, but only the team leader is allowed to allocate these hours.

Once again, the coach asks whether the team commits to the plan. The answer is now a more emphatic "yes." "But ..." says one of the team members "... there are a number of goals of the week that are dependent on Carl, the team's most senior member. If Carl does not do the work, then others cannot finish their work and the whole plan will fail." This provides the start of a short discussion about the skills and knowledge available in the team. The "Carl-issue" weighs on the team. Everyone knows that this is the elephant in the room; it has been for the last two years. The team agrees that investigating the skills and knowledge of the team has a high priority. Fortunately, the analysis is planned for this week. With 30 minutes to go, the team turns to the "Customer" section of the week board. The coach explains the aim of getting feedback from customers and the three Voice of the Customer questions to ask. A frisson of fear edges its way through the team. They understand that it means actually asking customers what they think. The room stays silent, no volunteers. The team goes back to the goals of the week. The coach asks which of the goals involves a discussion or meeting with a customer or user. Eight goals are identified. The owners of the goals agree to ask the questions and bring back the customer's answers.

The "Team" section of the week board is next. The team leader has collated the data from the Team Barometer and presents the results. Scores are all around the six to seven mark with a few small dips and peaks to five and eight. The team is typical of many teams at this point in the transformation: No one sticks their neck out to indicate that they think things are poor in a certain area. The lowest marks tend to center on the speed of decision-making and, if the team has not yet done a team purpose session, they may indicate that the goals of the team and the contribution to the strategy are unclear. In this case, the results tend to be tepid. The coach challenges the team to identify a single improvement they would like to make based on the speed of decision-making. This engages the team leader and the team members in a discussion of which decisions are currently pending. The team leader commits to ensuring that the decisions are made by the next week start. With five minutes to go, the team discusses which two performance indicators they would like to track. One of the team members agrees to collect and present the data, something about calls (incidents and service requests) and something about changes. The team adjourns and gets on with their work.

This is a fairly typical first week start. But there are also other reactions. In many teams, there is someone who will declare the whole exercise "a complete waste of time." The person "could have got a whole lot of work done in the two hours just sitting around." There are also team members who have great difficulty identifying their goals of the week. On occasion, this has been the case because the person did not have much to do, all the while attempting to appear busy. The week start is a first major step to transparency in the team. The general consensus is that it is a good thing that everyone knows what each other team member is doing. Often, for the first time, team leaders feel like they have a complete overview of what is going on in the team.

In some teams, there is someone who finally sees their opportunity to voice some grievances they have with the team. The tool they use is the team barometer. The team member will score the statements in a very extreme way, to challenge the rest of the team and, particularly, the team leader. Often, the aim is to send the team leader away with some kind of action that will probably not be very successful, a wild goose chase. Often, this will have been a successful strategy in the past. The best response to this behavior is to get the team member to focus on the statement they would like to see improved most and identify an action that involves that team member getting together with one or two other team members and the team leader to find a solution.

There are also week starts that are the stuff of nightmares. The key reason is lack of support for the Lean IT Transformation from the team leader. One team leader was positive about Lean during the individual preparation of the week start, said he believed in the goals and agreed that visual management would be a great help to both himself and the team. Come the week start, his demeanor changed as he sided with two senior members of the team who loudly proclaimed that the week start was a "charade" and a "song and dance," that it made a farce of their seniority, as if they were "not able to manage the work properly." And worst of all, "using sticky notes is like going back to kindergarten."

Not everyone takes instantly to the benefits of visual management. As a coach, the sign you are looking for is the declaration that "there are more important things to do than this." This statement always gives an opportunity for identifying the improvements that can be used to turn the negative reaction into a positive action. Generally, the week board does not elicit such a negative response but it has been known to happen. The day board, on the other hand, can give rise to full-scale mutiny if introduced too early.

The "Carl-issue" provides an opening for an analysis that was already planned, and that is now fully accepted and anticipated by the team. They realize that having an overview of the skills and knowledge in the team will provide an opportunity to take steps in resolving the "key man risk," the "single points of failure" in the team.

Skills and knowledge are, next to time usage, the second measurable part of people. The vital aspect here is to determine whether the team or the IT organization as a whole has access to the right amount of skills and knowledge to provide the value that customers expect from IT. The objective of the Skills and Knowledge analysis is to balance the skills and knowledge necessary to deliver the current and future customer demand and, thus to provide people in the team with development opportunities. Understanding the needs of the IT organization starts at the team level. A lack of skills and knowledge is a driver of mura, and a contributor to all kinds of waste. For example, an IT organization's customer requires more Java than .Net expertise. This is the result of the organization servicing an application developed by an external party. However, the IT team cannot match the Java demand since the customer migrated to the Java-based application, and the IT organization did not ramp up its Java knowledge at the same speed. The consequence is that the IT organization has .Net-skilled people who are under-utilized and a lack of Java knowledge. This amounts to a mismatch leading to Talent waste and variability in delivery of value (mura).

Knowledge is the technical theoretical understanding and practical know-how that team members have regarding the components used by the team while delivering customer value. Within IT organizations, it is vital to ensure that everyone continuously works to improve and update their knowledge. Technological developments within IT are so rapid that standing still in knowledge development presents IT organizations with a huge issue. In practice, specialists on a specific topic tend to be kept in their area of expertise for too long. Eventually, technology is superseded by newer technology. As long as the specialist is maintained on the "legacy" technology, he will not develop new skills and will become obsolete. It is vital that leaders provide IT people with the opportunities to progress to newer technologies.

Skills are the demonstration of knowledge-based practice, resulting from learned abilities, and are required to be successful in the IT team. Skills may include such aspects as analytical abilities and ability to work under time pressure, but also customer orientation. Leaders must focus on identifying and developing the most important skills. The best place to start when defining skills is the organization's True North values.

To improve the performance of a team or department and to develop a group of people, we need to understand their current capabilities. IT organizations tend to focus on the development of expertise in narrow technology areas which takes years to mature, when they should aim to develop people who are more flexible, agile and adaptable to the changing needs of the customer. Of course, a team needs a mixture of experts and more multi-skilled people.

The Skills and Knowledge Analysis is a Lean IT assessment tool that analyses current team skills and competencies and matches that to current and future customer demand in types of skills and volume. How does it work? The team determines what skills and knowledge are needed to deliver the customer value. This is based on an understanding of what has been asked of the team in the past and an estimation of what will be asked in the future. Using the Voice of the Customer and associated CTQ, the team can identify where more or different skills and knowledge are required. The result is a gap analysis showing where there is a mismatch between the skills and knowledge available and those required. Based on the gaps, the team can manage its own development by creating a plan to drive the development of existing people from single skilled to more multi-skilled, thus removing personnel bottlenecks and increasing the flexibility and consistency of performance within the team. A skills and knowledge analysis also provides the team members with the opportunity to voice their preferences and ambitions for the direction in which they wish to develop.

Analyzing skills and knowledge can be done using a simple spreadsheet model (Figure 23.10).

Start by identifying which skills and knowledge are required. It is advisable to create a spreadsheet for knowledge and a separate one for skills. When defining the knowledge required by the team, everyone must be involved. The result is a tailored list of knowledge per team. Be careful about subdividing technical areas into an unworkably large amount of small units. However, there may be more than 20 knowledge areas. Mostly, we focus on no more than ten skills.

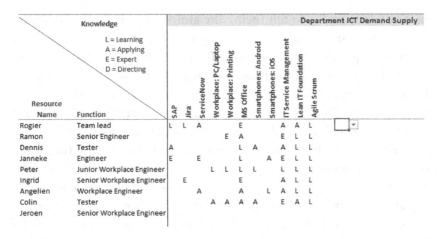

Resource Name	Function	SAP	Jira	ServiceNow	Workplace: PC/Laptop	Workplace: Printing	MS Office	Smartphones: Android	Smartphones: iOS	IT Service Management	Lean IT Foundation	Agile Scrum	
Rogier	Team lead	L	L	A			E			A	A	L	▾
Ramon	Senior Engineer					E	A			E	L	L	
Dennis	Tester	A				L	A			A	L	L	
Janneke	Engineer	E	E			L		A		E	L	L	
Peter	Junior Workplace Engineer			L	L	L	L			L	L	L	
Ingrid	Senior Workplace Engineer	E				E				A	L	L	
Angelien	Workplace Engineer		A			A			L	A	L	L	
Colin	Tester			A	A	A	A			E	A	L	
Jeroen	Senior Workplace Engineer												

Knowledge
L = Learning
A = Applying
E = Expert
D = Directing

Department ICT Demand Supply

FIGURE 23.10
Example of a skills and knowledge matrix.

Based on the workload (i.e. numbers of each unit of work) received by the team, the necessary capacity and level of knowledge and skills can be determined. The skills and knowledge are scored using a five-level ability scoring scale based on a person's ability in a certain area. The scale is:

- **None**: the person has no relevant knowledge in the specific area.
- **Learning**: the person works in this area, has some knowledge and experience but needs guidance.
- **Applying**: the person has sufficient theoretical knowledge and practical experience, masters most of this area.
- **Expert**: the person has much experience, can teach others, and advises regarding this area.
- **Directing**: the person influences the team and the content, demonstrates deep knowledge and has vision and ideas.

Each member of the team scores themselves on the various knowledge and skills areas independently. The team leader completes the matrix as well. Note: When scoring skills, it is important to be aware that the perception of ability in skills is (generally speaking) more subjective than perception of knowledge. Follow up with a short interview of each team member to validate the scores. Combine all input into a single team sheet and share the overall results with the whole team. Preferably, print the results on a large piece of paper and post them on the wall. The team leader should gather the team around the results and discuss what the analysis is trying to tell them. The aim is to identify the gaps (and excesses) between the ideal team composition based on the analysis of customer requirements of the team. The team, together with the leader, must determine whether sufficient knowledge and skills are present in the team to ensure the team can deliver the required customer value. In most cases, there will be discrepancies between the available and required skills and knowledge. The team leader must challenge the team to initiate improvements where necessary. This means setting time aside for specific knowledge sharing activities (Learning Capacity). The skills and knowledge analysis helps to provide a record of the state of the team, and all work done to share and acquire knowledge must be recorded in the Skills and Knowledge Analysis, through a regular update of the analysis. The Skills and Knowledge Analysis can also be referred to during coaching sessions with team members. It is important to repeat the skills and knowledge analysis two to four times per year because the Voice of the Customer—the key driver for required skills and knowledge—will change, and the team members will see the fruits of their own labors as they move from None through Learning to Applying and further. This has been found to be highly motivating for both individuals and the team as a whole.

The Functional Support Web team carried out their Skills and Knowledge Analysis. They chose to focus on the knowledge aspect to start with. The analysis uncovered not just one "Carl-issue." It turned out that about half of the work could only be done by one person, each time a different single point of failure. Together the team realized that they desperately needed to create a common basic level of knowledge for everyone in a very short space of time. For the past months, the team had "worked around" the lack of knowledge of some team members rather than focusing on remedying the problem. The result was that a series of one-hour one-on-one meetings were organized to get team members up to speed with the basics of their work. Some meetings were one-on-two but never more. The aim was to give intense attention to learning the work. The effect was that one member of the team decided to find other work because she realized that this was not what she wanted to do. She had moved to IT from the business to help support the web services but found that she was not interested in going deeper into the technical side of the services. The deeper technical knowledge had been identified by the team during their investigation of the necessary knowledge to be a successful team as described in their team purpose. Interestingly, there was one team member who was at a

"Learning" level of a particular area. Logically, he would be expected to develop to "Applying" in this area. However, he chose to develop into an area of which he previously had no knowledge at all. The team agreed that this was possible because the gap would be filled by another team member who did want to develop in that direction.

An interesting side note: The work of the person who left the team was picked up by the rest of the team during the subsequent weeks and months. As a result of more efficient work, the team was able to compensate very well for the loss of a team member. Previously, the departure of a team member would lead to the team clamoring for a replacement because the team perception was that they could not handle the increased workload.

Once the team has become comfortable with the fact that their skills and knowledge are posted on the wall, and this happens quite quickly, the team leader can discuss the knowledge analysis with other team leaders to see whether there is untapped potential in other teams. This is an excellent way to find new challenges and development steps for team members.

In the first week, the team looked at their units of work and they created SIPOCs. The second week involves going a step further with one or two of the processes. Using Value Stream Mapping (VSM), the team is helped to understand waste and improvement potential in a value stream. It is used to visualize the current and future states of a particular value stream. This visualization is used to facilitate the communication within the team improving the value stream and the stakeholders, such as other resources in the process or managers responsible for the process. The most important output of the Value Stream Map is to determine which improvement actions need to be implemented to achieve the desired future state. The team knows which process(es) it needs to improve based on the customer's CTQ requirements and wishes.

The goal of Value Stream Mapping is to visualize a process in such a way that the process can be analyzed. The team builds the Value Stream Map by taking the SIPOC and detailing the flow of the process steps, by adding basic information so that the Value Stream Map is easily understood by anyone who wishes to review it. This means giving insight into the input and output of the process. The key activity is to draw in the process steps. The SIPOC has given us a broad insight into the activities. The VSM needs to be more specific. The key reason for being specific is that the team will try to quantify as much of the process as possible. This means creating logical and measurable process steps. Also, the ability to define clear steps makes it easier to identify waste. The aim of the VSM analysis is to understand where the process fails to provide the value that the customer requires. Understanding these issues gives us input for continuously improving the value stream and the value it provides. Value Stream Mapping is an analytical exercise that supports the achievement of all of the Lean principles. However, it is also an exercise in understanding the behavior that exists in the team and across the IT organization.

The team starts with creating the Value Stream Map of the current way of working, reflecting on their current processes and identifying bottlenecks and other impediments. The next step is to determine improvements together with the team. The team then creates an improvement plan with a maximum timeframe of three months, during which selected improvements will be carried out. Having determined the improvements to the process, the team can then show the future state of the value stream and communicate with all stakeholders on which improvements will be made. The team will be able to differentiate between high and low impact improvements (Figure 23.11).

Before we can identify improvements, the team must gain a deep understanding of the performance of the process. A number of measurements need to be made. The waiting and cycle times of each step are measured, on top of performing a Value / Non-Value Analysis on each

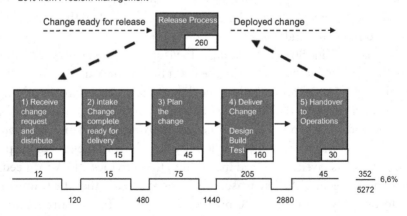

Unit of work: Request for Change
Takt time: 6 hours
Lead time: 11 days

CUSTOMERS:
80% from Service Delivery Manager
20% from Problem Management

FIGURE 23.11
VSM.

step. In this way, we can identify where there are issues of flow and waste in the process.

The first piece of information is the standard time. This is the time that a particular step should take to carry out by design. We record the standard time in a block in the right bottom corner of each step. The standard time for the whole process is the sum of all the standard times of the steps. Standard time is not necessarily the same as the actual time spent. It has more to do with our expectations. For example, the team may determine that it should take ten minutes to accept and record a change request from a customer. On measuring the step, the team may come to the conclusion that it takes twice as long. The aim of standard change is to set a level of performance that is realistic and recognizable for the people carrying out the process. As with all standards in Lean, it should represent the best known way of doing the step. The Standard Time helps the team to design processes that are capable of delivering value at the rate required. We can then measure how much time it takes in reality. The difference shows us where the process can be improved. In practice, differences between the standard times and measured times reveal waste in the process step.

One of the important measures that provides insight into the process is the takt time, which can be called the "heartbeat" of the process. Takt time is defined as the pace the process must maintain in order to keep up with the pace of incoming customer demand. It is in effect the average rate at which customer requests enter the process. This determines the speed of the process. Takt time allows the team to determine which standard times are necessary for the process to match customer demand. If the process is too much slower than the takt time, inventory will build at the beginning of the process. If the process is faster than the takt time, resources may remain idle or inventory will build up at the end of the process. Takt time is calculated by dividing the net working time available by the number of incoming customer requests during that time. Takt time is vital for managing the flow of a process and understanding how long can be spent on the steps in the process. Takt time is especially relevant for service desks because of the volume of units of work entering it, but the diversity of units of work in technical teams means that an understanding of takt time can help to segment and distribute work efficiently within the team.

A service desk receives on average 100 calls per working day. Measured over opening hours from 08:00 to 18:00, the takt time is 6 minutes, based on an average of 10 calls per 60 minutes. Unfortunately, the distribution of calls is uneven over the day with 70% of the calls being received during the first half of the day. During the first five hours, the takt time is now calculated as 14 calls in 60 minutes, i.e. 4.2 minutes. The takt time in the afternoon is increased to 10 minutes (6 calls per hour). This has a significant effect on the resources required to meet the customer's requirements.

The next piece of information we need to add to the VSM is lead time, the time between the moment a customer requests something and the moment that it was delivered. To calculate lead time, we subtract the time the request was submitted from the time the customer received the requested performance. The lead time is strongly related to work-in-progress. Shortening lead time often goes hand-in-hand with the reduction of the work-in-progress.

Time metrics are added to the VSM. These must be based on measurements. Most measurements can be derived from tooling. However, it may be necessary to go the gemba to measure how the work gets done.

The four most important measures to start with are cycle time (sometimes known as process time) which is the time we actually spend on creating the product or service. In the ideal situation, this is only Value-Add time. In the first pass of analysis, the cycle time will include time spent on Necessary Non-Value-Add and Non-Value-Add activities because the data has not yet been split into these categories. In the course of the execution of a non-standard change, the measurements derived from the tool may readily provide information on the time between steps in the process based on status information. However, it may be difficult to identify how much of the time in the step is VA, NNVA or NVA.

The second type of time is waiting time. This is time spent on waiting for the next activity and is relatively easy to identify. Together, cycle time and waiting time make up the time spent in a process. These are recorded on the serrated line, the time line, underneath the process steps. A key measure of the flow of the process is Process Cycle Efficiency (PCE). This is the percentage of total lead time spent on Value-Adding activities and is stated at the end of the timeline in a Value Stream Map. Dividing cycle time by the lead time provides a good indication of the process cycle efficiency, without having to do detailed analysis of each step to split out the VA activities.

Two other useful time measures are machine time and changeover time. Machine time is the time the product is worked on by a machine. In the case of IT, we see machine time when database reorganization needs to take place or when a Business Intelligence system needs to load data. Changeover time is the time needed to reconfigure a device between two units of work. Within IT, we find this kind of time when we need to adjust a development environment between different program changes. Within IT, there is another form of changeover time that is much more difficult to measure: the effect of changing the unit of work that a person is working on. Otherwise known as the time related to context-switching, teams may be particularly affected by this form of waste if they tackle many different units of work on a single day. This is something that team leaders must be aware of when goals of the week are set. Having too many goals will inherently include context-switching. The largest single cause of context-switching, however, is entirely self-imposed: not finishing work first time round and having to go back to it. For example, a team member is trying to solve an incident but needs a colleague to help with the solution. The incident solver chooses to set the incident aside rather than contact the colleague at that moment. Setting the incident to one side in favor of another unit of work creates the first bit of context-switching. Going back to the incident is the second bit of context-switching. Incidents that are bounced through an IT organization constitute huge amounts of changeover time. Machine time and changeover time are really specific forms of waiting time.

For each step in the process and for the process as a whole, we can also add process metrics. The capacity is the calculated maximum production volume of a process or process step. This helps to identify what the theoretical capability of the process or process step is. The throughput is the actual production volume of a process or process step, taking all constraints into consideration. Throughput shows us how far we are from using the available capacity to its fullest. Work-in-progress (WIP) is the average volume of work that is in the process (step) at any point in time. WIP is an absolutely vital measure. It is about understanding how many units of work are being worked on at once, and gives an indication of the level of flow in the process. Lastly, parallel lines is the number of simultaneously operating lines of work. Having insight into the number of parallel lines can help us to understand whether there are bottlenecks that may be remedied by adding extra processing capacity. This could mean both people and machines are added to increase the capacity of the process step. Each of these metrics gives us a richer understanding of the process, and helps us to analyze the process.

There are two calculations in a Value Stream Map that help to understand how it is performing. These are Process Cycle Efficiency (PCE) and calculation related to Little's Law. PCE is calculated by dividing the time spent on Value-Adding activities by the total lead time. This tells us what percentage of the total lead time, the unit of work is actually being worked on. This measure is vital as it indicates whether a process is in flow or not. To be clear, most IT processes have very low PCEs. Little's Law helps us to understand the relationship between lead time and work-in-progress. By dividing the number of units of work in the process (inventory) by the average completion rate, we can calculate the average lead time for a unit of work. These calculations can be done over the entire process, but also for each process step. This helps to create a richer picture of the dynamics of the process, and identify where the issues exist.

The final step is to add symbols to the Value Stream Map. These symbols come in two categories: Waste and Other Symbols. The first type of symbol is waste. Here, the aim is to define where types of waste are present. It is reasonable to assume that where there are waiting times, there is probably inventory. We do not necessarily need to put the inventory symbol at each location. It is about identifying and recording the wastes with the most influence on the process. On top of the waste symbols, there are a few other symbols that help us create a readable Value Stream Map. We can distinguish between physical flows and information flows. In IT processes, the most important flows are information flows. The core IT process of developing software to making it available to customers is an example of an information flow. However, it could be argued that this is a physical flow of a product through, for example, a continuous delivery pipeline. This is where we see the IT context causing some challenges as compared to Lean in a manufacturing environment. When we investigate the delivery of hardware, we must take the physical flow into account. One very useful symbol is called the kaizen "burst." This symbol illustrates the areas where more investigation is required; we know something is wrong but we have not been able to identify it sufficiently. We need to define a problem statement and work towards a solution. It may be necessary to produce a new SIPOC and more detailed VSM for that part of the process (Figure 23.12).

It is rare for all information and numerical data to be available during the first session of creating a VSM. Mostly the session will be adjourned until week 3, and in the meantime, measurements will be done regarding the time aspects of the VSM.

During the four-week analysis phase, the Lean IT coach plays an important role in coordinating the collection of data and measurements. In this phase, the coach ensures that the team leader can focus on

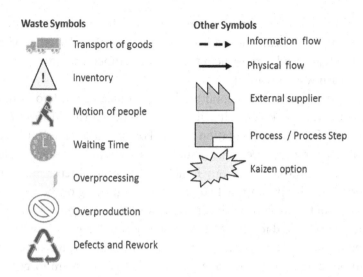

FIGURE 23.12
Common symbols used in a value stream map.

understanding and practicing the changing role of leadership, while the coach ensures that the activities related to the analyses are carried out. This means that the coach must know how all of the tools work, what they are used for, what needs to be done to gain the insights that the tool provides, and how to analyze the results of the tool.

The week ends with a review of the commitment document in which improvements the team intends to make are recorded. This does not mean that improvement cannot already start; preferably the team should start right away, improving their way of working.

WEEK 3

The team has reached the halfway mark of the Analysis phase. Mostly, teams are quite pleased with what has happened so far, although there is a growing realization that this Lean stuff is for real. When the team realizes that there will be more analysis this week and there is an expectation that some of the improvements identified must be implemented as well, some resistance starts to appear. It mostly comes in the form of team members saying they "just want to get back to work." Remember, we are still in the Know What stage. Team members still see work and Lean as two separate things. Through the Leadership transformation, the team leader is starting to understand that Lean and work are one and the same. Together with the coach, the team leader must help the team to embed the Lean principles into the team way of working.

Week 3 starts with the second week start. Once again, two hours are planned for the week start. It will gradually be shortened to one hour by the end of the Implementation phase. For now, the team must spend the time learning the week start ritual. This second week start is often a bit of a disappointment. For our Functional Support Web team, it is no exception. The disappointment comes at the beginning of the week start, as the goals of the week from the previous week are evaluated. One by one, each ticket is checked for completion. Usually about a quarter of the goals are deemed to be complete. There is a number of reasons for a goal of the week to be marked as incomplete. The first is that the team forgot about the goal, or did not get round to doing it. The second is that the deliverable is missing a component, usually documentation or communication to one or more stakeholders. Some of the decisions to declare a goal unfinished are contentious, because delivering a change without documentation was never a reason to mark it as incomplete in the past. Here, the concept of Definition of Done is very useful. A short time-out is sometimes useful at this point, to put together a list of criteria which allow the team to identify whether a goal of the week is truly finished. Alternatively, the list of criteria is set up as part of a daily kaizen exercise. Another reason for a goal of the week to be deemed incomplete is that the deliverable was misjudged in terms of size or a key meeting for the deliverable was postponed; both reasons cause a delay. The final reason is simply that the team or an individual chose to do something different. The question here is of course, why?

At the end of the evaluation, the team sees that most of last week's goals of the week have spilled over into the current week. This is a defining moment for the team as a number of mechanisms that explain the "busyness" become painfully clear. The next half-hour is spent analyzing what actually happened. Mostly, the team members place the blame for the incomplete goals of the week on outside factors. The coach is there to challenge this fatalistic mindset. The question is: "What could *you* have done to ensure that the goals of the week were completed?"

One of the main reasons is that team members accept work that is not in the plan. They did it without discussing it with the team leader, even though it was agreed the previous week that any work not on the week board would only be accepted after approval from the team leader. After all, the slack time was owned by the team leader. "Yes, but ..." is the standard response, "the customer came to my desk and I could hardly say no." This one sentence is probably the most prominent driver of work not getting done by the team. Based on a slightly distorted sense of customer orientation, team members drop work that was committed in favor of work that someone pressures them into doing. To be clear: IT has the right to stick to a planned set of goals of the week, since they represent previously requested customer value. There are very few things that cannot wait a couple of days, until the next week. I hear you say: "Incidents" and you would be right, but the team has reserved time for those, so nobody needs to wait for those to be solved.

At this point, one of the team members points out that they wanted to consult with the team leader regarding a bit of unplanned work, "but the team leader was never there." The "never" bit is exaggerated, but the signal is clear. The behavior of the team leader needs to change. Often, they will spend as little as 10% of their time with the team, spending the rest of their time in their office or in meetings, out of sight of the team members. The fact that team leaders need to increase the time spent with the team to at least 50% often comes as somewhat of a shock. Team leaders who are not accustomed to spending time with their teams, choosing to focus on fulfilling demands from higher up the hierarchy, tend to feel very awkward as they increase the time spent with the team. This awkwardness is also a result of the team's reaction to their presence. As the team leader learns how to interact with the team, the awkwardness subsides. This is part of the "Go to the Gemba" mantra from the Leadership Transformation.

Another big excuse is: "Yes, but ... I had an incident to solve." The coach or team leader usually joins in at this point reminding the team that time was reserved for incidents. This should not have affected the goals of the week. A discussion then starts about the number of incidents and whether the time reserved for incidents was correct. Based on the averages, the chance of receiving substantially more incidents than for which time was reserved is small. And even if there were more incidents, there should have been some slack time available to accommodate for at least some, if not all, these incidents. The interesting aspect is that usually nobody has bothered to keep track of the number of incidents nor inform the team leader when the planned time is exceeded. The monitoring of this kind of metric must become a daily occurrence for both the team and team leader (see Leader Standard Work).

One leader cautioned me for the use of averages. "When we do a large release," he said, "we can expect to get more incidents than average, but we don't know how many. Even with Scrum teams bringing code live every week or fortnight, we have moments when all of the delivered value is brought together. At these moments, there are often peaks in the number of incidents." And many have delivered the same caution over the years.

There are two key points here.

1. Why do we necessarily need to have more incidents? If the team (and the leader) focus on building in quality at the source, the team should be able to integrate changes into the production environment without excessive incidents. Especially through the use of the concepts and tooling associated with continuous delivery, teams can—continuously—improve their ability to carry out faultless changes.

2. If the team knows when the release moment is going to happen—and they know—then they can factor in an additional level of reserved time in the capacity planning for that week, to ensure they can deal with the expected increase in customer demand in the form of incidents.

Either way the use of averages is still valid but does not mean that they should be slavishly followed.

A fourth reason for not achieving the goals of the week is: "I had a project I was working on." Then a discussion starts as to what work needs to go on the week board. The conclusion is: *all work*. Many IT organizations work with two separate flows of work. There is "regular" work and there is project work. The project work gets doled out by the project managers and regular work comes from different sources. The "different source" is usually the work recorded in the service management tool. The lesson learned is that work required of the team *must* be on the week board. The problem with project work is that team members are allocated to a project for a particular percentage of their time, irrespective of whether that time is actually used. This allows project managers to work in a very ad hoc way. A project manager knows, for example, that a person is allocated to the project for 40% of their time. Without notice, one project manager let one of the team members know on Wednesday that they were needed on Thursday and Friday. The team member had not expected to have to work on the project any more that week, and had allocated time on

Thursday and Friday to goals of the week. The team learned that both team leader and team members should ensure that project work is part of the goals of the week, otherwise both the project and the goals of the week will face delays. Unplanned goals of the week do not get done, unless the team leader agrees. A project manager can pull the stunt of submitting an emergency change twice before he gets a reputation of not being on top of his project. And no project manager wants to go there. Take a look behind the last two reasons and we find two problem areas: dependencies and "unplanned" work. Both have the capacity to destroy flow.

Dependencies are probably the largest cause of waiting time for IT teams. One of the challenges in this phase is for the team to start identifying the dependencies that create the most delays. There are three categories of dependencies: other teams within IT, suppliers and customers. They need to be worked on in that order. Reducing the dependencies within IT calls for teams to allow other teams into their "domain." A classic case is that an application team needs the network team to open a port. Segregation of duties (muri) and lack of capability (muda—talent waste) are two reasons why this dependency exists. Teams need to investigate how they can co-operate in order to reduce this waste. This will be picked up in the implementation phase.

Unplanned work is another concept bandied around within IT. Its rise to prominence comes from Scrum and, although there is no formal definition of the concept, it basically includes any work that was not on the (planned) backlog. Since most of what is on a backlog is made up of user stories (i.e. changes), units of work like incidents and service requests are often defined as unplanned work. It is important for the team to realize that this work is "plannable" to a certain extent and that is that the team can reserve time to tackle these units of work. Through the capacity planning exercise as carried out during the week start, the team can start to identify which work is truly unexpected and unplanned, and which work is predictable, only its exact timing is uncertain. Unplanned work should focus exclusively on the work that is submitted to the team during the week, for which no time was reserved. The decision as to whether this work should be done resides with the team leader.

The team is faced with a simple question that is not always easy to answer: How will the team ensure that it does achieve its goals of the week? The first answer is almost always "by having fewer goals." After some discussion, it becomes clear that the team will not make any progress if it does not take on a realistic number of goals. Reducing the number of goals to a handful only ensures that less value is delivered to the customer. And the aim is to deliver *more* customer value. More solutions are suggested, until someone says "Why don't we just stick to the plan and refer any interference to the plan to the team leader? She can decide what needs to be done and defer the rest of the demand until next week."

The other practical solution is that the team gathers at the week board on Wednesday afternoon for a quick check whether the goals are being met. This one solution opens the door to discussing the day board ... maybe next week or the week after that. There may still be some resistance in the team regarding the day board in this second week. Experience shows that the day board gains greater acceptance as time goes by.

Fast forward to Wednesday: The team meets at the week board and checks the progress of the goals of the week. The goals of the week are not ordered neatly on the board, so the team has to go through them one by one asking the team member carrying out the goal of the week what the status of the goal is. If you ever wanted to hear the sentence "I'm working on it," now is the time to be with the team. After a series of I'm-working-on-its and a fairly inefficient process of understanding where the team stands with their goals of the week, usually a small group gets together to think up a better way to monitor progress. Support for the introduction of the day board, or kanban board, starts to grow.

This is actually quite a good moment to introduce the concept of pull into the team. Pull is one of the five Lean principles, but what is the difference between a Push and a Pull system?

A Push System produces a product or service before the customer has actually ordered the product or service. The product is so-called "pushed" through the process. The key effect is that we produce to stock: Push processes always have inventory. In general, this is mostly final product but also work-in-progress. Push systems use a mechanism called Batch and Queue. We produce a certain number of products in one go and then store them in stock until the next step in the process takes place. Push production systems tend to work with forecast demand schedules rather than actual demand. This type of production always accentuates the bottlenecks in the system since each process step produces at maximum capacity. The process step with the lowest capacity will become the step with the greatest inventory preceding it. In IT, the introduction of the ITIL Problem Management process is a classic case of "Push." When the organization starts, it encourages the teams to identify the problems they intend to solve, with a complete disregard for when these problems will actually be tackled. The result is that a large inventory of problems is identified, most of which remain on the pile for … a very long time.

A Pull System works differently. The value stream starts when the customer places an order. In effect, we let the customer pull the product or service through production. The ultimate version of a Pull System is just-in-time production in which inventory is brought into the process at the moment that it is needed in a Value-Adding step. In reality, most Pull Systems have small inventories to support the leveling of production. The ideal situation is that a single product is pulled through the process as and when the customer needs it. This is known as Single Piece Flow. In this situation, there will be no bottlenecks since each step in the process is capable of processing, at least, a single unit of work at a time. The key to a Pull System is that the team knows how much capacity it has and understands the throughput. They know how many units of work can be in a single process step at any one time. As a slot opens up in one step, work can be pulled from the earlier step, creating space for work to be done earlier in the process. The aim is to ensure that there is always some capacity available in the process to accommodate variability in customer demand. At the same time, the team works to reduce the variability in demand. Take our Problem Management case above. A Pull System for Problem Management involves creating a particular capacity per week (in the weekly capacity plan) and then solving problems in the reserved capacity. A workable strategy for most IT teams is to reserve 8–12 hours of team time and commit to solving one problem per week. This may not seem like much but, if this is done every week for a year, most IT teams will have structurally halved (if not more) their incoming incidents.

Kanban is a key part of the pull/replenishment system, as opposed to a push/scheduling system. It uses signals to ensure that production is leveled. The ultimate form of production is single piece flow, which enables mass-customization. Kanban is not an inventory control system; it is a scheduling system that helps determine what to produce, when to produce it, and how much to produce. A simple example is that an empty slot on the day board means that there is space for new work, the empty slot works as a replenishment signal for a new kanban. Again, this is a visual system that benefits from clear simple information that can be identified at a distance. Often, different colors are used to identify different types of work. These kanban tickets are typically used on the day board. The benefit is that the requirements for information processing can be simplified as a result of

Kanban, since we know exactly what information is needed to ensure the progress of the unit of work.

Scrum is a classic Lean case of managing demand to match the capacity of the team. A sprint backlog contains the amount of work that the team expects to carry out in two weeks. Experience has shown that working with week starts effectively means working with a one-week sprint. This is perfectly adequate and, in fact, more suitable for most IT teams.

In the second week, the team started looking at the value streams in which the team is involved. Removing the TIMWOOD waste (muda) is an important aspect. However, the team needs to look at the variability in the process as well. The Lean concept for this purpose is production leveling or heijunka. Heijunka is vital for achieving flow. It means ensuring that each process step can handle the same number of units of work per unit of time. The aim is to produce intermediate products and services at a constant rate so that further processing may also be carried out at a constant and predictable rate. One of the ways to achieve heijunka is through reducing bottlenecks. We can do this by adding parallel lines or other capacity, or increasing the efficiency of steps so as to bring the process time into sync with other steps in the process. Combining the concepts of pull and heijunka helps the team to understand what type of board they need to manage the progress of work. As we saw when starting out with visual management, the board could either be a time-based board (day board) in which the team can manage the progress work and the capacity of the team based on the days of the week, or they can choose a kanban board which focuses on the progress of work through the main delivery process, monitoring the capacity of each step in the process rather than directly relating capacity to individuals as is done with the day board.

The discussion of pull, production-leveling and kanban brings us back to the processes. The team has built and analyzed the current state of the Value Stream Map. In week 3, the Value Stream Map must be completed with the numbers. The numbers to be collected will have been identified in the second week and small measurements will have taken place in the meantime. With the help of the various VSM-related measurements described earlier, the team can identify steps in the process where improvements are needed.

Once the VSM has been produced, the team must analyze it. Areas to investigate include what policy-based waste is associated with the process (muri)? Where do we find variability and what is causing it (mura)?

What kind of waste is in the process (muda)? How can we understand and improve the flow of the process? Lastly, but certainly one of the more important aspects, how can we ensure that each step is carried out "first time right"? These questions lead to the identification of improvement areas in the process.

Next, the team must plan which improvement to implement and how this will be done. Notice that the team starts with a single improvement. There is a tendency for the team to become overambitious, create a long list of improvements and then fail to implement any of them. The plan must cover no more than twelve weeks, preferably within the eight weeks of the implementation phase. In fact, mostly, the chosen improvement can be carried out within one week. Ideally, the team should ensure that the improvement is delivering the intended benefits before working on the next improvement. Often, the effect of introducing an improvement in a process is wider than just the area where the improvement is introduced. This is why you should wait to see the effect of an improvement; you may get more benefits than you expected. Whatever happens, the situation in the process will have changed, meaning that previously identified improvements may no longer be suitable.

If the plan is longer than twelve weeks, then the team must focus on smaller improvements that can be carried out more quickly. Obviously, there may be improvements that may take longer, for example, increasing server or network capacity, but even these improvements can be broken down into smaller steps. The team must discuss the proposed actions with the stakeholders. When it comes to process improvements, this will mean talking with other teams that deliver work to or receive work from the team, or discussing changes with customers or suppliers. It is important to have their commitment and to ensure that where decisions are required, they are made. Finally, the team and other people in the process must act as owners of the improvements and must carry out the improvements themselves. This has been shown to help in the acceptance of changes among other people in the process. There is a tendency at the beginning for team members to expect the coach or the leader to take the lead in implementing improvements. However, a key behavioral change is to ensure that the team starts to take responsibility for its own processes and work.

Value Stream Mapping helps the team to effectively understand, analyze and identify improvements to processes. In small steps, they take a process from its current state to a future state which, through implementing and sustaining of improvements, becomes the new, improved current state of the process.

Week 3 is an important one from the perspective of measurement. There are three areas where measurements that were started in the first two weeks need to start delivering results: performance indicators, time writing (ECA) and Value Stream Mapping. We have discussed the VSM measurements. Let us turn our attention to the performance indicators and time-writing.

At this stage of the analysis, the team may have identified performance indicators they wish to measure. However, there may currently not be sufficient data available to actually do this. Often, the team must resort to measuring what it can measure. In week 2, the team focused on finding the data. Now it is time to process that data into metrics that can be used to steer team performance. Most teams can measure the following performance indicators of the key units of work (incidents, service requests and changes): the number of units of work opened and closed per day/week, the average lead time over time, the number currently open (inventory) and the age of open units of work. These indicators are mostly available per technology type, customer (group), location and other such specifiers. Given either real or fictitious service levels, it is possible for the team to determine what percentage of units of work fall within and outside the service levels.

The first graphs concern the numbers of opened and closed incidents and service requests (Figure 23.13, Figure 23.14).

This is the first moment of contention within the team, regarding the measurements. More will follow. The team works on incidents and service requests that they do not close and therefore are not part of the count. This causes an underestimation of the number of units of work processed. The team resolves to maintain a check sheet of incidents and service requests that they are asked to work on but do not close, so that they can gain insight into additional work. One of the key metrics is the average number of incidents and service requests received per day. These numbers are fed into the capacity plan to make it more accurate.

Next, the average lead times are analyzed. These are almost always fairly disappointing, especially for second line teams. The average lead times of incidents and service requests tend to be longer, sometimes much longer than expected (Figure 23.15).

There is disbelief and assertions that the data is wrong. Looking through the source data proves that the data is correct. The calculation of lead time

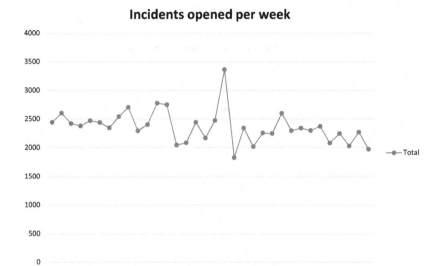

FIGURE 23.13
Incidents opened per week.

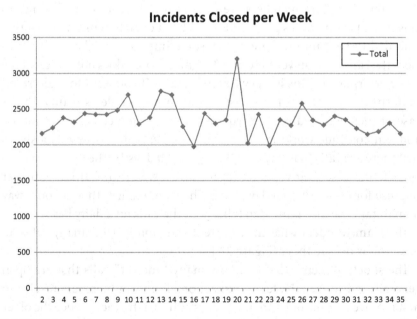

FIGURE 23.14
Incidents closed per week.

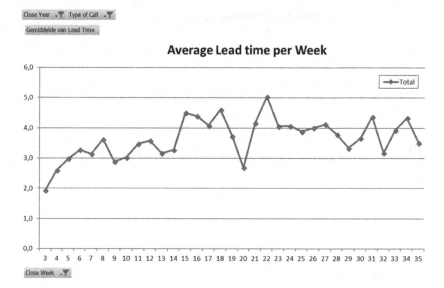

FIGURE 23.15
Average lead time of incidents per week.

cannot be faulted. The conversation turns to the behavior of the team. It turns out that team members are not always diligent when it comes to closing calls, sometimes purposefully ("I left it open to remind myself that I needed to look into the problem"), sometimes by mistake ("I forgot to close the call"). Whatever the cause, the information does not represent the true performance. This is a key lesson learned: If you want to understand performance, the team must ensure that the data reflects reality. In the case of incidents and service requests, if the customer has their answer and can continue working, the call must be closed. The raw data shows that there are calls that stay open for up to 300 days(!). The team members agree to increase their vigilance regarding calls. But how? This is a further impulse for establishing a day board. The team realizes that the only way to maintain the discipline is to talk about the calls on a daily basis.

The team wonders what their current situation is. How many calls are open? How old are they? (Figure 23.16)

The shock of seeing that there are many "ancient" calls that are open generally galvanizes the team into action. The team members resolve to first remove all calls older than 100 days and then further reduce the older calls, until there are only calls that are less than 15 days old. An associated measure is the number of days of inventory. Knowing how many calls are open and the average number received per day, we divide the former by

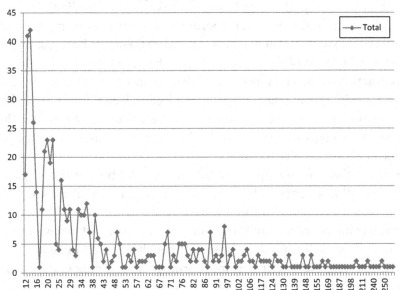

Age of Open Incidents

FIGURE 23.16
The long tail.

the latter to calculate a "number of days of inventory" metric. This number should be a maximum of one. Most teams have inventories amounting to between five and seven days of inventory. In the spirit of Lean, this is waste.

An average resolver group (i.e. not the service desk) receives five to ten incidents per day, and a similar number of service requests. Generally, the numbers amount to one to two calls per team member. Teams that receive more will need to work on stabilizing their (part of the) service quickly. The team agrees that they have sufficient time to solve these incidents and service requests. The problem is now the time needed to catch up.

There is another angle to the excess inventory: coordination (derived waste). At an organizational level, we may see, for example, that there are 200 incidents and 300 service requests per week (100 calls per day). Usually half to two-thirds of these calls are handled at the service desk. The rest go through to resolver groups. Even so, there will be some 500–600 calls open at any one time across the organization. The automatic reflex of most IT managers is: "We need coordinators." And so each team appoints an incident coordinator who doubles as a dispatcher within the team. This is all overhead, people spending time shuffling open tickets when they could be solving them. Fast forward to a moment that the teams have one day's worth of inventory. The team leader can take on the coordination of the calls; better still, the team can coordinate the calls between them. The numbers are so small that it is easy to monitor them. We have just saved a substantial portion of time. Depending on the size of the IT organization, coordination of calls may amount to many man-hours of work per week. All it takes is ensuring the team gets daily feedback on the number of days of inventory, and driving this down relentlessly. The added benefit is that the team no longer feels swamped by the negativity caused by a large pile of incidents and service requests.

Some of the most anticipated results are those of the Earning Capacity Analysis. This is often a huge surprise to the leader. Previously, the team voiced a complete aversion towards time writing. Now, the team is extremely interested in what their time-writing of the past two weeks says about their work. The result looks something like the table in Figure 23.17.

The subcategories under Earning, Burning and Learning Capacity may vary from team to team depending on the level of detail and the specific type of work per team, but the results are almost always surprising in some way or another. It starts with the overall ratio. Learning Capacity is more often than not sorely under-represented, and the amount of Earning Capacity is generally disappointing to the team. They find that they spend far too much time on NVA activities. One IT organization turned out to have coordination alone (part of Burning Capacity) at over 30%, a ratio of almost 2:1, with the 2 representing Earning Capacity *and* the other Burning Capacity categories. This excess of coordination was a result of muri (policy-based waste). Each change was supplied with a coordinator who was allowed book time on the change. Some changes contained more coordination time than work time. Agreed, these are the excesses but coordination time is like wire hangers in a wardrobe, they have a strange habit of mysteriously multiplying while we are looking the other way.

EC/BC/LC	Sum of Hours	Sum of Uren %
Earning Capacity	304470	52,36%
Burning Capacity	80126,3	13,78%
Burning Capacity (Coordination)	145795,4	25,07%
Burning Capacity (Rework)	30932,2	5,32%
Learning Capacity	20126,9	3,46%
Grand Total	581450,8	100,00%

FIGURE 23.17
Results of ECA.

Therein lies the problem, leaders do not appreciate the value of time data and do not use it to question the wisdom of choices made. Management roles represent sufficient coordination capacity without creating more.

Another interesting finding is the effect of interruptions. Most team members accept as a fact of life that they will be interrupted in their work. The perception is that short interruptions are not a problem. The ECA of a number of teams has revealed that interruptions often lead to distractions amounting to on average 40 minutes. The team members commit to being more respectful of each other's time, i.e. only interrupt if an impediment threatens to stop work from progressing.

Lastly, the team turns to the numbers on the VSM. These confirm the impression given by both the metrics and the ECA: There is a lot of waiting time. The problem with the waiting time is that it is barely visible to the team members as they can always be busy; if work on one unit of work is impeded, there is always another unit of work that can be worked on. The effect of waiting time falls squarely in the lap of the customer. This realization comes not so much as a surprise but as a confirmation of something the customers have been saying for some time. The team resolves to attack this problem in the implementation phase (Figure 23.18).

Figure 23.18 represents a fairly typical change management process for non-standard changes. The Process Cycle Efficiency (PCE) is also fairly representative. Of the total time that changes exist, they are worked on for 3% of that time. This was the VSM for a relatively small IT organization. In larger IT organizations, the PCE only gets worse as a result of technical silos and competing priorities. A PCE of 1% is quite normal.

Just to check your understanding of PCE. If you were to raise the PCE from 1% to 2%, what would the reaction of your customers be?

1. They would be thoroughly annoyed with such a small improvement.
2. They wouldn't notice the difference.
3. They would be mildly happy.
4. They would be ecstatically happy, singing your praises from every rooftop.

If you chose D, you were right. Raising the PCE from 1% to 2% involves reducing the waiting time by 50% while keeping the time worked on the change the same. Imagine your average lead time for changes is six months (not uncommon) and you reduce it to three months. Your customers will

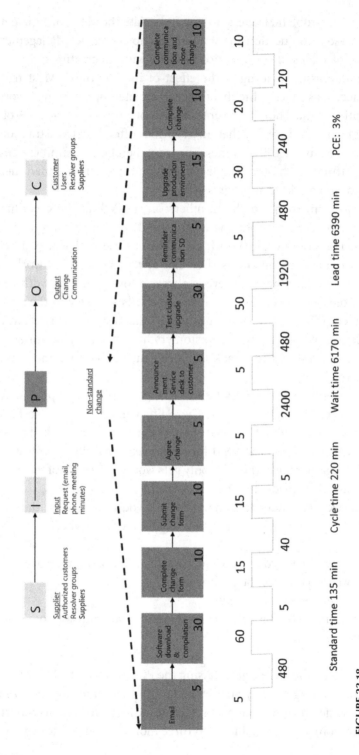

FIGURE 23.18

VSM change management.

think you are simply brilliant. How far we have sunk, to give our customers such pleasure with such, on the face of it, poor performance.

When it comes to improving processes, there is a Lean concept that helps to improve the basic health of a process and the work environment, 5S. 5S provides us with a set of hygiene rules that help to, for lack of a better word, clean up our processes: Sort, Simplify or Set in Order, Shine, Standardize and Sustain. Sort is about eliminating all unnecessary tools, parts and instructions. We aim to keep only essential items and eliminate what is not required, prioritizing items based on their importance to the process and keeping them in easily-accessible places. Removing all obsolete work instructions, manuals and software is part of Sort. Simplify or Set in Order ensures that everything is in the right place. There should be a place for everything and everything should be in its place. Also, the place for each item should be clearly indicated. This is about getting SOPs and other instructions in the right place on your document repository so that people can find them easily. Standard use of the Configuration Management Database (CMDB) is a "Set in Order" activity. Shine is simply about keeping the workspace and all equipment clean, tidy and organized. At the end of each shift or working day, the work area must be cleaned and everything must be put back in its place. For IT, this means, among other things, a clean desk policy or ensuring that work is checked in. Standardizing is a very important activity within Lean. Work practices should be consistent and standardized. All employees doing the same job should be able to work in any station with the same tools that are in the same location in every station, with the same standard procedures. Standardizing makes doing work easier, particularly routine work, and it makes it easier for resources to take over work if necessary. Given that we have seen that non-standard changes can take a significant time to get through the process, there is a substantial incentive to standardize changes so that they can be carried out more quickly. Unfortunately, many IT organizations do not see the value in standardizing, perceiving it to take more time than it saves, especially when you take into account that you need to keep the SOPs up-to-date. In fact, standardizing *always* saves time, especially because it opens the door to the automation of standardized work. Lastly, we must Sustain what we have created. This means maintaining and reviewing standards. Once the previous 4 S's have been established, they become the new way to operate. Investigating each of these aspects in relation to each process step can help to ensure that processes become more efficient through simple improvements.

The measurements serve as a baseline, an initial measurement against which future measurements can be plotted to check whether improvements have had an effect. At the same time, as a result of the application of 5S, a number of improvements have been identified. These are in danger of being lost, if not recorded. To ensure all problems are captured, an improvement board is posted on the wall. All identified problems and potential improvements are written on sticky notes and posted on the improvement board. The coach encourages the team members to post new problems or potential improvements on the board.

The initial reaction to week starts is often not universally positive because a known habit, the traditional fortnightly team meeting, is changed. The greatest change is the fact that there is more emphasis on carrying out the agreed actions. This is often a feature of traditional team meetings. Any "extracurricular" activities, i.e. goals not directly related to customer delivery, were often forgotten or simply not actioned. In the week start, everything defined as a goal of the week is treated with equal importance in that everything needs to be completed. If the team commits to goals of the week, then it must be completed irrespective of whether it was internally or customer oriented. As the team members get used to the new ritual, a feeling of achievement settles on the team, replacing a feeling of inadequacy related to all the things that were not done.

The day start is a different proposition. Even though the team has clearly identified the need to monitor progress on a daily basis, the introduction of the day start still meets resistance. The key comment is that the day starts are a waste of time because having a team of, for example, ten people standing around for fifteen minutes is a classic case of waste. It is important for the team to realize that the fifteen minutes replaces or rather prevents a series of bilateral information discussions that occur throughout the day, in which who is doing what is discussed. It is important that the team starts feeling the reward of freeing up time that is currently lost, to do other more productive work. There are always people who see a direct benefit as they had become thoroughly disillusioned, bored and fed up with the lack of progress, or the fact that proposed actions always got delayed. The day start often requires more coaching and more attention as team members choose to turn up late or choose to plan meetings in parallel to the day start. This is behavior that needs to be dealt with swiftly by the team leader. The week start and day starts are cornerstones for the team. They help to cement the team feeling and collective performance ethic.

In a software development team, when a new piece of software is developed, it must be visible that this unit of work ("user story") needs to be processed. The unit of work must be posted on a visual Product Backlog containing the work that needs to be done. The software development team places the ticket for the new piece of software on their kanban board. This board may represent the most basic of processes with "To Do" items, "Doing" items and "Done" items. Alternatively, the kanban board may show the process steps in greater detail so that units of work can be tracked through the process and impediments can be identified as soon as it becomes clear that a unit of work is not progressing across the board as expected. The work selected from the backlog is put into the "To Do" section. Here we see alignment with the customer in that the team indicates what capacity it has for customer work in the next two weeks, and together with the customer determines which units of work have the greatest business value. Embedded in the To Do – Doing – Done flow is the Definition of Done concept. This describes the organizational and quality requirements for the finished product. The Definition of Done helps to establish and enforce standards.

In an IT operations team, the day board will mostly be filled with units of work that need to be done on a particular day. Carrying out standard changes, deploying software to the production environment and working on non-standard infrastructure changes often need to be done at specific times on specific dates. An operations team will therefore need to plan work for specific days of the week. First, they will appear as one or more goals of the week and, subsequently, they will be allocated to a person for execution on a particular day. On top of this, capacity will need to be reserved for solving incidents, doing operational work and answering service

Visual management at the service desk is a different proposition to that of a development or operations team. It is impossible and senseless to create a separate ticket for each call and post it on the day board. The day board will focus on understanding how customer interaction is being handled: What types of requests are coming in? Through which channels are these requests coming to the service desk? How much use is being made of self-service facilities? For what types of requests do customers use which channels? This means that much of the day board will be made up of metrics on the flow of calls to the service desk. The rest of the board will be made up of the exceptions, the calls that are not processed promptly

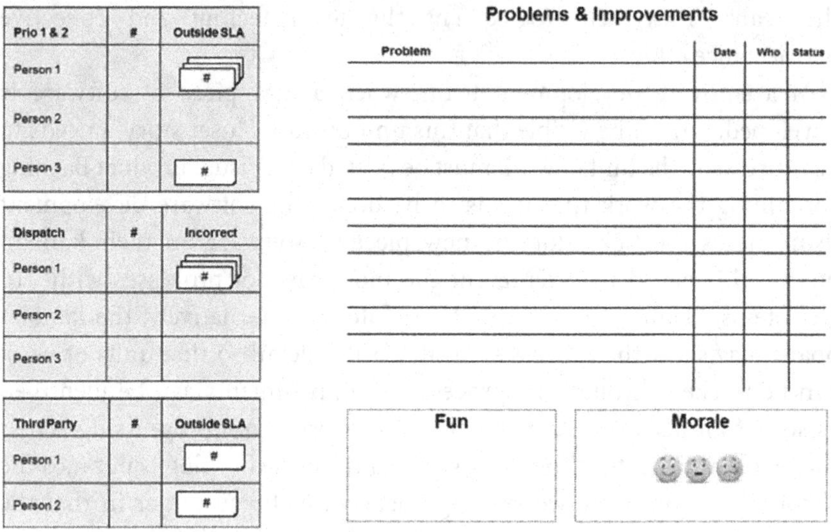

FIGURE 23.19
Example of visual management for a service desk.

through the process. During the day start, the service desk team will focus on special categories of calls, such as high priority calls that are overdue, calls routed to third parties, calls incorrectly dispatched and the number of overdue calls in each resolver group. The service desk will align with both the IT operations team and the software development team by feeding back information regarding the problems with IT services. In addition, they will present possible improvements to the way the teams work (Figure 23.19).

The discussion starts regarding the suitability of the visual management introduced into the team. The coach must emphasize that the current visual management is a starting point from which to improve. Similar to leadership teams, operational teams are initially reluctant to adjust their own boards, believing them to be "untouchable." It is vital that the team learns that the visual management boards are theirs to do with what they see fit. Leaders must reinforce the use of the boards to ensure the new habit of using the boards has a chance to take hold.

WEEK 4

Once again, the week is kicked off with the week start. This third week start is already more effective than the previous two. Often, it will not only be more focused, with new goals of the week being clearly defined as deliverables rather than activities with increasingly accurate time estimates, but it will also be shorter as a result of the team understanding the process and goal of the meeting better. Also, many of the team members come prepared with their sticky notes.

The most marked effect is that of the capacity planning. By ensuring every week that the work "fits" in the time available without conceding reserved time to other activities, the team is starting to gain confidence in the fact that everything they plan to do, can actually be done in the week. It will still take a number of weeks for a certain level of serenity to descend over the team, but the resignation that work will not be finished off the weeks before the week start is beginning to become a memory rather than a fact of life. The team members' perception of time is changing.

The team still needs to get used to the day board and the associated daily stand-up. In this fourth week, the day start will exceed its allotted fifteen minutes as team members get used to the fact that they need to be succinct in their communication. There are team members who feel they need to explain everything they will do on that day. The team leader will need to coach the person into being better prepared, focusing on the key deliverables of the day. One aspect that is part of this coaching is to help the team member to understand the "respect every individual" principle, since each team member must have equal opportunity to share their work with the rest of the team.

The focus of this week is ensuring that all analyses are satisfactorily completed and, more importantly, discussed within the team so as to identify improvements.

The improvement board has been standing in the corner of the team's space for the last two weeks and has filled with improvements, mainly from the analyses but increasingly from the week and day starts. It is not clear to the team how to deal with this set of problems and improvements. In this fourth week, a meeting is planned for one hour to go through the sticky notes on the improvement board. This is an optional meeting, meaning that whoever has time to discuss the improvements should turn up to the meeting. Those who have other things to do, do not need to attend. The meeting is planned as a recurring meeting once a week.

Five of the team members assemble at the improvement board at the allotted time. For the first meeting, the coach takes the lead. Next to the improvement board, the coach hangs up a 2×2 matrix showing impact versus feasibility (Figure 23.20).

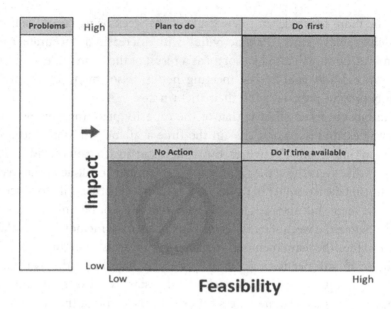

FIGURE 23.20
Improvement board "solution matrix."

The coach explains the process. Each sticky note will be read out and discussed by the team. The team members will then decide whether the improvement or problem has high or low impact first on the customer and then on the IT organization. Then the team looks at the feasibility of potential solutions. With improvements, this is relatively easy since the solution is often inherent in the proposed improvement. For problems, it is slightly more difficult because the solution is not yet clear. Team members must provide a best guess indication of whether they believe a solution has a high or low feasibility. The aim is to identify those improvements or problems that have the highest impact and feasibility. These will be tackled first. The improvements or problems with low impact and low feasibility will be discarded.

And so the team members pick up the first improvement and determine its impact and feasibility. As a result of a lack of comparison material, the improvement often ends up in the top right—let's do it—quadrant. It may take five to ten minutes to fully discuss a particular ticket. Tickets are slowly moved from the improvement board onto the 2 × 2 matrix. It is clear that not all of the improvements will be discussed. As an indication, ten to fifteen tickets can be discussed during a meeting of one hour. If a team member feels that an improvement or problem is truly urgent, then they indicate this so that the ticket can be discussed. The team must resist the urge to extend the meeting to try and deal with all of the tickets. Experience has shown that the number of tickets added per week is not extreme and the tickets will all be dealt with within a few weeks. Since only half the team is at the meeting, certain tickets may be "parked" because the person who submitted the ticket is not there to explain what they mean. Other improvements that have come from the analyses are known to the whole team.

The aim is to identify the "high-high" improvements and problems. The problems are input for kaizen sessions to be planned in the future, and the improvements for which the solutions and actions are clear, are candidates to get posted on the week board as actions for the next week. They are "candidates" because the team needs to decide how much of their discretionary time (i.e. goals of the week time) they will spend on improvements. Improvements come in all shapes and sizes which means that, for a chosen amount of time, the team may be able to carry out a single improvement or quite a few. The team sets a time limit for the execution of improvements, rather than a number. This ensures that the team knows it can fit the work into their week plan.

The implementation of the day board opens a new opportunity for the team leader to interact with the team on a different level regarding improvements. This is where the leader can practice activating daily kaizen in the team. As we saw earlier, daily kaizen is the act of responding to everyday occurrences such as incidents, mistakes and other quality issues. The focus of leaders on uncovering and dealing with problems is vital for encouraging employees to see and tackle problems they meet in their daily work. Daily kaizen is about "stopping the line" when a problem is uncovered. This is principally a kaizen mindset issue: Do we continue programming and let the testers find the errors in the code, even if this means stopping or delaying delivery? The word "actually" is quite a reliable trigger of daily kaizen: "Well, actually, we should be ensuring that we empty the log files every morning." Daily kaizen: improve the morning operations checklist. "Actually, the incident happened because I misinterpreted a step in the standard change procedure. We need to add a clarification." Daily kaizen: improve the standard operating procedure.

I have described the day board as being introduced in the third week. It is, however, possible that the team was not ready for it at that time. Its implementation then shifts to week 4 or later depending on the team's ability to manage its work using the week board. If the team can stick to its week plan, does not have many distractions in the form of incidents and service requests and/or has fewer, larger tasks rather than many smaller tasks, it is possible that the team dispenses with the day board. This makes the work of the leader more difficult because she loses a natural moment of interaction with the team. It is, however, rare that teams do not need some form of structured daily interaction. Where the daily interaction feels forced or unnecessary, there is a good chance that the "team" is not a team at all, rather a collection of individuals who have been placed together for management convenience. The leader should take the time with each individual to find out which day start (of a different team) is more suitable for their work.

The daily discussion of improvements also raises the question of the ability of team members to carry out structured problem-solving, according to the agreed problem-solving method. A short kaizen training will be carried out in week 4 or planned for week 5. Usually a half-day training by a kaizen lead including a new look at the entries on the improvement board is enough to create a common understanding. When the team intends to tackle a larger problem, it is vital that they have access to a kaizen lead who can guide them through their first few problem-solving sessions.

The most important task in week 4 is defining the goals for the implementation phase, the next eight weeks. Team members, leader and coach must review all of the evidence delivered by the various analyses of the past weeks and put together an improvement plan. The plan will focus on embedding structures that help the team to work in accordance with Lean principles.

It is time for a quick review of the past three weeks.

- The team has determined its purpose. The question is: Does the purpose still resonate with the team members? Does it need to be adjusted or clarified in any way?
- The customers of the team have been identified, and their needs have been broadly described. What improvements does the team need to make in its way of working and interaction with the customer to deliver more value?
- The units of work processed by the team have been identified. The team knows the volumes and expected time spend per category of unit of work. How does the team expect to improve the numbers in the coming time?

- The required performance has been defined in terms of performance indicators. It is now time for the team to set goals for the next eight weeks. What improvement in performance do they wish to see in the coming time? What do they feel is achievable?
- The team has investigated the way it spends its time. In what way will the team adjust the way it spends its time in the coming eight weeks, as a start to further improvements in the balance of time spend?
- The team barometer has identified areas of satisfaction and dissatisfaction within the team. What does the team intend to work on in the next eight weeks? What aspects are currently poorly addressed?
- One or more processes have been analyzed. What lessons has the team learned from this analysis? What improvements need to be made? Are there other processes that need to be analyzed?
- The team has introduced and is using visual management. What adjustments need to be made to the boards to ensure they increasingly support the team's work? What other information needs to be made available visually so as to support the team and the leadership's information needs?
- The team leader has done a leadership assessment together with the team. What behaviors does the team leader need to practice and improve in order to be more effective for the team?
- The cascade has been constructed. The links between the team and the leadership hierarchy have been instituted. Is the leader ensuring that problems escalated to a higher level of accountability are being resolved? Is the cascade providing the guidance regarding goals and vision? What improvements need to be made in this area?

The answers to the above questions should be recorded in a document and, as with all important information, posted on the wall for all to see! Usually, this will be done during a so-called commitment session in which the team voices its commitment to the goals. A significant ritual is for the team members, their team leader and the team leader's manager to sign the document, giving their commitment to the achievement of the goals. It may appear that the emphasis is now on the team to perform. To a certain extent that is true. However, through their statement of commitment, the leaders have attached themselves to the achievement of the goals as well. If the team fails, the leaders have failed as well. In this phase, it is more often than not the case that existing policies will form a barrier to improvements. We are, of course, talking about muri, policy-based waste, that leadership must work to remove.

So what are these existing policies that block improvements? It is probably more appropriate to ask which policies do *not* inhibit the creation of a high performance IT organization. Most of the structures created in the mass production phase need to be reviewed and, probably, adjusted.

The financial structures, particularly the way budgeting is done, cause all sorts of problems. One of the aims of Lean is that we organize for maximum flow. This means putting people who need to work together a lot in a team. The problem is that the budgeting rules are based on the fact that we have development departments who work on "change" and we have operations departments that work on "run." The budgets have been set up so that this duality can be monitored and managed. When we bring together the disciplines in order to increase flow, this separation in budgets no longer makes sense. The budget of the team is an expense dedicated to ensuring particular business processes or functions work well. In fact, the budgets become more aligned with their goals. As an example, an IT team has been assembled to support the sales and marketing processes. The team, made up of eight people, supports a Customer Relationship Management (CRM) system, a Content Management System (CMS) and a couple of associated systems. Let us assume the fully loaded cost of this team is one million (euros/dollars/pounds). On top of this there are license costs for the CRM, CMS and other systems, probably amounting to another million. We now know that the cost of automating the marketing and sales processes is two million. The only question that needs to be answered is: Is this amount worth it? Or: Are the marketing and sales processes gaining sufficient value from the two million invested per year? If they are, great! If not, how is the Marketing and Sales manager indicating to the team what is necessary for them to provide more value. Setting a balance of "run" and "change" spend is a pointless exercise since this will vary over time with the lifecycle of the systems. It also unnecessarily puts an administrative burden (muri) on the team.

A second financial aspect is authorizations. To what extent can the team make investment decisions based on their own insights? The chances are they will need to ask their team leader for authorization to spend money, and the team leader will probably need to have the expense authorized by other levels of leadership. Each level introduces new delays. The aim of Lean is to provide a high level of autonomy to the team. This means identifying a budget over which the team has control and which they can use as they see fit. The team is accountable for the use of the funds.

A good example of how budgeting and authorizations can stand in the way of Lean production, is how suppliers are contracted and managed. Currently, this is often a centralized function. The responsibility can be devolved, while retaining a small core staff of contracting professionals to help with specialist tasks. Looking at our Marketing and Sales team, they bear the final responsibility regarding customer data and must ensure that the customer information is both accurate and available to others who need to use it. They should be responsible for selecting, working with and managing the supplier of the CRM and CMS systems, in collaboration with the Sales and Marketing team. The team can be given the freedom to achieve an optimal contract within a given budget. In fact, if the team knows that they can spend one million on the software, hardware and communications, they can manage the budget themselves. The central purchasing function can support the team in negotiating contracts, with the team focusing on creating a working relationship with the supplier.

A third area of muri is the structure dedicated to managing projects and programs. It is not the case that there are no longer projects or programs in a Lean IT organization, it is just that the size and importance are much reduced. The coordination of large-scale developments is just done in a different way, using the various Lean mechanisms. Traditionally, a program structure aims to bring all projects together so that they can be managed in "harmony." As we saw earlier, all projects need to be represented in the obeya. In effect, the leadership team manages its own portfolio without the need to resort to a program management bureaucracy. The vast majority of projects will be managed within the teams. As with the team described above, Marketing and Sales "projects" will be managed within the Marketing and Sales department together with the IT team supporting the Marketing and Sales processes. In fact, as the team increases the flow of work, there will no longer be multiple projects on the go at any one time, but mainly the incremental improvement of processes. Obviously, there will be moments that a step change is required but this will be less frequent than is currently the case. The cascade will ensure that information regarding developments (large and small) are cascaded to the right level. All the rest should be visible through the (key) performance indicators. The IT organization remains accountable for the coherence of the entire IT landscape. However, the functional improvements become the responsibility of the "customer" organization.

Here we meet the next area of muri, the organizational structure and, more particularly, the associated areas of responsibility. A classic case is the subdivision of development and operations ("run" and "change") at senior management level. This usually translates to an IT organization that is split along these lines at the gemba, and embeds the contrast in the organization, rather than ensuring the collaboration of the two disciplines in delivering value to customers. There are many ways in which accountability can be allocated within a senior management team without having to resort to organizing the rest of the organization along the same lines. The interesting aspect is that the more accountability at the most senior level and organizational structure are aligned, the less the leadership team acts as a team. This is one of the greatest barriers to the transformation to Lean production.

Within Lean production environments, there is often talk of creating autonomous teams. Aside from the behavior of leaders which needs to evolve along with the behavior within the team, one of the main barriers to increasing autonomy are existing human resources (HR) policies. Lean IT organizations need different HR structures. The most important is the way in which evaluations are done. The use of tools such as the skills and knowledge matrix encourage the team to take responsibility for the development of the people within the team. There is no need for annual personal development plans, as team members work to acquire the knowledge and skills they need on an ongoing basis. (Semi-)Annual reviews become irrelevant as a result of regular coaching, as planned in the leader's standard work. Another classic HR tool, the RACI table (Responsible, Accountable, Consulted, Informed) is also a construct that needs to be reviewed in the light of the development of teams that bear integral responsibility for the services they provide. Also, the reduction of the coordination "overhead" means that the strict allocation of RACI becomes muri rather than a help to the people in the organization.

A final area of muri is legal. As we know, policies are often based on interpretations of legal and regulatory requirements. A significant inhibitor for Lean IT organizations is the segregation of duties requirement. This is a classic solution for a variety of problems, which often causes more problems than it solves. Segregation of duties is a kneejerk mass production response to situations where it may be inadvisable for a single person to complete a task for fear of a conflict of interests. For IT, this has been one of the drivers of the split between development and operations ("We can't have developers putting their own code into production. What if they haven't tested properly or cause some kind of problem? Or worse they have manipulated the code to their own benefit?"). Many of the conflicts can now be solved through automation. The regulations usually stress the auditability of activities, i.e. do we know who did what when? The availability of continuous delivery pipelines, a beautiful mechanism for improving the flow of value to customers, with their (almost) infallible records of who did what and their ability to stop failing code from passing through the process ("andon cord") provide extremely effective jidoka tools that allow IT organizations to dispense with segregation of duties, as long as everyone works on a personal systems account. Segregation of duties can be replaced by a more constructive process of active peer review, like pair-programming. It is therefore important to review legislation and regulations to check whether they are being interpreted in a Mass Production way and whether a Lean Production interpretation can lead to more effective, less obstructive solutions.

As you can see, there are many areas in which leaders must redefine the environment so that teams can truly achieve their potential in a Lean environment. In fact, *not* dealing with these areas proactively or at least promptly when they arise can cause the entire transformation to stagnate. In many cases, it means curtailing entrenched, acquired power in the aforementioned staff organizations.

The leaders signing for the goals of the team need to realize that there may be far-reaching consequences to their commitment. They will need to be prepared to do significant problem-solving in the leadership team. This means that the leadership team must have intimate knowledge of the structured problem-solving mechanism (DMAIC) and must take the time to measure and analyze the problems before determining their solutions. It is quite surprising how often it is the leadership teams that jump to conclusions when faced with a problem. In one situation, the customer complained about the speed with which calls were being solved. The leadership team came together and concluded within about five minutes that it was necessary to decree that all teams must have a dispatcher of calls who was responsible for making sure people picked up calls quickly. Each team implemented the dispatcher role in a different way; some with a person taking on the role, others rotating the role on a daily basis. Predictably, the intervention failed miserably to increase the speed with which calls were solved. The leadership team had chosen a recognizable solution ("force them to do it") rather than investigate the underlying reasons for why calls were not picked up quickly. First of all, the fact was that 95% of calls were picked up in a way that could be called "quickly." One part of the problem was the intervention of managers putting people on other work while they were in the process of solving a call, thereby giving off a clear signal that calls were less important than changes. This led to team members making their own choices regarding the priority of calls. By agreeing (leadership and teams) that calls had precedence over other work because the customer was not able to continue their work, the speed of resolution of calls was improved. The organization had learned the value of flow when working on calls. Leadership had learned the value of thoroughly investigating a problem before decreeing a solution that only aggravated the situation.

24

Implementing

We have looked at the transformation from both the leader's and the team's perspective. We will now look at the eight weeks of the implementation phase of the team transformation from the coach's perspective. During these eight weeks, few (if any) new tools will be introduced into the team. These eight weeks focus on implementing the improvements identified, raising the level of performance of the team and embedding the rituals into the team's behavior so that they become habits. During these eight weeks, the leadership and team transformations will need to work together to achieve the results. In the end, it is not just about achieving the results. It is also about the way they are achieved. Resorting to non-Lean methods defeats the point. The aim is for both leaders and team members to learn how they can achieve their results in a different way, for example by changing the focus from resource efficiency to flow efficiency.

This is where the coach role changes. In the previous four weeks, the coach was very much focused on ensuring that the analyses got done, partly by doing them herself but also by training and coaching both leaders and team members. The emphasis of the role now shifts to observing and giving feedback on behavior. This is the essence of steering an organization and it is what leaders need to get good at.

It is in this phase that we start to see the need for and emergence of the Lean IT Expert. Prior to this phase, we see leadership focusing on learning Lean leadership, kaizen leads focusing on kaizen, coaches focusing on ensuring that the lean "structures" are identified and followed, and the team members focused on understanding how the Lean principles affect the way they work. During the implementation, and thereafter, the focuses will start to merge. This process will create individuals who are capable in all areas.

To start with everyone must know the basics of Lean. This is the minimum knowledge required in the leaders and the teams, and creates the basis for a constructive conversation across the organization. If everyone "speaks the same language," there is a greater possibility of adopting that language as the standard. One of the first areas where the capabilities start to merge is leadership and coaching. There is a substantial synergy between these two practices. Leaders need to adopt the skills of coaches and learn how the Lean tools work so that they can repeat them on a regular basis. Looking at the Lean Leadership Development Model, this step represents Commitment to Self-Development in order to make the step to Helping Others to Develop.

Another area of development and overlap is from the basic knowledge to kaizen. As kaizen leads are given the opportunity to practice their skills and share their knowledge with the teams, more and more people will become knowledgeable in kaizen. The team members learn through taking part in improvement kaizen; leaders gain experience with the method through acting as a sponsor to kaizen teams.

As leaders move through the Development Model, they acquire kaizen skills, thus completing their knowledge cycle. They now need to continue applying all of the acquired knowledge, turning themselves into practicing Lean IT Experts. Once the leadership has acquired the knowledge and skills of Leadership, Kaizen and Coach, they become the role model for every future leader. This provides the "lead by example" basis for all team members to aim for building the full range of Lean behaviors. Of course, it will take some dedication, commitment and time to reach this state.

Looking at the implementation phase from the coach's perspective, it becomes clear what their role is. We saw in Leadership workshop 3 (Go See), how leaders must be aware of the comfort, learning and fear zones of people. The coach needs to be even more acutely aware of this model. The coach needs to help create an environment in which learning can happen. This means supporting, teaching and challenging both team members and leaders. Straightaway, this presents us with a problem. At this early stage of the transformation, getting leaders to take internal coaches seriously has been proven to be difficult. Leaders tend to see the Lean IT coaches as extensions of themselves especially when it comes to the difficult work of getting people to act differently. In many transformations, leaders push *their* responsibility of ensuring behavior evolves in the right direction onto the coach. The comment often heard is: "What is the coach responsible for if they are not going to tell people how to do things differently?" It is actually quite a good question. Why do we need coaches in a Lean IT transformation?

The answer is that you do not need separate Lean IT coaches … *if* leaders pick up the role. The end-state we are looking for is that leaders do their own coaching and act as a coach to their teams, with more senior management acting as coach to lower levels of leadership, and on occasion for the teams as well. It is important to remember that a coaching role is necessary in a Lean IT environment because it is almost impossible to gauge and assess one's own behavior. Since Lean is all about learning and a personal assessment will rarely uncover the need to adjust behavior, the (separate) role of Lean IT coach is necessary for the duration of the transformation and for a substantial period beyond.

Looking at the role of Lean IT coach, it all starts with knowledge of Lean IT. This is the same knowledge as everyone else, supplemented with knowledge of kaizen and leadership. Good coaches aim to acquire more knowledge and more understanding of Lean than others in the organization. Not out of a sense of achievement but because it is the best way to be able to help others to acquire the necessary skills. Having said this, the coach is not there to teach and lecture others, rather to have broad knowledge so that they can ask the right questions, and help others do the thinking for themselves. The coach must also acquire basic generic coaching skills, including dealing with resistance, giving feedback effectively, active listening and understanding motivation and how to encourage it in others. Next, the coach must gain intimate knowledge of the environment in which they are acting. This is where many Lean coaches have failed to have a significant impact within IT. As we discussed in Part I, the context of IT has its own peculiarities. This means that the basic Lean knowledge and coaching skills will not always be enough for a coach from a different area of business or sector to be effective within IT. Last but not least, the coach will need to interact with both leaders and team members to ensure the adoption of Lean principles. Dealing with individuals is one level of complexity, the coach will also need to deal with teams both at the operational level and at managerial levels. The group dynamics in these teams (or groups as they initially may be) add another level of complexity to the coaching task. In the context of the Lean IT transformation, it is important to realize that a coach acts at the level of an organizational coach, as opposed to a personal coach who helps an individual investigate their own particular situation. The Lean IT coach aims to help people acquire and improve behaviors that are consistent with Lean principles.

What does a coach do in the context of a Lean IT transformation? In the teams, the main role of the coach is to support team members in using the right Lean tools to gain insight into their problems, then help the team to find the root causes and solutions for these problems. They may need to use the full DMAIC cycle; on other occasions they will help to uncover what turns out to be an obvious problem with a relatively straightforward solution. Alternatively, the root cause may be investigated with a Five Whys investigation. The coach advises leadership on building new capabilities, the best way to transform the organization and will escalate problems to the correct level, while the cascade is not yet working properly. The coach is a facilitator for both teams and leaders, through developing expertise in Lean and the way to transform IT organizations. It is important for coaches to use their personal drive and openness to challenge the status quo. They must be able to convince people from a rational perspective and also encourage people to take steps based on empathy. The coach also injects energy for change into the system. As you may recognize, many of these skills are what is expected of leaders.

A coach is not a manager, nor is he a secretary. They are also not a free resource to be inserted into the operation if gaps are identified. The coach is not necessarily an expert on all Lean IT tools, but is someone who can ensure that a knowledgeable coach can be brought in, if necessary. One thing for everyone to remember is that a Lean IT coach will certainly not tolerate people continuing to work in the old way. The coach will ask questions to challenge the thinking and acting in the right direction.

The extension of the "what is the coach responsible for ..." question is: How do we know whether a coach has been successful or not. The coach is successful if the effects of the coaching are still visible when the coach has left the room. This, paradoxically, is when the coaching actually starts, whether the coach is a leader or a dedicated coach. The coach must start by creating learning experiences that help the person being coached to move towards their intended goal. Take a leader who wants to become a Lean IT leader. The coach must identify learning steps in which the leader can practice new behaviors, for example carrying out a gemba walk, acting as sponsor to kaizen or helping teams to develop their visual management. A clear indication of the success of a coach is when the coached person tries something new. This means that the person is probably in their learning zone. It is up to the coach to check whether this is actually the case.

In summary, the Lean IT coach must bring skills, expertise and energy. Skills include being a strong problem-solver, analytical and a systems thinker looking across silos. The coach must be a clear communicator, empathetic and a good listener, who is sensitive to the atmosphere of and feedback from the organization. Creativity and pragmatism help teams to collaborate towards decisions and actions. The expertise required is knowledge of Lean IT and Lean IT tools, methods and structures, knowledge of coaching and people management and knowledge of the IT context. The Lean IT coach must have the eagerness to challenge the status quo through the ability to ignite motivation in others. The coach must have a hunger for learning and development, and wish to share this. Personal drive and energy, with a bias for action and outcomes are also vital for the success of the coach. The coach must also be comfortable with ambiguity and with a willingness to try and, possibly, fail, followed by learning and another try.

A coach cannot coach without being open to coaching as well. This helps the coach to understand what it feels like to be coached. When being coached, it is important to be prepared to see the problem, understand it and understand one's own role in the problem. This first awareness step is followed by acceptance. Does the person being coached accept their part in the problem? This is particularly difficult for leaders who were brought up in the Mass Production "infallibility-of-leadership" paradigm. A key step is accepting responsibility for changing the situation. With this acceptance, the person being coached can turn to action, engage with the environment regarding the problem and try something new in order to alleviate or remove the problem.

In *Toyota Kata: Managing People for Improvement, Adaptiveness and Superior Results*, Rother (2009) describes what is called the Coaching Kata. This kata is focused very specifically on embedding the improvement mindset into the organization. It is not about coaching people to do anything else; coaching is aimed squarely at learning to improve. As we have seen, this is a broad topic including all manner of tools to help support the investigation part of learning in relation to the different aspects of an IT organization.

The coaching kata is basically a 5-step model that helps the coach and the person being coached to move forwards. First the need, target, direction or vision must be defined. Then the person being coached must describe how they understand the current condition. The next step is to establish the next target condition, then use the Five Whys questioning method to identify which steps are necessary to move towards the next target condition. Lastly, the person being coached reflects on the lessons learned.

During this process, the coach may give a deliberately vague assignment, need or challenge, followed by questions to understand what the person is thinking. For example, how can you get your teams to start improving? The coach challenges the person being coached to think further about the assignment. Questions may include: What is stopping the teams from improving now or why do you think they do not spend time on structural improvements? This may be repeated several times to clarify the thinking and the ideas behind the thinking, and may include some fact-finding to validate the thinking. The person being coached must then define the next step to achieve the next target level. Then comes the important step: Carry out the action. Both parties reflect on what happened and extract lessons learned to be used in the next cycle of the coaching kata.

An interesting aspect of the coaching relationship is that the coach and the person being coached have interlocking learning (Plan-Do-Study-Act) cycles. The coach starts with planning the coaching activities, by considering what the person being coached needs to learn and determining a suitable challenge or assignment. The Do of the Coach supports the Plan step of the person being coached. While the person is carrying out the actions, the coach is in her Study step. The coach then Acts to ensure that the person being coached evaluates the actions in their Study step. The coach's Plan phase is related to the Act phase of the person being coached in that the Act is about deciding what to do differently next time. The coach needs to adjust their plan accordingly (Figure 24.1).

One of the more difficult phases in the coaching process is the coach's Do phase. This involves presenting a deliberately vague challenge. Many

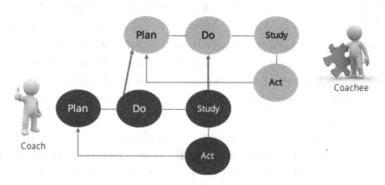

FIGURE 24.1
Interlocking learning cycles of coach and person being coached.

people, especially leaders, being coached get irritable and impatient, as they have a tendency to feel that they may not be giving the "right" answer. Leaders are particularly susceptible to giving up quickly with the question-and-answer process. They ask what the answer is rather than thinking through the challenge while explaining their thinking. Many leaders have stated that the reason for their irritation is the efficient use of time. However, on questioning their reaction, it turns out to have more to do with the "infallibility-of-management" paradigm than most will initially admit. In this case, it is not about efficient use of time, the effectiveness is far more important. Teams and team members tend to be more accepting of the challenge. They do not feel they need to give the "right" answer, and tend to be more open to the search.

This leads us to the most challenging phase of coaching and that is the Do phase of the person being coached. This is also the most important phase for the entire transformation. If individuals, particularly leaders, do not try new behaviors on a daily basis then there will be no new insights or realization that the new behavior can create different, more positive results, which means there will be no change to the culture. In short: Practicing new behaviors every day will create a high performance IT organization. There is one assumption here, the behavior must be consistent with the Lean principles and the Lean Leadership Development Model.

During a Lean IT transformation, coaches have a broad role that is reflected in the coaching relationship. There are four levels of autonomy that the person being coached achieves during the process. Coaching the day start is one of the challenges for coaches and leaders during the early days of the transformation. It is a clear example of getting people to try out new behavior on a daily basis. The most critical outcome to achieve is that the day start has a positive effect on the team. It is this positive effect that ensures the team continues the behavior. Once this behavior has become a habit, the culture of the team has shifted.

The first step in the coaching model is showing what the behavior looks like (Show). The coach shows the behavior. In the case of the day start, the coach will ensure that the meeting request for a 30-minute meeting is in everybody's calendar and may even go round the team a few days before telling everybody individually that there will be a day start, starting in a few days' time. The 30-minute timeslot will be reduced to 15 minutes as the team gets used to the ritual. The moment arrives for the day start to happen. There are two possibilities: Either everyone arrives on time in anticipation of the new "thing" or half the team is on time and the rest show the embedded behavior of turning up a little bit late because of some important work. Mostly, this will be accompanied by a statement that the person was doing something for a customer and "that's what Lean is all about, delivering value to the customer. Well, that's what I was doing. Am I wrong?" As a coach, you should not get drawn into the discussion rather, thank the person for turning up and continue with the day start. Usually, there has not yet been an explicit discussion about turning up to meetings on time. More about this later. The coach explains the day start. It is important to position the day board next to the week board so that the team can refer to the week board when filling the day board. For the sake of this example, we will assume that the team works with a day-based day board rather than a Kanban board. The coach hands out sticky notes and asks everyone to create the notes for the work they will be doing in the coming days. It usually takes 2–3 minutes for the tickets to be ready and placed on the board on the day that the work will be done. The coach then explains to the team that they should explain how they did with their work yesterday, what they will be doing today and whether they need any help. And that they have one minute to tell their story. Most team members carry out the task as indicated. There are always team members who exceed their minute. Since the coach has clearly indicated the rules, she must give feedback when the minute is exceeded, asking the team member to summarize the rest of the activities. Always remember, if someone talks for longer than a minute, they are either giving too much detail or they have too many tasks. After the tasks for the day have been discussed, the coach asks about the morale of the team members. This is a ritual that will be moved to the start of the day start in order to gauge the mood in the team. Most team members are unaccustomed to sharing their "feelings" in the team and will generally score either positive or neutral. The coach asks whether anyone would like to elaborate on their mood, whether the team members need to be aware of anything that may affect the way a team member reacts. By now, the first day start will have exceeded its "ideal" fifteen minutes. The remaining time, usually five minutes, is used by the coach to discuss the rules of the meeting. The coach asks the team what they would like the rules of the meeting to be. The first rule is almost invariably: We turn up on time. The second is: We tell our bit within one minute. Later, rules such as "we come to the meeting with our sticky notes prepared," "we are interested in each other's work" and "we prepare our sticky notes prior to the meeting" may appear. The coach asks a team member to write down the agreed rules on a sticky note and post them on the day board. The coach thanks the team and wishes them a good workday.

The coach evaluates the day start with the team leader, particularly focusing on what the team leader saw and learned. The question of the late team member comes up. The team leader wonders why the coach did not tell the team member that he should turn up on time. The main reason is that there was not an explicit agreement regarding this "performance." The coach reminds the leader of the structure of the performance dialog in which a performance needs to be agreed, then feedback and support can be given. The next time a team member is late for the day start both the team leader and the team members can give feedback. This is also the case for the more verbose members of the team. The coach and team leader discuss whether the team leader feels ready to try running the day start. Mostly, leaders like to observe up to five day starts before taking on the task. The coach should do no more than five day starts before the team leader takes over. In some cases, the team leader may try to avoid running the day start by suggesting that the team members know what to do and can run the day start in turn. The day and week starts are the responsibility of the team leader and they cannot delegate this duty until they are sure the team has embedded the behavior into the team rituals. Most team leaders take over the role within three days.

The leader (the person being coached) moves to the next level, Do It Together. The day start is prepared and run together with the coach. The team leader takes the lead and requests help from the coach as and when needed. The coach may on occasion remind the team leader of what needs to be done. During the day start, the team leader and coach help the team members to carry out the day start effectively. Efficiency (doing it within 15 minutes) will come later. After the day start, the coach and team leader evaluate how the day start went; what went well and what could be improved. In teams where the team leader has been infrequently present in the past, the team may need to get used to the fact that the team leader is taking a visible and active role towards the team. This generally upsets a balance in which one or more of the team members may have taken an informal leadership role within the team. The team leader needs to "earn" the position as the team's recognized leader. This will be achieved through, among other behaviors, consistently taking charge of the day start.

As the team leader gains experience and confidence with running the day start, they move to the next level of coaching, Prepare, in which the team leader and coach prepare the day start together. The coach will ask what the team leader expects will happen. They may also discuss the leader's response to a number of scenarios, for example, people turning up late, team members not coming prepared or content discussions happening at the board. For each case, the leader will be challenged to define their response. For each new situation, the team leader will ask the team whether it is necessary to create a new day start rule, e.g. "we discuss content after the day start." The coach gives feedback on the leader's performance and, if necessary, suggests improvements. Once the behavior has become second nature, the leader moves to the final level of coaching, Do It Yourself, in which the coach is only present once in a while to observe and give feedback. The team leader is now experienced enough to start coaching team members to take over when the team leader is on holiday. Generally, a team leader should be independently running a day start within about ten working days (Figure 24.2).

The day start is a very suitable ritual for building the coaching relationship and helping the team leader and the team members to experience explicitly learning new behavior. Throughout the process, it is important to discuss the positive effects that the day start has on the ability of the team to get work done, achieve the goals of the week and deal effectively with ad hoc

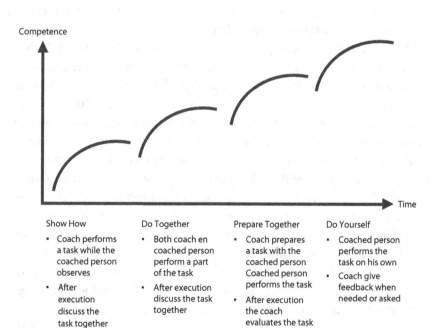

FIGURE 24.2
Four coaching phases.

or unplanned work that enters the team. The team leader is well-positioned to correct behavior before it escalates. This may mean that a team leader must talk to a customer about their behavior of disrupting the team's work with new priorities. These are ways in which the team leader shows value to the team by facilitating their ability to achieve their goals of the week. A breakthrough moment is when, during the day start, team members are able to avoid double work or can optimize the way work is done. This provides significant positive reinforcement to both the leader and the team members, thus causing this successful behavior to become embedded into the team's culture. I have witnessed a number of transformations that have stagnated as a result of changes in leadership in which the new leader is not a supporter of the transformation to Lean IT. In all cases, if the day start ritual is understood and embedded in the teams, they are extremely reluctant to give it up, even if the new leadership does not support it.

The interesting aspect regarding the day start's influence on the team is that it increases the openness of communication. Team members more readily share their mood in the team, explaining why they may not be fully effective. As trust builds, teams have been known to share their mistakes of the previous day. This is a collateral effect of the day start. As we saw in leadership knowledge session 4, building the trust is the start of the creation of a high performance team. The week and day starts also support and encourage the other aspects. These rituals help to identify and surface conflicts which need to be discussed after the meeting. Determining goals of the week and ensuring they are planned for execution on the day board is a ritual that encourages commitment to the goals. Discussing work done and, by association, work not done is all about being accountable for the work that team leader and team members have committed to. Last but certainly not least, the goals of the week are results and the day starts ensures that attention is paid to achieving the results. The day and week start rituals have considerable depth when it comes to building a high performance culture.

Taking a step back from this example of coaching, we can identify that coaches, in essence, carry out three activities: teach, support and promote. You may recognize these activities as those central to doing a gemba walk. A coach must be able to share knowledge, i.e. teach. Examples of this are performing analyses to define value and waste and teaching others how they are done, implementing visual management and capacity management, facilitating kaizen events, creating content on Lean for awareness sessions or for training staff members and providing training.

The Lean IT coach must support others in their journey towards becoming a Lean IT Expert. This is about driving action planning and bringing together necessary resources, providing feedback and supporting others as they use the various Lean IT tools. They will also support more junior Lean IT coaches and act as a role model for leaders and team members in their daily work. Lastly, the Lean IT coach must be prepared to promote the direction being taken by the IT organization. This does not mean becoming a Lean IT evangelist or, worse, a fundamentalist. The aim is to support leadership with the clear communication of organizational goals and how Lean IT and its associated tools will help to achieve the goals. The Lean IT coach must use their knowledge of Lean IT to influence leaders and team members effectively, at the same time, walking the talk. So, if doing a gemba walk and coaching are essentially the same, should leaders not be coaches and vice versa? This is a question faced by all IT organizations. As we discussed earlier, ideally the entire IT organization should be populated by Lean IT Experts who have mastered all aspects of the three roles (leader, kaizen lead and coach).

The Lean IT leader is responsible for creating the vision and aligning goals, thus giving direction to the transformation as a whole. The leader is responsible for taking decisions when necessary, taking care to only take decisions on the right level. The leader must develop coaching skills to be effective. During the transformation and, mostly, for some time thereafter, the Lean IT coach is a member of the guiding coalition of the transformation. Coaches work based on informal influence, rather than the formal hierarchical position of the leader. As stated in part I, the coach is the conscience of the organization and must indicate when Lean principles and values are not being applied. In this way, they help to keep the transformation, and in particular the leaders, on track.

In carrying out this role, the coach will need to develop or enhance certain skills. There have been many books written on coaching and I do not pretend for one moment to be complete in describing the skills that are necessary for a coach. Within the context of a Lean IT transformation, a coach must master a few skills. First and foremost, the coach must learn to observe behavior and give objective feedback on what he sees. It is vital that the coach is aware of the ABC behavior analysis model described in part III. The awareness of the effect of consequences means that the coach will continue to observe what is happening after the behavior has happened to identify clearly how its consequences affect the person being coached and their surroundings. As Aubrey Daniels says in his book *Bringing*

Out the Best in People: How to Apply the Astonishing Power of Positive Reinforcement, "antecedents get us started, consequences keep us going" (2016). By consequences, he principally means *positive* consequences. Having observed behavior that has not been effective, the coach must be able to give feedback. This feedback should be given in the context of a performance dialog. The challenge for the coach is to understand whether the objectives were sufficiently clear before giving feedback. Providing feedback on someone's behavior without there having been a clearly agreed objective against which the behavior can be measured leads to pseudo-feedback which tends to end up in the person giving feedback purely venting frustration about the behavior of the other person (Figure 24.3).

The feedback model above is embedded in the performance dialog, as is one of the essential coaching skills: active listening. The role of the coach is to elicit as much information from the person being coached as possible to ensure that their thinking is made explicit. This helps both actors to understand what is driving the behavior. What is the coach listening for? The coach is particularly trying to understand whether there are blockages in the person that cause resistance to the changes taking place. The essence of resistance is one of two blockages: "I don't want" and "I can't do." The coach must help the person being coached to identify which blockage is stopping them from taking action. Remember that the blockage will probably be associated with where someone is on the Parker & Lewis transition curve as discussed in Part II. The aim of the coach is then to help the person to identify which (small) step they will take in order to make progress in the direction required.

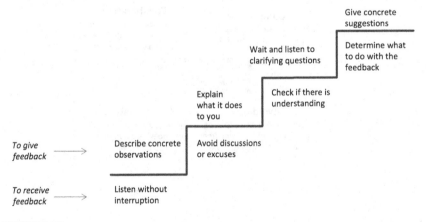

FIGURE 24.3
Feedback model.

Related to dealing with resistance and blockages, a Lean IT coach must know how to deal with conflicts. As shown by the Thomas-Kilmann instrument, conflict is about balancing assertiveness with cooperation. Too little of both leads to people avoiding the conflict. In the case of the team member who was late for the first day start, avoiding the conflict is about downplaying the importance of this person in favor of the entire team. If the behavior continues, there will be a conflict between the team and the individual. This needs to be solved in a way that creates a win-win situation for all involved. In terms of the model, this is about maximum assertiveness and maximum collaboration. If this does not lead to a solution, parties can choose to meet each other half-way i.e. compromise. Compromise can lead to both sides feeling they have not achieved a good result. If both parties choose to stick by their point of view, the conflict ends up in a competitive state in which the protagonists feel they will lose face if they back down. These conflicts will tend to escalate and become entrenched, until someone "loses." The last possibility is accommodation in which one party yields to the other's point of view. This feels like obeying an order and mostly does not resolve the conflict. Lean IT coaches should aim to reach a collaborative solution to the conflicts they face. This is not always possible as Lean views clash with the existing paradigm. The aim is to keep the dialog open, creating an opening for trying out new behaviors. Often new insights from trying out new behaviors will help people to see how effective Lean behaviors can be (Figure 24.4).

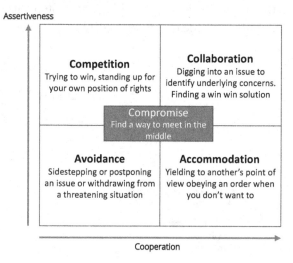

FIGURE 24.4
Thomas-Kilmann Instrument.

One of the capabilities that Lean IT coaches need to develop is understanding Lean IT tools, many of which have been described in the analysis phase of the team transformation and in the leadership transformation. The coach must know how they work and, maybe more importantly, how they fit together. The importance of this understanding is that teams may have different problems they wish to tackle first. Some may wish to focus on getting their capacity planning right, others may need to do a detailed investigation of the Voice of the Customer, while another team may feel that they need to work on multi-skilling the team members. The starting points are in fact all connected and the coach must be able to help teams solve their primary problem while knowing what potential next steps could be.

One of the key goals in Lean IT is to ensure the flow of work. Let us take a look at how the coach would introduce the various tools in order to give the team insight into the components necessary to improve the flow of work through the team. If each individual in each team understands the concepts, the team members can collaborate to create flow through the entire IT organization (Figure 24.5).

The aim is to ensure that all aspects of the organization are in place to ensure flow. The first step is to understand customer value. This is made up of two parts: the volume of demand and the qualitative aspects of the value. The historical volume of demand can be determined during the data

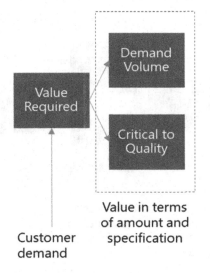

FIGURE 24.5
Deconstructing value into its component parts I.

analysis. The questions for the team are: What will be future demand? Is there a pattern in the arrival of value demand? And can the team influence and iron out any variability in demand? The qualitative aspects of the value demand are collected based on conversations with the customer and summarized in the Critical to Quality tree. Both aspects (demand volume and quality) have associated metrics that help the team to understand whether they are performing well.

The next steps involve understanding the units of work (Figure 24.6).

The demand volume and the specifications help to identify units of work. We saw the generic types of units of work within IT organizations. In this step, it may be necessary for the team to specify the units of work more precisely so that the associated value streams can be better understood. One team may be able to subdivide its changes into two categories while another may need to define more categories of changes, depending on the type and volume of customer demand. Each of these units of work has a value stream which can be investigated using the combination of SIPOC and VSM. This investigation will result in understanding the waste (muda, mura, muri) in the system.

Moving further along the sequence, we find that each unit of work requires a certain amount of time to process and needs certain skills and knowledge to be completed (Figure 24.7).

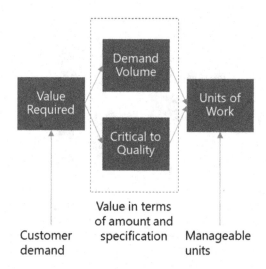

FIGURE 24.6
Deconstructing value into its component parts II.

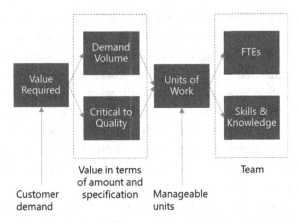

FIGURE 24.7
Deconstructing value into its component parts III.

The units of work analysis include understanding how much time is spent on the various types of work, i.e. the average time value of each type of unit of work. This gives the team insight into the amount of effective time needed to fulfill the demand. By multiplying the number of a particular unit of work by its time value, we can understand how many FTEs we need to fulfill demand. It should be clear that this represents an optimum use of time which is rarely achieved in practice. Taking the example of incidents, analysis in tens of IT organizations shows that the average time spent working to resolve an incident is around 45 minutes. This is a combination of shorter average times at the service desk, approximately 10 minutes, and longer times in second line teams, on average 75 minutes. Based on these numbers, a team can calculate how much time they need to reserve in their capacity plan. This is why identifying units of work that are similar in time value is important. Service requests are often an area where there is much contention. If we take the general definition, a service request could range from 5 minutes to many days. By specifying the difference between a service request and advice, we can define two categories with different dynamics. A service request now has an average time value of about 30 minutes, whereas advice resembles a non-standard change. The main reason to not merge these latter two categories is the difference in the outputs of the processes. The insights of the time value of units of work can come from the Earning Capacity Analysis.

The next challenge is to ensure that knowledge and skills are available in sufficient amounts to process the work. In essence, the team must understand the number of parallel lines it needs to meet demand. For example, are three developers necessary to create enough code to meet demand, or will two suffice? This will be a combination of understanding how many units of work need to be worked on simultaneously and what knowledge is needed in these units of work. Together, this will enable the team to define how many people with what skills and knowledge are necessary to make the team successful. Again, these aspects will have associated metrics that allow the team to measure how they are doing.

The last step is to combine these aspects into a just-in-time capacity plan that will allow the team to monitor whether the requested value is being delivered (Figure 24.8).

In building this flow, we have touched upon ten different tools that give insight into different aspects of the problem of delivering customer value in flow. And we have not even broached the subject of continuous improvement, which should be embedded in each of the steps.

The Lean IT coach must be able to help teams to work through the various aspects of improving flow. The above description is merely an example of the kind of links that can be built between one Lean IT aspect and another. The main point is that coaches must be able to help teams to move seamlessly from one area to the next taking logical and understandable steps to ensure buy-in for the next step. It should be clear that depending on the perceived problem of the team, the coach can start anywhere in the flow and move upstream or downstream to provide new insights.

In the eight weeks of implementation, the coach must help the team to achieve the goals to which the team has committed. This will be done by continuously creating insight and understanding of the situation at hand.

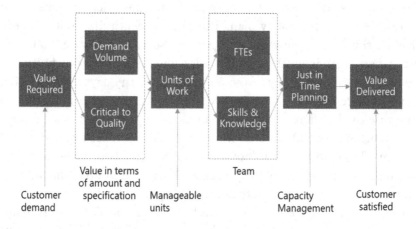

FIGURE 24.8

Deconstructing value into its component parts IV.

At the same time, the aim of the coach must be to ensure that the team knows how to use all of the tools and structures correctly by the end of the eight-week period, all the while helping the team leader and team members to transcend the basics of the tools and structures to truly understanding the principles they are meant to support. This is where danger lurks when it comes to transformation in larger organizations. Once the coaches have carried out three waves of analysis and implementation within the teams, there is a strong tendency for the coaching to become tool-focused and mechanistic. This is encouraged by senior leaders who want to know how the transformation is progressing. In some cases, the leaders have requested an overview of which teams have implemented which aspects of the Lean infrastructure. This type of report should be avoided at all costs, since it is a small step from having this overview to translating it into a number (preferably on a scale of 0 to 5), subsequently creating a spreadsheet in which the progress of all teams can be "managed." More importantly, the numbers can then be aggregated and averaged to give an overall number defining the progress of the entire transformation. The entire transformation will be deemed complete when the total score is 5. As time progresses and the transformation appears to be advancing more slowly than anticipated, the number for declaring success will be reduced to 4.6, then to 4.18 and subsequently to 3.73, to ensure the transformation finishes when it was planned to be finished.

Just for clarity: The previous paragraph is infused with an increasing amount of sarcasm. If you find yourself headed in this direction, pull the andon cord extremely hard.

But, I hear you say, my senior management wants to know how the transformation is progressing. There is only one answer to this need: *Go to the gemba!* The beauty of a Lean IT organization is that all important information is on the wall and the number of reports that need to be produced declines dramatically. Through the use of A3, the volume of the reports that still need to be produced declines substantially as well. As we saw in the leadership transformation, coaching leaders into doing gemba walks is one of the key behaviors that they need to learn, practice and master.

So who should be a coach in your IT organization? Selecting coaches is relatively simple. We have seen what qualities a coach needs to have: skills, expertise and drive. When selecting coaches, drive is the most important criteria, followed by skills. With those two in place, expertise can be quite easily acquired. A potential coach must be someone who dares to speak their mind and who is committed to helping the organization move in a new direction. Once again, the Lean IT coach is a role in which individuals can show their leadership capabilities. And, since they fully understand and support the new Lean management system through their coaching, they are candidates for a future leadership role in the organization.

Before we move on to the final phase of the transformation, we must investigate a number of specific situations that crop up during the implementation phase, and sometimes earlier.

Can teams use electronic boards rather than whiteboards with sticky notes?

We are helping IT teams to transform. As technology-oriented people, they will naturally want to use electronic tools to support their efforts. The reasons most stated for wanting digital visual management are, among others:

- Sticky notes fall off the board, they don't fall off the screen. Critics have a point here. Sticky notes have a tendency to lose their stickiness. There are excellent alternatives in the form of magnetic plastic sleeves in all shapes and sizes that can hold tickets.
- The writing is illegible. Again, good point. Most IT people could qualify as doctors if it were judged by the readability of their handwriting. On many occasions, I have seen tickets being created using a word processor or spreadsheet template. These are then printed out and put into magnetic sleeves. This works best for Kanban boards where tickets spend more than just a couple of days moving across the board.
- The system gives us a history of what has been done. This is an interesting argument. Why do you need a history of your visual management? Changes to the systems will be documented through a development pipeline or in a service management tool. The same counts for incidents and other units of work. The effect of improvements should be visible in the measurements we make. In all of these cases, having a historical record of the visual management is excess to requirements. The question is: Who is going to do something with the data recorded? It is vital to understand that information systems and visual management serve two distinct goals. The information systems are there to record the details of units of work so that performance data can be derived. Visual management is there to manage the flow of work. Can these two not be combined?

Yes, the two functions can be combined, but only once the team has learned the distinction between the two.

- We will have single entry of data. This follows on from the previous argument. What do you aim to do with the visual management data that is collected and archived for posterity?
- Sticky notes are childish. That is just a matter of opinion, and in a Lean IT organization, we work based on facts. The fact is that a sticky note on a board serves as a powerful reminder for what needs to be done.

I have experienced the introduction of electronic visual management at various moments during the transformation. In general, the earlier the tool is implemented, the less successful the transformation. If people do not understand the reasons for having visual management, jidoka and just-in-time (and if you need to look up jidoka, you are not there yet), then implementing a tool will be an expensive waste of time. Teams must become highly proficient with the manual visual management boards, before moving to electronic alternatives.

But what do I do if team members are not co-located? This is the second big argument that teams and team leaders raise. My first (rather facetious) response is: "So you've got a problem. Solve it!" In fact, the answer is not as facetious as it may seem. There is a tendency to view non-co-located team members as a reason to give up on visual management before it has even been started. This is the kind of non-Lean behavior that needs to be identified and addressed. In Lean, we believe that there is a solution to every problem, only we may not have looked hard enough for it yet.

Non-co-located teams come in many forms. There is the traditional case of people being spread over multiple locations. But also people who work part-time or have "work-at-home" days fall into the same problem area. To be clear, Lean IT (and Agile and DevOps) teams should be co-located as much as possible. If this is not the case, then the first analysis that needs to be done is to understand whether these non-co-located people are actually part of the same team, as defined in Part II. If they are a real team, then they should be set the task of defining how they wish to create the same effect as a week start and a day start. That's the problem. Solve it!

Solutions to this problem are usually quite simple. Most importantly, the team makes the solution work for them. They tend to accept any accompanying inconvenience because of their need to work together. If the team is in fact a group, then it is almost irrelevant whether the people are co-located or not, the visual management will not provide the benefits gained by a real team. Doing a day or week start with remote participants is always a challenge regarding the attention of the participants. Again, if the participants *need* to be interested in what the others say because their own work depends on it, then almost anything will work.

The main facilitator of non-co-located teams is a good communications system. A good conference call system or, preferably, video-conferencing system is an absolute necessity. The basic requirement is for people to be able to hear each other and see the board. Seeing the board can be solved in a couple of ways. Aiming a camera at the board allows everyone to have an overview of the layout, but mostly it means people cannot see the details. If it is a live camera feed, then remote team members will follow the proceedings. It is also possible to adjust the tickets prior to the meeting, take a high-resolution photo of the board and send it round to the participants. They can then zoom into the photo on their computer to see the details. This way of working requires the discipline of preparing the tickets prior to the meeting, which is quite difficult early on. Some teams have supplemented their conference call with an electronic board.

There are many obstacles small and large that arise during the implementation phase. Each of these challenges provides coaches and leaders with opportunities to reinforce key aspects of Lean thinking and acting. Common aspects that come up are:

- Acknowledging that good is not an end state but a step towards further improvement. Perfection is about delivering quality at the source and the eradication of waste through continuous improvement based on Lean principles;
- In the same way, problems are seen as opportunities to improve customer value, rather than a reason to apportion blame;
- Lean challenges people to think differently in the process of delivering value. In Lean organizations, people do not talk about the procedure but the "best known way" of doing something. This implies that there is a better way, only we do not know it yet. Thinking counter-intuitively can lead to new "best known ways" of doing work;
- Invest in people to create long-term relationships. In IT, we also need to look at how we develop long-term relationships with external service providers. They can play a crucial role in the value delivered to customers;

- Being Lean in the long-term depends very much on what you do in the next five minutes. If you behave in such a way as to deliver value in the short term, the ability to meet long-term goals will be much easier. In this way, we can sustainably deliver value;
- We have a tendency to look at our department or its immediate surroundings. It is vital to look at the whole picture to avoid sub-optimization. For IT, this means at least taking an integral view of a service towards a customer. This view helps teams to make decisions about priorities.

The central behavior underlying these aspects is learning. People working within Lean IT organizations distinguish themselves from other organizations by the fact that they are prepared to learn and that their environment encourages them to learn. Coaches and leaders play an important role in ensuring that this learning can and does take place.

Lean IT is about thinking and acting. The thinking is based on a number of beliefs that support Lean behavior. In Lean thinking, there is a fundamental desire to add value to customers. The vast majority of people come to work to do the right thing, especially if it means having a happy customer. One of the more difficult aspects of a Lean attitude is to be critical *and* to bring a solution. Most people are capable of being critical but forget to bring the solution. The last two beliefs are related to a positive view of people: their ability to rise above themselves and to work together to produce better results than what an individual can do alone. If we believe that improvement is possible, it is a small step to take the responsibility to make the improvement happen. We will look at continuous improvement from a methodical perspective in Part V. However, it is important to understand the impact of continuous improvement in terms of behavior. Understanding that small concrete adjustments can make a considerable difference from one day to the next is vital to ensuring that these adjustments are made. These adjustments can only be made if learning is turned into part of the daily routine within the Lean IT organization.

What makes a Lean transformation a long-term success? When an organization starts with Lean, the first improvement proposals are often evolutionary. These are often quite quickly identified and these quick wins are swiftly implemented. At the start, the success of Lean is quite visible. As time goes by and many improvements are identified and implemented, it becomes more difficult to identify new improvement opportunities. The low hanging fruit has been taken. This leads to comments such as "we're finished with Lean; there's nothing left to improve." Generally, people forget that every improvement is a step forward.

How do organizations succeed in integrating the Lean way of thinking into a long-term source of success and truly adopt a continual improvement attitude? One of the key challenges is for continuous improvement to become an integral part of the paradigm used by leaders for steering the organization.

Part V

Continuous Improvement

"Lasting Improvement is achieved only when people work to higher standards. Maintenance and improvement have thus become inseparable."

Masaaki Imai

25

Improving

This is the most difficult phase to achieve and, more importantly, maintain. The reason is that teams and management will seek to reduce the amount of energy they need to expend. So far, the effort has been considerable, and leaders and teams work to embed habits. As habits set in, the way of working and the choices that are made are no longer or insufficiently challenged. The IT organization that is able to build the habit of challenging, learning and carrying out improvements on a long-term basis is the organization that has reached the Know Why stage and can claim that Lean has become its modus operandi. Both types of kaizen (daily and improvement) must be present in an IT organization for it to continuously improve. As one of the pillars of Lean and Lean IT, ensuring that an IT organization is competent at ensuring continuous improvement in line with the interest of the customer(s) is absolutely vital to the success of Lean within IT.

In this part, we will look at the last piece of the Lean IT Expert puzzle: mastering continuous improvement and becoming a Lean IT kaizen lead. The Lean IT kaizen lead is someone who is involved with Lean improvement at any level of the IT organization, in any "department" or team.

Lean is particularly known for its desire to improve using small steps. This is the preferred method because of the relative ease with which small improvements can be achieved. Small steps do not require much effort in managing organizational change. In fact, small changes often feel highly logical, even desirable, for those being asked to incorporate the change into their work. This does not mean that there cannot be situations within a Lean environment where larger changes are necessary. To this end, Lean recognizes three words used to define different types of improvement: kaizen, kaikaku and kakushin.

Kaizen is the Japanese word for continuous improvement using small incremental changes. It translates as "change for the better." Kai means "change" and zen means "for the better." Kaizen is an approach to continuous improvement that involves solving problems. When applied to the workplace, kaizen means continuous improvement involving everyone, leaders and team members alike, every day and everywhere, providing structure to process improvement. Kaizen is about continuously improving: everyday, everyone and everywhere. Many small improvements implemented with kaizen produce faster results with less risk. In IT, we can equate this to a minor update to a piece of software.

Lean also recognizes that there are moments where more radical, step change is necessary. This type of change is known as kaikaku. This refers to a revolutionary change to the existing situation. Following the software example, kaikaku would be the upgrade of an application currently in use from a release level to a new release level. Software providers will often substantially change both the technical basis of the software and its functionality. For both IT and the user community, this means a large step change.

A third type of improvement known within Lean is kakushin. The idea contained within kakushin is that some change will form a complete deviation from the current situation. It is about innovation, transformation, reform and renewal. Again, in our software example, this may mean implementing an application to support a process previously not supported by automation, leading to an altered business process, for example a web-based application that fully automates the registration of orders, the submission of invoices and the generation of a picking order at the order fulfillment. This kind of change will entail the disappearance of roles and functions within a business, both from technological and business process perspectives. The example represents a complete deviation from the current way of working.

Before we can dive into the methodology of solving problems, in the spirit of Lean as a way of thinking and acting, we must investigate the starting point of kaizen: developing a kaizen mindset. This is fundamentally about believing that improving IT services and the way they are delivered can and must be done on a daily basis.

Just to remind you, the core elements of a kaizen mindset are:

1. Seeing and prioritizing problems: Are leaders and team members truly prepared to uncover problems, accept them as a part of daily life and initiate action to identify the problems that most need solving?

2. Solving problems: Are leaders and team members prepared to invest time and other resources to understand the root causes of problems and resolve problems completely?
3. Sharing lessons learned: Are leaders and team members driven to share the lessons learned as a result of solving problems with others in the IT organization so that they may benefit from the lessons learned?

It is important to note at this point that problem solving is not about reactively waiting for problems to appear and then resolving them as they occur. A problem-solving mindset involves first establishing a desired state of the service or process, understanding the current baseline and gap and, then, to incrementally closing the gaps toward the desired state through improvement steps. The essence is that identifying problems and solving their root cause drives learning. In Lean IT, our mindset is that we accept that our world is filled with problems and we act to solve the problems on a continuous basis.

A problem is a difficulty that has to be resolved or dealt with. If we look at problems more specifically in relation to the Lean definitions, we find that standards are at the core of understanding whether we have a problem or not. The first type of problem we can identify is quite simple: the lack of a standard. Without a standard, there is no basis for improvement. The second type of problem we have is when we have a standard but are not able to achieve the standard. The gap between the current performance and the necessary performance is defined as the problem. Problem-solving is then focused on defining how we can ensure that the standard is achieved. This type of problem is sometimes referred to as an impediment because there is a blockage in the ability to deliver as desired. The third type of problem is when our existing standard no longer meets the requirements, for example, customers or regulators require us to work at a new level of quality. This type of problem is often referred to as an improvement (Figure 25.1).

Within Lean IT, we also recognize the Plan-Do-Check-Act cycle as an integral part of continuous improvement and recommend its use in all circumstances. For the specific task of problem-solving, the preferred method is DMAIC. This method has a proven track and it is easy to understand and adopt, and suitable for the majority of problems encountered within IT. DMAIC is suitable for both kaizen and kaikaku situations.

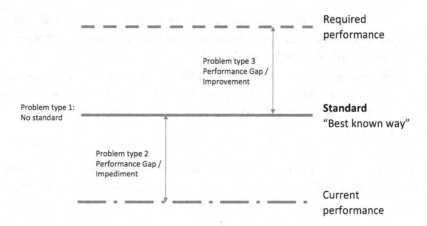

FIGURE 25.1
Three types of problems.

For kakushin, DMEDI (Define, Measure, Explore, Develop and Implement), an approach similar to DMAIC, is strongly based on data and statistical analysis, and can be used for more radical improvements. It requires the application of creativity in using data to design new processes, products and services. DMEDI aims at taking a step-change leap over existing processes, products, or services, and seeks to generate a competitive advantage. DMEDI is principally used in situations where existing processes, products or services work so poorly that they need to be designed from scratch, or where the gap between the desired state and the current performance remains huge. DMEDI can be used if an IT service or process continues to fail to meet customer expectations even after DMAIC has been used. The application of DMEDI requires a longer lead-time and considerable resources compared to DMAIC.

Lean has a relatively relaxed relationship with problems. In many organizations, problems do not always appear to be welcome. There is an inclination toward believing that higher levels of management prefer to hear a positive story and are not open to hearing about problems. This is represented by the statement often attributed to managers (and has on occasion been said to the author) "Don't bring me problems, I want solutions." The inference of this statement is that problems are not interesting, it is the solution that counts. Lean takes a completely different approach. Problems are fully accepted as a part of people working together. In fact, in Lean, there is a strong belief that problems are solvable, partially solvable, or at the very least their impact can be reduced, while the search for the root cause continues. Problems are seen as opportunities in disguise, and are challenges that encourage people to overcome them. Lean sees problem solving as a leadership activity regarding the identification of future or desired state and the relentless pursuit of closing the current gaps between the desired state and the current situation. Problem solving is about establishing the way forward, making the difference between the status quo and a better situation. When we solve a problem within an IT organization, in essence, we are removing muri, mura and/or muda from people, process and/or technology.

As a result of the speed of development of the IT industry, we are continuously confronted with new situations. Inevitably, new situations generate new problems that need to be solved. However, not only new situations require problem solving. Within IT, we are confronted on a daily basis with disruptions to existing services. These unplanned outages or failures impact the users of IT services who then require support. Providing this support means restoring the service by solving an incident but also the application of Problem Management practices to identify the root cause and establish solutions to ensure the disruption does not occur again in the future. The necessity to solve problems permanently has been long recognized within IT. The term "Problem" is defined as "the cause of one or more incidents." The Problem is one of the key units of work within an IT organization. Problem Management is one of the core operational IT processes, as defined in ITIL. Its aim is to prevent problems and incidents, eliminate repeating incidents and minimize the impact of incidents that cannot be prevented.

Problem Management is made up of two parts. The first part is aimed at uncovering the root cause of incidents. A Problem for which the root cause and a workaround are known, is called a Known Error. A workaround is a way of reducing the impact of the problem and associated incidents when the full resolution is not yet known. The second part focuses on removing the Problem from the IT service infrastructure. In many cases, this is done by carrying out a change. The DMAIC methodology is completely compatible with the Problem Management process. In fact. using DMAIC to solve technical problems provides additional structure and discipline within the IT organization.

An anecdotal example of problem-solving without DMAIC is fairly typical for non-Lean IT organizations. An incident has occurred with an important business application. The traditional flow has taken place. This means the incident call has been placed with the service desk. The service desk has routed the call through to the department that appears to be most closely related to the cause of the failure, in this case the server department. After some research, the department can see that the application is "in distress" but determines that nothing is wrong with the server. After some delay, they pass the call through to the network department, where the problem appears to be. Again, after a delay, the call is picked up and investigated. Once again, the department determines that it has nothing to do with them. The call is bounced back to the service desk. The service desk team member, who by now has had to answer a number of "status" calls ("when is this disruption going to be resolved?"), passes the call to the application team. The application team can see something is wrong but cannot work out what is going on. By this time, the incident has been escalated by the users to a hierarchical level in the business that automatically means the IT manager is called and is "helped to understand" how important it is that the application is restored. The IT manager comes out of his office, walks around the various departments and then calls together the three technical experts who have had a look at the situation. Then part II of the charade starts. The experts start by pointing out that the incident is not the fault of their part of the technology. They are each able to explain what is "probably" wrong in the other domains. The next step is that the experts start throwing solutions at each other: "Have you tried restarting the application?", "Have you looked at the OS?", "Have you checked the firewall settings?" and so on. This can take some time. All the while, the customer waits.

The situation is very different if the IT organization has adopted DMAIC as the standard structured problem-solving method. This may not prevent the first round of individual investigations, but the investigations will be more thorough. When the team comes together, each expert will bring their definition of the problem, the associated data, their analysis and potential solutions. They will then go through the same process of defining the problem collectively, understanding the measurements and maybe doing some more, followed by collective analysis and so on. Since all of the participants know the problem-solving procedure, they can carry it out quite efficiently. Problem management using DMAIC is an excellent way to get team members to practice using the structured problem-solving method to improve the quality of IT services.

Kaizen needs to be organized. Even in the high-pressure situation of an incident, bringing together the right resources to tackle the problem is important. Although I will spend a fair amount of space describing the details of kaizen, it is important to realize that this process can be carried out quickly by people who are well versed in the method. When you start out, it can be a fairly slow, pain-staking affair. Remember, it is about building habits. Once the method has become a habit, you and your team will be able to carry it out more efficiently.

In order to solve a problem, we must first accept that the problem is often not solvable by an individual; that it is only with the power of a diversity of points of view that the problem will be adequately addressed. This brings us to two major questions: How many people are necessary in the kaizen team? And do they have specific roles

To start with the first question, practice has shown that five to eight people is the optimum range. This includes all roles. With fewer than five participants, the diversity of points of view can be compromised and the work that needs to be done is spread over a small group. If you find yourself needing a larger team, then the scope of the problem is probably too large. There are basically three roles in a kaizen team.

First and foremost is the kaizen team member. These are people doing the required work. They must be involved with the problem as it occurs in the work. They must have intimate knowledge of the process in which the problem occurs, i.e. they must work in the process on a daily basis. It is useful to have people who are "upstream" and "downstream" of where the problem occurs. Also, having someone who is involved with the problem but can look at it from a dispassionate point of view, can be useful to avoid tunnel vision. Selecting the correct team members for a kaizen team is the next challenge. It is clear that we need diversity. This means the team must include people who work in the process, maybe a manager who is close to the process, but not necessarily the manager of the process (who may be the sponsor). The team will need a variety of skills and knowledge, for example, technical, business and regulatory rules governing the process.

The second role is the kaizen sponsor: This person is the owner of the problem, the person who has a direct interest in having the problem solved. The kaizen sponsor must have an affinity with the problem and must also be prepared to do what is necessary to get the problem solved. The kaizen sponsor is someone at a higher level of management who truly feels the pain of the problem, and therefore the need for its resolution. This does not mean that the resolution can be at any price. Without this person, there is no point carrying out a kaizen event. Especially, when time (and maybe some money) will be spent understanding and solving the problem.

The final role is the kaizen lead. This person manages the kaizen process on behalf of the sponsor and the team. This role ensures that the correct steps are followed as efficiently as possible so that the right actions can be taken as quickly as possible to remove the problem. This person must be experienced in managing the kaizen process and ensuring that the team stays on track. A kaizen lead must have facilitation and team-building skills in order to turn the group into an effective team in a short time.

When an IT organization starts with problem solving, getting the various roles to work properly is a challenge. The first issue is that the kaizen lead, being the one who knows the process is also seen as the scribe and an additional pair of hands. This is not the case. The role of kaizen lead is actually much more taxing than it may seem. The kaizen lead must ensure that the process is followed, which means being alert for jumping to conclusions, tunnel-vision, groupthink, dominant behavior and other such barriers to reaching the right conclusions. The kaizen lead also needs to be aware of whether the team needs to use a specific tool and to teach the team how to use the tool. Often, the kaizen sponsor will be unclear about what they need to do. The kaizen sponsor must describe the problem as they see it to the team, and must be prepared to discuss their view of the problem with the people experiencing the problem on a daily basis i.e. the kaizen team members. Regularly, the sponsor presents a statement which includes a "preferred" solution, thus killing any chance of having a meaningful discussion about the problem at hand. The other, more serious, problem is that the sponsor is not able to deliver a believable feeling of desire or sense of urgency to have the problem solved. The team needs to feel that the sponsor is losing sleep or has a stomach ache because of the problem. This is where most IT leaders do not provide the right impulse to get things done. When it comes to organizational problems, which is what most Lean problems are, leaders seem to have a "long-term" view. Only not the right long-term view. They tend to assume it will take a long time to solve the problem. Changing the way processes work is seen as something that will not happen in the short term. This is because adjusting processes is lumped into the "Organizational Change Management" basket. And changing organizations is seen as a long-term, slow and painful process. Lean IT does not see it this way. Adjusting processes, changing ways of working, in fact any change is seen as the short-term implementation of small, low-cost solutions to alleviate the symptoms of problems while working toward understanding the root cause. Leaders, and particularly those acting as sponsors for kaizens, must learn to look differently at the problems their organizations face. In many IT organizations, I have encountered leaders who literally give process problems a lower priority, even when they are identifiably the cause of customer dissatisfaction. Often saying that there are more important problems to solve, by which they mean technical glitches in the IT services or projects that are behind schedule. To be clear: You have technical glitches and problems with your projects *because* you have process problems. Solving process problems is the key to the solution of all other problems. Focus on getting the processes right and the results will follow! It is important to remember that the selection of the problem to be solved is always a cooperative affair. This means that a sponsor selects the problem they feel has the highest priority. However, if the team believes a different problem needs to be resolved first, then the sponsor must respect that fact and select a new problem. In the meantime, the sponsor may need to collect more evidence that the problem not selected needs to be looked into next time around.

In day-to-day working within a Lean IT organization, we have seen that problems are brought up on a daily and weekly basis, and posted on an improvement board. There is thus always a ready inventory of problems to be solved. This inventory of problems will contain both daily kaizen initiatives that need to be picked up; there will also be problems that need some more attention in the form of a kaizen event. The fact that a problem has found its way onto an improvement board means that there is someone who thinks it is important to be resolved. The question is: Does this person have the support of others, especially those in the position to allocate resources for the resolution of the problem? Assuming there is sufficient need to solve a particular problem, usually the kaizen sponsor or a small team of people including the sponsor will create a short kaizen charter in which the problem is described and an indication is given about the requirement for resources (people, time and money) for the resolution of the problem. Also, the time within which a solution should be found will also be indicated. This means that an initial stakeholder analysis must have been done. Based on the kaizen charter, the event can be planned and prepared. This means organizing basic things, such as a location where the kaizen team can meet with whiteboards, flip-overs, marker pens, sticky notes and access to data sources. The sponsor must also ensure that the participants are invited.

Planning a kaizen may appear to be simple. Just get a bunch of people in a room and get them solving a problem. The reality is more complicated. Ideally, a kaizen is planned within a short time, in which the kaizen team dedicates their time to solving the problem. In practice, within an IT organization, this kind of planning is quite difficult. Especially at the start of a Lean IT transformation, the organization is not attuned to the fact that people are out of the "production" process for a number of days, even full weeks. To be clear, the optimal way to run a kaizen is to have a team focus on the problem in a dedicated fashion for as long as it takes to come up with one or more suitable solutions. This tends to meet fierce resistance, particularly from the leaders who find it impossible to envisage "losing" up to eight people for any length of time. Conveniently, leaders forget that people go on holiday or get sick. No, the issue is that we are now consciously *choosing* to remove people from the work process in order to solve a problem. Herein lies the crux, leaders need to understand the benefits of solving the problem and that a couple of days of absence is often a miniscule price to pay for the effect achieved. One of the effects is that leaders start to realize that improvement is not optional and time must be reserved to solve problems. It is the application of the systemic thinking and constancy of purpose leadership principles that help leaders to ensure problem solving is factored into the regular work.

Generally, IT organizations start by experimenting with carrying out kaizen based on five or six meetings of two to three hours per meeting at regular intervals over a period of maybe two weeks. This gives engineers the time to carry out operational work in the meantime. On top of this, the kaizen team members also need to do kaizen work, for example data collection, processing of data, preliminary analysis, communicating the intermediate outcomes of the kaizen with their own team or discussing the feasibility of solutions with people outside the kaizen team.

In almost every case, the result of the first few kaizen carried out in a scattered way, is that planning an initial period of two days for the team to work in a dedicated way on the kaizen works best. In the run-up to the two-day session, the initial problem statement will be created and the team members selected. During the time before the start of the kaizen, the team members can already start collecting data they feel is relevant. One solution to the planning problem is to plan kaizen moments into the IT organization's calendar, for example two consecutive days every two weeks. The problem to be tackled can be identified two to four weeks in advance giving the sponsor time to select team members, and giving team members the time to prepare themselves (Figure 25.2).

Having planned the kaizen sessions, the problem now becomes: Can we find 26 problems per year to solve? The answer is that once the organization truly opens itself to the problems that it has, finding something for a kaizen team to do is easy. Most IT organizations have no shortage of known

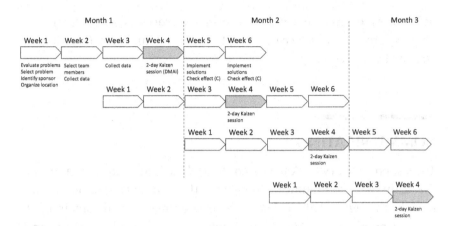

FIGURE 25.2
Planning of fortnightly kaizen.

errors or opportunities for improvement, if they look properly. Deciding which kaizen initiatives deserve the resources, involves deciding which is most important to the customer and the organization as a whole. Having made this primary decision, we must check the feasibility of the initiative.

As we saw earlier, problems can be signaled by one or more of four "Voices." The most important voice is the Voice of the Customer (VoC) which gives the IT organization feedback on how the customer, the user of the IT service, actually experiences the IT service. Voice of the Process (VoP) indicates which processes may not be working correctly. Again, the VoC may indicate that the results of the process may be satisfactory and the VoB may not have any issues with the costs or quality. However, process measurements may indicate that, for example, even though changes are delivered on time and with few incidents, the variability of the process gives cause for concern. The Voice of the Business (VoB) tells us whether there are issues in the IT organization itself; not to be confused with the fact that the customer of IT is regularly referred to as "the business." Even if the VoC does not identify any problems, the VoB may well find problems to be solved. An example could be that the customer is very happy with the quality of the IT services, but the Voice of the Business tells us that cost levels are too high and that budgets will be exceeded before the end of the year. Finally, the Voice of the Regulator (VoR) identifies where the organization must improve to meet regulatory requirements. IT may also be directly affected by regulators. The Sarbanes-Oxley Act specifically stipulates that IT must create an audit trail of changes and for user authorizations. As IT becomes more entwined with the primary processes of business, or even replaces these primary processes with systems that only require humans to see the exceptions, IT will find itself more directly affected by the regulator.

COMMUNICATING

The last preparatory work that needs to be done is to define how and when the team will communicate progress. The minimum communication must be through a daily update of the improvement board containing the relevant problem. This should be supplemented by regular submission of the current state of an A3 report. One of the powerful tools that Toyota has institutionalized within Lean is working with A3 reports. This tool supports and promotes continuous improvement, and is based on the PDCA cycle. A3 is not a clever acronym, it simply refers to the size of a piece of paper. A3 is 29.7 cm by 42 cm (11.7 in by 16.5 in). It is twice the size of A4 and half the size of A2. The beauty of the A3 sheet is that it provides enough space to explain a relatively complicated story, but limits the writers in their verbosity. The aim of the A3 is to encourage conciseness in the communication of a message. A templated version of the A3 also works as a checklist to ensure adherence to the chosen problem-solving methodology. It is important to understand that there is no hard and fast way to complete an A3 problem-solving sheet. In fact, the most basic form of A3 is an empty sheet of paper. It is however much easier to create an A3 report if you have some guidance as to what needs to be written on the sheet.

Most A3 templates tend to have up to eight sections. A quick search on the internet will reveal a multitude of variants. It is important that the problem-solving A3 covers the complete PDCA cycle. In any case, it must help the team compiling the A3 to follow a structured problem-solving method and it must help people to understand the logic behind the solutions chosen.

One of the well-known templates of the A3 problem-solving sheet (Sobek and Smalley, 2008), includes the following elements:

- Background: In this section, the context in which the problem exists is described. This may include a brief history of the IT organization or department in which the problem exists. The background section will include a description of the problem.

- Current Condition: Here we describe the current condition surrounding the problem. This may include complications that cause the problem to remain in place.
- Future State Goals: This is a description of the way the situation should be if the problem did not occur. Preferably, we should be able to define in concrete terms what would happen if the problem no longer existed. "Concrete" may even mean setting a numerical target that should be achieved as a result of the resolution of the problem.
- Analysis: This section includes a short description of the analysis that was done to discover the root cause of the problem.
- Proposed Options: Here we find the list of possible solution candidates to the problem.
- Plan/Improvement: This is where the improvements to be implemented are described and a brief plan is created for their implementation.
- Follow-Up: After the chosen solutions have been implemented, there must be one or more follow-up actions to ensure that the adopted solution remains in place. There must be at least one action to inform others of the lessons learned from the problem-solving action and/ or to communicate the solution to other parts of the organization where they may be suffering from the same issue.

The associated A3 may look like the template in Figure 25.3. You may, however, wish to have an A3 that more closely mirrors the chosen methodology, with five sections focusing on DMAIC (Figure 25.4).

As we stated earlier, within IT, we not only recognize problems to be solved; we also recognize Problems (ITIL definition). These tend to be issues of a technical nature that are the root cause of incidents. An A3 model for the resolution of these Problems could look like the one shown in Figure 25.5.

In their book *Understanding A3 Thinking: Keys and Tools for PDCA Management*, Sobek and Smalley (2008) describe two other forms of A3 report: the A3 status report and the A3 proposal. These are again variations on the above themes, but with different purposes. The A3 status report is aimed at informing all stakeholders of the progress of the execution of a long-running project or action. This type of A3 is not so much focused on analysis, rather it aims to continually check whether the assumptions made continue to be correct and ensure that it is clear which actions need to be taken.

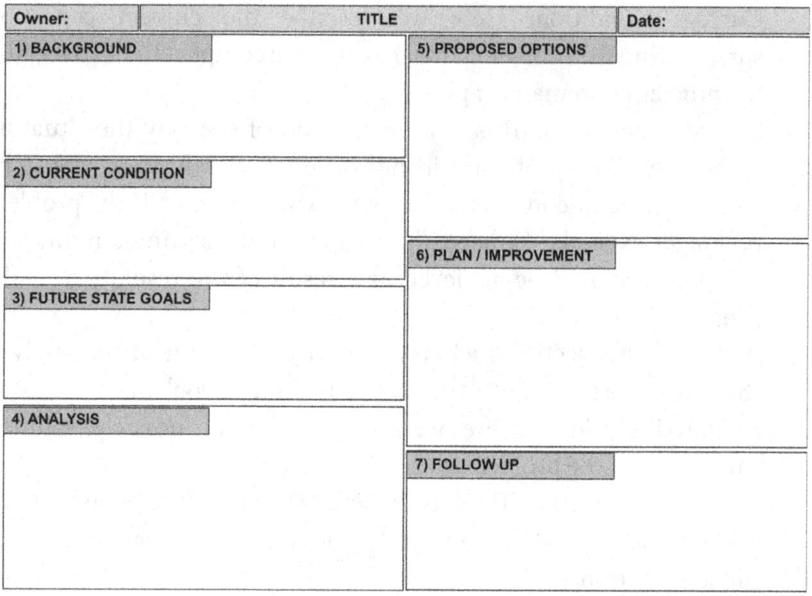

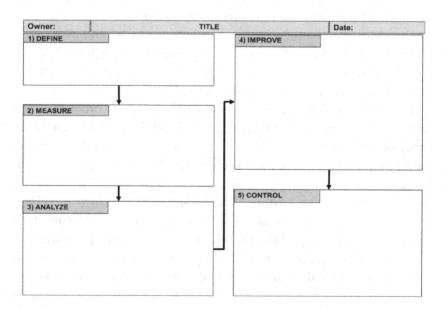

FIGURE 25.3
Example of an A3 problem-solving template.

FIGURE 25.4
Example of an A3 problem-solving template based on DMAIC.

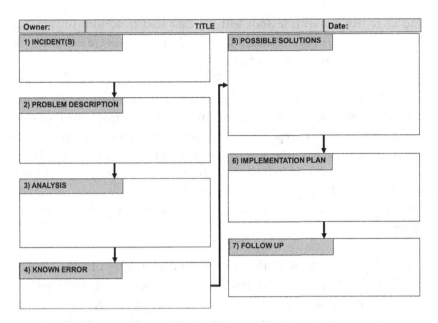

FIGURE 25.5
Example of an A3 problem-solving template based on ITIL problem management.

An A3 status report will tend to focus on the Check and Act aspects of the PDCA cycle.

The key components of the A3 status report are:

- Background: In this section, the context is described. This may be a concise version of the problem-solving A3 for which the A3 is a status report.
- Current Conditions: Here, the progress of the project is described. The changes that have already been made are described.
- Results: This is the key section of an A3 status report. The current conditions are the consequence of actions taken. These actions have led to results. It is the results on which the decisions are taken whether to continue and, if so, which course of action to take.
- Remaining Issues/Action Items: The A3 status report ends with the upcoming actions. These may be based on issues encountered during the process of getting into the current condition or they may be actions based on the original plan.

The A3 status report is an important document to support the learning process within the organization. Each status report must lead to some kind of reflection, with lessons learned that lead to action. In this way, the A3 status report is embedded into the daily kaizen, and enhances the continuous improvement mindset.

The A3 proposal is used for creating a recommendation for action. Generally, the A3 proposal will be aimed at implementing new policy or for carrying out a project that entails substantial investment of time and/or money. This A3 report focuses principally on the Plan phase of the PDCA. It will also describe how the Do, Check and Act phases need to be carried out, i.e. it should indicate how the proposal will be monitored as it is being executed and post-implementation phase.

The A3 proposal report is more similar to the A3 problem-solving report.

- Background: As with the A3 problem-solving report, this section includes the context within which the proposal is being written.
- Current Condition: This is the key section of this A3. It should be clear from this section why the proposal needs to be made and why it is important to seriously consider its execution. The main issues must be clear to the reader.
- Proposal: This is a description of the proposed course of action.
- Analysis/Alternatives: This section is all about the business case for the proposal.
- Plan Details: In this section, the reader is given the details of what will be involved with carrying out the proposed change. It is vital that stakeholders, necessary resources and consequences are made clear.
- Unresolved Issues: In this section, issues that are not (sufficiently) addressed that may have an impact on the execution of the proposal, are dealt with. In essence, these are risks that may affect the proposal.
- Implementation Schedule. This is a high-level plan of how the proposal would be implemented.

In all cases, the text in an A3 must be created in such a way that the audience clearly understands what problem has been solved, what the status is of a particular project, or what the proposal is. The A3 must be written from the perspective of the reader!

Now for the reality check: Completing an A3 takes practice. Creating a high-quality A3 complies with the statement "If I had more time, I would have written a shorter letter." It takes time and skill to turn the A3 into a powerful communication tool. There are four basic skills that are necessary for a kaizen team.

The first key skill, summarize, is the ability to express thoughts, facts, and other information concisely. Although an A3 sheet looks quite large when it is blank, the act of filling it with the relevant information can be quite a challenge. It is vital, therefore, to stick to the information that has a direct bearing on the issue at hand, be it a problem, a proposal or a status. In order to summarize, we need the two other skills. The ability to analyze and synthesize. Analysis is part of most A3 reports in some form or other. The aim of analyzing is literally to separate something into its constituent parts or elements. It is vital when writing an A3 report to understand the parts of the problem so that only the right information is given. If we are able to discern the parts of a problem, we can also determine which of these parts are relevant to the reader. The opposite is also true. One of the best ways of summarizing is by combining parts or elements. The ability to synthesize can be defined as combining a number of discrete elements to make a coherent whole. This is important when the parts do not immediately appear to have individual relevance to the issue. These skills support the need for systemic thinking when solving problems. Once we have analyzed, synthesized and summarized, we need to tell a story succinctly. In line with the "a picture paints a thousand words" adage, it is strongly recommended to turn your story into a visual experience using pictures and graphics to explain what has been investigated and what is proposed as a solution.

Using the aforementioned skills will help to determine the parts of the story about your kaizen. You will then need to construct the story in a way that is easy for the stakeholders to understand. This will help stakeholders to accept the solution you are proposing. There are many ways to construct a story. The one we will deal with in this publication is Barbara Minto's *The Pyramid Principle: Logic in Writing and Thinking* (2008). This is a method that is fully compatible with A3 thinking. In fact, it helps to structure the information and insights gained during the kaizen event.

The problem is framed using the Situation-Complication-Key Question sequence: The situation represents the current situation and ambition of what the situation will look like when the problem is solved. The complication describes the things that are keeping the current situation the way it is or preventing the problem from being solved. And the key question is the question to be answered; the problem to be solved (in question form). In effect, this is one way of creating a problem statement. We will look at another similar method in the Define phase.

In fact, the most important part for the A3 is how the answer is structured. This is where the elements of the analysis are structured in order to present a coherent set of motivations supported by arguments, completed by the proposed course of action. The answer includes the structuring process required to bring the Measure, Analyze and Improve steps together (Figure 25.6).

Using the Pyramid Principle means using a bottom-up approach for grouping arguments (the A's in Figure 25.6) in a logical way such that they support a motivation for the answer you give. The Answer should be supported by three clear motivations as to why this answer is the best answer to the key question. The arguments and motivations will come from the Analyze phase of your kaizen event. The answer will be the result of the Improve phase. A useful technique in constructing an argumentation pyramid is MECE. This stands for Mutually Exclusive, Collectively Exhaustive. Mutually Exclusive means that all items in a particular category only belong to that category, and no other category. Collectively Exhaustive means that all possibilities have been covered. In an IT context, we may encounter a situation where there is a lack of satisfaction with two services. Based on a data set including a variety of calls, we would need to have each call put into a single category, e.g. the call may be an incident, a service request, a request for information or a complaint. These categories would need to be defined in such a way that all calls in the data set fall into one of the four categories, and only one of the four categories. In this way, the analysis on which the data is

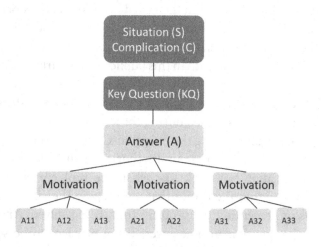

FIGURE 25.6
Structuring a story according to the pyramid principle.

based would be assured to be MECE. Subsequent conclusions drawn and proposals suggested would also be relevant to the correct calls. Analysis may show that the calls for a particular application are distributed 80% incidents and 20% service requests, whereas a second application may have 20% incidents, 40% requests for information and 40% service requests. Assuming for one moment that the absolute volumes of calls are the same, the analysis may conclude that application 1 is technically unsound since it has many technical disruptions. Further analysis may identify the causes of these disruptions. Secondly, the analysis may show that there has been insufficient training of users regarding application 2 because there are many calls for support.

The result is two motivations: Resolve the technical problems and train the users, and a series of arguments leading to these motivations. The answer to the key question may then be: We need to invest differently in applications 1 and 2, to increase the user satisfaction of the two services.

By this point in your transformation, the leadership team should be working with an obeya which will have an improvement board. Each of the teams that has been through its analysis and implementation phases will have an improvement board. So there should not be a shortage of problems to choose from when it comes to kaizen. Your problem should be selecting the next problem to solve. The best kaizen selection is based on identifying the problems that best match the current needs, capabilities and objectives of the IT organization, related to the Voices.

Each problem needs to be investigated at a high level from three perspectives: results for the customer or business benefits, feasibility and organizational impact. The aim is to create a broadly prioritized list of possible kaizen initiatives. Each time a kaizen initiative is selected, the previous prioritization needs to be reviewed to ensure that it is still valid. Kaizen candidates on the list may in the meantime have a lower priority due to a series of daily kaizen actions, or as a result of changes in the customer's environment. The initial high-level understanding of business benefits, feasibility and impact will be reviewed in the Define phase of the kaizen. If we turned out to have chosen the "wrong" kaizen, it is always possible to "pull on the andon cord" and stop the process. Remember: It is important to not get lost in a "mini-kaizen" when investigating which problem needs to be solved.

26

Investigating Problems

DEFINING THE PROBLEM

"The beginning of wisdom is the definition of terms" is a quote attributed to Socrates (c. 400 BC). He might just well have said "The beginning of solutions is the definition of problems." And, in practice, it turns out to be true. Once a problem has been defined, the problem can appear to diminish in size or importance. As our understanding increases, so does our feeling of our ability to solve the problem. This issue of the perceived diminishing size of a problem gets more significant the more we understand about the problem. We will return to this issue as we go through the DMAIC cycle.

Unsurprisingly, "Define" is the starting point for DMAIC, namely with the definition of the problem to be solved. Before we can start, we need to identify which problem we are going to solve. This may appear to be simple, especially since one of the most prevalent starts to a sentence within IT is "The problem is ..." followed by a problem statement of dubious quality. On top of this, the "problem statement" usually includes the preferred solution somewhere in an adjoining sentence, e.g. "The problem is that [x] is not possible with Windows/Linux, but is possible with Linux/Windows," or "The problem is that development doesn't provide us in Operations with a decent handover document." A good way to start developing the kaizen mindset within the IT organization is to have a standard response to these "The problem is ..." statements. The standard response could be something like "But is that the real problem?" Experience has shown that this simple question gets IT people reconsidering their initial assertions about problems in a constructive manner.

Problems are mostly visible difficulties which confront the IT organization or individuals. However, problems never exist in isolation. There is always a cause. The cause and factors that keep the cause in place are the entities that we are trying to understand when we seek to solve a problem. One of the most difficult parts of defining a problem is that every problem has symptoms; phenomena that accompany the problem or serve as evidence that the problem exists. They are, however, not the problem itself.

Before we can start to investigate our problem, we must have a statement that helps the team investigating the problem to focus its attention. We call this a problem statement. A complete problem statement should include a description of the current situation, the reason why this is not acceptable and an indication of what the ideal situation looks like. Next, the problem itself is described, followed by the question to be answered. It is vital that the problem statement is Specific, Measurable, Achievable, Realistic, Time-bound (SMART) to ensure that the team solving the problem knows when it will be successful. The other reason for using a question as the form to describe the problem statement is that we can then discern the problem statement from any hypotheses we may have. A hypothesis is "a proposition, or set of propositions, set forth as an explanation for the occurrence of some specified group of phenomena, either asserted merely as a provisional conjecture to guide investigation (working hypothesis) or accepted as highly probable in the light of established facts" (Dictionary. com). A hypothesis is a statement that will start with the words "I/We think/believe that …". The hypothesis is as yet not supported by any factual basis. The hypothesis is based on people's beliefs as a result of their observations. These are by definition selective and biased, and very much in need of testing through thorough analysis of the data and facts that can be found. People can be very convincing in their assertions of the causes of problems. This is where the kaizen lead needs to be very alert during the kaizen event. It is very easy to take a hypothesis for fact, especially when it feels true to everyone in the room.

Let's investigate a common problem in IT organizations. We need all of our software changes to go into production seamlessly, without defects, where everyone is aware of and informed about the outcomes and status of the change. Right now, there are too many release failures, requiring rollbacks. If we do not address this problem in the short term, we will need to increase the number of resources needed to handle the ensuing incidents and rework. Consequently, we may miss future customer deadlines potentially resulting in lost revenue, SLA penalties, lost business and further damage to our quality reputation. The question to be answered by the kaizen team is: How can we halve the number of release failures in the next two months? This is specific. It is measurable. The team may debate whether it is achievable and realistic, but it is certainly time-bound.

As the discussions start, "solutions" will start flying around the room: "We need to test more thoroughly," "Nobody follows the change and release process," "We need to get a better development pipeline." At this stage of the proceedings, these are all hypotheses, and the kaizen lead needs to recognize these as such and feed this back to the team. In time, the individuals in this kaizen team will learn how to recognize hypotheses themselves and bring this skill into future kaizens they may be involved in.

Three associated hypotheses that need to be tested while investigating this problem could be formulated as:

1. We think that our ability to test changes is not good enough.
2. We believe that the adherence to the change and release process is inconsistent across the IT organization.
3. We think that the technology supporting certain software development and release processes is unstable.

These hypotheses will also help the team to identify what needs to be measured to understand the problem. More on the Measure phase in a little while.

There are many problems and in order to solve them, it is essential to know the characteristics of a problem. In 2007, David Snowdon and Mary Boone published the *Cynefin* (Welsh for "habitat") *model*, in which he categorized decision making into one of five types. Decision making is directly related to the underlying problem about which a decision must be made. It is, therefore, possible to use the same categorization to identify the type of problem we are dealing with. The Cynefin model contains the following five types: obvious, complicated, complex, chaotic and disorder (Figure 26.1).

The first type of problem is the obvious type. This is a problem that is caused by the fact that the rules have not been followed. The relationship between cause and effect is obvious to the people closely associated with the problem. It is reproducible, repeatable, and the outcome is predictable. This type of problem is often seen as operational problems and can be solved using best practices, ranging from technical user manuals to IT best practice frameworks. Where the problem is the result of people not following the required steps to achieve the desired outcome, a Standard Operating Procedure can be used. As long as the SOP is used, the problem

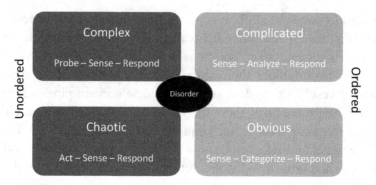

FIGURE 26.1
The Cynefin model.

should not reoccur. Obvious problems are particularly suited to daily kaizen. More often than not, obvious problems keep recurring because no one actually takes the time to solve them.

The second type of problems are the complicated problems. The relationship between cause and effect requires analysis which implies that expert knowledge is necessary. Having said this, the problem does follow rules. However, the rules may be more difficult to unravel than expected. In IT, there are many technical components that work together to deliver an IT service. Each of these components works according to pre-defined rules, which in the end boil down to 0's and 1's. Unfortunately, the rules of one component may interfere with the rules of another component. This is how complicated problems arise. This type of problem can be solved by using good practices, scenario-planning and systems thinking. Once understood, the rules for resolution can be defined and followed. There is a right answer that can be found. These are the types of problems where technical experts may disagree because they focus on the elements of the problem they recognize.

Obvious and complicated problems always require analysis, that is, breaking the problem down into a sequence of technical events. This is one of the reasons why it is important to record what activities have been carried out within an IT organization as it makes understanding the causes of obvious and complicated problems easier and quicker.

Complex problems are problems for which the cause and effect are explainable in retrospect. The issue has not been seen before and there are no known solutions or best practices available. The team needs to look for new ways to solve the problem. This kind of problem does not repeat in exactly the same way; outcomes may be unforeseen, and patterns emerge over time. To understand these problems, these patterns must be investigated. This means learning while solving the problem. This type of problem is frequently related to the human factors within IT organizations. We may need to carry out several different experiments to understand the dynamics of the problem and find a solution. There is not necessarily a single right answer and we can use guidelines to solve the problem. Generally seen as more strategic decisions and problems, they tend to affect social systems, rather than technical systems.

Lastly, there are chaotic problems. With these problems, no cause and effect relationship is directly perceivable. These problems are not detectable before the fact, there are no clear answers and there are elements of the problem that we cannot know when it is happening. These problems require crisis management that focuses on relieving symptoms to create some kind of stability. Typically, a leader will have to act quickly based on the information available to stabilize the situation in order to buy time for experimentation and learning. The crisis team must act to change the existing situation. All action must be aimed at trying to create order. When taking action, it is important to do a risk analysis of the action to understand what its consequences could be.

As opposed to obvious and complicated problems, complex and chaotic problems require synthesis. The team solving these kinds of problems needs to investigate how factors and symptoms interact to create the problem.

The final area to address is disorder. This is the situation in which we do not know into which of the four other categories the problem falls. Causality is not understood at all. From disorder, we can use the Cynefin model to determine which state the problem is in and then act accordingly. The danger with the disorder is that experts see the problem's symptoms as being part of an obvious type of problem. This may cause the problem to be underestimated or incorrectly diagnosed.

Generally, within IT, we use kaizen to investigate complicated and complex problems. If a problem turns out to be obvious, the solution will probably be found during the Define or Measure phases. We generally refer to the solutions found before the team starts the Analysis phase as quick wins.

Prior to the start of the kaizen, the sponsor, often together with the kaizen team, will select a problem and will assess whether it is worthwhile to spend time and effort on solving the problem. This assessment needs to be validated in the Define phase of the DMAIC cycle. In terms of business benefits, the kaizen team will need to consider aspects such as the impact on external customers, the business strategy and the financials of the business. On top of this, the urgency of the problem, whether the problem is getting worse and any dependencies related to the problem need to be considered. The sponsor and kaizen team members must then try to understand what effort must be expended to solve the problem, in other words, assess the feasibility of tackling the problem. The following aspects may be investigated: resources needed to tackle the problem, availability of the necessary expertise, complexity of the problem, the likelihood of success and the amount of support for solving the problem. Lastly, the team must look at whether solving a particular problem will provide the organization with the following additional benefits: learning benefits, cross-functional benefits and benefits in developing competencies or capabilities. A useful question to ask is: What will happen if we do not solve this problem, but a different problem instead?

Having validated the problem, it needs to be investigated. This is done by creating a Critical to Quality tree related to the problem, in which the customer's perspective of the problem is mapped out. This gives a first indication into the drivers of the analysis and which measurements need to be made in the Measure step. A second tool that needs to be used is the SIPOC. As we have seen this is about scoping the process; who is the supplier of the trigger to the process? What is the trigger? What is the output of the process and who receives it? What are the main steps that transform input to output? It is important to realize that every problem is a process problem. Even technical problems find their origins in poor process. As IT people, we have a tendency to think of ITIL processes when we hear the word "process." When solving a problem, we need to think more flexibly about processes. In the case later on in this chapter, the process that will be tackled is the "infrastructure work allocation process."

One of the pitfalls of the Define phase is putting too much detail in the process map (SIPOC). At this phase, you should strive to cover about 80% of all possibilities. The other pitfall is to bite off more than you can chew; ensure the scope is not too big. You should use some basic data and a refined SIPOC to re-scope the problem.

Within IT, there are always problems to solve. Some may seem trivial, whereas others are clearly quite significant. Table 26.1 shows a summary of typical IT problems. This list is merely a selection from kaizens commonly carried out within IT organizations and by no means complete. If you find yourself without problems to solve, consider this list. If none of these

TABLE 26.1

Common Problem Areas in IT

Problem	Explanation
Technical performance problems	This problem may come in a multitude of forms. Every piece of technology (hardware or software) may be a source of problems. Often, a piece of technology does not so much fail as just not perform well for any number of reasons.
"Fire-fighting," focus on solving incidents rather than structural resolution	IT organizations seem to have the time to repeatedly solve incidents, but do not make the time to remove the sources of these incidents. This leads to a highly ad hoc way of working, in which the number of incidents (both per unit of time and open at any one moment) continuously creeps higher.
Balance operational and change work	The classic statement here is: "I couldn't complete the change on time because I had to solve an incident." The key issue is that IT people are involved in all sorts of work, not just a single type.
Releases or "technical weekends" that cause problems the following work day	A key question within IT organizations is: Why do changes need to lead to more incidents? It should be possible to implement changes without causing further disruptions.
Planning and execution of work	This causes a huge amount of stress within IT organizations, as poor planning has a correlation with switching priorities.
Collaboration between development and operations, or applications and infrastructure	This is probably one of the most classic problems within IT organizations, departments that throw work "over the wall" to each other.
Changes applied without informing users	IT organizations and people are not renowned for their ability to communicate. However, this is a skill that must be mastered especially in a world where IT services are pervasive.
Constantly changing priorities	This causes context switching and work to be left incomplete (particularly the documenting). It is highly disruptive for the IT organization and ensures that not much gets completed in a satisfactory way.
Focus on achieving SLA KPIs	Engineers no longer focus on providing a great service but only look at whether they are achieving the numbers, and sometimes they do not even care about the numbers
Shared resources, dependency on specific individuals	IT people, especially the experts, are often required to be in multiple places at one time. They are allocated to multiple projects and continue to have a role in the operations. This often causes huge delays and highly stressful situations, leading to errors.
Lack of availability and capacity planning	Every IT organization knows that it should plan for the future and understand how its services will perform given the projected developments in their customer's organization. Very few actually do, leading to network capacity problems, disk space incidents, insufficient processing power, or poor human resource planning.

is a problem in your organization, you are one of the top-performing IT organizations in the world. Have a party to celebrate. If not, tackle the problem. And have a party anyway, you probably deserve it for some other reason.

Undoubtedly, while reading the list, you will have recognized problems; others may not be relevant in your IT organization. There will also be problems for which there are "standard" solutions ("if you use [standard IT solution], you can solve the problem"). Although the above problems may be recognizable, their specific causes may be diverse and different per IT organization.

A kaizen without support from stakeholders must not be attempted. Much attention is paid to sponsorship of the kaizen. However, if the team members, the primary stakeholders of any problem to be solved, do not see the point in solving the problem, then choose a different problem. If the team members are not convinced that the problem needs to be solved, then the acceptance of any solution will be very low. In many IT organizations, the term "problem owner" is used. In most cases, the problem owner is the same person as the kaizen sponsor. In larger organizations, the owner may be at a more senior level of leadership, and the sponsorship of the kaizen team may be delegated. In a situation where a particular problem exists across the entire IT organization, the owner may be the end-responsible IT leader (IT director, CIO, IT manager). In order to make the investigation of the problem manageable, the owner may choose to only investigate the problem in a single department. In this case, the manager of the department may act as sponsor for the kaizen team that is made up of people from within the department. The expectation is that lessons learned from the kaizen can be replicated across the rest of the organization.

Other stakeholders include people up and downstream of the place where the problem is identified. In pretty much every case, the customer will have an interest in the resolution of the problem, be it from a qualitative perspective or a cost perspective. Carrying out a stakeholder analysis is all about understanding where the various people involved stand on a particular issue, and what impact their view has on the success of addressing the issue. Not all stakeholders should necessarily be involved in the actual kaizen event. Some stakeholders provide input or data into the Measure phase, others need to be kept informed, and others need to be actively involved in the actual meetings. Stakeholders are directly or indirectly involved with the problem, often referred to as the "chicken or pig dilemma." When it comes to having a cooked breakfast, the chicken is indirectly involved by having to provide an egg; the pig is fully and directly committed as it needs to deliver the bacon. In the stakeholder analysis, the sponsor and kaizen team will need to understand which stakeholders fall into which category. On top of that, they will need to identify whether a stakeholder is positive, negative or neutral regarding the problem. And whether they have a strong and explicit opinion on the subject or whether they are not outspoken. Also, the stakeholder's influence must be investigated. Do they have formal or informal power regarding the problem? Adjust the analysis regularly throughout the kaizen to understand how the stakeholder's stance changes. Based on the influence (power or impact) and involvement (or interest), the team can readily identify types of stakeholders (Figure 26.2).

For each of the types of stakeholders, there is a communication strategy involved in keeping the stakeholders engaged with the problem.

The Define phase can be more difficult than it may appear at first glance. Take the example of an IT organization of about 100 people. There were four customer-oriented teams, a business intelligence team, a team of project managers and architects, and a group of technical experts responsible for the core of the IT infrastructure: networks, servers, databases, operating systems. These technical experts were allocated to customer-oriented support teams based on an estimated number of hours. For example, the three network engineers were allocated to the four customer-oriented teams for an average of 16 hours per team. The other hours were reserved for projects (these hours were "given" to project managers) and other work. You could say that the allocation of hours was "hard-coded" into

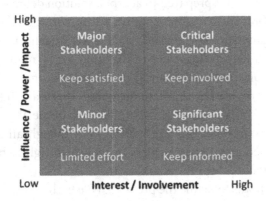

FIGURE 26.2
Example of stakeholder analysis model.

the organization. It was up to the technical experts to manage the time. Unfortunately, the actual requirements of the teams fluctuated over the weeks; some weeks they would need more time, other weeks they would need less. The effect was that these technicians faced an almost unmanageable flow of work from multiple teams, each clamoring for attention and putting pressure on the technicians to drop everything they were doing and come and help. In effect, the IT organization had created a situation of "shared resources." The result was a highly tense situation in which the management team was dissatisfied with the performance of the shared resources, the team leaders felt they did not get the service they had been promised and the engineers felt as though they were being pulled in all directions by four team leaders, multiple project managers and three management team members.

This situation existed for about a year and the situation had become explosive because neither the support teams nor the infrastructure technicians believed they were getting or delivering high-quality services. The primary stakeholders were the infrastructure engineers, the IT management team (MT) and the team leaders of the customer-oriented teams. The situation was, in fact, so explosive that the mere mention of the problem to any one of the stakeholders led to emotionally charged discussions about the quality and capabilities of the other stakeholders. The organization had recently started out on its journey to Lean IT. The teams had started with visual management and the choice had been made to start problem solving.

The first step was to understand whether there was a desire within the MT to actually solve the problem. The direct response was "of course." To the question, "Are you prepared to accept a solution defined in a kaizen?", there was a long silence. And here we encounter one of the key issues within IT organizations when they start using kaizen: the acceptance of the results of a kaizen. It is very challenging for IT managers to accept that the solution to a non-technical problem (as in this and many other cases) may be provided by the team members. This is a point that requires substantial coaching of leaders. Eventually, one of the MT members said he would act as sponsor for the kaizen, even though all MT members could be defined as problem owners in their own right. The other three agreed they would accept the result, as well.

The next step was to define the problem. Due to the emotionally charged nature of the discussion, we started with a pre-kaizen session with each of the three key stakeholder groups (experts, MT and customer teams).

In each of the sessions, the stakeholders were challenged to define their perception of the problem. They were also challenged to define the problem from the point of view of the other stakeholders.

After the exploratory sessions, a first kaizen session was organized, in which delegates from the three stakeholders came together. A total of nine people made up the kaizen team for the Define session. The lesson learned here is that nine people is too many. The main issue is that in a group of nine there are people who take a non-collaborative stance. When the group is smaller, it is easier to get the participants into a cooperative state of mind. The kaizen lead started the session by explaining the DMAIC procedure to be used throughout the kaizen. Then the discussion started. This first session was a complete disaster. It turned into a highly emotional exchange in which each of the parties involved voiced their entrenched gripes about the other parties. The experts bore the brunt of the complaints. The kaizen sponsor, the kaizen lead and two of the team members attempted to normalize the situation but failed as reproaches were fired across the room. The session was adjourned after a fraught hour.

The sponsor and lead evaluated what had just happened and determined that the group was too big and the approach too unclear for the participants. The second attempt, a couple of days later, was more successful. The team was reduced to six people, leaving the most vocal participants in the team. The sponsor took the lead by explaining from a very personal point of view why this problem needed to be solved. This took the participants somewhat by surprise but stressed the importance of solving the problem. This was a clear turning point in the kaizen and shows the importance of a kaizen sponsor who truly feels the pain of the problem.

The kaizen lead explained the procedure once again and set out the goal for this session: to agree on the problem statement to be solved. He stated the initial problem statement as defined by the problem owner or sponsor, and also asked all the participants whether they were prepared to do what was necessary to solve the problem, independent of personal preferences and opinions.

As a result of the previous sessions, it was quite easy for the participants to define the symptoms of the problem. It took a further two hours to finally gain full agreement among all parties regarding the problem to be solved. The result was particularly interesting because the problem statement was closest to that as stated by the technical experts. Management and team leaders did not use their hierarchical power to push through their idea of the problem to be solved. Other cases have proved that a two-hour session to define the problem statement for a complicated or complex problem is no luxury. In fact, it is often very necessary. This is because the team had to ensure that symptoms did not end up being defined as the problem. The kaizen lead had to continually keep the team focused on the goal and had to question the team members when he felt the symptoms were being turned into the problem. The key to agreeing on the problem statement is to determine the perspective from which the problem is being tackled. In this case, the problem could have been defined from the perspective of the customer teams, from the perspective of the individual experts or from the perspective of ensuring that the teams and the experts worked harmoniously together. In the end, the problem was defined in terms of getting the work done: How can we ensure that work is routed to the technical experts in a more manageable way? Another lesson learned from this session was the adage that "every problem is a process problem." We do not always know what the process is. This is why in the Define phase, you should always count on the fact that you need to produce a SIPOC related to the situation.

Having agreed on the problem statement, the team needed to agree on how much time they would take to solve the problem. The urgency and impact dictated that the team would work as fast as possible, setting two further meetings for the next two days.

This kaizen ended up focusing on the process for how work was to be brought to the technical experts and how it would be distributed among the experts. The result was that the technical experts were recognized as a team rather than a loose set of experts. They were given a team leader to help organize the team. The "hard-coded" hours were scrapped, and replaced by a prioritization mechanism, supported by visual management. As it turned out, the amount of work that entered the team was not excessive, it had been the inefficient work allocation mechanism that made it seem as though there was too much work. The customer teams had demanded that the technical experts join their week starts. This demand was dropped as a different communication mechanism was agreed: Once a month, a member of the technical team would join a meeting of the customer-oriented team in which the customer's plans were laid out. Within a month, the situation had become more stable and the relationships between the parties were improved. This does not mean that there were no embers of personal animosity, but the basis for better cooperation had been built.

The result of the Define phase is that the "Background" section of the A3 can be completed. Also, a start can be made on filling the Current

Condition and Future State Goals sections of the A3. These will be completed after the Measure phase, during which data will be found to further define both Current Condition and Future State Goals.

To summarize the Define phase, we find the following steps in the Define phase:

1. Problem Selection and Owner Identification	Use the criteria to determine whether a problem is significant enough to warrant solving in the short term. Always ensure that there is a person who owns the problem and sponsors the kaizen event (the kaizen sponsor). It is vital that the sponsor is serious about solving the problem. The owner/sponsor must be able to maintain the drive to solve the problem. This is an important reason why the kaizen event must be kept as short as possible because there will always be another problem around the corner that clamors for attention. This step may already have been sufficiently addressed in preparing the kaizen.
2. Problem Statement and Kaizen Team Selection	Create a problem statement, complete the background section of the A3 and select the right team members. Kaizen team members can be selected using the stakeholder analysis. The team members will have been selected prior to the event. In the Define step, it is important to validate that everyone has a strong interest in solving the problem. All team members must agree on the problem to be solved. If there is no agreement, then it is possible that there are two different problems that need to be solved, or stakeholders have been incorrectly identified. The kaizen lead may use an Ishikawa diagram as a visualization tool for collating symptoms of the problem, even though it is usually used for analysis of factors causing the problem. The kaizen lead can also use the Five Whys technique to understand and scope the problem.
3. Validate Scope of the Problem	Once we have defined the problem, we must validate its scope. The team must understand whether it is reasonable to expect the problem to be solved. To do this, we draw a SIPOC for the process in which the problem occurs. The team may need to adjust the scope based on insights gained from the SIPOC. During this step, it is useful to understand what type of problem needs to be solved. This will be an indicative typology to guide the team's resolution efforts. It is very important not to jump into a problem too quickly. It takes time to define the problem, and particularly, to gain agreement among the team members. The time is often spent learning to listen to one another. Team members have the tendency to repeat themselves with different words. Here, the role of the kaizen lead is extremely important. The lead must ensure that team members take the time to listen, often the managers in the team have the most difficulty with this aspect. A technique that the kaizen lead can use is to ask the person wanting to say something to repeat what the previous speaker has said, in his or her own words. This technique ensures that the previous speaker feels heard and the following speaker must address what has been said.

4. Collect Voice of the Customer Information	Having understood the scope of the problem, we need to bring together the Voice of the Customer information that is relevant to this specific problem. Use the Critical to Quality (CTQ) to collate and structure the information. Note that you may well have selected your problem based on feedback from the customer. Having validated, and possibly adjusted, the scope of the problem, you may need to go back to the customer for more specific requirements and wishes regarding the problem at hand. The team must formulate specific questions for the customer. Likewise, if the problem is based on a signal from the Voice of the Business or the Voice of the Regulator, the team must formulate clarification questions for the business or regulator.
5. Create a High-Level Plan	You will need to agree on a plan for the execution of the kaizen event. This will include practicalities, such as the availability of team members and the sponsor, availability of meeting facilities and agreement on the main deadlines. This needs to be done during the Define meeting. All participants must clear their agenda to ensure that the kaizen can be completed in a short period of time. Within IT organizations, this can be a considerable issue since IT people can rarely take off their work to do a kaizen full time. This is certainly one of the key challenges of doing kaizen in an IT organization. A suitable strategy is to plan five meetings (one for each phase) and ensure that there is time between the meetings so that actions can be carried out. The meetings should be planned as 3-hour meetings, which can always be finished early if the goals for the meeting have been met. The plan should also include how the (interim) results should be communicated, preferably using the A3 problem-solving template.

It is critical that all aspects of the Define phase are completed prior to moving to the Measure phase. If the problem statement is not fully defined and agreed by the kaizen team, there will be no basis to complete the following phases. This invariably leads to going back to the Define phase.

MEASURING THE PROBLEM

The second phase in the DMAIC cycle is the Measure phase. In this phase, we refine the problem statement based on measurements. The goal is to ensure that there is a detailed understanding of the current situation surrounding the problem area. This is done by collecting reliable data on the variables related to the problem. The aim is to provide information to help identify the underlying causes of the problem. We do this by creating a data collection plan based on the variables that we believe influence our problem, followed by the actual collection of as much of the data as we can. It is possible that we identify data that cannot actually be collected or would require a substantial effort in time, manpower or lead time to collect. Knowing we would like to collect the data may result in the creation of a measurement system for future use.

First, the team must define the data to be collected. The data obviously needs to be related to the problem statement. During this phase, we need to fully understand the role of variables in the resolution of problems. There are essentially three types of variables:

- Independent variable: This is an input. In the case of problem solving, the independent variable can be seen as something that may or may not contribute to the problem. The aim is obviously to find the independent variables that have the greatest effect on the problem.
- Dependent variable: This is the output; in effect, this is the problem.
- Control variable: This kind of variable is particularly useful in experiments. This variable is kept constant while others are changed so that they can be investigated.

The mathematical notation for the relationship between independent and dependent variables is: $y = f(x)$, where y is the dependent variable and x is the independent variable. The f means that the problem (dependent variable) is a function of independent variables. In fact, a clear notation would be $y = f(x1, x2, x3 ...xn)$. In this equation, we see that the problem may in fact be caused by any number of independent variables. The aim in the Measure phase is to find the independent variables (the x's) and understand their impact on the problem (the y). The latter will be further investigated in the Analyze phase.

Take the example of a desktop support department's inability to deliver laptops to customers within the agreed time. This is the y, the definition of the problem. The equation could look like this:

$$y = f\left(laptop, knowledge\ of\ employees, process, software, holidays, sickness, ...\right)$$

We would need to collect data regarding each of the independent variables to understand their effect on the problem. The task in the Measure phase is to determine the independent variables of the problem and to collect data regarding these independent variables.

In part II, we were introduced to the IT units of work. It is also useful to understand the characteristics of the units of work. This is a slightly different cross-section of the units of work. Within Lean IT, three categories of units of work are identified: runners, repeaters and strangers (Bicheno, 2008). A further refinement of the IT units of work is based on the time value of the work and the process dynamics.

- **Runners:** These are units of work that occur on a daily basis and tend to require up to one hour of work to be in a state of completion. Within IT, we can say that incidents, service requests, standard changes and operational activities fall into this category. The dynamics of these processes is that work is statistically predictable (per week), but the exact occurrence of the work is not known. This work cannot be planned as such, but time can be reserved for these units of work. These represent up to three quarters of the work in IT organizations.
- **Repeaters:** These units of work occur regularly; indicative frequency is weekly. Within IT, high impact incidents, small to medium-sized non-standard changes and the smaller advisory services fall into this category. This category is partly plannable (advice and changes). The average amount of time associated with repeaters within IT is two to four hours. However, the high impact incidents require a direct response, and therefore have a dynamic that more closely resemble runners. Unfortunately, their impact means that solving the incident can require a different effort than regular incidents. Repeaters may represent up to a quarter of units of work.
- **Strangers:** These are units of work that have an irregular occurrence. IT "strangers" are large non-standard changes, large requests for advice and plans, all of which tend to occur, or need updating on a monthly, or quarterly basis. The time associated with these units of work is very diverse, ranging from four hours to many tens of hours. Strangers do not include projects, as a project should be seen as a collection of standard and non-standard changes, i.e. a combination of runners, repeaters and strangers. This category generally does not exceed 10% of the work done in an IT organization.

Once we have identified the units of work and the type of unit of work with which the problem is associated, we can go and find data. During the Analysis phase of the Team Transformation, we took the opposite route. We use tools to identify where problems may exist. During the kaizen, we have a problem and use tools to find out what is causing the problem. Either way, we need to find data and facts to help us understand what is going on.

One of the most important aspects of collecting data is to understand its context. In Lean IT, we understand the context by going to the gemba, the place where the work is done. The key question is: What do you look for when you go to the gemba? The aim is to find out how specific data is used within the organization. This means going to the place where the data is used, understanding its usage and purpose. Observe the person using the data and ask questions to clarify how the data is used. Going to the gemba, observing the work being done, and understanding how data is used can help to determine what other data should be recorded. It may also lead to understanding unused, unrecorded or unrequired data.

In essence, there are three types of data that we need to collect: unit of work, technical and people data. Unit of work data is closely related to processes data. Technical data helps us understand the "behavior" of the technology and includes data from log files, monitoring and technical performance. Together, these give us information about events and other occurrences within the various IT components, alerts based on thresholds and data about CPU, memory, network speed/capacity and storage usage. People data focuses on time usage and the availability of skills and knowledge.

Data comes in two forms: quantitative data and qualitative data. These two forms of data require different measurement systems in order to collect the data meaningfully. Quantitative data is numerical data that is always expressed as a number. Quantitative data is data that is not influenced by people. The main measurement system of this data is automated data collection. Most systems register data in the course of their operation. In some cases, the amounts of data are quite substantial. This data is generally held in log files that can be consulted to find out when something exceptional happens or shows the trends of how the system is working. When using quantitative measurement systems, it may seem as though the data is objective. However, having a huge amount of data does not necessarily translate into information, since we may not have understood correctly what the data is telling us. In many cases, we will need experts to interpret what the systems are saying.

Qualitative data is generally expressed in non-numerical terms. Often, qualitative data is transferred to numerical data by giving it a scale on which answers are scored as numbers. Especially for qualitative data, visits to the gemba are necessary to check whether the data is being interpreted correctly, and to understand the context within which the data is generated and its variance from standard work. Qualitative measurement systems principally measure capability or maturity from the perspective of the people involved. Through the data collection method, qualitative measurement systems do attempt to create objectivity in the subjective data. This can be done by using a framework of criteria; most maturity models work on this basis. However, the maturity model is also based on human perception. This means that qualitative measurement systems are always open to bias, be it based on the questioning or on the answers. Three forms of qualitative measurement system are:

- Annotated Observation: This basically means watching what happens and noting the number of times something happens, the amount of time spent on a task, the number of errors made in finished products and other such objectively observable occurrences. The tool often used here is the check sheet, and an example is the Earning Capacity Analysis. The question for the researcher is whether they are actually watching a representative set of actions and does the fact that someone is watching have an impact, positive or negative, on the performance. By observing different subjects at different times, influence can be taken into account.
- Interview: One of the preferred methods of gathering qualitative information is through interviewing people involved or people associated with the aspect that is being investigated. An interview can involve one or more people involved with the subject matter. Generally, multiple points of view are sought when gathering information through interviews, since information from interviews is always biased. Interviewees do not always answer questions, they tell the stories they want to tell. Statements from interviews should be backed up with evidence. Carrying out multiple interviews often can remove any personal bias.
- Registration: During the course of work in an IT organization, data is recorded on work units (incidents, changes, problems and service requests). This data provides valuable input for understanding how the organization performs regarding these units of work. In registering units of work, the system records time stamps and other data either automatically or as a result of the action of a user. As a result of the dependency on human action, registration is seen as qualitative rather than quantitative. Often, registration data is

accessed through reports that are embedded in the tool where the information is stored. This can lead to misunderstandings because it is not always clear how the report has been built up. Taking the raw data out of the database can help mitigate this problem.

In order to create a valid qualitative measurement system, ensure the goal of the observation or interview is clearly formulated. Define the framework against which answers will be checked. Determine the questions to be answered and ensure the answers can be unambiguous. With observation, this can be relatively simple, using "Yes" or "No" type answers, counts or time measurements. During interviews, answers will often be narrative. Answers must be clearly noted. Ensure that answers can be, and are, recorded in a way to ensure that processing the answers to a suitable result of the measurement is possible. Both the processing and the raw data must be auditable. Lean IT examples of qualitative measurements are collecting data for Voice of the Customer or Skills and Knowledge Analysis. In both of the cases, the information is based on the opinions of the people involved.

Baselines and benchmarks are necessary to understand the relative value of the performance, as derived from the data. A baseline is the measurement of a situation in order to understand whether a change occurs based on an intervention after the baseline has been set. This is particularly useful in kaizen because we are very interested in the effect of changes that have been implemented in the IT organization. It is vital that during the Measure phase, a baseline is set which can be used to measure progress. A benchmark is a standard or set of standards used in evaluating the performance or level of quality of an organization. Benchmarking is a measurement used to compare the organization's position in relation to other organizations. Benchmarking can also be done between teams within a single IT organization. Benchmarking may be used during a kaizen to understand how well others perform a particular activity. This may help to identify what improvements are possible. Generally, benchmarking serves little purpose once an IT organization has truly entered its Continuous Improvement phase. The IT organization itself with its own standards serves as the benchmark for improvement. Seeking solutions from outside the organization is useful, but only understanding how another organization performs, usually without understanding the context within which the performance is taking place, does not help.

The result of the Measure phase is a data collection plan and collected data. This data will be processed in the Analyze phase (Figure 26.3).

	Variable	Data	Type of data	Sample or complete set	Reason for collecting this data	Data Collection Method	Analysis tool	Insight gained
1								
2								
3								
4								
5								
6								
7								
8								
9								
10								
11								
12								

FIGURE 26.3
Example of data collection plan.

Customers of an IT organization were highly dissatisfied with the service. A part of the IT organization was responsible for carrying out network installations and changes. Delivery times were completely unpredictable and were consequently experienced as too long. Expectations were not managed. Quite often, there would be a workload peak as a result of sales activities or management pressure. This led to stress, because the team needed to spend extra hours. New requests balanced fulfilled requests, and the backlog remained the same, causing intense frustration within the team. Unfortunately for the team, the expectation was that the number of requests they need to process would increase by 100% in the next two years. These needed to be processed by the same people. Inevitably, this led to despondency in the team since they were not able to keep up with the current workload. The organization's hypothesis was that processes were not implemented such that they would help customers.

Having defined the problem, data needed to be collected. Most of it was available in the systems used by the team. The data that was collected was a data dump of the previous 12 months of requests. The data required was the date of receipt of the request, the starting date, the completion date and the closure date. Also, the department responsible for the execution of the request was included in the data set. Preliminary data processing provided new insights including the average lead time of requests, WIP inventories, numbers of opened and closed requests per time period, and how long requests spent on each status.

The data was validated, and the three key conclusions were drawn from this part of the kaizen. Data was incomplete, for example, the start date of the work was not always recorded. Data was unreliable, for example, the time stamp of status 2 was sometimes earlier than that of status 1 and data was not used to manage the process. This meant that the kaizen team needed to be careful when drawing conclusions. It was also a trigger for the operational team to improve their data registration.

Based on this data, the kaizen team was able to construct a VSM. The VSM provided insight into where the data was missing, particularly details about waiting times. These gaps were filled in using an ECA adapted to the specific situation. The sheet allowed registration of NVA, NNVA and VA activities. This time registration lasted for two weeks to ensure representative data. The VSM further uncovered that there was no standard process for each of the three basic request types.

During the Measure phase, the following quick wins were identified.

- Daily (manual) measurement was instituted straightaway. It was carried out by the team and communicated twice daily in short stand-up meetings.
- Specified knowledge-sharing sessions were organized every day based on identified needs.
- Resource planning was initiated to reduce context switching, such that. per day people were allocated to a single task thereby increasing their effectiveness. Rotation schemes ensured that all team members became proficient at processing all types of requests.

The data was enriched and processed into graphs and other graphics so that the kaizen team could close the Measure phase and proceed to analyzing the data in the Analyze phase.

At the end of the Measure phase, the kaizen team should be able to complete the Current Condition and Future State goals sections of A3. This often involves revisiting the text already written in the Define phase. There is a tendency to fill the space available in the Define phase without realizing that the Measure phase will deliver a numerical specification of the current situation and can help to define the future state goals more precisely. There may even be some data to support the background.

Bringing together the important aspects of the Measure phase into a series of steps, we find the following points to take into account when carrying out the Measure phase of the kaizen.

1. Identify the Outputs and Inputs of the Process in Which the Problem Occurs	Problems invariably have an effect on the output of one or more process since it is often the recipient of the output who indicates that it does not meet the expectations of said recipient. Having defined the output relevant to the problem, we need to define the input. This leads to an understanding of which value stream causes the problem. Much of this work will have been done while making the SIPOC in the Define phase. This step entails collecting the data concerning the inputs and outputs of the process. Within IT organizations, it is not always clear that there is a process associated with the problem. Take the case in the Define chapter. This was identified as a people problem, a time-constraint problem, an attitude problem and many other types, but not as a process problem. In the end, the key issues were identified by treating the issue as a resourcing process problem. This allowed the emotion to be removed from the discussion.
2. Create a Value Stream Map of the Process	As we stated above, the value stream map (VSM) describes the current situation of the process at this phase of the kaizen. Describing the current situation may seem easier than it actually is. Often, people working in the same process have different perceptions as to how the process actually works. It is vital to go and look at the gemba to see how the process is actually executed. Within IT organizations, there is a tendency to say "we already have a process picture" when the kaizen lead recommends creating a VSM. The process document is usually quite old and must have been based on a process-oriented implementation. These documents are essentially useless since they describe a desired situation that has never been achieved; nobody knows the document except the people who wrote it and it distracts the team from the focus of creating a description of how the process currently works. Always take a clean sheet of paper when making an initial VSM.
3. Create and Execute the Data Collection Plan	Once we know what the process looks like, we can identify the independent variables that may affect the problem. When we know the independent variables, we can define the data that needs to be collected in order to investigate the problem. There is a strong tendency to believe that IT organizations are difficult to measure. As a result, kaizen teams within IT may try to take a shortcut in the Measure phase. Often, the involvement of a powerful sponsor will lull the team into a false sense of security. Powerful sponsorship does not mean we do not need to collect the right data to support the resolution of the problem. The data is a continuous reminder of how important it is to completely solve the problem. However difficult collecting data may be, it still must be done. In fact, measuring the various aspects of IT is not so difficult. The team just needs to be prepared to extract data from databases. And if there's one business that has people who know how to do this, it is IT.

4. Validate the Measurement System	We have already discussed possible inaccuracies within measurement systems. This is why the kaizen team must validate the measurement system(s) it uses. The idea here is to show that the data collected can be reproduced and repeated, in exactly the same way. Any assumptions made must be stated explicitly. Any manipulation of data must be documented and explained so that it is clear on which premises, analysis is being done in the Analyze phase.
5. Assess the Capability and Performance of the Process	For each measurement we make, we must set a baseline. In the case of the IT units of work, we tend to create time series charts and determine average performance over a defined period. Setting a single data point as a baseline tends to create an arbitrary and highly contentious baseline. Although there are organizations that sell benchmark data and reports for considerable amounts, there is also doubt as to whether benchmarking truly helps IT organizations. The problem is that IT organizations are service organizations in which the factors influencing performance and cost may be similar but may have very different effects from one organization to another. It is therefore vital to baseline while benchmarking is optional.
6. Identify Quick Wins	During the execution of measurements, it may become clear that there is a course of action that everyone involved agrees on; a solution that can be implemented straight away. This so-called quick win should be implemented as soon as possible. On rare occasions, a problem thought to be complicated or complex may turn out to be obvious.

As with the Define phase, it is vital to ensure that the key deliverables from this phase are completed before moving on to the Analyze phase. In practice, it is almost impossible to think of everything that needs to be measured. Often, further necessary measurements will emerge as a result of gaps in the analysis. This should, however, not be a reason for rushing the Measure phase or too easily accepting that something is not measurable.

FINDING THE CAUSE

The Analyze phase is aimed at finding the root cause of the problem (finding the most important x's). From the Define phase, we have a clear problem definition. This has been refined during the Measure phase and data has been collected. The data will have been processed to a certain extent during the Measure phase. In the Analyze phase, the goal is to translate the data into information that will provide insight into the variables that have the greatest impact on the problem. By determining these main variables, we will be able to provide input for the Improve phase, in which we will try to find the possible actions that will reduce the negative impact of the variables. In short, the Analyze phase is about the identification, quantification, interrogation and prioritization of the root causes of the problem, we are investigating. We do this using a number of tools. There are tools that help us make sense of the data we have uncovered during the Measure phase and there are tools that help us to further decompose the problem into its constituent parts.

As early as the 1950's, there has been a list of the seven basic tools of quality. It is speculated that Kaoru Ishikawa created the list as a result of exposure to the teachings of W. Edwards Deming. Whatever the source, the list of the seven Basic Tools of Quality has been standardized and is used universally. The list suggests that all data quality related data can be visualized using one of the tools. My experience supports this suggestion. Sure, it is nice to vary the types of visualizations you use to analyze data, and spreadsheet programs provide ample opportunity for variation. In the end, the seven tools of quality are sufficient. The seven tools are: histogram, Pareto chart, scatter diagram, flow chart, control chart, fishbone (Ishikawa) diagram and check sheet.

According to Webster's online dictionary, a histogram is "a representation of a frequency distribution by means of rectangles whose widths represent class intervals and whose areas are proportional to the corresponding frequencies." In short, this means that we create a graph in which groups of numbers are plotted based on how often they appear.

The power of histograms is that they allow us to analyze extremely large datasets by reducing them to a single graph that can show one or more peaks in the data. The histogram also visualizes the significance of the peaks. The Long Tail diagram (see Figure 22.16) is an IT example of a histogram. This one shows the number of open incidents with a certain age (time that they are open).

The Pareto chart is a way to visualize the relative importance of the root causes of problems. It is based on the principle (the Pareto principle) that a limited number of factors account for most of the impact on the problem. The Pareto principle is sometimes referred to as the 80–20 rule, that is, 80% of the impact is caused by 20% of the factors.

The Pareto diagram in Figure 26.4 shows the prevalence of particular causes of an incident, both absolute (in numbers) and cumulative (in percentage).

A scatter diagram is a graph that aims to demonstrate the relationship between two sets of data. We try to understand whether there is a

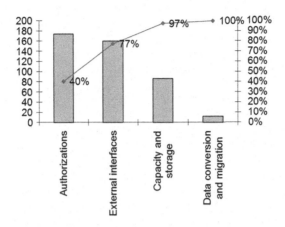

FIGURE 26.4
Example of Pareto chart.

correlation between two sets of data and whether this correlation is positive or negative. This type of diagram can be used to both interpolate and extrapolate.

The scatter diagram in Figure 26.5 shows the relationship between the average time to repair of incidents in days and the days of inventory within an IT organization. In effect, this is a chart depicting Little's Law.

A flowchart is one of the simplest of the seven quality tools. The flowchart is the visual representation of a series of steps in a process and helps to break down a complicated process into a simple series of steps. This simplification ensures that the process becomes understandable to anyone. A flowchart shows actions and decisions at points where variations occur in the process. These decision points are always marked by a question that can be answered with "yes" or "no." The basic forms are blocks (actions) and diamonds (decisions). There are many other symbols used for drawing flowcharts. A further elaboration is the use of so-called "swimming lanes." These are horizontal or vertical lines that separate the activities of different roles or groups responsible for completing a particular task in the process. In Value Stream Mapping, a very simple version of the flowchart is used. The goal of the VSM is to understand waste and time usage within the process.

The control chart is essentially a time-series chart. A time-series chart is one in which data is plotted on a chart where the horizontal axis is a time sequence. The vertical axis can be numbers or another variable whose value can be different over time. The difference between a time-series chart and a control chart is that the control chart is used to identify variation in a repeating process. This is done using control limits. Control limits are

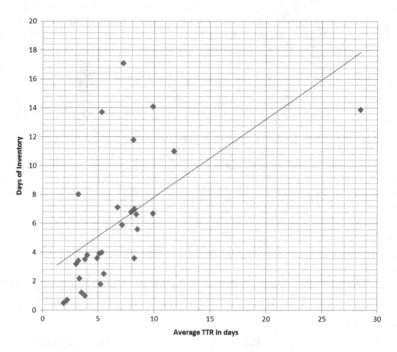

FIGURE 26.5
Example of scatter diagram.

sometimes also called action limits (control limits are calculated; action limits may be assigned). A control chart helps to understand variation. There are two important types of variation: common cause variation and special cause variation.

Common cause variation is due to random shifts in the variables that are always present in the process. As a result, the pattern shows the variation with "noise," the collective effect of many minor influences. A process affected by common cause variation is called stable or in control. It makes no sense to figure out what the causes are. The only way to improve the performance is to redesign the (parts of the) process to reduce common cause variation. An example of this is when a process, for example, the ability to deliver a new piece of standard software to the customer, performs consistently at a level that does not meet the requirement of the customer. We would need to completely redesign the process to improve the performance (Figure 26.6).

Special cause variation can be assigned to a specific cause which can usually be discovered. Special causes generate patterns in the data. They provide signals about the problems in the process and how they can be

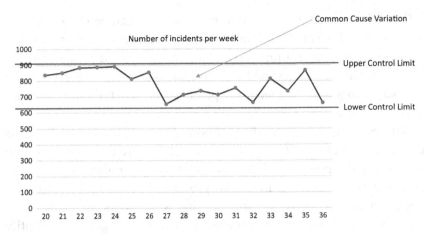

FIGURE 26.6
Example of a time series chart with common cause variation.

resolved. You cannot predict if and when the special cause variation will occur and what will be the impact. Therefore, the process is unstable and unpredictable. Continuing with the example above, if the ability to deliver the software shows a spike in lead times, we can investigate and possibly remove the reasons for the spike (Figure 26.7).

The control chart can thus be used to identify whether a process is under control (statistically) or it suffers from special and/or common cause variation. It can also be used to detect statistically significant trends in measurements, for example, to identify whether improvements have had an effect on performance.

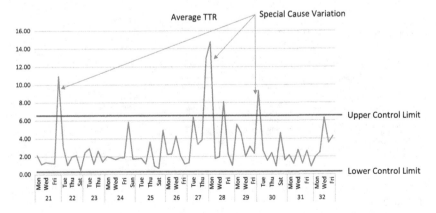

FIGURE 26.7
Example of a time series chart with special cause variation.

Control charts are best suited to processes that can be measured on a regular basis. Typically, this is in processes that repeat within a reasonably short span of time. Within IT, we look at the processes that work on incidents, service requests and standard change. Control charts are also very suited to monitoring technical processes, such as the ability to load a data warehouse.

Ishikawa diagrams (also called fishbone diagrams) are causal diagrams that show the causes of a specific event. They were designed by Kaoru Ishikawa in the 1960's. The Ishikawa diagram is generally used to identify potential factors causing an overall problem. Each cause or reason for imperfection is a source of variation, that is, an "x" or an independent variable. Causes are usually grouped into major categories to identify these sources of variation. Depending on the industry, there may be up to seven categories. Within IT, we commonly use four categories: people, process, technology and policy

In practice, these categories are Collectively Exhaustive. The factors affecting a problem can, however, often be placed in one or more categories, that is, the set of categories is not Mutually Exclusive. An example: Is the fact that people do not follow a process, a people factor or a process factor? The answer is that it does not matter as long as the factor is posted on the Ishikawa diagram and its impact on the problem is analyzed accordingly (Figure 26.8).

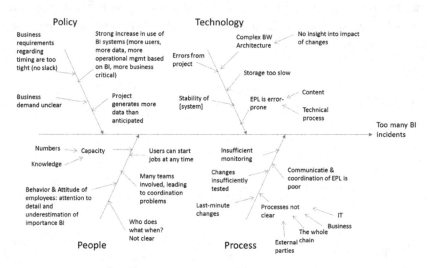

FIGURE 26.8
Example of Ishikawa diagram.

The check sheet is a simple and highly effective tool for collecting quality-related data in a structured way. It is a way to assess a process and can function as input for other analyses. The check sheet helps to quantify the causes from the Ishikawa diagram, for which there is limited or no numerical data to be analyzed.

The seven basic quality tools help us to process the data we have collected and visualize the data in a way that facilitates getting to the root cause of the problem we are investigating in our kaizen. There are also tools to help us take a step further and actually get to the root cause.

The Five Whys analysis is a simple root cause analysis that requires the kaizen team to question a failure through sequential causes. "Why" is asked to find each preceding trigger until we supposedly arrive at the root cause of a problem. A why question can often be answered with multiple answers. Each answer should be supported by evidence that proves the answer is right. Failure to do this may send the team on a wrong failure path. By asking three times "where," narrow down the location of the problem. Make a table with two columns and five rows and write the question from the problem statement at the top of the table. Ask the question: "Why did this happen?" Find the answer, supported by evidence, and write the answer in the left-hand column of the top row. Repeat this question and answer cycle, four more times. List the answers in the left-hand column of the table. Determine a solution for each of the answers and record these in the right-hand column.

A cause-and-effect matrix helps determine which factors affect the outcomes of the process being investigated. It maps the value connection between inputs (the Xs) to outputs (the Ys). With these relationships visible and quantified, you can determine the most influential factors contributing to value.

Failure Modes and Effects Analysis (FMEA) is an analysis for identifying all possible failures in a design, process, product or service. The failure modes are the ways in which something might fail. Failures are any errors or defects and can be potential or actual. The effects analysis is about understanding the consequences of those failures.

Failures are prioritized according to their consequences. The aim of the FMEA is to take actions to remove the sources of failure, that is, the root causes, starting with those with the greatest impact. FMEA can be used throughout the lifecycle of an IT service, from design to operation and retirement of the service.

The VSM is a mine of useful information. This information is used to identify the places in a process where a solution is most needed. Having carried out the chosen calculations, there is a series of aspects that we must analyze in more depth.

There are process steps that introduce a delay into the process; these are time traps. A classic example is the need for an approval. This is not a capacity constraint. A time trap is based on a policy decision (muri). The waiting times in the VSM must be analyzed carefully to determine the reason for waiting times. Removing time traps will improve the efficiency of the process. Capacity constraints are process steps that do not have sufficient capacity to process all of the work that it needs to process in a particular timeframe. These steps are also referred to as "bottlenecks." Removing capacity constraints allows the process to deliver the value in the quantities required to meet customer demand. Takt rate is an important metric for understanding bottlenecks. Each process step for which the takt time is higher than the takt time for the entire process is a bottleneck. Capacity constraints can cause variability (mura) throughout the process. The main drivers of capacity constraints in IT are lack of resources or knowledge.

Time traps and capacity constraints are important causes of waiting time. Obviously, we need to analyze the other types of waste (TIMWOOD) in the VSM to ensure that these are not causing delays or quality issues (muda). We do this by analyzing each step in the process and determining whether a particular type of waste is present in the step. This waste is identified with a symbol on the VSM.

Much of what has been dealt with in this chapter is not specific to IT. Does this mean that the analysis within IT kaizen is same as non-IT kaizen? From a tool perspective, maybe. However, within IT, we find that there are specific challenges based on the context that we discussed earlier. Looking at people, process and technology, we find a number of characteristic analyses.

There is a massive amount of data available within IT organizations regarding the "behavior" of the technology. Technology delivers data that is very suitable for the creation of control charts and histograms. Having said this, Murphy's Law dictates that the bit of technology that you need to investigate does not have the right set of monitors in place to ensure that the technology can be researched. It is vital that monitoring can be put in place quickly to understand the technological aspects of a problem.

The analyses mostly related to technology are control charts, Pareto charts and scatter diagrams. Control charts help to understand the behavior of technology over time, Pareto charts help to rank the importance of the causes and scatter diagrams are used to understand whether there is a relationship between symptoms. The analyses described above in relation to VSM are all used in relation to IT processes. It is important, as already stated in the Measure phase, that people within IT organizations (especially those involved in kaizen) know the difference between the IT units of work and the associated processes. The dynamics of each unit of work must be understood so that the effects can be understood. People-related analysis is particularly related to the availability of skills and knowledge, and the usage of time. Skills and knowledge can be analyzed using a skills and knowledge matrix. The aim is, particularly, to understand in which ways muri and mura are caused by choices made regarding people. One of the IT-specific analyses is time-related. Where traditional Lean analyses look at the time aspects of processes, within Lean IT, we also manage time on an organizational level. In essence, we look at the VA time versus NNVA and NVA time at an organizational level, i.e. per team, department or the whole IT organization. This helps us to understand whether teams are faced with substantial amounts of ad hoc work or whether they have a high diversity of units of work, leading to muda and mura.

In a large utilities organization, the use of Lean principles had been steadily and rapidly increasing within operational departments. The engineers were starting their days with daily stand-ups and the operational costs were showing improvements. The business leadership was enthusiastic and had commissioned a large number of reports created in the Business Intelligence (BI) system. The IT organization was happy to see this increase in interest in the BI service. However, as a result of carrying out lots of changes for the customer departments, the IT department supporting the BI system had not paid attention to how this was affecting the BI service. The number of incidents and complaints were exploding. Worst of all, the reports so critical to the business were only being made available by the end of the morning, due to slow data loading and system crashes. This meant that the benefits that had been achieved by the initial business teams were now being nullified by the fact that many other business teams were now causing the performance of the system to deteriorate. The problem was escalated to board level and a kaizen was started.

The problem definition was developed quite rapidly: How can we ensure that all reports are available at 07:00 every working day? The kaizen sponsor, lead and team came to an agreement on this question to be answered within about an hour. In the first iteration, the kaizen team focused on creating an Ishikawa of the problem. The team subsequently set about creating clear control charts of the performance of the load processes, supplemented by those of the use of memory, network bandwidth, processing power and disk space. These were accompanied by histograms of the occurrence of incidents and the implementation of changes. For each of the branches of the Ishikawa, a Pareto chart was produced. Initially, no VSM was made, because the problem was deemed to be a technical and behavioral problem. In the end, the VSM provided vital insight to solving the problem. It turned out that a number of steps had been determined to be sequential in the past, when they could be carried out in parallel. This was the result of a challenge to the "common sense" assumptions that had been made many years back and, since then, had not been challenged. The VSM including both human and technical actions showed where time was being wasted. During the Analyze phase, the sponsor played an unsettling role for the team, pushing for solutions. The kaizen lead needed to have a discussion with the sponsor to ensure the team was not put under pressure to jump to conclusions. Here, it was found that no clear timelines had been agreed between the team and the sponsor. And team members were unclear as to how much time they could spend on the kaizen, outside of the five meetings that had been planned. The five meetings had been set based on the DMAIC phases, with an agreement that work would be done in between the sessions. However, no one had any idea of how much work would be required in between sessions.

In the end, based on the aforementioned analyses supplemented by the use of the Five Whys technique at various points during the Analyze phase, the analysis was completed, with sufficient factual support to warrant a complete overhaul of the Business Intelligence (BI) environment. The technical analysis and VSM showed that the primary causes of the problem could be found in the way the process was structured from the close of business on one day until 07:00 the following morning and in the way the entire system made use of storage and memory.

In both, causes were addressed in the short term alleviating the key problem. However, the structural program was needed to ensure the improvements were sustainable.

The Analysis phase tends to be the phase in which most time is spent. The team will spend much effort trying to bring together the various symptoms, causes, effects and indications of how these may be mitigated.

There are two major pitfalls to avoid in this phase:

Don't fall in love with your analysis. All the hard work that goes into the Analysis phase is in fact only a step to determine the correct course of action. Most of the charts, graphs, matrices, etc. will not find their way onto the A3; only the most significant. This does not mean you should throw away the analysis once made. All analyses should be stored as a baseline for checking the effect of improvements made and for starting future improvement initiatives.

Don't jump to conclusions. Based on the insights gained in the Analysis phase and the relief that the solution of the problem is getting close, the team may have a tendency to think that they have found the solution as they uncover root causes. Jumping to conclusions will mean that other, possibly more significant, root causes may be overlooked. This is where a kaizen lead proves their value, by keeping the team on track.

Completing the Analysis part of the A3, ensures that the team must focus on the essence of the analysis. To wrap up the Analyze phase, let us take a brief look at the main steps that need to be accomplished before moving on to the Improve phase.

1. Determine the Critical Independent Variables	The first and probably most important step is to identify the key X's, the independent variables that most influence our problem. If we do not identify these correctly, we may spend a lot of time and effort in analyzing aspects that really have little bearing on the problem at hand.
2. Perform the Data Analysis	We must use at least seven basic tools of quality to analyze the data collected in the Measure phase, with the aim of determining which of the X's have the greatest influence on the problem.
3. Perform the Process Analysis	We also need to take a detailed look at the VSM we created in the Measure phase. In the VSM, we will be trying to identify where there is waste, where the balance between Value-Add and Non-Value-Add activities is clearly tipping the wrong way, i.e. too much NNVA and NVA activity. We also need to do the necessary calculations (PCE and Little's Law). Our highest level goal is to understand the flow (or lack of it) in the process by analyzing the throughput and constraints.

4. Determine the Root Causes	Based on the data and process analyses, we can generate theories to explain potential causes. Use the Five Whys, C&E Matrix and FMEA to narrow the search for the most important root causes. If the kaizen team does not feel it has found the real cause or does not have sufficient evidence to support the root causes found, do not hesitate to go back and collect additional data to verify root causes or find new ones. Remember: It is vital to not jump to conclusions, especially once one or two root causes are known. Do not start formulating solutions before you have finished the analysis. It may be a solution but is it the best solution or the one that will actually solve the problem completely rather than partially? Let the analysis run its course and see where the data, the facts, the calculations, the visualizations and the dissecting of the problem take you.
5. Prioritize the Root Causes	Lastly, we must prioritize the root causes we have found. This priority will be passed on to the Improve phase, so that the kaizen team can focus on finding solutions for the most pressing root causes.

Closing the Analyze phase is probably the most critical change of phase. The reason is that prior to the closure of the Analyze phase, significant attention must be paid to the solutions. As we have seen, quick wins may be found early in the cycle. However, the danger of jumping to conclusions is always present. The kaizen lead must therefore be continuously vigilant that the team stays focused on the current phase. This is absolutely vital for the Analyze phase where the temptation to go for the solutions is greatest. The other danger that can raise its head at this point is distraction; there are more than enough problems that need to be tended to. As the team works through the DMAIC cycle, the problem and its causes become clear. When we do not understand a problem, it seems more threatening. As we understand the problem better, the threat decreases, and people have a tendency to downplay the problem. In the worst case, this can lead to the problem sponsor being distracted towards a different problem that is demanding attention. With this distraction, the kaizen team may lose interest and the kaizen itself may peter out before the solutions have truly been found and implemented. It is absolutely vital that a kaizen is brought to its logical conclusion, with at least one solution of the problem being implemented. This solution must have a visible impact on reducing the problem.

27

Embedding Solutions

GETTING TO SOLUTIONS

At the end of the Analyze phase, the kaizen team basically has a list of the most important X's, the factors that cause the problem. The next goal is to identify improvement options. This is the aim of the Improve phase.

The Improve phase is really the moment that we start thinking about solutions. Earlier in the cycle, we may have come across a solution, especially if the problem turns out to be an obvious one. Assuming that we are dealing with a complicated or complex problem, the Improve phase is the time to start gathering solutions

In this section, we will look at ways of generating solution ideas, techniques for selecting and prioritizing the solutions and testing solutions. All of these methods are useful but the one that stands head-and-shoulders above all of them is going to the gemba.

Observing the gemba and validating solutions at the gemba are two of the most important ways to ensure that the right improvements are implemented in the right way. Going to the gemba facilitates the generation of ideas for solutions, especially because ideas can be discussed with the people. Gemba validation ensures that the implementation of improvements is carried out in a way that garners support with the people doing the work.

The IT management team had recently received a number of complaints from customers about the intake of projects within the IT organization. Their complaints revolved around the number of times they had to tell their "story" before IT actually got down to execute the project.

The Measure and Analysis phases of the kaizen showed that, depending on the sensitivity of a topic, up to six different people may have a meeting with the customer to define the goals for the project. First, an account manager would ask what the customer wanted. Second, an information manager would request a meeting to gain some more insight into the technological impact of the project. Then a project manager would turn up and pretty much repeat everything the account manager and information manager had just done, but then from a project execution perspective. If there were budgetary or governance issues, the financial director or operations manager may require an explanation similar to the one that had already been given. And, finally, if there was any kind of problem the CEO would get involved as a referee. There seemed to be many projects with "any kind of problem." In short, the process of getting a project started was extremely time-consuming.

The kaizen involved creating a Value Stream Map of the process and the analysis focused on the roles involved. Each of the roles had documented responsibilities some of which either overlapped, conflicted or caused handovers. The analysis determined that, in fact, no one was actually responsible for ensuring that a project was defined so that it could be executed.

The Improve phase was novel in that the kaizen team, which did not include the customer, actually invited all of the known project owners (the principal project customers of IT) to listen to the analysis and help to generate solutions to the problem. The team, and the invited customers, used classic brainstorming to generate solutions. The kaizen lead introduced a 20-minute period of reverse thinking when she felt the options were drying up. This had the added effect of causing hilarious exchanges between business and IT people. Later, in the evaluation, the team realized that this period of fun actually improved the acceptance of the changes that had previously been non-discussable. The "non-discussables" were especially related to people having to relinquish part of their responsibility or authority for the sake of a more efficient process. The result was quite surprising: The customer recognized that they themselves had caused part of the problem by insisting on a fairly bureaucratic governance on the business side; a classic case of muri.

Policies were adjusted and the information manager was given an overall responsibility for ensuring that the project was fully defined. This was done in such a way that a project manager, who was allocated to the project at a later date (sometimes weeks after the project had been defined), could easily infer the requirements and start executing the project.

There are many options when choosing idea generation techniques. The techniques described below are well-known, often-used, proven techniques that generate many ideas. Brainstorming is about generating as many ideas as possible. It is vital that ideas are not evaluated during the brainstorming session as this limits the creativity. Typically, the brainstorming session will start with a recap of the key factors causing the problem. These may be posted on a flipchart or on the wall; a visual solution is recommended. Per factor, the team must generate as many solution ideas as possible. As time passes, the solutions become more outlandish and strange. This is when you know that the brainstorming session is reaching its goal. Often, in the absurdity of a proposed solution is a core truth that helps to develop a more realistic solution. Once all the ideas have dried up, the team can move on to selecting and prioritizing the ideas. An alternative to brainstorming is brainwriting. In this technique, the principal factors causing the problem are posted on flipcharts around a room. The team members walk around the room in silence posting sticky notes with their ideas on them. Participants read each other's posts and use them as inspiration to generate new ideas. The fact that a particular post is not explained means that another person can freely associate or interpret the post as they wish. This again leads to ideas that are generated out of the ordinary phase.

Reverse thinking is about describing what you would like to happen and then working out how to make the opposite happen. This method helps to understand what the team should definitely not do. Once this is clear, the step to understanding the possibilities becomes much easier. Usually developing 10 to 15 reverse ideas provides sufficient input to look for desired solutions. This method works because it is fun. Looking at the absolute opposite of what you are trying to achieve means, from an IT perspective, how can I aggravate the current, problematic situation? This leads to amazing definitions of how the IT service infrastructure and organization can be comprehensively sabotaged. Many additional insights have been collected during a reverse-thinking session, as particularly engineers try to out-do each other with better ideas. The challenge is to then identify the opposite solution. A single negative solution may lead to multiple positive solutions.

A third idea generation technique uses action verbs as triggers to generate ideas. SCAMPER is an acronym with each letter standing for an action verb which in turn stands for a prompt for creative ideas.

S – Substitute, **C** – Combine, **A** – Adapt. **M** – Modify, **P** – Put to another use, **E** – Eliminate, **R** – Reverse

Again, the aim is to produce as many ideas as possible. Each cause of the problem is approached using the seven action verbs, with the aim of understanding what could happen if an aspect of the cause (or all of it) is substituted, combined, adapted, modified, and so on.

Having generated a large number of solutions, we need to make this number manageable. This can be done through bundling and/or elimination. The question is: How can we select the best solution(s) for solving the problem?

Also for this task, there are tens of tools. The selection presented below are among the more commonly used. Affinity mapping reduces the number of solutions by bundling solutions that are linked, similar or overlapping. The benefit of bundling solutions is that we are able to identify the central themes of a set of solutions. This in turn can provide further insight into the best solution. Affinity mapping is all about sorting the many solutions into a manageable set of clusters. As with brainwriting, the first part of affinity mapping is done in silence. Team members put sticky notes with possible solutions together, if they believe the solutions should be clustered for any reason. Then one by one the clusters are discussed, and a header describing the key theme is given to each set of solutions. The team then determines which solutions are most suitable from each of the clusters, or potentially they may develop a different solution based on the insight gained from the bundling exercise.

The solution matrix is a simple tool, that we saw earlier, made up of two axes: feasibility and impact. Feasibility represents the ability of the IT organization to actually implement the solution. Feasibility is high if the costs, effort and time involved are low. Impact is about judging the effect that the solution will have, if it was implemented. Impact is about the effect on the IT organization and its customers in financial, performance and/or learning terms. All of the solutions are then plotted by the team onto the solution matrix. The important part of the process is that team members discuss the reasons why they believe a given solution should have a particular impact and feasibility. This helps gain understanding of how the team members see the adoption of solutions within the organization. Once all the solutions have been plotted, there will be a group that is clustered in the high impact, high feasibility quadrant. These will be the solutions that need to be considered first for implementation.

Each of the above techniques helps to gain control over a large group of solutions. The solution matrix helps to make a broad prioritization of the solutions, as well. Multi-voting also focuses on prioritizing the solutions. This is done by each team member allocating votes to a set of solutions.

Let's assume that there are thirty solutions. Each team member is given ten votes (a third of the total number of solutions that can be voted for). After everyone has voted, the scores are tallied and the top ten solutions are selected. It is possible to conduct a second round in which everyone gets three or four votes in order to select the best solutions from the previously determined top ten. In this way, the kaizen team can reduce the number of solutions to a manageable number.

The last technique is one to use once the number of solutions has been reduced to less than a handful. The aim is to build comparable business cases for each of the solutions. Each business case will include both the costs and the returns for the same fixed period of time. The solutions of a kaizen should give a positive return within a maximum of six months. Anything more probably means that the solution is too big and costly; the team should look for smaller solutions, possibly only tackling part of the problem. It is advisable, where possible, to implement part of the complete solution to a problem at a fraction of the cost, rather than spend huge amounts of resources to completely solve a problem in one go. The key consideration here is the acceptance of the change: Smaller changes are more easily accepted and assimilated into the way of working than large changes.

Having selected one or more solutions to implement, the question that must then be answered is: How will we try out the solution to see whether it works. This will depend very much on the type of problem being solved.

Based on Table 27.1, we can deduce that there are situations within IT for which solutions have already been devised. Let us look at some typical solutions used within IT organizations. Best practices is an area at which the IT industry excels. There are many best practice frameworks

TABLE 27.1

Solution Test for Different Types of Problems

Type of Problem (Cynefin)	Solution Test
Obvious	Implement a pilot using the best practices available in the market
Complicated	Create a small production pilot to understand how the solution works in the live environment.
Complex	Use experimentation techniques to understand how the solution "behaves" in practice.
Chaos	Determine which actions to take and carry out a risk analysis for each action

developed for use within IT. These best practice frameworks present sets of rules that have been developed over many years with contributions from the IT community. The prominent examples are technical manuals, ITIL, COBIT, Scrum and Prince2/PMI. On top of the best practices, IT also has good practices. These are frameworks of principles and tools that help to improve the ability of IT to deliver and improve its services to customers. In this category, we find methods like Lean IT, Agile and DevOps.

The Improve phase leads to the review of the Future State section to see whether the solutions meet the requirements of the intended future state. The Proposed Options section of the A3 must be completed. Finally, the team must also describe the plan for implementing the solutions in the Plan/Improvement section. This last section will be finalized during the Control phase, when the relevant details of the control plan are added. The main steps that need to be accomplished before moving on to the Control phase are:

1. Generate Potential Solutions	Having understood the cause and effect relationships in the Analyze phase, the kaizen team must now generate as many solution possibilities as they can, using one or more idea generation techniques. It is important that maximum creativity is used in this step. The more solutions, the better the chance that there is an easy-to-implement solution that solves the problem. Remember: We are looking for small effective steps to resolve the problem, not large solutions that require considerable effort to implement.
2. Select and Prioritize Solutions	From the many solutions defined, we must now reduce the collection to a small number of solutions that have both an impact and high feasibility. We do this using the selection and prioritization techniques. If necessary, the team may need to perform small experiments to check whether a solution is suitable.
3. Apply Best and Good Practices	Within IT, we have a large number of best and good practices, it is very important to check the best and good practices for the particular area where the problem exists. Since IT problems, even complex problems, usually include parts that can be solved using best practices, it is a waste not to apply what others have already learned.
4. Develop "Future State" VSM	Once the team understands which solutions it intends to implement, it can create the future state VSM. Creation of future state VSM is important because it helps to focus the improvement efforts and to communicate the intended changes to the other people working in the process who were not part of the kaizen.

5. Pilot the Solution and Confirm Improvement Outcomes	During the Improve phase, the kaizen team must check whether the intended solutions actually work. Use the pilot to create documentation required to support the full-scale implementation, for example, SOP, checklists, KPIs (Key Performance Indicators) and metrics. The team may also use the FMEA (Failure Mode and Effects Analysis) to prepare for the possible challenges during the implementation.
6. Create Implementation Plan for Full-Scale Rollout of Solution(s)	Plan the implementation. This is primarily for communication purposes. Hopefully, the solutions to be implemented are small requiring a minor amount of training to ensure adoption. However, there may be aspects of the implementation that require substantial communication with people affected by the problem. The kaizen team and particularly the sponsor must agree on the fact that the solutions will help to alleviate the problem. It is only then that the Improve phase can be closed and the implementation of the solution(s) can begin.

EMBEDDING THE IMPROVEMENTS

You have come a long way through this book. Embedding improvements into the IT organization is the summary of what Lean is about. This can only happen if you identify the right improvements, based on Lean principles, and if you embed them with respect for people. Without these elements, people will not accept the improvements and no progress will be made.

The Control phase is the last step in the DMAIC cycle. In this phase, the goal is to successfully implement and, more importantly, maintain the gains achieved, i.e. it is all about ensuring the sustainability of the improvement. The question that the kaizen team is trying to answer is, "How can we *guarantee* the improved performance?" Ensuring that the successes from the Improve phase will continue means transferring the responsibilities for performance to the process owner. One way to look at the concept of establishing controls is to ask yourself what elements, activities, roles, policies, etc. you need to put in place to make sure that the next time you go to the gemba, the improvement is still in place and preferably better than you left it.

Achieving control is one of the important aspects of leading an organization. Leaders need to be in control of what is happening in their organization.

A control, in essence, is a procedure or policy; a way to identify whether work is done in the correct way. There are specific IT controls that provide assurance that the information technology used by an organization operates as intended, for example, with the correct authorizations, sufficient audit trails and processes that deliver the correct results. The aim of this phase is to implement controls to ensure that work is done the correct way. It is important to realize that, in the ABC model, controls are antecedents. They do not cause the right behavior. At best, they help to identify the desired behavior. This is why there are elements in the Control phase that also help to ensure behavior is practiced.

In the previous kaizen phases, we successfully investigated and, eventually, made improvements to alleviate the causes of the problem. To make structural improvements, we have focused and dealt with the underlying causes that prevented the performance needed to meet the requirements from the four voices discussed earlier. Now that we have achieved the performance improvements, we need to look at controlling the delivered quality. The Control phase has two main focus areas: guarantee the increased performance and the hand-off of the improved process to its process owner.

Making changes to the way organizations work is challenging and sustaining those changes is even more so. We need to be diligent and develop the habits and practices necessary to maintain our current state and pursue improvement in the future. That is why we need a kaizen mindset, which means enjoying the challenge of counteracting the descent into chaos and continually seeking improvements. To help the process owner and the people doing the actual work, we must develop a control plan. This plan consists of four basic parts: documentation, monitoring, response and training. Without implementing a control plan to ensure problems do not reoccur, the kaizen cannot be successful in the long run!

Our improvements in the way of working need to be institutionalized as habits and routines. One ingredient to achieve this is through documentation. Of course, we all know that documenting alone is insufficient. However, without documentation, it is difficult to create a baseline to establish the right routines and habits. Examples of new documentation include new process steps, standards, procedures, policies and instructions for new or updated systems or tools. Creating policy often results in documents that resemble legal documents, not least because they aim to be complete, covering all eventualities and exceptions. A policy should be clear and concise, and should stay within the intended scope. The policy should clearly state its intent and the spirit that should be followed when applying it. New or rewritten policy must obviously not contradict any other policy. Establishing clear ownership and accountability for results is one step towards gaining control. This needs to be documented so that the ownership and accountability are available for all involved. These roles and responsibilities can also be used in the process documentation. Process documentation is always a contentious issue: If it is not there, people complain that they do not know what is expected; if it does exist, nobody reads it. Traditionally, process documentation comes in one of two forms: a process flowchart accompanied by a RACI (Responsible, Accountable, Consulted, Informed) chart or a process flowchart with "swimming lanes" (as described in the Analyze phase). Whichever method you use, the document should be short and simple so that it is easy for people to understand. This style of process documentation is often required for compliance purposes. An additional way to document a process is to post the Value Stream Map on the wall, and regularly organize short meetings to determine which improvements need to be implemented. Creating a Value Stream Map has the effect of keeping the improvement of the process at the top of people's minds. A final piece of documentation is the SOP, a written procedure that describes how a specific task should be carried out. The idea is that by following the SOP, the desired outcome can be guaranteed and created in a consistent and efficient manner. Within IT, the key area where we use the SOP is in describing the execution of Standard Changes. A good SOP has a name for each step. It describes what needs to be done per step and how this should be carried out. An excellent and highly effective SOP also includes why a step needs to be carried out in the way described. If people do not understand the "why," they will not often ignore that step, especially if it is an administrative step (see the case at the end of the chapter). An alternative to the SOP is the checklist. Checklists are particularly helpful when the process is non-standard or has limited aspects of repeatability. Although this document works principally as a reminder to carry out particular activities (as does the SOP), it does not guarantee a specific outcome. Rather, it ensures that things are not forgotten. It is very important to determine the detail of the documentation. This should be based on the risk of not having sufficient detail versus the value of a short and easy-to-understand document. As with everything in Lean, start by focusing on the value.

These documents need to be supplemented with action in order to make sure they do not just remain antecedents that have no effect on the organization. We need to be able to detect irregularities through monitoring. To detect any irregularities, we need to know how the implemented changes are affecting performance. The approach for monitoring should focus on monitoring the process using the updated metrics and measurements made during the Measure phase, evaluating the improvements made in the Improve phase and assessing the capability of the process over time, ensuring that the solutions work for the long term.

This is done by using metrics. During the Define and Measure phases, we identified and created measurement systems for metrics related to the problem. Some of these can be re-used. The improvement we have chosen to implement will undoubtedly be related to a Critical Success Factor for which there is a KPI. The credibility of measurements is highly dependent on their consistency and coherence. Consistency means that they are measured in a repeatable way that is the same across the whole IT organization. Coherence means that the measures are self-consistent across any number of assessments. Ideally, we will identify leading and lagging indicators. The former will identify whether the performance will decline in the future; the latter will look at performance. Within IT, an example of a leading indicator is the number of problems solved. This is a leading indicator for reducing the number of incidents. Untested changes on the other hand are a leading indicator for an increasing number of incidents. The decrease or increase in the number of incidents is the lagging indicator.

Aside from the usage of metrics, we need to establish a dashboard. The input for the dashboard is the information from the metrics. A dashboard is a visual tool to ensure that both managers and engineers know how they are performing. The dashboard ensures consistency in the use and interpretation of metrics and KPIs since everyone looks at the same consistent and coherent measurements.

We have also seen that an excellent way of spotting irregularities is to talk with the people related to the problem area about performance and the issues they face. To do this, we can setup visual management and engage in meaningful performance dialogs with the team members and leaders. Visual management is about effective communication and real-time updates regarding the work. Performance and workload are shared for visibility and effective communication. Visual management covers steering the work, planning and reviewing progress and, of course, managing improvements on a daily and weekly basis. Visual management tools, therefore, make sense as control mechanisms. Visual management helps to create consistent and effective communication. It removes the need for a series of one-to-one communications that inherently has the risk of an inconsistent message. The communication is effective because the entire team hears the same message at the same time. Lastly, frequent feedback loops are established. This is based on common knowledge of the chosen solutions to problems. Measurement is vital to understand the dynamics of the processes. Measurement must lead to the changes in behavior and we must ensure that our behavior helps us to achieve our goals. Once again, we can apply the performance dialog to better understand what good performance is and how to collaborate in order to create value for customers.

Quite often, support from other organizational units is required when implementing improvements. Therefore, we must establish rapid and effective communication that can easily cascade through all levels of the IT organization. This may require changes to the structure of the meetings relevant to the problem area. The goal is to propose changes to the structure so that ideas, suggestions and requests for help can flow readily through the channels of the organization.

Although we never know when and what kind of irregularities we will be facing, we can prepare by setting up responses in advance. This means establishing checks that will signal out-of-control conditions and define actions to be taken. During the Analyze phase, we looked at the use of the FMEA to understand what could go wrong in a certain situation. To the FMEA, we can add OCAP procedures (Out-of-Control-Action-Plan).

As we saw before, a good FMEA defines the activities such as inspection, checks or measurements aimed at control, the frequency of these activities, who is responsible and the tools involved, and the standard or norm that defines acceptance and rejection criteria. The interventions are grouped together in what is called an OCAP or Out-of-Control-Action-plan. It prescribes what to do in case a failure occurs. It is a living document, which stores knowledge about possible or known issues and related solution strategies. The OCAP makes exception handling and firefighting efficient and effective. It is vital that team members are involved in setting up the FMEA and the OCAP to ensure they know the requirement. By adding the OCAP to the FMEA, it is possible to prepare for disruptions. Also, the responsibility for the activities was anchored in the workplace. In effect, the OCAP is like a small-scale contingency plan.

Finally, having identified how the improvements will be monitored and deviations responded to, we must ensure that everyone involved knows the behavior required. The training part in our Control plan is focused on ensuring that each person executing a particular role knows the required behavior, understands the documentation, can monitor the process and knows how to respond to deviations. To aid in setting up the necessary training, a Skills and Knowledge matrix can be used. With this tool, we can readily identify the current and desired knowledge and skills for those involved in the problem area. If a knowledge and skill matrix already exists, it will need to be updated to include any improvements. The training takes the form of actually trying out the new behavior. Many kaizens result in the creation of an A3 that is hung on the wall for all to see. However, insufficient time is spent helping team members and leaders to truly understand what the associated behavior actually looks like. It is assumed everyone will understand. We must therefore build a communication plan to ensure that everyone is informed of the changes.

Building a communication plan is essentially about ensuring that the right people are given the right information at the right time. When putting together a communication plan, we must include the following variables: Content: What are we communicating about? Audience: For whom is the communication? Purpose: Why are we communicating about this content? Timing: When will the communication take place? Is it a one-time event or will it recur? Format: Will the communication be presented in the form of a newsletter, email, interactive meeting, presentation, training or any other form? Input: From whom do we need input or consultation prior to the communication event? Actions: Who will ensure that the communication happens? And capacity: How much time is needed to carry out the communication event? (Figure 27.1)

A classic problem for many IT organizations is the use and, particularly, the maintenance of the Configuration Management Database (CMDB). Mostly, considerable effort is put into ensuring that the Configuration

Content	Audience	Purpose	Timing	Form	Input	Actions	Capacity
Status update for Kaizen Sponsor	Kaizen Sponsor, Kaizen Team	Assuring commitment, Kaizen tracking/progress/ issues	Daily	Status Update by mail 3 days before meeting. Final version on the kaizen sharepoint	Kaizen Team	Kaizen Lead makes report.	2 hr
Kaizen Team meeting	Kaizen Team	Kaizen tracking/progress/ issues	Daily 09:00	Daily stand-up	Kaizen Team, Kaizen Sponsor	Kaizen Lead leads meeting	30 mins
Performance reports	Kaizen Team	Trigger weak areas where improvement initiatives apply	Daily	On paper/mail/ sharepoint	Service Management Tool	Kaizen Team makes reports	1 hr
Explanation New SOPs	Infrastructure Teams	Provide audience with material to train their members in order to start up processes	Week after kaizen completed	SOPs, presentation material	Kaizen Team	Kaizen team: produce SOP and presentation	2 hrs
Share Best practices	IT employees	Introducing best practices and lessons learned in other areas of the IT organization		Lessons Learned meetings	Lessons Learned from kaizen	Kaizen Team, Kaizen Sponsor	2 hr
Kaizen Update	IT employees	Update the audience with the goals + progress of the kaizen	Daily	Kaizen A3	Kaizen Team, Kaizen Sponsor	Kaizen Sponsor explains status of Kaizen based on current A3	15 mins

FIGURE 27.1
Example of communication plan.

Items (CI) are recorded in the CMDB. The problem is that within months (sometimes weeks), the CMDB is no longer up-to-date, CIs are missing, details of new CIs have not been entered and people start complaining about the quality of the CMDB. This leads to general apathy towards the CMDB, and it spirals into disuse.

One IT organization decided to take this problem seriously. The kaizen resulted in the conclusion that many of the aspects necessary for the CMDB to be used were in place. What was missing was a comprehensive set of controls to ensure that everyone was focused on keeping the CMDB up to date. The result of the kaizen was a complete control plan, which was written by both managers and engineers, thereby stimulating the adoption of the agreed actions.

Starting with the documentation, it was found that process documentation existed. Its quality was fine and it turned out to still be relevant. Two pieces of documentation were missing. The first was a policy. This document was created and consisted of nine points covering definitions, authorizations, the allocation of responsibility for particular CIs to teams, the basic set of data to be collected and the way quality should be monitored. The second piece of documentation was not so much missing, as in need of improvement. This concerned all Standard Change procedures. It was decided to include the "CMDB update" step at three-quarters of the way through the set of steps to ensure that everyone would carry out the update before the end of the procedure. In the SOP, it was explained why the step was so important.

The next step was to define the monitoring activities. First, a set of simple metrics was defined: the number of CIs with no relationships, the total number of CIs under management per team and the number of CIs not containing the basic set of data. The metrics were used during the visual management meetings and results were used in both performance dialogs and communicated through the cascade. The management levels agreed that if the metrics did not show a steadily improving result, management would ensure that corrective action was taken. The responses were pre-determined and communicated to the teams.

Lastly, everyone in the whole IT organization was trained in the new way of working. The training was primarily done by team members, not by management. In general, team members were very persuasive in their communication to their colleagues as to the why, how and what of the way of working surrounding the CMDB. The result was a much better acceptance of the need to maintain the CMDB. The quality of the CMDB improved over the ensuing months. The quality improvement did not spike and fall back, rather it showed a steady improvement trend.

The final step in our kaizen is its closure and the hand-off from the kaizen team to the kaizen sponsor. We consider the kaizen closed when the kaizen sponsor has accepted a set of deliverables. The main deliverable is improved performance, including the before and after data on metrics, to be used as a baseline for further improvements. This will be described in a completed kaizen A3, including lessons learned (both successes and failures) and recommendations for further improvements. There will be associated documentation, including SOPs, policies, data, VSMs and other documentation produced during the kaizen. Also, any training material created will be transferred so that it can be used to support sharing knowledge gained and new best practices.

One of the powerful aspects of running kaizens is to transfer successful implementations across the entire organization, through replication and standardization. Replication means taking the solution from the team and applying it to the same type or a similar type of problem. Standardization means taking the lessons learned from the team and applying those good ideas and solutions to other problems. The kaizen team should consider standardization and replication opportunities to significantly increase the impact on the business, so as to far exceed anticipated results. The transfer of best practices demands great care and a well-devised implementation method. Never assume that your proposed improvements would work perfectly at once somewhere else. Usually the improvements encounter complications when translated to different environments. Fine-tuning the improvements may be necessary and can provide a great opportunity to involve the others. Ensure that any feedback given is captured and used.

When the kaizen event is officially over, a team evaluation may be done to assess how each individual did as a team member, leadership should recognize the team's work, and the team should be encouraged to share their experiences of how to run a successful kaizen.

In this last step of the kaizen, we finalize the A3. This will entail reviewing the entire A3 to ensure that the story that needs to be told is actually told. As the team moves through the DMAIC cycle, each phase that is completed appears to be the most important. The key message of the A3 is: What are we doing to remove the problem we initially defined? The analysis that the team spent so much time on, producing valuable insights through measurements, may be reduced to a few sentences, results or graphs. The proposed options from the Improve phase may be limited to the top three. In finalizing the A3, we focus on creating a consistent story based on the prior documentation and, principally, describe the solution to the problem defined in the background section. In the Plan / Improvement section, the chosen solution to the problem is described. It is accompanied by a plan defining how the chosen solution will be implemented in the IT organization. The Follow-up section is where we describe the activities that we have devised to ensure that the solution remains embedded in the IT organization, or, if necessary, how the solution will be disseminated throughout the IT organization.

To complete the Control phase, let us take a brief look at the main steps that need to be accomplished.

1. Create a Measurement System	Institute the metrics to control the improvement. Ensure that these are included in a dashboard for use by all people involved. The basis for this measurement system will probably have been laid during the Define and Measure phases.
2. Create Documentation	It is vital to record the changes made. At the same time, we must be careful about creating too much documentation. Keep policies and process documentation concise. Ensure that the documentation is written for the right audience. Make use of Standard Operating Procedures and checklists wherever possible.
3. Create Control Plan	Ensure that the kaizen team makes a control plan, preferably with help from colleagues outside the kaizen team. This involvement helps to generate a plan that is supported by a greater number of people and that contains acceptable controls. The control plan must include all of the four key aspects: documentation, monitoring, response and training.
4. Communicate to Stakeholders	Communicating the results and control measures to the stakeholders is vital. This is the only way to ensure that everyone involved knows what to do. Part of the communication is achieved through training; the rest will be achieved through information sessions. Sending an email to inform someone of the change does not constitute communication to the stakeholders.
5. Present the Results as Described on the A3	We need to finalize the kaizen A3. The key reason is to ensure that all pertinent information is collected in one place, and that the results of the kaizen are explained simply. This document can obviously be used to support the communication of the solution and the control activities to the stakeholders.
6. Transition Ownership	The last step is for the kaizen sponsor to take ownership of the results of the kaizen. In effect, we move the responsibility from a "project team" back to the hierarchical line. The kaizen sponsor should be pleased with the result, since a (part of the) problem has been solved. So, do not forget to celebrate the success with all involved.

28

The Road Goes On

You have come a long way through this book. There may have been a moment that you stopped recognizing your own organization in the description. Go back to this point to identify what you need to do next to advance the transformation of your IT organization. The point you aim to achieve is creating an IT organization that can identify and embed improvements into its people, way of working and products and services on an ongoing basis. This is the aim of Lean IT.

In order to achieve this, the IT leadership must understand what it means to have and use a Lean-Agile Management System. Their meetings include talking about how well the LMS is working, identifying where it needs to be improved.

As Bob Emiliani indicates in his 2018 book *The Triumph of Classical Management Over Lean Management: How Tradition Prevails and What to Do About It*, the adoption of Lean has not been as widespread as one could expect based on the rational arguments that support Lean. Emiliani suggests that the adoption of Lean has stagnated as a result of the interests of the existing leaders and the perpetuation of an old managerial paradigm. The solutions we have tried are through rational argumentation and behavioral adjustment, and Emiliani contends that the problem is a political one. I do not disagree. In the transformation from a well-known way of working to one which is not yet fully understood, there is always going to be a lack of clarity. And politics are important in environments where clarity is lacking. From the perspective of IT organizations, the leeway for leaders to play the politics card is rapidly shrinking, to the point that delaying a transformation has become more dangerous for existing IT leaders than taking the plunge and moving to a Lean (or Agile or DevOps) paradigm.

Politics have been part of IT organizations since their inception. Too much to do with too few people always means there are trade-offs in which political maneuvering can take place. This is nothing new. The question is: whether you as a leader within IT are prepared to do what is necessary to help your business to survive the coming digital transformation-fired episode of extinctions. In 2018 and the previous years, we are living in a time of economic boom; recessions or worse are sure to follow. The businesses whose IT organizations are most rapidly able to adapt, and these will be the IT organizations that have adopted a Lean-based Production and Management System, will be more likely to survive the downturn.

This brings us back to the need for Lean IT Experts; people who have taken the time to deepen their knowledge of Lean as applied in IT. Does this solve the political aspect of the problem? Not directly. However, the more the leaders of IT organizations agree that Lean Production in IT, whether it is in the form of Lean, Agile, DevOps or some variant still to be defined, is the way forward, the more chance there is that Lean Production will become the modus operandi of IT organizations. Let us not forget that it took many years for Mass Production, based on Taylor's ideas of Scientific Management, to be accepted. There is hope, especially if you take the step to become a Lean IT Expert.

References

Bell, S. 2012. *Run Grow Transform*. Taylor & Francis.

Bell, S. and M. Orzen. 2010. *Lean IT*. CRC Press.

Bicheno, J. 2008. *The Lean Toolbox*, 4th edition. Picsie Books.

Collins, J. 2001. Level 5 leadership: The triumph of humility and fierce resolve. *Harvard Business Review*, July–August.

Covey, S. 1989. *The 7 Habits of Highly Effective People*. Simon & Schuster.

Daniels, A. C. 2016. *Bringing Out the Best in People: How to Apply the Astonishing Power of Positive Reinforcement*, 3rd edition. McGraw-Hill Education.

Deming, W. E. 1982. *Out of the Crisis*. MIT Press.

Deming, W. E. 2000. *Out of the Crisis*. MIT Press.

Dictionary.com. http://www.dictionary.com/browse/hypothesis?s=t, accessed 26 May 2018.

Duhigg, C. 2013. *The Power of Habit: Why We Do What We Do, and How to Change*. Random House.

Emiliani, B. 2018. *The Triumph of Classical Management Over Lean Management: How Tradition Prevails and What to Do About It*. The Center for Lean Business Management.

Ford, H. (in collaboration with Samuel Crowther). 1922. *My Life and Work*. Garden City.

Gawande, G. 2011. *The Checklist Manifesto: How to Get Things Right*. Profile.

Goldsmith, R. 2014. *Toyota's 8-Steps to Problem Solving*. CreateSpace Independent Publishing Platform.

Harada, T. 2015. *Management Lessons from Taiichi Ohno*. McGraw Hill Education.

Humble, J. and D. Farley. 2010. *Continuous Delivery*. Addison-Wesley Professional.

Imai, M. 1997. *Gemba Kaizen*. McGraw Hill.

Ishikawa, K. 1985. *What is Total Quality Control? The Japanese Way*. Prentice Hall.

Katzenbach, J. R. and D. K. Smith. 1993. The discipline of teams. *Harvard Business Review*, July-August.

Kotter, J. 2007. Leading change: Why transformation efforts fail. *Harvard Business Review*, January.

Larman, C. n.d. www.craiglarman.com/wiki/index.php?title=Larman%27s_Laws_of_Organizational_Behavior.

Lean IT Association. 2014. Lean IT Foundation Official Publication.

Lencioni, P. 2002. *The Five Dysfunctions of a Team: A Leadership Fable*. Wiley.

Lewis, R. and C. Parker. 1981. Beyond the Peter principle: Managing successful transitions. *Journal of European Industrial Training*, 5(6).

Liker, J. 2014. *Developing Lean Leaders at All Levels: A Practical Guide*. Lean Leadership Institute Publications.

Liker, J. and G. Convis, 2011. *The Toyota Way to Lean Leadership: Achieving and Sustaining Excellence through Leadership Development*. McGraw-Hill Professional Publishing.

Minto, M. 2008. *The Pyramid Principle: Logic in Writing and Thinking*. Financial Times Prentice Hall.

Modig, N. and P. Ahlstrom. 2012. *This Is Lean: Resolving the Efficiency Paradox*. Rheologica Publishing.

Ohno, T. 1988. *Toyota Production System: Beyond Large-Scale Production*. Taylor & Francis.

Ohno, T. 2012. *Taiichi Ohno's Workplace Management: Special 100th Birthday Edition*. McGraw-Hill Professional Publishing.

Rogers, E. 2003. *Diffusion of Innovations*, 5th edition. Simon and Schuster.

Rother, M. 2009. *Toyota Kata: Managing People for Improvement, Adaptiveness and Superior Results*. McGraw-Hill.

Sarbanes–Oxley Act, 2002, Public Law 107–204, 116 Stat. 745, enacted July 30, 2002, also known as the Public Company Accounting Reform and Investor Protection Act.

Seddon, J. 2003. *Freedom from Command and Control*. Vanguard Education.

Shook, J. 2011. How to go to the Gemba: Go See, Ask Why, Show Respect (https://www.lean.org/shook/DisplayObject.cfm?o=1843).

Snowdon, D. and M. Boone. 2007. A leader's framework for decision making. *Harvard Business Review*, 85(11): 69–76.

Sobek, D. K. and A. Smalley. 2008. *Understanding A3 Thinking: Keys and Tools for PDCA Management*. Taylor & Francis.

Toyota Motor Corporation. 2001. *The Toyota Way*.

Womack, J. P. and D. T. Jones. 1996. *Lean Thinking: Banish Waste and Create Wealth in Your Corporation*. Free Press.

Glossary

Term	Description
5S	A set of hygiene rules that help to, for lack of a better word, clean up processes and workplaces.
A3	Refers to the size of a piece of paper that provides enough space to explain a relatively complicated story but encourages conciseness in the communication of a message.
A3 Problem-solving Report	The A3 problem-solving report is a document informing all stakeholders of the results of an improvement kaizen.
A3 Proposal	Is an A3 report used for creating a recommendation for action.
A3 Status Report	The A3 status report is aimed at informing all stakeholders of the progress of the execution of a longer-running project or action.
Accountability	Being prepared to offer an explanation for attitude, behavior and actions, without necessarily being asked.
Affinity Mapping	Bundling solutions that are linked, similar or overlapping in order to reduce the number of solutions.
Agile	A set of principles, originating from the development of software, that can and is applied to a variety of areas (e.g. Agile Project Management).
Agility	Increasing agility means being more able to adapt to customer value requirements.
Analysis	An A3 skill where the aim is to separate something into its constituent parts or elements. It is vital when writing an A3 report to understand the parts of the problem so that only the right information is given. If we are able to discern the parts of a problem, we can also determine which of these parts are relevant to the reader. What was done to identify the root cause of the problem (vb. Analyze).
Analyze (Phase)	Third phase of the DMAIC cycle, in which the analysis of the problem is done.
Andon	Literally, this is a signal. Refers to a system to notify management, maintenance and other workers of a quality or process problem. An andon system or cord is one of the principal elements of the jidoka quality-control method pioneered by Toyota as part of the Toyota Production System and is now part of Lean. It gives the worker the ability, and empowerment, to stop production when a defect is found, and immediately call for assistance.

Annotated Observation	Watching what happens and noting the number of times something happens, the amount of time spent on a task, the number of errors made in finished products and other such observable occurrences.
Application Development	A function within an IT organization in which software products ("applications") are created.
Baseline	Baselines and benchmarks are necessary to understand the relative value of the performance. A baseline is the measurement of a situation in order to understand whether a change occurs based on an intervention after the baseline has been set. This is particularly useful in kaizen because we are very interested in the effect of changes that have been implemented in the IT organization. It is vital that during the Measure phase a baseline is set that can be used to measure progress.
Batch and Queue	A Push production model where products are created before customer demand and in a certain quantity at production cycle. After production the products are stored (queued) in stock until the customer's demand is received.
Behavior and Attitude	The way people think and act.
Benchmark	A benchmark is a standard or set of standards used in evaluating the performance or level of quality of an organization. Benchmarking may be used during a kaizen to understand how well others perform a particular activity. This may help to identify what improvements are possible.
Capacity	The maximum amount of output that the process can deliver over a period of time.
Cascade	A mechanism that involves aligning meetings so that the information shared in one meeting can quickly be brought to a different meeting in which the information is needed.
Catch-Ball Communication	A method of idea generation and sharing based on the communication of goals through the organization's hierarchy.
Cause and Effect Diagram	See *Fishbone Diagram*.
Cause and Effect Matrix	A cause-and-effect matrix helps to determine which factors affect the outcomes of the process being investigated.
Change Over Time	Time needed to change from processing one unit of work to processing a different one. Within IT, this is the time lost due to context-switching.
Change Story	A clear description of which changes need to be made and why: The change story gives direction. In the change story, the motivation behind the desire to change is described.
Check sheet	The check sheet is a simple and highly effective tool for collecting quality-related data in a structured way. It is a way to assess a process and can function as input for other analyses when there is limited or no numerical data to be analyzed.

Closed Loop Thinking	This considers how changes within the system ripple across the value stream, affecting the work and behavior of other employees in the same department, in other departments, external customers, suppliers and other stakeholders.
Common cause variation	Sources of variation in a process that are inherent to the process, also referred to as noise.
Configuration Management Database (CMDB)	A repository that acts as a data warehouse for information technology (IT) organizations. Its contents are intended to hold a collection of IT assets that are commonly referred to as configuration items (CI), as well as descriptive relationships between such assets.
Constancy of Purpose	Principle (from the Deming/Shingo Model).
Continuous Improvement	Ongoing process in an organization with the objective to find, resolve and share solutions to problems. The objective is to achieve perfection, in other words, to improve value streams, product and customer value. A philosophy of frequently reviewing processes, identifying opportunities for improvement, and implementing changes to get closer to perfection.
Control (Phase)	The fifth and final phase of the DMAIC cycle. This phase ensures that improvements are implemented and anchored into the way of working
Control Chart	The control chart is essentially a time-series chart. A time-series chart is one in which data is plotted on a chart where the horizontal axis is a time sequence. The vertical axis can be numbers or another variable whose value can be different over time. A control chart helps to provide understanding of variation.
Control Plan	A plan aimed at maintaining the changes that were made in order to sustain the improvements. This plan consists of four basic parts: Documentation, Monitoring, Response, Training.
Control Variable	This kind of variable is particularly useful in experiments. This variable is kept constant while others are changed so that they can be investigated.
Cost of Poor Quality	The price you have to pay for poor quality products or services. For example, claims, fines and loss of customer confidence.
Critical to Quality	Critical to Quality is an attribute of a part, assembly, sub-assembly, product, or process that is literally critical to quality or, more precisely, has a direct and significant impact on its actual or perceived quality.
Cross-Functional Alignment	Share common objectives, make appropriate prioritization and resource allocation decisions that add value to the customer across a value stream that goes through multiple functional areas.
Customer	The person or group of people who buys, uses or derives value from your product or service OR the person next in line in the value stream. The person "next in line" is sometimes referred to as a "partner in the value stream," or an "internal" customer.

Customer Value	A capability provided to a customer at the right time at an appropriate price, as defined by the customer. The more a product or service meets a customer's needs in terms of affordability, availability and utility, the greater value it has. Thus, a product with true value will enable, or provide the capability for, the customer to accomplish his objective.
Cycle Time	Cycle Time is the total elapsed time to move a unit of work from the beginning to the end of a process.
Cynefin (Model)	A model, in which categorized decision-making is placed into one of five types: obvious, complicated, complex, chaotic and disorder.
Daily Kaizen	Act of responding to everyday occurrences such as incidents, mistakes and other quality issues and addressing quality issues at the source rather than being satisfied with quick fixes.
Day Board	A board used to share information and updates within the team focused on identifying short-term priorities, blockages and dependencies. The day board is used during the Day start meeting and is a key element and enabler of Lean visual management.
Defect	Output of a process that does not meet requirements. For example, a product that does not function as specified. Defects generate rework.
Define (Phase)	The first phase of the DMAIC cycle, in which the problem to be solved is defined and agreed.
Definition of Done	The description of the completed product in the form of a simple list of activities (writing code, coding comments, unit testing, integration testing, release notes, design documents, etc.) that verifiably add value to the product.
Dependent Variable	This is the output; in effect, this is the problem that is captured as part of the Measure phase.
DevOps	DevOps is a solution that derives its effectiveness from the integration of a number of critical areas: process, organization, performance, behavior and attitude and automation.
DMAIC	An acronym for the five steps in problem solving with kaizen, i.e. Define, Measure, Analyze, Improve and Control.
DMEDI	Acronym for the five steps in problem solving with kakushin, i.e. Define, Measure, Explore, Develop and Implement
Dynamic Thinking	This is about creating a vision for the near or distant future. It aims to increase understanding of what has happened, what is happening and identifying what may happen in the future.
External IT Organization	An IT organization that is its own enterprise providing specific services to a variety of customers.
Failure Demand	Demand from the customer based on a failure of the IT service as opposed to a request for value, e.g. findings from an acceptance test or resolving an incident.

Failure Modes and Effects Analysis (FMEA)	Failure Modes and Effects Analysis (FMEA) is an analysis for identifying all possible failures in a design, process, product or service. The Failure modes are the ways in which something might fail. Failures are any errors or defects and can be potential or actual. The effects analysis is about understanding the consequences of those failures. The aim of the FMEA is to take actions to remove the sources of failure, i.e. the root causes, starting with those with the greatest impact. FMEA can be used throughout the lifecycle of an IT service, from design to operation and retirement of the service.
Failure Stream	A sequence of activities triggered by a customer as a result of failure in the product or service, aiming to resolve a defect, or to provide information on how to best use the system. Opposite of a value stream. A failure stream does not add value to the customer. For example, resolving an IT incident.
First in First Out (FIFO)	Work is processed on a "first come, first served" approach.
Fishbone Diagram	The fishbone diagram identifies many possible causes for an effect or problem. It can be used to structure a brainstorming session. It is also known as an "Ishikawa Diagram"
Five Whys	A root-cause analysis tool used to identify the true root cause of a problem. The question "why" is asked a sufficient number of times to find the fundamental reason for the problem. Once that cause is identified, an appropriate countermeasure can be designed and implemented in order to eliminate re-occurrence.
Flow	The smooth, uninterrupted movement of a product or service through a series of process steps. In true flow, the work product (information, paperwork, material, etc.) passing through the series of steps never stops.
Flow Efficiency	Efficiency based on processing a unit of work through the IT organization in the most efficient way.
Flowchart	A flowchart is one of the simplest of the seven quality tools. The flowchart is the visual representation of a series of steps in a process and helps to break down a complicated process into a simple series of steps. This simplification ensures that the process becomes understandable to anyone.
Gemba	The place where the work is done. Within a Lean context, gemba simply refers to the location where value is created.
Gemba Walk	Go to the place where the work is done with the intention of understanding what is actually happening there. The opposite is a Gallery Walk, in which management walks around but does not take time to understand problems.
Genchi Genbutsu	This means going to the gemba to observe what is happening without judging.
Ha	The second phase of the Shu-Ha-Ri learning cycle, is about diverging from routines, based on full understanding of the kata.

Habit	A routine or behavior that is executed automatically based on a trigger or cue.
Histogram	A histogram is "a representation of a frequency distribution by means of rectangles whose widths represent class intervals and whose areas are proportional to the corresponding frequencies." In short, this means that we create a graph in which groups of numbers are plotted based on how often they appear. The power of histograms is that they allow us to analyze extremely large datasets by reducing them to a single graph that can show one or more peaks in data. The histogram also visualizes the significance of the peaks.
Holistic Thinking	This means understanding the interconnectedness of the aspects of larger systems.
Horizontal Alignment	See *Cross-Functional Alignment*.
Hoshin Kanri	A cyclic planning and management concept applied at the strategic level to achieve breakthrough objectives, and at the day-to-day level to manage the operation to keep the business running.
Humility	Having a clear perspective and respect for one's place in context. The concept of humility addresses intrinsic self-worth, relationships and socialization as well as perspective.
Hypothesis	A hypothesis is a statement that will start with the words "I/We think/believe that …". The hypothesis is as yet not supported by any factual basis. The hypothesis is based on people's beliefs as a result of their observations. These are by definition selective and biased, and very much in need of testing through thorough analysis of the data and facts that can be found.
Improve (Phase)	Fourth phase of the DMAIC cycle. The kaizen team thinks up possible solutions to the problem based on the analysis done.
Improvement Board	A board that presents current problems and the follow-up to resolving or addressing that problem (also kaizen Board); an element of visual management.
Improvement Kaizen	Carrying out kaizen events to bring about incremental change. It is often referred to as kaizen.
Incident	An unplanned interruption to an IT service or reduction in the quality of an IT service. Failure of a configuration item that has not yet affected service is also an incident.
Independent Variable	In the case of problem-solving, the independent variable can be seen as something that may or may not contribute to the problem. The aim is obviously to find the independent variables that have the greatest effect on the problem.
Inflexibility	Inability to meet customer demand with a certain resource. For example, you have sufficient employees, but they do not have the right skills to work on the current customer demand.
Input	The resources used or transformed by a process; also known as the Xs or the input variables.

Internal IT Organization	An IT organization operating within an enterprise, providing a wide range of IT services to that enterprise.
Inventory	All components, work in process and finished products not being processed but stored and waiting.
Ishikawa Diagram	The Ishikawa diagram identifies many possible causes for an effect or problem. It can be used to structure a brainstorming session. See *Fishbone Diagram*.
IT Operations	The functional area of IT responsible for the production environments and all activities associated with these environments.
IT Outcome	The delivery of IT products or services to the business (customer).
Jidoka	Creating an environment in which disturbances to the flow of work through the value streams are made visible, i.e. problems are not left covered up. Japanese word for autonomation, which aims to prevent the production of defective products or services.
Just-in-Time	A system for producing and delivering the right items at the right time in the right amounts so that inventories are kept to a minimum.
Kaikaku	The Japanese word for "radical change," it is a business concept concerned with making fundamental, transformational and radical changes to a production system, unlike kaizen which is focused on incremental minor changes.
Kaizen	An improvement philosophy in which continuous incremental improvement occurs over a sustained period of time, creating more value and less waste, resulting in increased speed, lower costs and improved quality. When applied to a business enterprise, it refers to ongoing improvement involving the entire workforce including senior leadership, middle management and frontline workers. Kaizen is also a philosophy that assumes that our way of life (working, social or personal) deserves to be constantly improved.
Kaizen Board	See *Improvement Board*.
Kaizen Charter	The document in which initially the problem is described, and an indication is given of what resources (people, time, money) are to be allocated to the resolution of the problem. At the end of the kaizen, the kaizen charter includes all aspects of the kaizen.
Kaizen Event	See *DMAIC*.
Kaizen Lead	This person manages the kaizen process on behalf of the sponsor and the team.
Kaizen Mindset	A belief throughout the IT organization that improving IT services and the way they are delivered can and must be done on a daily basis through seeing and prioritizing problems, solving problems and sharing lessons learned.
Kaizen Sponsor	This person is the owner of the problem and has a direct interest in having the problem solved.
Kaizen Team Member	The people executing this role will do the required work. They must be involved with the problem as it occurs on the work floor.

Kakushin	This is the third form of improvement. Kakushin focuses on innovation, reform and renewal. It differs from kaikaku in that kaikaku deals with transformational change of existing structures, systems, etc. kakushin deals with the introduction of completely new structures, systems, etc.
Kanban	Literally, a signal. Kanban is a scheduling system for Lean and just-in-time (JIT) production. Kanban is the embodiment of the pull/replenishment system (see *Pull*).
Kanban Board	A kanban board is a workflow visualization tool that enables team collaboration focused on monitoring the flow of work. Physical Kanban boards often use simple work records like sticky notes on a whiteboard to communicate status, progress and issues.
Kata	When taken literally, this term means "form." The defined routine for thinking and acting in a particular situation.
Known Error	A problem for which the root cause and a workaround have been documented.
KPI	Key Performance Indicator, a measure indicating a key performance metric of a process, condition or state. A KPI should be in line with the strategy, long-lasting, and consistent in the cascade from top to operational level.
Last In First Out (LIFO)	Work is processed in a "last arrived, first handled" approach.
Lead Time	The time between the moment the customer submits their request to the time they receive the requested item or service.
Leader Standard Work (LSW)	The standards that can be found in a leader's work. LSW helps to identify where issues and deviations are happening in the leader's work.
Little's Law	Little's Law = the number of units of work in the process (WIP) / average completion rate. This helps us understand the relationship between lead time and work-in-progress.
Machine Time	The time a unit of work is worked on by a machine. This is a type of waiting time.
Measure (Phase)	Second Phase of the DMAIC cycle. In this phase, facts and figures are collected to understand the problem we are trying to resolve.
MECE	Acronym for Mutually Exclusive, Collectively Exhaustive. Mutually Exclusive means that all items in a particular category only belong to that category, and no other. Collectively Exhaustive means that all possibilities have been covered.
Metric	A measurable characteristic of a variable that is regarded as a performance indicator.
Motion	People or equipment moving or walking more than is required to perform the processing.
Muda	A Japanese word for waste. See *Non-Value-Added* and *Waste*.

Multi-Voting	Multi-voting focuses on prioritizing the solutions by allowing each team member to allocate votes to a set of solutions.
Mura	A Japanese word meaning unevenness; irregularity; lack of uniformity; variation.
Muri	A Japanese word meaning overburdened, unreasonableness; excessiveness. Often related to policy-based waste.
Necessary Non-Value-Added (NNVA)	Activities that add no value from the customer's perspective but are required in order to operate the business. This could include legal and regulatory requirements as well as certain internal business processes which would put the business at risk if eliminated in today's environment.
Nemawashi	The informal process of laying the foundation for a decision, change or project.
Non-Value-Added (NVA)	Activities that add no value from the customer's perspective nor are they necessary to properly run the business. These activities are often legacy in nature ("we've always done it that way").
Obeya	Japanese word for "big room," sometimes translated as "war room." This is the room in which management teams have their visual management which provides insight into the current state of all aspects of the organization.
Organization	Lean IT is structured in five dimensions. Organization is the dimension that covers all aspects related to the way the company is structured.
Output	Products or services created as a result of a value stream or process.
Over processing	Type of waste. It means doing the work better than requested by the customers. Also referred to as gold-plating.
Over production	Type of waste. It means producing more than requested by the customer.
Overburden	See *Muri*.
Parallel Lines	Number of lines of production that can operate in parallel. For example, three cashiers in a supermarket handling customers at the same time.
Pareto Diagram	Bar chart showing the causes of problem or condition order from large to small contribution. Effective tool to show what the big contributors to the problem are.
PDCA Cycle	Plan, Do, Check, Act is a well-known continuous improvement method often referred to as the Deming or Shewhart Cycle. The PDCA cycle is applicable in any situation and forms the basis for all improvement within Lean.
Perfection	A key objective of Lean to bring a product or service into a state where the number of defects is zero or as close as possible to zero. Relates to continual improvement.
Performance	Performance is the ability to achieve defined goals in time, related to customer value.

Performance Dialog	A structured and objective discussion of performance. These discussions consist of three elements: define an objective, offer support and evaluate achieved results.
Performance Indicator	Measure that gives a visual representation of a defined performance.
Plan-Build-Run	This is the short description of the basic functions/activities of an IT organization.
Poka Yoke	Literally, to prevent an unintentional error, this is a concept aimed at ensuring that activities can only be done in one way, the right way; foolproofing an activity.
Principle	An accepted or professed rule of action or conduct.
Problem	An undesired situation that stands in the way of providing the necessary customer value; an opportunity to improve. Also, the root cause of incidents (ITIL Definition of Problem, denoted with a capital P).
Problem Board	See *Improvement board*.
Problem Management	A Core ITIL Operational process with an aim to prevent problems and incidents, eliminate repeating incidents and minimize the impact of incidents that cannot be prevented.
Problem Statement	A statement that helps the team investigating the problem to focus its attention. The problem statement may be in the form of a question or in the form of a statement. The former is preferable because it is then clear when you have found the answer to the question.
Process	A series of actions that must be performed correctly in the correct sequence at the correct time to create value for a customer.
Process Cycle Efficiency	A measure of overall process health focused on the percentage of value-add time (work that changes the form, fit or function as desired by the customer) divided by process lead time. PCE = Value Add Time / Process Lead Time. PCE is an indication of how efficiently the process is converting units of work to process outcomes.
Process Throughput	The number (volume) of products or services that a process can produce within a timeframe.
Process Throughput Analysis	A tool to perform a process analysis with the objective of calculating process output, e.g. process throughput and constraints. Used to improve the capacity of a process.
Pull	A system of cascading production and delivery instructions from downstream to upstream activities in which nothing is produced by the upstream supplier until the downstream customer signals a need.
Push	Push Production is a system where an upstream process produces as much as it can without regard to the actual requirements of the next process and sends them to the next process whether they have capacity to begin work or not. Push Production typically results in queues of work building up, which result in delays.

Pyramid Principle	Developed by Barbara Minto. The Pyramid Principle is a method that is fully compatible with A3 thinking. In fact, it helps to structure the information and insights gained during the kaizen event. The problem is framed using the following framework: Situation-Complication-Key Question-Answer
Queue Time	The time a unit of work is in a queue. This is a type of waiting time.
Repeater	These units of work occur regularly; indicative frequency is weekly. As an example, within IT, we find high impact incidents, small to medium sized non-standard changes and the smaller advisory services.
Resource Efficiency	An efficiency measure based on how much work is completed by an IT employee.
Re-Work	Activities required to fix defects of a product or service produced by a process to meet the requirements.
Ri	The third phase of the Shu-Ha-Ri learning cycle, Ri is about transcending routines, based on mastery of the kata.
Root Cause	The underlying or original cause of an incident or problem.
Root Cause Analysis	Studying the fundamental causes of a problem, as opposed to analyzing symptoms.
Runner	Units of work that occur on a daily basis and tend to require up to one hour of work for them to be completed. Within IT, we can say that incidents, service requests, standard changes and operational activities fall into this category.
SCAMPER	A third idea generation technique uses action verbs as triggers to generate ideas. SCAMPER is an acronym with each letter standing for an action verb which in turn stands for a prompt for creative ideas. S – Substitute, C – Combine, A – Adapt, M – Modify, P – Put to another use, E – Eliminate, R – Reverse
Scatter Diagram	A graph that aims to demonstrate the relationship between two sets of data. We try to understand whether there is a correlation between two sets of data and whether this correlation is positive or negative.
Sensei	When taken literally, this term means "teacher." A coach within the Lean context.
Service Desk	The customer contact center of an IT organization.
Service Manager	A role or function responsible for ensuring that a defined IT service is delivered to the customer.
Shu	The first phase of the Shu-Ha-Ri learning cycle is about "automating" routines, learning the kata and developing positive habits.
Shu-Ha-Ri	A Lean learning cycle. It is a model of learning based on the kata. The process of self-development is guided by the principle of Shu-Ha-Ri.
SIPOC	Supplier, Input, Process, Output, Customer. Diagram used to establish the kaizen project team, create the project charter and planning, get stakeholders' support and start the project.

SIPOC	This acronym means Supplier, Input, Process, Output, Customer. It is a diagram used to establish the kaizen project team, create the project charter and planning, get stakeholders' support and start the project.
Skills & Knowledge Analysis	Skills and knowledge analysis is used to steer team development to meet skills demand. The objective is that team skills are aligned with the customer demand for those skills.
SMART	Specific, Measurable, Achievable, Realistic, Time-bound.
Solution Matrix	A matrix in which solutions can be plotted according to two axes: feasibility and anticipated cost.
Special Cause Variation	Source of variation that can be assigned to a specific cause which can usually be discovered. Special causes generate patterns in the data and provide signals about the problems in the process and how they can be resolved.
Standard Operating Procedure (SOP)	An SOP is a written procedure that describes how a specific task should be carried out.
Standard Time	Estimated time within which a specific process or process step can be executed, e.g. we should be able to complete, receive and record an incident in 10 minutes. The average time may, in practice, be higher or lower.
Standard Work	A collection and implementation of the best practices known at that point.
Stranger	Units of work that have an irregular occurrence. IT "strangers" are large non-standard changes, large requests for advice and plans, which all tend to occur or be updated on a monthly or quarterly basis.
Summarize	An A3 skill that is the ability to express thoughts, facts and other information concisely.
Synthesis	Refers to a combination of two or more entities that together form something new; alternately and is required to address complex and chaotic problems (vb. Synthesize).
Systemic Thinking	A principle that unifies all the other principles of operational excellence and enables companies to sustain Lean and develop a constancy of purpose centered on continuous improvement.
Takt Time	The pace at which work must be completed to meet customer demand. Takt, a German word meaning pace, is the heartbeat of any Lean system. Process Time divided by Takt Time yields the number of workers required to support a specific product. To calculate, divide the available work time by the customer demand for that period.
Tally Sheet	See *Check Sheet*
Team	A small number of people with complementary skills who are committed to a common purpose, set of performance goals and approach for which they hold themselves mutually accountable.
Throughput	The actual amount of output over a period of time. This is invariably lower than the capacity as a result of waste.

Transformation	A change in form, appearance, nature, or character. Used to define the overall process of moving from a traditional IT organization to a Lean IT organization.
Transportation	Movement of products in a factory. It is a type of waste if products are transported more the strictly needed.
Trend	A gradual, systematic change of a metric over time
True North	The important and constant focus that organizations should have on value.
T-Type Leader	The combination of deep understanding of a technical area supplemented by broad knowledge of leadership and IT service delivery.
Unit of Work	Describes the unit (the thing) that goes through the process, for example, incidents, cars, designs etc.
Value Stream	A value stream is a set of specific actions to create a product or service. The specific activities required to design, order and provide a specific product or service from the point of product (or service) concept, through launch, ordering raw materials, production and placing the product (or service) in the hands of the customer. From a shareholder's perspective, the value stream could also include the steps and time required until the receipt of revenue.
Value Stream Mapping (VSM)	A technique used to analyze the flow of materials and information currently required to bring a product or service to a consumer. A visual representation of all of the process steps (both value-added and non-value-added) required to transform a customer requirement into a delivered good or service. A VSM shows the connection between information flow and product flow, as well as the major process blocks and barriers to flow. VSMs are used to document current state conditions as well as design a future state. One of the key objectives of Value Stream Mapping is to identify non-value-adding activities for elimination. Value Stream Maps, along with the Value Stream Implementation Plan are strategic tools used to help identify, prioritize and communicate continuous improvement activities.
Value-Add (VA)	Activities that add value in the eyes of the customer. The customer is willing to pay for this work.
Variability	Variation in the output of a process in quality and demand volume. Fluctuation in cost, quality or throughput time in the delivery of value. See also *Mura*.
Variable, Control	This kind of variable is particularly useful in experiments. This variable is kept constant while others are changed so that they can be investigated.
Variable, Dependent	This is the output; in effect, this is the problem.
Variable, Independent	This is an input. In the case of problem-solving, the independent variable can be seen as something that may or may not contribute to the problem. The aim is obviously to find the independent variables that have the greatest effect on the problem.

Vertical Alignment	Ensures the goals of all stakeholders, from the boardroom to the work floor, are aligned; goal setting and review, goals are set and adjusted so they continue to fit.
Visual Management	Visual management concerns the use of displays, metrics and controls to help establish and maintain continuous flow and giving everyone a view of the work along the value stream. Its aim is to ensure transparency and understanding of the situation. Visual Management is about effective communication and real-time updates regarding the work.
Visualize	An A3 skill used to turn your story into a visual experience using pictures and graphics to explain what has been investigated and what is proposed as a solution.
Voice of the Business	Concerns the "business" of the IT organization itself; not to be confused with the fact that the customer of IT is regularly referred to as "the business."
Voice of the Customer	Gives the IT organization feedback on how the customer, the user of the IT service, actually experiences the IT service. It captures customers' expectations, preferences and aversions with the objective of creating products or services that meet the customer's needs and preferences.
Voice of the Process	Defines the needs and requirements of the processes. Provides information about processes that are not working correctly.
Voice of the Regulator (VoR)	Defines the needs and requirements of the external regulator.
VSM	See *Value Stream Mapping*.
Waiting Time	Waiting for the next production step to begin.
Waste	Any activity that consumes resources but does not provide value as defined by the customer. Also referred to as muda or Non-Value-Adding activities.
Wave	A phase in the Lean IT transformation in which one or more teams are helped through a step in the transformation.
Week Board	A board used to share information about the team's performance over the previous week and objectives for the coming week; an element of visual management
Work in Progress (WIP)	The number of uncompleted units of work that are still in the process. This number is directly related to the lead time (Little's Law).

Appendix A: Lean IT Foundation Syllabus

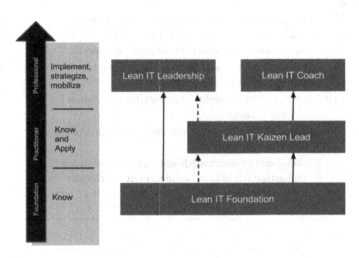

FIGURE A.1
Lean IT Association certification scheme.

Syllabus Area Code IN		Syllabus Area: Introduction (IN)	Chapter Reference
Level	**Topic**		

Know the historical development of Lean, the key principles underlying Lean and the dimensions for structuring Lean IT specifically to recall:

01	01	The historical development of Lean and the importance of the Toyota Production System.	4
01	02	The key principles underlying Lean: Customer value, value stream, flow, pull, perfection	4
01	03	The concepts of waste (muda), variability (mura) and overburden (muri)	4
01	04	Classification of activities: Value-Add, Necessary Non-Value-Add, Non-Value-Add, particularly as related to specific IT activities such as solving incidents, developing applications, testing	4

01	05	Plan-Do-Check-Act cycle as the generic method for quality improvement	4
01	06	Definition of Lean IT (Lean IT Association definition)	1
01	07	Dimensions of Lean IT: Customer, Process, Performance, Organization and Behavior and Attitude	10
01	08	Key "players": Shingo Prize (show high-level model and explain), Lean IT Association, author community	5

Understand the following aspects dealt with in the Introduction specifically to identify:

02	01	Lean principles: How these are related to one another	4, 5
02	02	Waste: Ability to identify types of waste within an IT organization or process (TIMWOOD with Talent)	4
02	03	The cost of poor quality and reasons for using Lean Principles to improve performance	4
02	04	Types of activities: Ability to define what IT activities fall into which category	4
02	05	PDCA: Ability to describe how the PDCA cycle works on the most basic level	4
02	06	Relationship to other models and methods used within IT: Understand where Lean IT differs from and complements other methods. The connection of Lean IT with IT service management is specifically investigated.	5

Syllabus Area Code CU		Syllabus Area: Customer (CU)	Chapter Reference
Level	**Topic**		

Know the key components of the Customer dimension specifically to recall:

01	01	The Voice of the Customer (VoC) and the types of customers	22
01	02	Types of customer value	22
01	03	The concept of Critical to Quality (CTQ)	22
01	04	Ways to analyze the Voice of the Customer	22
01	05	Sources of continuous improvement opportunities: Voice of the Customer, Voice of Business, Voice of the Process, Voice of the Regulator	22

Understand the following aspects related to the Customer specifically to identify:

02	01	Types of customer value and the factors that influence customer value	22
02	02	The link between the Voice of the Customer and Critical to Quality	22
02	03	How to construct a Critical to Quality tree	22

Syllabus Area Code PR		Syllabus Area: Process (PR)	Chapter Reference
Level	**Topic**		
Know the key aspects of the Process dimension specifically to recall:			
01	01	Definition of process and the basic processes in an organization	22
01	02	Key components of a process: Goal, result, input, throughput, output, customer	22
01	03	The concepts of Push and Pull, including justifiable inventory to ensure reduction of variation	22, 23
01	04	The definitions of the SIPOC model	22, 23
01	05	The key aspects of a Value Stream Map (VSM), including the identification of waste in the VSM and adding metrics to the VSM	22, 23
01	06	The most important metrics in a process: Cycle time, Takt time, Lead time, Waiting time, Changeover time, Work in Progress, Parallel Lines, Throughput, Capacity	22, 23
01	07	Value improvement in processes: Possible sources of improvements including specifically heijunka and 5S	22, 23
01	08	The concepts of value demand and failure demand and the related value and failure streams	22
Understand the following aspects of the Process dimension specifically to identify:			
02	01	Relationship of process (value stream) with the other Lean principles	22, 23
02	02	The difference between Push and Pull systems	22, 23
02	03	The steps for creating a Value Stream Map, using SIPOC and Value Stream Map	22, 23
02	04	Waste in a Value Stream Map, ability to identify the symbols for the TIMWOOD waste	22, 23
02	05	Explain the SIPOC and VSM using IT examples e.g. SIPOC: Software development, VSM: High-level Change process (other examples are permitted)	22, 23
02	06	The difference between value and failure demand within IT	22

Syllabus Area Code PE		Syllabus Area: Performance (PE)	Chapter Reference
Level	**Topic**		
Know the key aspects of the Performance dimension specifically to recall:			
01	01	Definition of performance, as compared to a result	9
01	02	Definition and requirements for a Key Performance Indicator (KPI)	9

01	03	The concept of Process Cycle Efficiency (PCE) as a method for understanding time usage. Importance of time in an IT organization	19, 23
01	04	The goal of understanding the availability of skills and knowledge	23
01	05	The combination of Performance Indicators, Time and Skills and Knowledge to steer performance	23

Understand the following aspects of the Performance dimension
  Specifically to identify:

02	01	Relationship of performance with the PDCA cycle	9
02	02	The key aspects of a KPI	9
02	03	Why time is the most important production factor within IT	19
02	04	The relationship of PCE with VSM	23
02	05	The role of skills and knowledge in ensuring performance	23

Syllabus Area Code OR		Syllabus Area: Organization (OR)	Chapter Reference
Level	**Topic**		

Know the key aspects of the Organization dimension specifically to recall:

01	01	Organizational requirements for Lean IT structuring for customer orientation, empowerment of frontline to act in delivery of value to customers and speed of communication through the organization	9
01	02	The principle for organizing: Customer orientation and speed of communication	9
01	03	Goal of management to empower employees	9
01	04	Concept and components of the performance dialog	17
01	05	Concept and goals of visual management including use of boards (day, week and kaizen/improvement).	8
01	06	Explain the concept of Kanban and its role in visual management	23

Understand the following aspects of the Organization dimension
  specifically to identify:

02	01	Why organizations need to be customer-oriented	9
02	02	What the goal is of a performance dialog	17
02	03	The use of each of the visual management boards – day board, week board and kaizen/improvement board	8

Syllabus Area Code BA		Syllabus Area: Behavior and Attitude (BA)	Chapter Reference
Level	**Topic**		
Know the key aspects of the Behavior and Attitude dimension specifically to recall:			
01	01	Characteristics of the Lean mindset, Empowerment of the individual to stop the production line (jidoka/andon)	4, 6
01	02	Types of Lean behavior, Quality at the source (First Time Right)	6
01	03	The role of managers within a Lean environment — role in welcoming problems	11
01	04	Lean Leadership – Go See, Ask Why, Show Respect. Go to the gemba as concept for Go See.	17
01	05	Valley of despair in relation to people's expectations over time (Kubler-Ross)	11
Understand the following aspects of the Behavior and Attitude dimension specifically to identify:			
02	01	The difference between behavior and attitude	6
02	02	The difference between traditional management and Lean management	15
02	03	The behavior and attitude required for successful use of Lean	6
02	04	Behavior and Attitude in relation to expectations surrounding a change in way of working	6

Syllabus Area Code PS		Syllabus Area: Problem Solving/Kaizen (PS)	Chapter Reference
Level	**Topic**		
Know the key aspects of Problem Solving/Kaizen Specifically to recall:			
01	01	Definition of kaizen and kaikaku as the two forms of improvement within Lean (continuous and step)	24
01	02	Overview of steps in the DMAIC method	24
01	03	Define phase: Definition of a problem	24
01	04	Measure phase: Definition of a Pareto chart and its use	25
01	05	Analyze: Definition of an Ishikawa (Fishbone) diagram and its use	25
01	06	Analyze phase: Five Why method for root cause analysis	25
01	07	Improve phase: Inputs for future state: VoC (Voice of the Customer), VoB (Voice of the Business), VoP (Voice of the Process), VoR (Voice of the Regulator)	26

Understand the following aspects of Problem Solving/Kaizen specifically to identify:

Appendix B: Lean IT Kaizen Syllabus

Syllabus Area Code IN		Syllabus Area: Introduction (IN)	Chapter Reference
Level	Topic	Goal: Introduce kaizen concepts	
Know the most important concepts regarding kaizen specifically to:			
01	01	Recall and understand definitions of kaizen (continuous improvement), kakushin (innovation) and kaikaku (revolutionary change/"transformation of mind") as the three forms of change for the better within Lean	25
01	02	Recall the phases in the DMAIC method	25
01	03	Understand DMEDI: Define, Measure, Explore, Develop, Implement the innovation cycle as compared to DMAIC	25
01	04	Recall Continuous Improvement models, specifically ITIL Continual Service Improvement and Plan-Do-Check-Act	25
01	05	Know the difference between daily kaizen and improvement kaizen	25
01	06	Understand the kaizen mindset in relation to daily kaizen and improvement kaizen	25
Understand the following aspects dealt with in the Introduction specifically to:			
02	01	Describe the kaizen mindset	4
02	02	Identify the core elements of the kaizen mindset	4
02	03	Identify the difference between improvement kaizen and daily kaizen; identify benefits and drawbacks of each	20
02	04	Understand the difference between a problem and the IT Service Management definition of a problem	25
02	05	Identify muri, mura and muda as elements that can be removed using kaizen	25
Apply the following aspects dealt with in the Introduction specifically to be able to:			
03	01	Differentiate between situations where DMAIC is used as opposed to DMEDI	25
03	02	Identify how Lean looks at problems	25

Syllabus Area Code OK		Syllabus Area: Organizing Kaizen (OK)	Chapter Reference
Level	Topic	Goal: Governance and Organization of kaizen events	
Know the key components of Organizing Kaizen specifically to:			
01	01	Recall the sources of improvement initiatives – Voice of the Customer, Voice of the Process, Voice of the Business, Voice of the regulator	25
01	02	Understand kaizen team roles: Kaizen sponsor, kaizen lead, kaizen team member	25
Understand the following aspects related to Organizing Kaizen specifically to:			
02	01	Identify the correct team members for a kaizen team	25
02	02	Identify the way to select kaizen initiatives	25
02	03	Identify the activities for which each of the kaizen roles is responsible	25
Apply the following aspects related to Organizing Kaizen specifically to be able to:			
03	01	Gain support for the kaizen event	25
03	02	Plan and prepare a kaizen event	25
03	03	Select the correct team members for a kaizen team	25
03	04	Select kaizen initiatives	25

Syllabus Area Code A3		Syllabus Area: A3 Method (A3)	Chapter Reference
Level	Topic	Goal: Learn conciseness	
Know the key components of the A3 Method specifically to:			
01	01	Recall the origins and goals of the A3 Method and specific use of A3 Problem-solving report	25
01	02	Recall the role of the key sections on an A3 Problem-solving Report: Background, Current Condition, Future State goals/setting targets, Analysis, Proposed options, Plan/ Improvement and Follow-Up	25
01	03	Identify the aim of A3 Problem-solving report, A3 Status report and A3 Proposal	25
01	04	Understand the MECE concept: "mutually exclusive and collectively exhaustive"	25
Understand the following aspects related to the A3 Method specifically to identify:			
02	01	The differences between Summarizing, Analyzing and Synthesizing	25
02	02	Whether information is "Mutually Exclusive and Collectively Exhaustive" (MECE)	25

| 02 | 03 | The situation, complication and key question of a situation | 25 |
| 02 | 04 | Difference between A3 Problem-solving report, A3 Status report and A3 Proposal | 25 |

Apply the following aspects related to the A3 Method specifically to be able to:

| 03 | 01 | Summarize information into the A3 format | 25 |
| 03 | 02 | Structure communication according to the Pyramid principle | 25 |

Syllabus Area Code DE		Syllabus Area: Define (DE)	Chapter Reference
Level	Topic	Goal: What types of problems/how to write a problem statement/creating problem definition	

Know the key aspects of the Define phase specifically to be able to:

01	01	Recall the Key Steps of the Define Stage Select Problem and identify owner Create Problem statement and select kaizen team Validate the scope of the problem Collect VoC information Create high-level kaizen plan	26
01	02	Recall the definition of a Hypothesis and a Problem Statement	26
01	03	Understand the basic types of problems: Simple, complicated, complex, chaotic, disorder, based on Cynefin model	26
01	04	Recall the perspectives required to validate a problem statement	26

Understand the following aspects of the Define phase specifically to:

02	01	Identify the types of problems: Simple, complicated, complex, chaotic disorder, according to the Cynefin model	26
02	02	Validate a problem based on business benefits, impact and feasibility	26
02	03	Which tools to use to define and scope a problem statement (SIPOC, CTQ)	26
02	04	Explain the difference between a Hypothesis and a Problem Statement	26

Applying the following aspects of the Define phase specifically to be able to:

03	01	Know how to write a problem definition	26
03	02	Complete an A3 "Background Section"	26
03	03	Map the key stakeholder for the kaizen activity; carry out a stakeholder analysis	26
03	04	Identify typical problems in an IT context	26

Syllabus Area Code ME		Syllabus Area: Measure (ME)	Chapter Reference
		Goal: Refine the problem statement based on measurement	
Level	Topic		
Know the key aspects of the Measure phase specifically to:			
01	01	Recall Key Steps in Measure	26
		Identify the outputs and inputs of the process in which the problem occurs	
		Create Validate Value Stream Map of the process	
		Create and execute data collection plan	
		Validate the measurement system	
		Assess the capability and performance of the process	
		Identify Quick Wins improvements	
01	02	Recall IT units of work: Incident, Service Request, Problem, Standard Change, Operational activity, Non-standard Change, Advice, Plan	2
01	03	Recall three types of variable: Dependent, independent and control	26
01	04	Explain the definitions of Baseline and Benchmark	26
01	05	Explain the three generic types of units of work: Runners, repeaters and strangers	26
01	06	Recall VSM metrics (Lead time, Takt rate, Changeover time, Queue time, Work-in-process, Capacity, Throughput, VA/NNVA/NVA time) and calculations (PCE, Little's Law)	26
Understand the following aspects of the Measure phase specifically to identify:			
02	01	The difference between Qualitative and Quantitative Measurement systems	26
02	02	The difference between a Baseline and a Benchmark	26
02	03	The relationship between IT units of work and the three generic types of units of work	2, 26
02	04	Types of Qualitative and Quantitative Measurement systems	26
02	05		
Applying the following aspects of the Measure phase specifically to be able to:			
03	01	Create a Value Stream Map with metrics and calculations (Exercise)	22
03	02	Complete Current Conditions section of A3	26
03	03	Set up measurement systems	26

Syllabus Area Code AN		Syllabus Area: Analyze (AN)	Chapter Reference
Level	Topic	Goal: Get to the root cause of the problem	
Know the key aspects of the Analyze phase specifically to be able to:			
01	01	Recall Key Steps for Analyze Phase Determine the critical independent variables Perform the data analysis Perform the process analysis Determine the root causes Prioritize the root causes	26
01	02	Recall the seven basic tools of Quality: Histogram, Pareto chart, scatter diagram, flow chart, control chart, fishbone (Ishikawa) diagram, check sheet	26
01	03	Recall common cause variation and special cause variation	26
01	04	Recall Time Trap and Capacity Constraint	26
01	05	Recall the tools for investigating root cause: Five Whys, Cause and Effect matrix, Failure Mode Effects Analysis	26
Understand the following aspects of the Analyze phase specifically to be able to:			
02	01	Identify each of the seven basic tools of Quality	26
02	02	Visualize and analyze root cause Five Whys Cause and Effects matrix Failure Mode Effects Analysis (FMEA)	26
02	03	Identify the difference between Time Trap and Capacity Constraint	26
02	04	Identify the difference between common cause variation and special cause variation	26
Applying the following aspects of the Analyze phase specifically to be able to:			
03	01	Identify ways for dealing with common cause variation and special cause variation	26
03	02	Use all tools described in this section	26
03	03	Complete the Analyze section of A3	26
03	04	Analyze a Value Stream Map	22, 26
03	05	Identify whether a process is in control or out of control	26

Syllabus Area Code IM		Syllabus Area: Improve (IM)	Chapter Reference
Level	**Topic**	**Goal: Identify improvement options**	
Know the key aspects of the Improve phase specifically to:			
01	01	Recall Key Steps for Improve Phase Generate potential solutions Select and prioritize solutions Apply best and good practices Develop "Future State" VSM Pilot the solution and confirm improvement outcomes Create implementation plan for full-scale roll-out of solution(s)	27
01	02	Recall idea generation techniques: Brainstorming, reverse thinking, SCAMPER	27
01	03	Recall solution prioritization techniques: Affinity mapping, solution matrix, multi-voting, business case development	27
Understand the following aspects of the Improve phase specifically to identify:			
02	01	How to test a solution depending on the type of problem (Cynefin) to which it is related	27
02	02	Idea generation techniques, specifically: Brainstorming, reverse thinking, SCAMPER	27
02	03	Solution selection and prioritization techniques, specifically affinity mapping, solution matrix, multi-voting, business case development	27
02	04	Best practice solutions within IT: ITIL, COBIT, Scrum, Prince2/PMI	27
02	05	Good practice (principle-based) solutions within IT: Lean IT, Agile, DevOps	27
Applying the following aspects of the Improve phase specifically to be able to:			
03	01	Apply idea generation and solution selection techniques	27
03	02	Complete A3 Section Future State/Targets and Proposed Options	27

Syllabus Area Code CO		Syllabus Area: Control (CO)	Chapter Reference
Level	**Topic**	**Goal: Ensuring the sustainability of the improvement**	

Know the key aspects of Control phase specifically to recall:

Level	Topic		Chapter
01	01	The definition of a control	27
01	02	Measurement of improvement Critical Success Factor/Key Performance Indicator Consistent and Coherent measurements Lead and Lag Measures Creation of Management Dashboards	27
01	03	The components of a Control plan: Documentation, monitoring, response, training	27
01	04	Types of documentation: Policy, process, standard operating procedure	27
01	05	Types of monitoring: Metrics, visual management, performance dialog, cascade	27
01	06	Key steps in the Control Phase which are: Create measurement system Create documentation Create Control plan Communicate to stakeholders Present the results as described on the A3 Transition ownership	27

Understand the following aspects of Control phase specifically to be able to:

Level	Topic		Chapter
02	01	Identify a Standard Operating Procedure	27
02	02	Identify the level of documentation, based on risk/value	27
02	03	Capture the lessons learned (of failure and success)	27
02	04	Replicate improvements to other areas	27
02	05	Identify the components of a communication plan	27

Applying the following aspects of the Control phase specifically to be able to:

Level	Topic		Chapter
03	01	Create a measurement system to control the improvement, present in a dashboard	27
03	02	Complete follow-up section on A3 and finalize all items on the A3	25
03	03	Create a communication plan tailored to the stakeholders	27

Appendix C: Lean IT Leadership Syllabus

Syllabus Area Code LL		Syllabus Area: Lean Leadership (LL)	Chapter Reference
Level	Topic	Goal: Understand the basics of Lean Leadership	
Know the key components of Lean Leadership specifically to recall:			
01	01	Shingo Model: Four key Guiding principles – Respect every individual, Lead with humility, Create constancy of purpose, Think systemically	15
01	02	Key components of systemic thinking: Holistic thinking, Dynamic thinking and Closed-loop thinking	15
01	03	The definition of a True North value	15
01	04	Lean style of Leadership	15
01	05	Four aspects of the Lean Leadership Development Model	15
01	06	Five flows of IT value as defined by Bell	2
Understand the following aspects of Lean Leadership specifically to explain:			
02	01	Shingo Model Guiding and Supporting principles that directly impact on Lean Leadership	15
02	02	True North Values	15
02	03	Organizational context of the IT Leader	2
02	04	Leadership aspects applied to the IT organizational context	2
Apply the following aspects related to Lean Leadership specifically to be able to:			
03	01	Use the comparison between Lean Leadership and Level 5 leadership (Collins, 2001) to identify differences	15
03	02	Use the comparison between traditional Western leadership and Lean Leadership to identify the differences	15
03	03	Identify the Five flows of IT value	2

Syllabus Area Code CS		Syllabus Area: Commit to Self-development (CS)	Chapter Reference
Level	**Topic**	Goal: Understand the importance of self-development and seeing what is actually happening both to self and within the organization	
Know the key aspects of Commit to Self-development Specifically to recall:			
01	01	Self-development principles: Shu-Ha-Ri – Shu: Execute and learn exactly – Ha: Standard with some improvisation – Ri: Mastery of standard; focus on deepening skill and understanding	16
01	02	Leader Standard Work	16
01	03	Resource efficiency v. Flow efficiency	19
01	04	Kaizen mindset: Always seek improvement	4
01	05	Accountability: Role of taking responsibility in a Lean IT setting, getting people to take responsibility	6, 9
01	06	Kata of Leadership – creating habits	16
01	07	PDCA cycle for practicing Lean Leadership	9
Understand the following aspects of Commit to Self-development specifically to be able to explain:			
02	01	Forms of standards in both IT work and IT leader work	16
02	02	Establishing accountability: How to identify whether people take responsibility and how to encourage it	16
02	03	Requirements for self-development	16
02	04	Three tools for structuring the Kata of Leadership	16
02	05	Examples of Leader Standard Work in IT	16
Apply the following aspects of Commit to Self-development specifically to be able to:			
03	01	Apply Shu-Ha-Ri to own situation	16
03	02	Create Leader Standard Work overview for own situation (Exercise)	16
03	03	Use the capabilities obtained through Self-development	16
03	04	Standardize meetings	16
03	05	Identify how and ensure that people take responsibility	16
03	06	Do a gemba walk within an IT organization – leveraging an IT reference model (investigation models for kata of a gemba walk)	17
03	07	Identify what to look for during a gemba walk (Exercise)	17

Syllabus Area Code HO		Syllabus Area: Helping Others to Develop	Chapter Reference
		Goal: Understand the importance of developing others as an integral part of Lean IT Leadership	
Level	**Topic**		
Know the key aspects of Helping Others to Develop specifically to recall:			
01	01	Definition of genchi genbutsu	17
01	02	Definition of nemawashi	18
01	03	Explanation of T-type leadership	9
01	04	Five Whys method for finding root causes	17, 20
01	05	Questioning techniques	17
Understand the following aspects of Helping Others to Develop specifically to explain:			
02	01	Importance of Lean IT Leadership in eliminating mura and muri	17
02	02	Go to the gemba and genchi genbutsu	17
02	03	Key goals of a gemba walk: Support, teach, promote; contrasted with a gallery walk	17
02	04	Relationship between jidoka and gemba walk	17
02	05	Role of T-type leadership	9
Apply the following aspects of Helping Others to Develop specifically to be able to:			
03	01	Use the Five Whys method (Exercise) - balancing Ask Why with Show Respect	17, 20
03	02	Apply the views to take when doing a gemba walk	17
03	03	Describe the IT gemba: Development, IT operations, Service desk, Supporting staff	2
03	04	Carry out a skills and knowledge analysis	23
03	05	Interpret skills and knowledge data	23

Syllabus Area Code CI		Syllabus Area: Continuous Improvement	Chapter Reference
		Goal: Understand the importance of practicing Continuous Improvement as an integral part of Lean IT Leadership	
Level	**Topic**		
Know the key aspects of Continuous Improvement specifically to recall:			
01	01	Definition of continuous improvement	20
01	02	Daily kaizen: Focus on smaller, daily improvement steps	20
01	03	Kaizen Event: Focus on solving larger problems	20
01	04	Definition of a team (Katzenbach & Smith, 2005)	21
01	05	The core elements of the kaizen mindset	4

Understand the following aspects of Continuous Improvement specifically to explain:

02	01	Difference between daily kaizen and kaizen event	20
02	02	Importance of standards or reference models as the basis for improvement	20
02	03	Importance of Lean IT Leadership in eliminating mura and muri	20
02	04	Key characteristics of a team, in comparison with a group	21
02	05	The five levels of team development (Lencioni, 2002)	21
02	06	Characteristics of IT teams – technically-oriented, project-based, customer-oriented	21

Apply the following aspects of Continuous Improvement specifically to be able to:

03	01	Describe the role of Continuous improvement within Lean IT	4
03	02	Apply the 5S technique in an IT context	20, 23
03	03	Identify when to use improvement kaizen and daily kaizen in IT	20
03	04	Use the team development model to determine whether an IT team functions as a team	21

Syllabus Area Code VG		Syllabus Area: Vision, Goals and Communication	Chapter Reference
Level	**Topic**	**Goal: Lean IT Leadership and its role in creating vision and aligning goals**	

Know the key aspects of Vision, Goals and Communication specifically to recall:

01	01	Performance dialog: Leading meetings and Listening skills	17
01	02	Nemawashi for ensuring adoption strategy and policy, and execution of projects	18
01	03	Definition of Hoshin Kanri: Method for translating strategy to operations	18
01	04	The key aspects of a Performance Dialog	17
01	05	Visual management – for development, IT operations, service desk	8
01	06	Cascade and Catchball mechanism	18
01	07	The aim of the Pyramid principle	25
01	08	Definition of MECE and its use	25
01	09	The goal of a change story	12, 15

Understand the following aspects of Vision, Goals and Communication specifically to explain:

02	01	Key characteristics of Hoshin Kanri	18
02	02	The goals of Catchball communication	18

| 02 | 03 | When a performance dialog is carried out | 17 |
| 02 | 04 | Key components of the Pyramid Principle in structuring communication | 25 |

Applying the following aspects of Vision, Goals and Communication specifically to be able to:

03	01	Create a vision for an IT organization	18
03	02	Explain how the cascade mechanism works	18
03	03	Carry out a Performance dialog: Leading meetings and Listening skills (Exercise)	17
03	04	Design cascade and Catchball mechanism for own IT organization (Exercise)	18
03	05	Define visual management for software development, IT operations, service desk	8

Syllabus Area Code TR		Syllabus Area: Lean IT Transformation (TR)	Chapter Reference
Level	**Topic**	**Goal: Organize strategy for operations implementation and how to execute a Lean IT Transformation**	

Know the key aspects of Lean IT Transformation specifically to recall:

01	01	Basic components of the business case for a Lean IT transformation – customer satisfaction, strategic advantages, cost advantages	3
01	02	Eight mistakes when carrying out a transformation, and their mitigation (Kotter, 2007)	3
01	03	Key phases in accepting change (Lewis & Parker, 1981)	11
01	04	The importance of a change story	12

Understand the following aspects of Lean IT Transformation specifically to explain:

02	01	5 Lean IT Dimensions for structuring Lean IT Transformation	10
02	02	7 phases of the transition curve (Lewis & Parker, 1981)	11
02	03	3 key phases of the Organizational Level of a Lean IT transformation	11
02	04	Role of Lean IT Leader in relation to the Lean IT coach	10, 22
02	05	The top-down and bottom-up aspects of a Lean IT transformation	7

Apply the following aspects of Lean IT Transformation specifically to be able to:

| 03 | 01 | Plan and structure a Lean IT Transformation, using the 5 Lean IT Dimensions | 10, 22 |
| 03 | 02 | Define plan for transformation of own IT organization (Exercise) | 10, 22 |

03	03	Make change story for own situation (Exercise)	12
03	04	Complete A3 proposal for the execution of a Lean IT transformation	24
03	05	Know which Lean tools and methods must be applied at what moment in a Lean IT transformation	14
03	06	Know the reasons for lack of success during transformation	3, 13

Syllabus Area Code A3		Syllabus Area: A3 Method (A3)	Chapter Reference
Level	**Topic**	**Goal: Lean Leadership and Communication**	
List the key components of the A3 Method specifically to recall:			
01	01	Goals of the A3 Method	24
01	02	Sections of A3 Report	24
01	03	Advance-Prepare-Do-Check cycle	9
Apply the A3 Method specifically to be able to:			
03	01	Organize information into the A3 format	24
03	02	Communicate the key message and create involvement	24
03	03	Define personal Lean IT Leadership goals in relation to reference model	10

Index

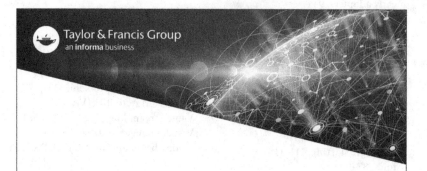

Printed in the United States
by Baker & Taylor Publisher Services